CHRISTIANITY IN OCEANIA

Ethnographic Perspectives

CHRISTIANITY IN OCEANIA

Ethnographic Perspectives

ASAO Monograph No. 12

Edited by
John Barker

Lanham • New York • London

University Press of America®, Inc.
4720 Boston Way
Lanham, Maryland 20706

3 Henrietta Street
London WC2E 8LU England

Printed in the United States of America
British Cataloging in Publication Information Available

Co-published by arrangement with the
Association for Social Anthropology in Oceania

Library of Congress Cataloging-in-Publication Data

Christianity in Oceania : ethnographic perspectives /
edited by John Barker.
p. cm. — (ASAO monograph ; no. 12)
"Co-published by arrangement with the Association for Social
Anthropology in Oceania"—T.p. verso.
Includes bibliographical references and index.
1. Christianity—Oceania. 2. Ethnology—Oceania.
I. Barker, John, 1953- . II. Association for
Social Anthropology in Oceania. III. Series.
BR1490.C47 1990 306.6'795—cd20 90-41768 CIP

ISBN 0–8191–7906–X (alk. paper).
ISBN 0–8191–7907–8 (pbk. : alk. paper).

The paper used in this publication meets the minimum requirements of American National Standard for Information Sciences—Permanence of Paper for Printed Library Materials, ANSI Z39.48–1984.

CONTENTS

Figures vii

Plates vii

Tables vii

Editor's Preface ix

CHAPTER 1
Introduction: Ethnographic Perspectives on Christianity in Oceanic Societies 1
John Barker

CHAPTER 2
Some Next Steps in the Study of Pacific Island Christianity 25
Charles W. Forman

CHAPTER 3
God and Ghosts in Kove 33
Ann Chowning

CHAPTER 4
Keeping the *Lo* under a Melanesian Messiah: An Analysis of the Pomio *Kivung*, East New Britian 59
Garry Trompf

CHAPTER 5
Christianity, Cargo Cultism, and the Concept of the Spirit in Misiman Cosmology 81
Martha Macintyre

CHAPTER 6
Fathers, Aliens, and Brothers: Building a Social World in Loboda Village Church Services 101
Carl E. Thune

CHAPTER 7
Christianity, People of the Land, and Chiefs in Fiji 127
Martha Kaplan

CHAPTER 8
Catholicism, Capitalist Incorporation, and Resistance in Kragur Village 149
Michael French Smith

CHAPTER 9
Mission Station and Village: Religious Practice and Representations in Maisin Society 173
John Barker

CHAPTER 10
Inventing the Mormon Tongon Family 197
Tamar Gordon

CHAPTER 11
Catholicism and Pulapese Identity 221
Juliana Flinn

CHAPTER 12
Christianity and Maori Ethnicity in the South Island of New Zealand 237
M. Jocelyn Armstrong

CHAPTER 13
Afterword 259
John Barker

References 265

Contributors 307

Index 311

FIGURES

FIGURE 1
The Religious Field and Indigenous Christianity 18

PLATES

PLATE 1
Village Boundary Marker, with the Sign of the Ten Commandments, Pamalmal Village, East New Britain (1981) 71

PLATE 2
Kivung Money House, Palmalal Village, East New Britain (1981) 73

TABLES

TABLE 1
Denominational Affiliation in Tonga, 1931-1976 200

EDITOR'S PREFACE

This volume is the product of two Association for Social Anthropology in Oceania sessions on "The Ethnography of Christianity in the Pacific" held in New Harmony, Indiana in 1986 and in Monterey, California in 1987. The sessions generated much interest and lively discussion, the fruits of which appear in the chapters below. Participants discussed several themes raised a decade earlier at the ASAO symposium on missionary activities, published as *Mission, Church, and Sect in Oceania* (Boutilier, Hughes, and Tiffany 1978). As a consequence, the Pacific Christianity session was soon dubbed "Son of Mission." Yet, if we are to trace descent thoroughly we should also credit the many ASAO sessions explicitly concerned with change and modern conditions in Pacific societies (e.g., Lieber 1977, M. Rodman and Cooper 1983, W. Rodman and Counts 1983).

The present volume, however, continues to develop new perspectives on Christianity in the south Pacific islands. *Mission, Church, and Sect in Oceania* focused primarily on the figure of the missionary and on the missionizing process. Most of the authors approached Pacific Christianity in terms of its introduction, dissemination, and transformation through time. From a historical perspective, Christianity is primarily a Western import. Yet, as Sharon Tiffany (1978a:305) noted, "Pacific islanders have... made Christianity their own in a complex variety of ways." Hence the final section of that collection explored through four case studies the ways that islanders understood and experienced Christianity at the time of fieldwork. The present volume builds on this insight. While not neglecting historical roots, the authors here are primarily interested in Christianity as an established and developing Pacific island religion in its own right. We explore, in a diversity of circumstances, how islanders understand, live, reproduce and modify their Christian ideas and institutions in the post-mission era.

On behalf of the authors, I would like to thank the participants whose papers are not part of the present collection but whose ideas, comments, and encouragement permeate these pages: Stephen L. Eyre, Leslie Marshall, Mac Marshall, Susan P. Montague, Elizabeth M. Roach, Karen Sinclair, Geoffrey M. White, and Darrell Whiteman. The late Peter Lawrence acted as an unofficial discussant during the Monterey sessions, contributing his prodigious knowledge of Pacific people decisively to focus our minds on key problems. Finally, I am grateful to Charles

Forman, who, as our discussant, concisely and sympathetically drew our attention to the historical and regional contexts in which to place our particular ethnographic analyses.

As a novice editor, I have been most fortunate in enjoying the good natured patience and cooperation of all the contributors. In addition, I am grateful for the support and critical advice of M. Jocelyn Armstrong, Charles W. Forman, Miriam Kahn, William McKellin, and Michael French Smith. The ASAO series editor, Margaret Rodman has offered consistent encouragement and sound direction; she deserves much of the credit for the final preparation of the manuscript. Thanks also to McMaster University and the University of Waterloo for their support of the ASAO monograph series, especially to Virginia Freeman MacOwan who painstakingly and expertly typeset and corrected the manuscript. My greatest debt is to my wife Anne Marie Tietjen and son Jacob, who sustained the long hours I was preoccupied with this project with love and patience. With the help of these and many friends inside and outside of the ASAO, this book has truly been a joint project.

John Barker

Department of Anthropology and Sociology
University of British Columbia
Vancouver, British Columbia, Canada
December 1989

1

INTRODUCTION: ETHNOGRAPHIC PERSPECTIVES ON CHRISTIANITY IN OCEANIC SOCIETIES

John Barker

"Oceanic religion" conjures up exotic images of ancient temple platforms, elegant cult houses, dramatic male initiations and bizarre cargo cults. "Christianity" suggests a contrasting set of images: white missionaries, small square churches, mother-hubbard dresses. These tenacious images are increasingly anachronistic. Christianity is today the most widespread and pervasive religion in the region, and the original peoples of the South Pacific are steadily making it their own. National churches under indigenous leadership have replaced most of the older missions. Churches with long histories in the islands proudly perpetuate distinct traditions of worship, combining imported and indigenous themes; politicians, some of them prominent clergymen, draw upon Christian values to promote social development and self-reliance; villagers gather in local churches to celebrate Christmas and Easter festivals in which they competitively raise funds to further Christian expansion; indigenous prophets and healers awe followers with powerful visions of Jesus and Mary; and isolated peoples listen raptly to sermons and gospel hymns beamed to them in their language from Evangelical radio stations in the islands and beyond. The emerging religion is pervasive, diverse, and vibrant.

As students of daily life in village societies, anthropologists have a special interest in Pacific Christianity, especially as it is emerging in different cultural communities. Several anthropologists have called for studies of "missionization" in recent years and some have published innovative ethnohistorical studies of conversion in a number of societies. But few have attempted ethnographic appraisals of Christianity as it is currently experienced and practiced in Pacific societies. The essays in this volume are exploratory in two senses: they inquire into an aspect of island life of which we know little; and they explore ways of expanding and revamping ethnographic methods and analytic frameworks in order to include modern conditions.

Some might argue that it is still too early to speak of "Pacific Christianity" as an aspect of indigenous culture. For although the Pacific islands have long been dominated by Western interests, their cultures often remain oriented to indigenous traditions and ideologies. To form an authentic part of the religious experience of Oceanic peoples, Christianity must enter into local world-views, aspirations, and concerns of Pacific islanders within their particular socio-historical circumstances. The contributors to this collection show in numerous ways how Christian forms and ideas are part of the circumscribed religious fields of small societies. Yet they also explore Christianity as a world religion with numerous symbolic and practical links to systems spanning many communities. Pacific Christianity thus possesses both a local and global face. The tension within Pacific Christianity between its local and global expressions is the key problem explored in this book.

In the chapters that follow the authors pursue these issues through a fascinating assortment of ethnographic circumstances and through the lenses of a number of distinct thematic concerns and theoretical perspectives. My main concern in this introduction is to set out analytic frameworks with which to approach the collection. I see four related areas of interest: denominational expansion and divisions across the Pacific region; scholarly approaches to missionization; the local face of Christianity as part of popular religions in Pacific communities; and the global face of Pacific Christianity as part of regional and international systems. The latter two sections discuss the main issues dealt with in the collection. I take the opportunity there to introduce each chapter. In chapter 2, Professor Charles W. Forman takes this discussion a further step by reviewing what has already been done and suggesting future avenues for ethnographic exploration.

THE EXPANSION OF CHRISTIANITY IN OCEANIA[1]

Interest in Pacific islanders' understanding and practice of Christianity goes way back, but it has not been supported by reliable information. Almost everything we know about what islanders have thought of their adopted religion comes from reports and commentaries written by Europeans. This literature is huge, written in vastly different circumstances by individuals with varying opinions and abilities of observation. Rich and diverse as these sources are, they collectively reinforce a misleading image: the European as the active agent of history and the Native as history's passive or reactive recipient.

Viewed from the outside, Pacific Christianity does indeed look like an extension of the Western original. The geography of denominations closely reflects the movements of the missionary bodies. Spanish missionaries came to the Marianas in 1668 and established Roman Catholicism, which remains the principal religion. Protestants, however, took the initiative in most of Micronesia and Polynesia. The most famous organization, the Congregationalist-dominated London Missionary Society, arrived in Tahiti in 1798 and, over the course of a century, expanded into the Cook Islands, Samoa, Niue, Tuvalu and Kiribati, the Loyalty Islands, and southern Papua. American Congregationalists commenced work in Hawaii in 1820 on behalf of the American Board of Commissioners for Foreign Missions. From there, they advanced across Micronesia. Anglicans of the Church Missionary Society along with some Methodist missionaries entered Maori communities in New Zealand at about the same time. In the following decades, English Methodists won large congregations in Tonga and Fiji after powerful indigenous leaders converted to Christianity (see Kaplan, chapter 7). The Protestant churches now dominate in most of Polynesia, but Roman Catholics, who re-entered Oceania later, gained converts in French Polynesia, New Zealand, and parts of Micronesia (see Flinn, chapter 11); and American Mormons since the turn of the century have made significant inroads in Tonga and New Zealand (see Gordon, chapter 10).

The progress of the missions tended to be slower in Melanesia than in eastern and northern Oceania because of the absence in most places of large political units. Converts had to be won village by village. Still, the general pattern here is much the same: the present-day denominations descend from the first mission societies to enter the region and most of these dominate large areas. Protestant organizations often entered into comity agreements with each other, sometimes with the formal sanction of colonial administrations, dividing regions into distinct areas of influence. Roman Catholic mission organizations never agreed to these arrangements; nor did some small sects, such as the Seventh Day Adventists, which arrived after the larger Protestant missions were well-established. Where there was rivalry between missionaries, it tended to occur between Protestants and Catholics. The Catholic missions, however, also occupied areas where they were the only or the dominant Christian representatives: in New Caledonia, parts of Bougainville, a large region of hinterland in southern Papua, and parts of New Guinea and Irian Jaya.[2]

In Vanuatu, the Presbyterians arrived first and now form the major religious group. Anglicans of the Melanesian Mission began visiting islands in northern Vanuatu and the Solomon Islands from the mid-nineteenth century. Today they share the Solomons with Methodists in the west, Seventh Day Adventists in the Morovo Lagoon, the South Sea Evangelical Church on Malaita, and Catholics on several islands.

Papua New Guinea, as the largest country in Melanesia and the last part to be evangelized, presents the most complex picture. Beginning in the 1870s, some long-established and some new missions began working along the coasts. In the Australian colony of Papua, the London Missionary Society shared the southern region with French Catholics and a small Seventh Day Adventist mission. The north coast was divided between the Methodists in the eastern islands and the Anglicans on the mainland. Australian Methodists and French Catholics arrived in the Bismarck Archipelago in the 1870s. After the Germans assumed control over northwest New Guinea, Lutheran and Catholic missions began steadily to penetrate the interior. The four major Christian churches of Papua New Guinea — United (Congregationalist, and Methodist), Catholic, Anglican and Lutheran — developed from these early missions and continue to represent different parts of the coastal regions. The coastal missions began to penetrate into the densely populated New Guinea highlands in the 1930s. Since the 1950s, they have been joined by more than 40 sects of all theological colorings. Not only is Christianity relatively new in the highlands, it is far more sectarian than in most of Oceania.

Oceania, particularly Melanesia, has provided rich soil for millenarian movements. Chowning and Trompf, in chapters 3 and 4, document cases of millenarianism in New Britain. Some independent sects have also received attention in recent years (Barr and Trompf 1983; Loeliger and Trompf 1985). But few islanders have opted for autonomous churches, in sharp contrast to Africa (see Fernandez 1978). The main exceptions are the Maori messianic churches in New Zealand and some very small groups in parts of Melanesia (de Bres 1985, Trompf 1983). As Kaplan (chapter 7), Macintyre (chapter 5), Smith (chapter 8) show for Fijians, Misimans and Kragur villagers respectively, most islanders remain loyal to the churches even while participating in millenarian activities and ideologies.

To an extraordinary degree, even in the long-evangelized areas, outsiders still set church standards. The reforms of Vatican II, to give but one example, had a major impact on local church practices and attitudes (Arbuckle 1978; Huber 1988; Smith 1980, 1988). The Pacific churches struggle to build and maintain theological colleges to train clergy to "world" standards. In recent decades, they have established dozens of regional and international cooperative and educational bodies modelled on the World Council of Churches and similar organizations. Such efforts are, of course, enormously expensive, and many Pacific churches are deeply in debt to founding churches in the industrialized world (Forman 1985).

The Pacific churches are intimately attached to Western Christendom in yet another way: they are subject to many of the same stresses and strains of attempting to practice their faith within an increasingly secular and international culture. The churches today devote much of their energies and funds to addressing problems of unequal access to economic and educational resources, alcoholism, ubanization, pollution, and tourism. Fundamentalist and Pentecostal sects, although mostly small, have been very active and influential in the Pacific in the last twenty years (Orr 1976). Waves of religious excitement continue to sweep out of Western countries through Oceania, where Christian revivalism combines with local forms and aspirations (e.g., Barr 1983; Jorgensen 1981a; Robin 1982).

The Western sources of Christianity have been crucial in the past, and remain so in the present, moulding the outward face of Pacific Christianity. Yet this reality relates mainly to the formal organization of Christianity. It tells us little about Christianity within popular religion: as part of the general orientation towards problems of morality and practice in daily life. It also tells us little about why islanders chose to be Christian or of what their Christianity means to them. The European signature does not in itself reveal why and how Christianity remains vital in Oceania.

PERSPECTIVES ON MISSIONIZATION

Missionaries, historians, and anthropologists have for their own reasons been keenly interested in the diffusion of Christianity across the Pacific. They have certainly been aware that indigenous acceptance of the missions was a crucial factor in the success of Christian expansion, and that local peoples have continually reinterpreted Christian themes and practices according to their own received knowledge and traditions. Yet intensive studies of Christianity from the perspective of local communities are few and far between. The analytic frameworks adopted by scholars focus upon the activities of and responses to European missionaries. This has militated against recognizing indigenous expressions of Christianity as authentic and worthy of serious study.

The missionary encounter

The earliest and most voluminous literature on Pacific Christianity came and continues to come from the pens of missionaries and their supporters and critics. The "metropolitan-ecclesiastical school of mission history," as one Africanist dubs it, focuses upon European-defined goals, strategies, successes, and failures (Strayer 1976:1; cf. Etherington 1983). The contributions of local pagans and Christians are by no means ignored, but they tend to be evaluated in terms of missionary aims and values. This can take several forms. John Inglis, an early missionary to Aneityum in Vanuatu, for example, saw the Bible as a set of charter myths by which to understand the transformations of a Christianizing society. He argued that the Aneityum Christians by donning Western clothing re-enacted Adam and Eve's convenant with God upon leaving the Garden. History merely repeated itself (Inglis 1890). Mormons, as Gordon (chapter 10) shows, also incorporated Polynesians into their charter myths. Through the years, however, this has been an unusual attitude. Most missionaries have recognized that as Pacific Christians assumed responsibility for the churches they would bring the best of indigenous culture into their Christianity. Many have insisted that Pacific islanders should not be remade in the image of white Europeans. Yet few mission writers address what a truly indigenous Christianity might look like. When dealing with actual cultural practices rather than ideals of evangelization, missionary writers have often criticized what seemed to them "resistance," "disobedience," "back sliding," and so forth. The missionary literature is an invaluable source — sometimes the only source — for exploring native understandings of Christianity, motives for conversion, and responses to the missions. Missionaries have also contributed important ethnological studies (see Barker 1979; Lutkehaus 1983; Whiteman 1985). Much of the missionary literature, however, reveals more of missionaries' and their supporters' attitudes than of the indigenous Christianity.

There are important exceptions. One thinks in particular of Maurice Leenhardt's sensitive and insightful writings on the conversion process in New Caledonia, as a type of "deep translation" to which both evangelists and converts contribute and in which both discover new depths of meaning and faith (Leenhardt 1979; Clifford 1980, 1982). At the present time, a growing number of expatriate and indigenous clergy are exploring local Christianity and traditional religions as the first step towards developing Pacific theologies.[3] Finally, a number of missiologists and mission historians have been critically re-examining documentary sources and recording oral history in order to correct some of the biases of much of older perspectives. They are pointing in particular to the important roles played by women, Pacific island missionaries, and the local people themselves in shaping the conversion process.[4] Many of these studies draw upon age-old Christian themes and concerns, but they attempt to recenter them in a transcultural and dynamic context. As Burridge (1978) points out, an appreciation of the internal dynamics of Christianity, a perspective which arises from a close study of mission theology and practice, forms a critical aspect of understanding the nature of Pacific Christianity today.

Nationalist histories

As the Third World began the process of decolonization following World War II, a second approach to Christian expansion gained prominence: a post-colonial or nationalist history. Written primary by secular professionals and by indigenous nationalists, its evaluation of Third World Christianity has been, as Strayer notes, profoundly ambivalent (Strayer 1976:2). Many would argue with Beckett that in the final analysis Pacific Christianity must "be understood in terms of colonization" (1978:209; cf. Huber 1988). Yet colonization is a charged concept that often pushes scholars towards partisan positions (cf. Comaroff and Comaroff 1986:1). Some students of missionization would agree with the position of the Africanist T.O. Beidelman, who insists that missions represent "the most thorough-going... facet of colonial life" because their efforts are "aimed at overall changes in the beliefs and actions of native peoples, at colonization of heart and mind as well as body" (1982:6; cf. De'Ath 1981; Hannett 1970; Narakobi 1977). Most Pacific scholars have been more cautious, pointing out ways particular missions aided and impeded colonial domination (e.g., Beckett 1978; Gunson 1965, 1969; Hilliard 1974; Nelson 1969; Smith 1982a, 1984, 1988; Young 1980). Finally, several scholars have explored the multifaceted roles missions played in the development of independent nation states: protecting local peoples from the more virulent forms of exploitation, such as labor indenture; providing schooling and medical services and in this and other ways hastening secularizing trends; and providing a network of emerging national elites (e.g., Barker 1979, chapter 9; Miller 1970; Oram 1971; Smith, chapter 8; Trompf 1977). Whatever the differences in evaluation, the nationalist perspective on Pacific Christianity has deepened our understandings by widening attention from the missionary-islander encounter to the gradual incorporation of the region into regional and world systems. Yet, with few exceptions, these studies continue to be based upon European observations and Eurocentric concerns.

Anthropological perspectives

A few anthropologists, as noted in the references above, have contributed to the mission and to the nationalist literatures. However, anthropologists have shown less interest in Pacific Christianity as a religious development in its own right. This should not be surprising or necessarily a reason for criticism. Anthropology from its earliest days in the region was practiced as salvage ethnography, as an attempt to understand indigenous cultural and social systems before they were swept away by the forces of modernization. As the frontiers of Western expansion have been pushed forward, many anthropologists have been driven to more remote regions or into the archives in search of the last remaining "primitives." Others have narrowed their research focus from the whole of people's experience the more "traditional" aspects of cultures: kinship, exchange, myths, notions of gender, for example. It has only been in recent years that many anthropologists, particularly academics, have turned their attention to colonial and post-colonial changes in Melanesian society. Most of these studies focus upon economic, political, and legal innovations, but a handful of anthropologists have made detailed studies of Pacific Christianity in particular communities (e.g., Barker 1985a; Oliver 1981; Roach 1987a; Whiteman 1983).

Anthropology has made its most significant contribution to the study of Pacific Christianity in the enormous quantity of detailed research into millenarian movements, particularly Melanesian "cargo cults."[5] Chowning, Trompf, Kaplan, and Macintyre give detailed appraisals of Christian ideas and forms in sustained millenarian situations in the first part of the collection. All commentators have noted Christian elements in these movements, but there is no consensus on how they should be interpreted.

Forman (chapter 2) notes that some anthropologists report on church life within larger ethnographic descriptions of a people. However, most anthropologists continue to view Christianity primarily as a missionary imposition, especially in Melanesia. A significant number have been developing a third general perspective on missionization. Observers have long observed that indigenous religious attitudes and activities may continue within Christianity long after conversion (e.g., Hogbin 1939, 1958; Keesing 1942; Read 1952). But many seemed to have assumed, like F.E. Williams (1944) and Malinowski (1961:464-467) that conversion would eventually lead to the collapse of native cultures. This opinion began to shift in recent decades, and today many would agree with and generalize Lawrence and Meggitt's (1965:21) statement about the long-Christianized religions of the New Guinea coastal areas: "The changes introduced impinged mainly on the superstructure of native life, the external form of the socio-cultural order." For the most part traditional religions continue either hidden under the surface of village Christianity or resurfacing within a Christian idiom.

This perception of cultural continuity within Chrisitan forms finds much support in the literature. Many scholars, for example, have contrasted the hierarchical nature of Polynesian church organization, in which village pastors often enjoy the respect and prerogatives of traditional chiefs, with the much more egalitarian ambience of Melanesian village Christianity. Several anthropologists have systematically analyzed the persistence of indigenous religious themes in specific societies (e.g., Barker 1985a, 1985b; Kahn 1983; McSwain 1977; Schieffelin 1981a, 1981b;

Schwimmer 1973; Thune 1981; White 1978; Young 1977). Given a growing interest in anthropology with processes of cultural reproduction and with structuralist reinterpretations of Pacific ethnohistory, we should expect to see more studies of this type in the future (e.g., Dening 1980; Hooper and Huntsman 1985; Sahlins 1985). Indeed, this orientation is evident in most of the chapters below, but especially in Kaplan's analysis of Fijian Christianity (chapter 7), Thune's interpretation of a church service on Normanby Island (chapter 6), Gordon's study of Tongan Mormonism (chapter 10), and Flinn's (chapter 11) evaluation of Pulapese Catholics' construction of cultural identity.

Each of the three perspectives on missionization, developing at different times in response to different interests — scholarly and practical — pertains to distinct aspects of the expansion and growth of Christianity in Pacific societies. Although partisan assumptions may inform the approach a scholar adopts, there is no reason why they cannot be synthesized.[6] And, as recent work has demonstrated, each is capable of further refinement when applied to particular historical and cultural contexts. Yet it seems to me that many of the scholars who have developed these analytic frameworks have not taken local expressions of Christianity seriously enough as phenomena in their own right. The tendency is to return to the missionary. From the first church perspective, for example, Pacific Christianity may appear the product of mission Christianity or a general Christian systemic; from the second nationalist perspective, Pacific Christianity may be relegated to a side-show, one event in the Western conquest of the region; and from the third perspective, Christianity often seems epiphenomenal, a superficial form lying above continuing cultural structures.

I exaggerate this critique to point out a tendency to focus on the Western/indigenous encounter rather than people's experiences and understandings of Christianity. Perhaps nothing better illustrates the present peripheral status of Pacific Christianity as an authentic subject for research than the relative lack of attention to the nature and practice of Christianity in post-mission village societies apart from studies of new religious movements. Scholars, including anthropologists, focus most of their attention on the early period of missionary contact and on conversion (see Forman, chapter 2). Although as missiologists, historians, and anthropologists, we frequently deal with national church organizations, local clergy, and worshippers, our attention often seems to be elsewhere. The Christianity we encounter in the field and in the research library rarely appears on the pages we write.[7]

The contributions in this volume are intended to show how ethnographic perspectives can enhance and extend our understandings of

Christianity in Pacific societies. The authors here adopt a variety of approaches and perspectives. This seems both necessary and theoretically healthy. Although most of the studies deal with coastal Melanesia, they cover a broad range of communities with distinct religious and social histories, ranging from isolated Misima Island to urban New Zealand. Moreover, even within particular regions Pacific Christianity is too varied and dynamic to be understood within a unitary theory of religious innovation. There is much to be gained, however, through careful study of the minutiae of Christian ideas and institutions in community settings, and how they form part of larger popular religions. In part, then, this collection is intended to encourage more sensitive and attentive perspectives on the realities of Pacific societies by making better use of established tools. Its larger aim is to encourage a general reorientation to the realities of religious experience in Oceania.

The chapters, however, do explore common themes. Most importantly, they examine the two faces of Christianity in Pacific island communities and the tensions between them: the local face of Christianity as part of the popular religions of island communities; and the global face of Christianity as part of the larger regional and international social and political systems that increasingly penetrate local societies. In the remainder of this chapter I want to develop a framework within which we can understand the two faces of Pacific Christianity in island communities. This will also serve as an opportunity to introduce the other chapters.

THE LOCAL FACE: PACIFIC CHRISTIANITY IN POPULAR RELIGION

Where anthropologists have recognized Christianity as a legitimate ethnographic subject, the key issue has usually been conversion. Like many religious concepts, conversion is deceptively simple. It may imply no more than a change in religious affiliation. But many scholars think of conversion as a much broader process of personal and social transformation, as the movement from a localized to a universal religion.[8] There is a good deal of disagreement over the relative influence of indigenous and Christian ideas and forms in emerging Pacific religions. Clearly the pre-contact social systems, the intensity of mission efforts, the period in which "conversion" takes place, along with numerous other contingencies, determine this argument differently in different places. Yet it inevitably arises, even in regards to people like the Maori of New Zealand who have long been members of Christian churches (see Armstrong, chapter 12). This sort of debate is a red herring. Models of conversion often force scholars to make unrealistic choices between traditional culture and Christianity and to obscure the more immediate reality: local popular religions consist of both indigenous and Christian ideas and forms.[9]

Ann Chowning presents an admirably balanced appraisal of the complex mix of traditional and Christian elements in the popular religion of the Kove in West New Britain (chapter 3). Chowning divides the Kove into four broad categories: those who have not been baptized, those who claim not to belong to a church, nominal Christians, and "devout" members of the Catholic and Seventh Day Adventist churches. The composition of these categories varies between villages and continually changes as people shift their religious affiliations. Although members of different factions sometimes compete and clash, there is a good deal of ideological overlap. No one clings wholeheartedly to traditional beliefs; even the unbaptized accept the existence of God and support the Ten Commandments. On the other hand, Christians draw on both indigenous ideas and the teachings of both churches to make sense of sickness and encounters with ghosts. Many Kove from all of the factions accept the teachings of a durable cargo cult, notably the idea that God originated from their land (see also Kaplan, chapter 7). Cargoist ideology provides a general framework for religious experience. Chowning writes, "In the thinking of many Kove, Christianity offers versions of their own religion, whereas outsiders see them adapting Christian concepts both to those that existed prior to the coming of Europeans and to those reflecting reactions to European culture"(pg. 34). The implication is that "conversion" makes no sense to the Kove, for there is only one cosmological reality revealed to greater and lesser extents in indigenous and imported religious ideas. This assumption may be traditional, but it clearly does not give rise to a unified "religion." Kove religion is a very complex field in which various constellations of Christian, indigenous, and syncretist elements wax and wane.

The coexistence of traditional and Christian elements in Kove popular religion is not in itself remarkable unless one first assumes that religions form logically coherent systems that must necessarily displace one another. Although Christians often employ exclusivist rhetoric, Christianity in general has been amazingly syncretic — to the point that authorities find it difficult to determine what a Christian minimally is. Christianity has also undergone many schisms through its history; European schisms were imported into the Pacific where the process of division continues. Even in Tonga, where converts successfully married Christianity with core indigenous values, denominations divide the religious field (Gordon, chapter 10; Korn 1978). The notion that traditional religions form coherent and closed systems has also been questioned in recent years, especially in Melanesia (Brunton 1980; Chowning 1969). The coherence and consistency of the totality of a people's religious experience cannot be assumed *a priori.* Our studies show that many Pacific Christians tolerate considerable ambiguity and inconsistency within their popular religion. The overall coherence of a religious field, therefore, is a variable to be investigated.

In chapter 4, Trompf describes an interesting instance in which indigenous people attempted to create a coherent popular religion. Like the Kove, many Mengen in East New Britain are Roman Catholics and most have followed to varying degrees the teachings of a long-developing "cargo cult," the *Kivung* ('assembly' or 'movement'). The leaders of the *Kivung* appropriated certain teachings from the mission, most notably the Ten Commandments and notions of God and Jesus. Trompf writes that the followers "dissociated their Christianity from its supposed European origins and institutional trappings, and derived inspiration for a preferred new form of social cooperation from both select Christian elements and traditional principles of positive reciprocity"(pg. 77). The *Kivung* built its following initially by resisting European authority; but the movement is neither a total rejection of the new order, nor a rival institution. The leaders have tried instead to establish a "total way" that will unify the divisions of mission, government, and business. They have not forbidden followers from attending church services, but imply that their movement possesses a deeper connection to spiritual realities. The *Kivung* has been enormously successful by several standards. Much of this success is due to its flexible adjustments to changes in Mengen society. Beginning as a localized cargo cult borrowing from Catholic teachings, the *Kivung* has progressively developed a more universalistic and secular outlook as the Mengen have become more involved in the national economic and political systems. Leaders of the movement today are more likely to speak of economic development, maintenance of villages, education, and representation in government than of cargo and ancestors, although the latter themes remain important. The *Kivung* has enjoyed some success as a "total way" because it addresses the totality of Mengen experience and aspirations.

It would be misleading, I think, to identify the *Kivung* as Mengen popular religion and oppose it, say, to the Catholic mission. Clearly Christian, syncretist, and traditional organizations may develop in a religious field and engage in fierce competition. But if we make indigenous peoples and their religious experience our focus instead of organizational distinctions and politics, then we must pay close attention to the actual dealings people have with these various religious permutations. Frequently people are involved in more than one. This makes the analysis of the relations between these religious organizations very complicated indeed.

Martha Macintyre's study of Misiman island religion in southeastern Papua provides an excellent illustration of this point (chapter 5). Methodist missionaries arrived on Misima in the 1890s and enjoyed considerable success winning baptisms and suppressing a number of rituals they found "pagan" and otherwise objectionable. The United Church, the national body that succeeded the mission, is today firmly entrenched in the island society under indigenous leadership. All the same, traditional conceptions of the person, spirits, and death survive in modified forms, some on the borrowed authority of reinterpreted Christian teachings and some in apparent defiance. The community has also supported a "cargo cult" for decades despite the hostility of church leaders. There is thus a classic division of the religious field into Christian, traditional, and syncretic domains, their boundaries marked and maintained by varying degrees of tension. Yet it would be very inaccurate to think of these domains as autonomous religious systems. The islanders participate in the entire religious spectrum; repudiating Christianity in favor of tradition, or the cult in favor of Christianity would be tantamount to reputiating part of themselves (cf. Ranger 1978:489). Macintyre indicates that the totality of popular religion provides the best framework for making sense of these permutations:

> I do not see Misiman Christianity as a veneer, indeed many of the people I met there I consider to be devout and sincere Christians whose religious adherence imbues their whole existence. But in teasing out some of the strands of these complicated and enmeshed ideologies I have highlighted the ways in which contradictions can be virtually ignored in one context because they are seen to be resolved in others (pg. 99).

Different parts of the religious field, then, may address distinct religious aspirations. This is particularly true as Pacific islanders are drawn more into larger multicultural contexts in which they must deal with issues often remote from the intimate matters of kith and kin in the community. But there are further complexities. Macintyre notes "subtle mergings and conflations" between the modalities of Misiman religion. When we turn our attention to what people do and think, instead of merely how they are organized, we may find that the distinct Christian or traditional identity of a church or ritual turns out to be illusory.

Perhaps because they look so familiar and therefore understandable, Christian rituals and literatures in Pacific communities have rarely received scholarly attention. Yet what might seem trite or prosaic to a Westerner may appear exotic and puzzling to members of a different cultural tradition. This insight provides Carl Thune with a starting point for his remarkable hermeneutic of a church service in Loboda village on Normanby island (chapter 6). Methodist missionaries began working on Normanby at about the same time as Misima. Both the church and its teachings have in several generations become conventional parts of village life, even if they challenge village morality (as is true, of course, of the church in Western societies). Although the services in Loboda appear very European — unaltered by their cultural environment — Thune argues that they really are "a part of the Loboda village cultural world. If they make sense to Loboda villagers, it is because they address villagers' concerns that almost certainly long predate the appearance of Christianity in Papua New Guinea" (pg. 102). Thune sees the services as part of the larger corpus of Loboda "literature;" more specifically as "a literary exploration of the fundamentals, possibilities, and impossibilities of the social world" (pg. 101). The Loboda social world is matrilineal, egalitarian, and local. The prayers and Bible readings of the service confront this familiar world with images of patrilineality, absolute authority, and universality. The purpose of the sermon, according to Thune, is to reconcile these contraries. His analysis is ingenious and provocative, suggesting new directions for the study of Christian institutions in local communities.

If Christianity is not always what it seems, the same is true of "traditional" religions. In chapter 7, Martha Kaplan analyses a situation very similar to that described by Chowning and Trompf in New Britain, where a people have absorbed Christian ideas and forms into the matrix of a pre-existing religious ideology. Like other interior people on Viti Levu in Fiji, Drauniivi villagers believe they have a special relation with the ancestral gods of the land who originally created the islands. They claim also that Christianity is identical to their autocthonous religion, that Jehovah first appeared in their mountains to create their ancestors. As proof, they point to "Christian" traits of sharing, generosity, and kindliness — traits that are far more characteristic of Fijians than the individualism and greediness they suppose characterizes European morality. Kaplan argues that not only this ideology but its mode of propagation draw from Fijian cultural traditions. Faced with the concept of a singular, ultimate God, interior religious leaders in the nineteenth century enacted a familiar cultural logic in which stranger kings were encompassed by the original people of the land, thus at once tapping and domesticating the foreign power. The cultural logic of the land encompassing the chiefs has influenced the ways Fijians have approached new ideas and new arrivals to their shores long after colonial rule and Methodism were firmly established. But Kaplan is careful to point out that this cultural logic has itself been reshaped by the contingencies of history. Examining some of the rhetoric of the recent government coup, she shows that the identification of Christianity with traditions has served a variety of interests: from legitimating the great wealth and power of ruling chiefs as divinely sanctioned to providing an ideology of racial discrimination against Indo-Fijians. An indication of the resilience of Fijian culture in the context of Drauniivi village, the cultural logic has also been a fertile source of new "traditions" invented in response to political interests.

To Western observers, Pacific societies have often appeared as battlegrounds between internal and external systems: between distinct economies, cultures, or religions. It is by no means original to recognize the over-simplicity of many such formulations; but the critique is still valid, especially in the study of emerging Pacific religions. As I pointed out in the previous section, by focusing on the larger categories of Christianity, traditional religion, and colonial systems, scholars have tended to create conceptual models that downplay and sometimes even exclude the possibility of independent indigenous expressions of Christianity. The five chapters I have briefly summarized, and the five that follow, show that Christianity has had a vital but extremely diversified influence in the religious experience of Pacific islanders. The diversity and flux of much of popular religion, I would argue, needs to be recognized and grappled with. To this end, I suggest scrapping models of conversion which impose systems upon the data and replacing them with contextual approaches which view Christianity as part of larger popular religions. In turn, this compels us to abandon models that make islanders the passive recipients of external change and adopt perspectives that highlight their active part in religious innovation. As more ethnographic attention is given to local Christianity, it is clear that islanders have been active participants in their own conversions, creating new forms of religion that are both Oceanic and part of world Christianity.

A focus on the local face of Christianity can provide a valuable corrective to models that assume that religious systems are more or less discrete. By highlighting the ambiguities and creativity of indigenous peoples, however, a local prospect may introduce its own parochial distortions: for it is clear when one compares cases that people are constrained and influenced in their religious ideas and actions by cultural patterns, Christian orientations, and larger political and economic pressures. People frequently have only a dim awareness of these forces in their lives. It is not enough, then, to look at how Pacific islanders experience and adapt Christianity in local societies, we must return to the larger contexts that guide and constrain islanders in what they may create. Christianity after all is bound up in regional and global economic, political, and social organizations, and proclaims itself a universal religion.

THE GLOBAL FACE: PACIFIC CHRISTIANITY AS A REGIONAL AND INTERNATIONAL RELIGION

Thirty years ago, Ian Hogbin commented on the cumulative impact of Christianity on native societies:

> Although pagan beliefs linger beneath the surface for so long, one great change follows immediately on conversion. The religion of any primitive people inevitably reflects the social structure of the community in which it develops... Christianity reflects another type of social system in which genealogical relationship is not so significant. Every Church asserts its universality, and those who belong to it offer the same kind of prayers to the one Deity. A mission native may continue to believe for many years that his chief obligations are to the members of his own society, but a basis is now provided for broadening the concept of brotherhood until it embraces not only the inhabitants of neighbouring settlements but also strangers (Hogbin 1958:182).

Scholars are gradually discarding the image of pre-contact pristine, isolated village and island societies. In many instances Christianity expanded along the lines of pre-existing kinship, alliance, and exchange networks that embraced many communities.[10] And while missionaries organized followers into wider polities, they introduced divisions of their own into the social scene (e.g. Ross 1978). Nevertheless, Hogbin's point is well taken. Christianity, particularly in the early missionary stages, introduced its followers to an enlarged and vastly complicated world — indeed, cosmos. The introduction was both practical and ideological. Through schooling and the application of imported practical arts, missionaries began to familiarize islanders with the orientations and organization of the hegemonic colonial system the Europeans were then building. And, through the provision of the Bible and church liturgies and traditions, they introduced islanders to a language within which Christians could speak about their enlarged social and spiritual community.

Michael French Smith in chapter 8 explores the significance of this expanding context in a comprehensive analysis of Catholicism in Kragur village on Kairiru island near Wewak in Papua New Guinea. Mission fathers and the people themselves have long regarded Kragur villagers as model Catholics, ardent and faithful followers of the church. Yet their involvement is full of intriguing ambiguities. Catholic missionaries played a dominant part in Kragur villagers' early encounters with the outside world, and villagers' practical involvement in church activities continues to shape their notions of European values and work patterns. Their understanding is by no means accurate; but by encouraging villagers "to exaggerate their own...problems and to romanticize the European way of working" (pg. 159), the mission system serves to make the new order comprehensible and acceptable, if somewhat discomforting. All the same, Kragur villagers draw on a combination of Christian and indigenous forms to insist on their cultural uniqueness in a multicultural world. Like the Drauniivi Fijians (chapter 7) and Pulapese (chapter 11), Kragur people "assert that they are good Catholics because they have a long tradition of living in terms of a similar [moral] code" (pg. 164). Smith notes that outside of church ceremonies Kragur engage in a mixture of Christian rituals, traditional magic, ideas of spirits and local deities, and cargoism. As Kragur people become more involved in the larger society of Papua New Guinea, the tension between the local and Catholic elements of their identity leads to continuing innovation across the religious spectrum. As Smith argues, the process is characterized by indeterminacy: "Neither missionaries nor villagers have had full control or consciousness of the political and economic significance of their involvement with Catholicism" (pg. 150).

It would be misleading, I think, to suggest that Kragur villagers are creating a brand new religion. Clearly there is much inventing going on, both deliberate and through creative misunderstandings, but there is also much that is accepted or continued wholesale: church liturgical forms, magic, and the superiority of European work patterns, to name three. We need a way of talking about indigenous Christianity that does not reduce it to the status of a foreign import or an indigenous innovation. I suggest that in examining societies like Kragur village, we borrow from Fabian's critique of studies of African religious movements (1981:119-20), and imagine indigenous Christianity existing in a field of tension between distinct and often contradictory forces. Picture indigenous Christianity suspended between local, regional, and global ideal-type poles, each corresponding to a specific mode of production, mode of cultural process, and type of religious organization. The model might appear as in Figure 1.

The three poles in the model are somewhat arbitrary. One can easily imagine more numerous reference points in different situations. Moreover, the entities within each set are not unchanging; nor should they be reduced to one another. Smith makes this clear by showing, for example, that Kragur villagers interpret Roman Catholic teachings in variant ways that sometimes lead them to accept and sometimes to resist the hegemonic economic order. With these provisions in mind, the model has a number of advantages. First, it allows us to examine simultaneously numerous influences at work in a religious field while leaving the question

FIGURE 1: THE RELIGIOUS FIELD AND INDIGENOUS CHRISTIANITY (adapted from Fabian 1981).

of their relative strength open. One cannot assume, for example, that initiation ceremonies or cargo cults are more authentic or significant to a group of people than Western-style church services. Second, it allows for the possibility of religious pluralism, enabling us to distinguish elements that define separate religious organizations from the general influences that affect the entire religious field.

I attempt to tease out such elements and influences in my study of relations between the village and mission station in Maisin society on Collingwood Bay in Papua New Guinea (chapter 9). Although Anglican missionaries have long left the scene, Maisin continue to support a distinct mission institution in their villages which they regard as foreign to village life. They have solid historical reasons for this. The missionaries praised traditional village life (as they understood it) and encouraged the Maisin to maintain as much of their traditional culture as possible. At the same time, the mission station has provided the primary access point to Christian teachings and to outside jobs, the cash economy and the larger political system. Maisin are content to identify the station with Western values and orientations; and, indeed, the patterns of station and village life show a marked contrast that can be identified with cultural differences between Western Christianity and indigenous traditions. This is, however, a situation of religious pluralism, not of the confrontation of two distinct systems. The same Maisin who engage in healing rites attend church services, pay stewardship levies and send their children to school. The station and the village are aspects of a single society that, as a whole, adjusts to its gradual incorporation into larger economic and political systems. As I show at the end of the chapter, Maisin talk about the relations between the local station and village reflects a more profound issue: the relation between the aspirations of villagers and the larger society of

Papua New Guinea.

It is interesting to contrast religious pluralism in communities, such as the Maisin villages or Misima (chapter 5), in which divisions develop between mission Christianity and indigenous religious forms, with situations where the divisions are primarily between denominations. In several Polynesian societies, notably Tahiti, Samoa, and Tonga, Christianity was quickly absorbed into the local culture and most islanders today see no contradiction or separation between "tradition" and their faith (Latukefu 1988:89-90). Pluralism tends to develop as schisms within denominations and through denominational rivalries. Tamar Gordon's (chapter 10) study of Tongan Mormonism gives a revealing picture of the process. Mormon doctrine on the family implies a sharp break with traditional Tongan morality. Partly for this reason, the Mormons have been vigorously opposed at various times by other Tongan Christians, who have worried the new religion would undermine the very basis of their society. Gordon shows that Mormons in Tonga take their church's strictures on the family very seriously but, in numerous practical and ideological ways, they build bridges between them and conventional Tongan forms and values. To the degree that indigenous Mormons are "inventing" families that marry American and Tongan forms, they shift the controversy surrounding their church from an argument about culture to a debate about the most authentic expressions of Christianity.

The model of indigenous Christianity as part of a religious field in tension between distinct social and ideological poles has a third advantage. It suggests that people may engage in religious activities and ideologies in several contexts and at different social levels. In a study of religious pluralism in Java, Hefner (1987) argues that participation in different levels of social organization produces distinct types of religious discourse in village societies. He notes that "in all religious and ideological discourse there is a dual economy of knowledge, in which explicit doctrinal knowledge is informed by and mutually informs a less discursive, tacit knowledge constructed in a wider social experience" (*ibid.*:55). Embedded in small-scale communities in which knowledge is woven into the fabric of everyday life, local religious expressions are relatively flexible and unarticulated, informed by tacitly assumed moral and cosmological assumptions. In contrast, regional religious activities must be more explicit and vocal about their general assumptions for they "provide the discourse for the elaboration of a secondary moral and ideological identity beyond that given in the immediacy of local groupings." Regional religions form "a kind of secondary community built above and between those given by local social circumstances" (*ibid.*:74-75).

With an omnipresent and omnipowerful deity and universal conception of human history, Christianity naturally dominates the more general levels of religious discourse in the Pacific. Moreover, it is closely associated in the minds of many Pacific islanders with the larger contexts of their existence, as Hogbin's quote opening this section and the model of the religious fields suggest. Yet Thune and Kaplan (chapters 6 and 7), among others, clearly show that Christian elements may form part of local religious discourse; and Trompf's (chapter 4) study of the Pomio *Kivung* is one of many examples of indigenous cultural categories being enlarged to address more complex realities.[11] This evidence suggests that religious discourses, like other permutations within the religious field, draw from a number of points of reference. It also suggests that in many cases the same people engage in several levels of religious discourse. It would be amazing, indeed, if there was no feedback between these levels of conceptualization.

Juliana Flinn in chapter 11 provides an interesting example of feedback between internally and externally oriented discourses on Pulap island in Truk State, Micronesia. Unlike some Micronesian islands where involvement in Christianity encouraged an ethic of individualism (Nason 1978), the Pulapese, with the encouragement of a post-Vatican II generation of Catholic fathers, identified the "Christian emphasis on harmony and concern for others... with Pulapese concepts of cooperation and focus on descent group and community concerns" (pg. 229). They have constructed a cultural identity for outsiders and themselves in which they construe Catholicism as extolling "traditional core values." Flinn shows that this development of a cultural identity was a response to the challenges of living in a multicultural colonial state. An identification with Catholicism allows Pulapese to assert a common relation with Christians elsewhere; at the same time, they can point to cultural features that distinguish them and may even indicate they act out "Christian" principles, such as generosity among kin, more faithfully than Christians elsewhere. As Armstrong notes in chapter 12, Christianity provides a basis for asserting both a common identity and for nurturing differences between Pacific peoples. The Pulapese's image of themselves is as least as important for its internal implications as for outsiders' consumption. It forms part of a relatively conservative ideology in which, according to Flinn, individualistic actions on the part of youths or strangers can be effectively countered. The Pulapese tell themselves that they are "traditional," and they draw on the authority of Catholicism to make sure their society conforms to that image. Flinn compares Pulap to two other islands in Truk where Christianity has been used in support of quite distinct types of cultural identity with different implications for change in these societies. In Vanuatu and Papua New Guinea, like Pulap, proponents of cultural identity emphasize the compatibilities between *kastom* and Christianity. This has often been a consciously political process, as leaders try to forge regional coalitions by appealing to local people's sense of their past and to their religious affiliations (Howard 1983; Keesing and Tonkinson 1982; Latukefu 1988).

As well as contributing to developing notions of who they are, membership in Christianity provides islanders access to a variety of regional and international forums. Many church organizations have acquired considerable political clout. In chapter 12, Jocelyn Armstrong points out that while the mission churches in New Zealand for a very long time formally acquiesced to the government's policy of cultural assimilation of the Maori, they formed a fragile haven for Maori self-esteem, identity, and language. In recent decades, they have formed a crucial political base for a unified Maori effort. A sense of Maori identity overrides the denominational differences between the churches. Partly through this spirit of ecumenism, self-help, and cooperation Maori assert an identity distinct from the Pakeha (white) majority. The churches have been important for the Maori not only as a source of self-esteem, but as a lobbying body against government policies and the inequities of New Zealand society. Indeed, as Armstrong points out, the Maori churches today are in the forefront of the ecumenical movement in New Zealand and the political program to construct a truly bicultural nation.

Church organizations elsewhere in the Pacific, from the Pacific Council of Churches down to local Christian cooperative associations, are actively engaged in reshaping local communities and nations. Some of their projects, such as organizing competitive feasts to raise church funds, address themes that are peculiar to the region (Gregory 1980); but others — temperance movements against alcoholism and domestic violence, campaigns to control multinational corporations, promotion of local economic development, studies of tourism, formation of youth clubs — are familiar concerns of Christian organizations around the world, addressing common problems at the level of the world system (see Forman, chapter 2). While Pacific Christianity in its local manifestations continues to reflect and nurture the diverse cultural traditions of small-scale island communities, as a global religion it has also brought the world to Pacific islanders and encouraged their entry onto the world stage. Armstrong's comment about Maori Christianity is appropriate for Pacific island religions as they become further involved in international Christianity: "We should look for the past in the present but also for rearrangements and new outcomes over time" (pg. 257).

CONCLUSION

Christianity in various sectarian forms has spread quickly across the Pacific to become the dominant religious influence in the vast majority of local societies and all of the new states. The chapters in this collection, along with a sprinkling of other recent studies mentioned by Forman (chapter 2), reflect a growing awareness among anthropologists that Oceanic Christianity can no longer be adequately understood solely in terms of the missionary encounter with traditional religions. Christianity has become part of the indigenous reality: an important aspect of Pacific islands cultures, one dimension of the integration of local cultures into regional and global cultures.

I have not attempted a new theory of conversion or religious innovation in this introduction. It seems to me unlikely that a new theory will advance our understandings much beyond the work that has already been done on missionization. As we become more familiar with the local complexities, however, we will need to develop more nuanced, multi-dimensional approaches — much as anthropologists have learned to do in the study of kinship, politics, and rites of passage. An adequate study of any instance of Pacific Christianity will draw on the various perspectives developed in studies of missionization. It will consider the doctrines and underlying systemics of both imported and local religions; the social and political conditions influencing the local church from its foundation in the local society to the time of study; and the social, economic, cultural, and political conditions of the local community at the time of study (cf. Laitin 1987:27). The elegance of unilinear models of conversion or mission colonization will be sacrificed for a more ambitious attempt to understand emerging religious realities.

But an ethnographic appraisal of Christianity must also develop its own perspectives and models to better examine what I have called the two faces of Christianity in island communities. For some time now Pacific scholars have called for approaches that see Pacific islanders as active participants in their own history. The ethnographic approach to Pacific Christianity takes up this challenge in a particularly radical way by viewing islanders as the ultimate makers of their own religions. Anthropologists, therefore, have much to offer in understanding emergent Pacific religions. Yet they should also be cautious lest they substitute their own disciplinary myopia for those of others. In particular, anthropologists need to continue to explore perspectives that examine local communities in their larger political and economic contexts (cf. Carrier and Carrier 1987). As I have suggested here, Pacific Christianity spans several social levels. To understand popular religion in local communities, therefore, we must develop ethnographic frameworks that recognize that people live simultaneously in several kinds of social contexts, and that their religions are capable of looking inwards and outwards. The ethnographic study of indigenous Christianity encourages a growing trend in anthropology towards more contextualized and historical accounts.

Christianity poses another more peculiar challenge to ethnographic analysis. Kenelm Burridge (1978) among others has documented the long-standing ambivalence anthropologists feel towards missionaries and, beyond them, Christianity. It is precisely because Christianity seems familiar, and is so deeply embedded in European historical and colonial experience, that it becomes difficult for many Western ethnographers to approach Pacific Christianity with the same dispassion they show towards initiation rituals, beliefs about *mana*, or sorcery accusations. While Western scholars, be they theologians, historians, or anthropologists, cannot help but be influenced by their personal associations with a religious tradition they now in several ways share with Pacific peoples, the challenge is to hold these views in abeyance while attempting to see what islanders themselves are making of their religious lives.

NOTES

1. The literature on the foundation and expansion of the missions is huge. Two excellent general histories are provided by Garrett (1982) and Forman (1982). This section is based primarily on Forman (1987).
2. New Guinea and the surrounding islands were divided into three colonies during the latter nineteenth century. The west was originally controlled by the Dutch until 1962, after which it was incorporated into Indonesia as the province of Irian Jaya. The British annexed southeast New Guinea in 1888. This area became known as Papua after Australia took direct administrative control in 1906. The remaining northeast part of New Guinea and surrounding islands were a German possession until the First World War, after which it became a mandated territory under the League of Nations, administered by Australia as New Guinea. The two former colonies of Papua and New Guinea were combined as Papua New Guinea upon the independence of that country in 1975.
3. See, for example, Point (1977), Trompf (1987), and Forman (chapter 2). Unfortunately, many scholars based outside of the Pacific countries do not have easy access to much of this material, which is in the form of theses from theological seminaries, articles in local journals and newspapers, and privately circulated papers and reports. The writings of Garry Trompf and his students on religious movements in Papua New Guinea draws heavily from these sources and indicates their scholarly value (see Barr and Trompf 1983; and Chapter 4 below).
4. See, for example, Forman (1984), Langmore (1982), Latukefu (1978), Tippett (1977), Wetherell (1978), Whiteman (1983).
5. Although the so-called cargo cults are the best known of these movements, there have been many religious agitations with Christian elements that have not involved cargoist ideas: cooperative societies, proto-nationalist movements, protests against colonial

administrations and missions, and independent churches and sects. Loeliger and Trompf (1985:xi) suggest the generic category of "new religious movements" for the whole. Although Melanesia has tended to receive the most attention, new religious movements have occured across Oceania (e.g., Burridge 1969; de Bres 1985).

6. There have been a few notable attempts, particularly by missiologists (e.g., Tippett 1967; Whiteman 1983).
7. This is especially the case in Micronesia and Melanesia. For a detailed critique of anthropological writings on Christianity in Melanesia, see Barker (Ms.).
8. Rambo (1982) provides a review of the huge literature on the concept.
9. Some of the following argument draws upon Ranger's (1978) excellent critique of African religious typologies.
10. The expansion of Methodism and Tongan hegemony in Fiji (Kaplan, chapter 7) and the diffusion of Christian influence through the *kula* network among the Massim (Wetherell 1977:43, 157) are two examples that come to mind.
11. Horton's (1971, 1975) intellectualist analysis of African conversion is the most sophisticated statement of the notion that traditional ideologies are capable of developing macrocosmic perspectives. In a provocative "thought experiment," Horton goes so far as to assert that given only the economic and social changes of colonialism a transformation from ethnic to world perspectives in African religions "might well have occurred in some recognizable form even in the absence of world faiths" (Horton and Peel 1976:482). The argument is compatible with the more Durkheimian position advanced by Lawrence (1964) and others who see authentic religious change coming only once the social and economic conditions of peoples' have been altered to force them into a wider community.

2

SOME NEXT STEPS IN THE STUDY OF PACIFIC ISLAND CHRISTIANITY

Charles W. Forman

The field of study opened up in this volume is one that presses for further and fuller examination. For the anthropologist studying the adaptation of small-scale societies to modern, world-scale culture, Pacific Christianity offers particularly significant examples for investigation. The process of change which comes with the introduction of a world religion to small-scale societies moved more slowly in the Pacific islands than elsewhere, allowing more time for an indigenous reaction and adaptation. Here were peoples who remained fairly isolated after their initial contacts with the wider world. They continued many of the features of their former life and developed a fairly stable culture combining the old and the new. Christianity has been part of the combination and a part which reveals much about the whole.

Students of world Christianity, like the anthropologists, will find much to attract them to the Pacific. In this region of the world, more than any other, a non-Western expression of Christianity on a broad, popular level had an opportunity to establish itself and develop along its own lines. Again, it was the relative isolation of the islands that made this possible. Also, the fact that whole populations adopted Christianity encouraged an indigenous expression of the faith. A handful of missionaries from Western churches tried to hold the new converts to imported standards, but the relative inaccessibility of most of the people and the continuation of the former social groupings inside the church put severe limitations on what the missionaries could accomplish.

In consequence, both the anthropologist examining adaptations of traditional small-scale cultures and the student of non-Western forms of Christianity will find some of their most illuminating material in the Pacific Islands.

Thus far little attention has been paid to this material. Pacific Christianity, partly because of the smallness of the populations involved and partly because of the lack of outside contacts, has been largely ignored by the scholarly world. The one discipline which has begun to show a considerable interest is that of history, though only in recent years. Up to twenty years ago there were no scholarly histories of any part of Pacific Christianity except for one three-volume work in German and a short, partisan historical analysis in French (Guiart 1959; Pilhofer 1961-63). But in the past two decades a steady stream of histories has appeared dealing with various parts of the Pacific Christian past (e.g. Forman 1982; Garrett 1982; Gunson 1978; Hilliard 1978; Laracy 1976; Thornley 1979; Wetherell 1977; Williams 1972). Many suffered from a common weakness as far as island Christianity is concerned, which was that they gave dominant attention to foreign missions rather than to the local churches. This weakness can be regarded as, to some extent, inevitable because the source materials have been written by foreign missionaries rather than by islanders. In the future, however, serious effort must be made to concentrate on the history of the churches rather than the missions. To do this, ephemeral written materials produced by local people need to be gathered before they are lost (e.g., Crocombe and Crocombe 1968; Tuaivi 1983), and members of the older generation need to be interviewed and their memories recorded while they are still living (e.g., Nerhon 1969).

As part of the history it is important to investigate the process of conversion to Christianity, and also the resistance to conversion. The forces that have been at work in Pacific cultures, making them hospitable or inhospitable to Christianity, have not been carefully analyzed in most areas. Certain islands have been studied (Beaglehole 1957; Clifford 1982; Dening 1980; Firth 1970; Gilson 1980; Hezel 1983; Monberg 1962, 1967; Tippett 1954, 1971; Vicedom 1961), but over the region as a whole there has been little deep analysis of the process of conversion. Even less has there been analysis of those areas that have resisted Christianity, such as Tanna in Vanuatu, Woodlark in Papua New Guinea, and the Moro Movement area of Guadalcanal (Davenport and Coker 1967; Guiart 1956), to determine what made areas like these different from the majority of Pacific Islands.

Outside the discipline of history, less has been done. In anthropology, the volume published in 1978 by the Association for Social Anthropology in Oceania (Boutilier, Hughes and Tiffany 1978) was a path-breaker. A number of other anthropological or sociological analyses of Christianity in particular areas, most of them short, have appeared (Babadzan 1982; Barker 1985b; Bohm 1983; Brady 1975; Fugmann 1986; Hughes 1985; Kaltefleiter 1984; Keysser 1950; Roach 1987a; Schieffelin 1981a; Tomasetti 1976; Westermark 1987; White 1978). The two journals, *Point* and *Catalyst*, coming from the Melanesian Institute for Pastoral and Socio-Economic Service in Goroka, have provided useful articles dealing with Papua New Guinea. The first full-scale scholarly monograph on a section of Pacific Christianity was Tippett's work on the Solomon Islands (1967), and this has been followed by Whiteman (1983) also on the Solomons, and Barker (1985a) on northeast Papua. Full-scale studies of adjustment movements or cargo cults have been much more numerous (e.g., Burridge 1960, 1969; Gesch 1985; Lawrence 1964; Siikala 1982; Steinbauer 1979; Strelan 1978; Worsley 1968). But these have dealt with phenomena that lie on the fringes of Christianity, rather than with its major expressions. Some large ethnographic works have, in the course of broad description of a people, reported on church life (e.g., Belshaw 1957; Berde 1974; Donner 1985; Hogbin 1939, 1951; Jorgensen 1981b; Levy 1973; Lundsgaarde 1966; Mead 1956; Rosentiel 1953; Thune 1980). But such works constitute only the beginnings of what is needed.

A full picture of Pacific Christianity will emerge only as many more, intensive studies are carried out. There will be need to question informants in the same manner as has been customary in exploring traditional religion. There will be need to examine what the belief structure of Christians really is (e.g., Ahrens and Hollenweger 1977; Levy 1969; Lymang 1969; Moritzen 1974; Tuza 1977). Examination of beliefs can be followed by analysis of their sources: What beliefs are derived from traditional religion and what from foreign importation — and what may give the appearance of an importation but underneath maintain the old traditions? The ways in which foreign imports have been modified and adapted reveal much about the thought processes and value systems of the people. In some cases the indigenous sources may be so predominant that the researcher will be inclined to call the Christianity only a thin veneer or to deny that it can be called Christianity at all. But here the outsider needs to respect the decisions of the people. If they themselves call their religion Christianity, outsiders would do well to accept that name. Only an intricate argument using debatable theological norms could justify any other course.

Beyond beliefs, there is need to study religious activities. The ritual or liturgical actions of the Christians constitute an important part of their religion and may reveal much about their way of thinking and believing. Some forms of Christianity that have come to the Pacific are highly ritualistic while others have almost no ritual at all. It may be possible to discern whether Pacific islanders are more attracted to the one or the other type, and whether they have a tendency to transform one into the other. There have been some recent attempts to resurrect pre-Christian indigenous practices in the liturgy of the churches (see Deverell and Deverell 1986; Garrett and Mavor 1975; Point 1980), and more needs to be known as to how well these attempts have been accepted and what staying-power they have shown. Where ancient religious practices have never died out, there is need to know whether they have continued inside the church or outside and parallel to the church, approved, ignored, or condemned by the church, and what differences the church reactions have made to their effectiveness in the common life. Does it make much difference to the old practice of using magical fishing stones that the Presbyterian church of Vanuatu turns its back on the practice and ignores it while, I am told, the Anglican church acknowledges it and teaches that the power of the stones comes from Christ?

Ritual and liturgy relate directly to the arts. Much needs to be investigated about the relation of Christianity to Pacific island arts (cf. Tippett 1980). We need to know where the arts have been encouraged and where discouraged. Has there been a discouragement of traditional art, but an encouragement of imported art? This question applies most obviously to the architecture of the church buildings and to their decoration. But it applies equally to the performing arts, to dances and stories and oratory, and to the music of the churches. Why have a few island societies retained a rich treasury of hymns in a distinctive indigenous musical style — the Cook Islands and Tahiti being outstanding examples — while most have simply adopted the hymnody of the West?

In this day and age, when women are challenging the conventional roles assigned to them, the Pacific churches are not exempt from challenge. Investigation is needed into what women's roles have been traditionally, how Christianity may have changed them already, and how it is pressing or being pressed to change them still further. (Forman 1984; Schoeffel 1977). Local and sectional studies are important here because the different sections of Oceania have had very different, even opposite, views of the place of women. The desire among women for a radical change may be found to vary greatly with their location. It may also vary with their place in society: do women of chiefly rank show less interest in changing their church roles than do women of less exalted social position? The relation between men and women in the church also calls for attention. The extent to which they can work together and the extent to which they are isolated from each other in separate church structures is something we know little about. The same may be said regarding the social forces, local or foreign, that have made for differences in men-women relations.

Patterns of leadership in the church, whether male or female, are another subject for study. Careful analysis has been made of political leadership in the islands and also of economic leadership, but religious leadership has hardly been touched. The relation of church patterns in leadership to the pre-Christian and contemporary secular patterns is largely unexamined. (Brady 1975; White 1978). To refer to a specific problem, it has been noticed recently that the Roman Catholic seminary in Papua

New Guinea graduates only a small percent of its students, while the central Catholic seminary for the other Pacific islands graduates a high percent. Some contrasting attitudes toward religious leadership may well account for the difference, but what those attitudes are is not at present known.

The beliefs and values held by religious leaders may be markedly different from those of the rank and file of Christians. The long process of education to which leaders are subjected certainly has the intention of making a difference. But whether that intention is achieved and what convictions the leaders hold are matters needing further exploration. At this point, while interviews would be useful, there is also available for use the wealth of material found in sermons and the lesser amounts of material in the writings of church leaders (Boseto 1983; Bürkle 1978; Fugmann 1985; Linge 1978; May 1985; Struggling for Lutheran Identity 1983; Trompf 1987). Pacific Christianity still moves primarily in an oral, rather than written, milieu, and those who would study its leaders' views must look chiefly to oral sources.

Up to this point the proposals for further study have revolved around Pacific Christianity as it has existed under the fairly stable conditions that characterized most of Oceania until fairly recently. But now there has been a massive new incursion of outside influences. Technological innovations, advances in communications and transportation, higher levels of education, and new ways of thinking are transforming Pacific society at a breakneck pace. A whole new range of studies in Pacific Christianity is demanded by the new situation. Basically the question must be, how does a Christianity which lived with and adapted to traditional Pacific societies now deal with the new conditions which confront it, as they confront all other established Pacific institutions?

The directly religious challenge of the present situation is carried by the new religious groups that have entered the scene. For many years a small number of long-established Christian denominations have made up the Christianity of Oceania. But now, with easier travel and rapid social change everywhere, new missions, mostly of Pentecostal and conservative evangelical groups, are coming in and formerly marginal groups are showing new strength, challenging the hold of the long-established churches. A new wave of Christianity is trying to supplant the old (Britsch 1986; Cummings 1961; Douglas 1974; Hall 1980). There has been almost no critical analysis of the new wave, though its power is being felt throughout the Pacific. What success is it achieving? Where is it being rejected, and why? What appeal does it have for islanders? Does it relate to elements of the island psyche which the older churches have ignored, or is it attractive only to young cosmopolitans who have lost much of the island psyche? Questions like these have yet to be answered in any careful, informed way.

The new situation in the Pacific has other than religious dimensions and there is need to study the Christian responses to these as well. Urbanization, for example, is a phenomenon of Pacific life to which there has been a modicum of Christian response. The extent and adequacy of the response should be considered. It may well be that the churches lose the people who move to the cities, or it may be that certain churches lose them while others hold them or even gain them. The facts about Christianity and urbanization, together with their implications, have yet to be understood (Point 1975).

Urbanization and new missions result in religious pluralism, a condition which is little known in the older village life where one church was usually predominant (Fullerton 1969). Pluralism could well shake the whole world-view of Pacific island Christians, but how far it has done so we do not know. Pluralism could also break the well-established relation of Christianity to the communal sense of identity, as that has been shown in some of the chapters of this book. It could destroy the role of religion as provider of the ultimate coherence for the society and make it the challenger of the society. But whether any of these changes are taking place, and if so to what extent, remains to be discovered.

The relation of Christianity to the new force of nationalism is another matter that calls for investigation (cf. Black 1963; Lini 1980; Loeliger 1974). The activity of church leaders in the independence movements in Vanuatu and New Caledonia and the use of Christian national mottos in Samoa and Papua New Guinea suggest that nationalism and Christianity have walked hand in hand. But if this is the case, it would be well to know whether the partnership is laden with tensions or is harmonious, and whether Christianity is an independent and equal partner or is simply a pawn of nationalism. Of course, answers to these questions may differ enormously from country to country, and would differ from author to author.

Beyond nationalism there is the new regionalism, the consciousness of common interests and common problems, which is drawing the Pacific Islands together and leading to the formation of hundreds of regional organizations. The relation of Christianity to this consciousness needs to be considered as a factor in assessing the long-term strength of regionalism. The churches have formed their own regional organizations (Crocombe 1983; Forman 1986), but the extent of tension between regional and national Christianity has not been analyzed. Regional actions have been taken by both religious and non-religious bodies to protect Pacific interests (Biddlecomb 1982; Siwatibau and Williams 1982; Winkler

1982), though the interplay between the two groups remains to be investigated.

Finally, there is, above the regional level, the world as a whole. What part is Pacific Christianity playing in relating the islands to the rest of the world? Is it in the forefront of efforts at world-wide relations, or is it moving only grudgingly into the world arena? Doubtless there are forces within the island religion pulling it in both directions, but they need to be identified and their relative strength examined.

The topics for investigation which have been proposed here are only suggestive of the richness and diversity of the subject and the minimal extent to which it has been explored thus far. Some of these topics have been considered in the chapters of this volume, but the consideration here cannot be regarded as definitive because the field is constantly changing. The field of Pacific Christianity, even if it were completely explored today, would require fresh investigation tomorrow, simply because the islanders' religion is always moving and developing. Increasingly, too, the islanders themselves will be making studies of their own religious life and bringing a new perspective to bear on the whole field. Outsiders may learn much from the insiders' approach to the subject and may soon have to take a subordinate role to those who can see the subject from within. The prospects are full of challenge.

3

GOD AND GHOSTS IN KOVE

Ann Chowning

"They are good Catholics... but they believe that God originally came from Kombe" — remark attributed to F. Bischof, the first priest in Kove, about 1938 (Wright 1966:87).

During a period of almost 21 years, the Kove of West New Britain have shown a general response to the presence of Christian missions that differs from that which I have found in other Papua New Guinea societies.[1] The early identification of one of their supernatural beings with the Christian God — an identification strengthened by the teachings of a long-lived cargo cult — made it possible for the Kove to think of themselves as Christians without necessarily feeling that they need affiliate closely with any of the missions working in the area. Few seem devout, and a number report changes of affiliation unaccompanied by strong conviction, while others express skepticism about the teachings of all missions. None speak of themselves as atheists, however, nor could any be classified as adherents of a fully traditional religion. For a very large number of Kove, regardless of church membership, aspects of the cargo cult ideology have greatly affected their beliefs about God. Not only did God originate in Kove, but He has a particular interest in His people. They, however, have been frustrated in their attempts to make contact with Him, and He with them. Such contact would produce for the Kove all the blessings thought to be enjoyed by others, notably Americans, such as freedom from any physical labor, and the ability to return to life again shortly after death.

Attitudes about ghosts and apparitions are a mixture of traditional beliefs and new interpretations affected by and contributing to theories about the fate of the soul and of the individual personality. Some of these interpretations derive from the cargo cult, and some from the teachings of the missionaries, which differ between the Roman Catholics and Seventh Day Adventists. On the other hand, the missions do not seem to have conveyed differing ideas about the nature of God, although they disagree strongly about the behavior demanded of those who would gain access to him or avoid his punishment. Mission teachings about God strike few Kove as inconsistent with cargo cult ideology; adherents of the cult may claim affiliation with any mission, or none. Because doctrines of the long-established churches have not produced the results sought by the cultists, many Kove are willing to try out recently-arrived missions, especially those with American connections. They also hope that foreigners other than missionaries can be induced to tell them how to get what they desire from their own God, who differs to an extent that few appreciate from the deity described by the missionaries.The present and future fate of Christianity in Kove reflects major misunderstandings on the part of both the Kove and foreign missionaries as well as the influence of Kove hopes and desires far removed from those that the missionaries wish to inculcate. In the thinking of many Kove, Christianity offers versions of an ancestral religion, whereas outsiders, including myself, see them adapting Christian concepts both to those that existed prior to the coming of Europeans and to those reflecting reactions to European culture.

BACKGROUND

When I first went to Kove in 1966, my main purpose was to investigate the reasons for the reported resistance to both government and mission influences. This apparent conservatism contrasted with what I had found in other Papua New Guinea societies in which I had worked. As it turned out, the Kove were not so conservative as outsiders thought them (see Chowning 1969, 1972), and much of the resistance to Europeans derived from adherence to the doctrines of a cargo cult which the then Australian administration thought was quiescent. Because, like so many cargo cults, this one centered on America, it was to create many problems for me as an American (see below); I did not so much investigate it as have information about it forced upon me. For other reasons having to do with the rivalry between adherents of different denominations, I did not investigate attitudes towards Christian teachings as fully as I might otherwise have done.[2] Consequently this chapter is only a partial account of the situation in Kove during the period covered here.

The Kove, called Kombe by outsiders, live along the north coast of West New Britain just to the west of the Willaumez Peninsula. Most of the villages are located on tiny islets within paddling distance of gardens on the mainland. Their neighbors to the west are the Kaliai (Lusi), described by David and Dorothy Counts, who speak a very closely related language. Culturally, the two societies also have much in common, but their history of contact has been different, and they have been administered from different government stations.

Kove was brought under partial government control in German times, prior to World War I, but Christianity came considerably later. A Roman Catholic (MSC) mission station was established on Poi Island in 1930, and apart from the disruption caused by World War II, during which time all foreign mission personnel were withdrawn, has had a resident priest ever since. About 1970, after quarters had been built for nuns, the station moved to Sasavoru on the mainland across from Poi, and from that time offered hospital facilities and a school on the mission station itself. Earlier the priests gave some medical help in emergencies and provided powdered milk for babies who needed it, but their principal focus was on conversion. Catechists, most if not all Tolai from East New Britain, were assigned to most villages and in some cases ran village schools, which reportedly gave little but religious instruction. In time many of the Tolai were replaced by Kove, who normally worked in their own villages. After the war several Catholic schools were established on the mainland, and a number of boys attended, with those to be trained as catechists receiving further education in East New Britain. Until the nuns came to act as chaperones, most parents refused to allow daughters to board at these schools (one of which shifted to government sponsorship after the new school was established at Sasavoru).

For over 20 years the Catholics had Kove to themselves, but in 1952 the Seventh Day Adventists established a mission station, complete with boarding school and medical facilities, at Silovuti, within Kove. They also sent missionary teachers into the villages, where they set up village schools and conducted church services. Most of these teachers came from Mussau, an island north of New Ireland famous for the wholesale conversion of its population to a religion which insisted that they reject all of their traditional culture, but some came from other areas, such as Bougainville, in which the church had long been active. Like the Catholics, the SDAs eventually trained Kove teachers in their high school in East New Britain, but although some of these worked in their own society, they were normally not sent to their own villages, and a number were stationed for long periods outside Kove.

The shift from Catholicism is said to have begun with the children, who regarded the SDA schools as much superior to the Catholic ones and insisted on attending them. (The SDA teachers were better educated than the catechists, and were better equipped to teach English and world history, among other subjects regarded as useful). It was also easier for children to accept the many SDA prohibitions, particularly on smoking, chewing betel, and eating the main Kove protein foods, shellfish, and pork. Although some Kove were converted directly as adults, and others were reported to have followed their children or spouses into the church, almost no adult converts found it possible to observe all of these prohibitions. Indeed, a number of mission teachers or their spouses were known to transgress from time to time. To this day, the most fervent SDAs tend to be men, and a few women, who attended SDA schools from early childhood into high school. They are particularly opposed to eating pork and, in most cases, drinking beer, although some raise pigs and buy beer to sell to others as part of the elaborate affinal exchange system. Because Silovuti boarding school also accepted students from outside the region, a number of these men have non-Kove wives.

In the 1970s Silovuti was first damaged by a scandal regarding the pastor and some of the female students. Parents removed their daughters, and some who were not SDAs expressed greater reluctance to pay school fees there for their children. At the end of that decade Silovuti was selected as the site for a South Korean-run timber project, and the mission station was shifted. For some years there was little SDA activity in Kove, apart from sporadic visits by missionaries hoping to revive local interest, but as of 1987 at least two SDA schools were operating, one with a teacher's wife trained as a nurse who ran an aid post. More extended medical care had, however, passed to Sasavoru, where many mothers went to bear babies regardless of their own church affiliation.

During the postwar period, and to an increasing degree in recent decades, Kove has also received frequent visits from missionaries representing other religions and denominations. The most prominent have been the Baha'i, Jehovah's Witnesses, and New Tribes Mission, the last of which has established a large mission station in the interior of the Kaliai region. Each of these has attracted a handful of at least temporary converts. Nevertheless, most Kove identify themselves as either Catholics or SDAs, with the prime symbols of their affiliation their Christian names (from the New Testament and the list of saints for Catholics, and from the Old Testament for SDAs),[3] and their observance of the day of rest on Sunday or Saturday. Many Kove have changed affiliation at least once during their lives, including some schoolboys who after leaving a school belonging to one denomination have completed their education at one belonging to another.[4] Wives, or occasionally husbands, are often reported to have shifted after marriage to their spouse's religion. Many families are mixed in their affiliation. There is, however, a tendency for villages or village wards to be identified as Catholic or SDA. During the 1960s antagonism between the denominations was so high that the missionaries stationed in the villages had physical fights, but as far as I know, no such episodes have occurred for many years. I suspect that the Kove, with a few exceptions, no longer feel so strongly about church membership, but here I may be in danger of over-generalizing from the village I know best.

In 1966 I lived in Kapo, a village identified as Catholic, and switched from it partly for that reason.[5] It had a village church, but no school, and a catechist from the village who was fervent though shaky on points of doctrine, judging from his request that I give him information about contraceptives. While I lived there I noticed that very few men attended the services he conducted, and a number of residents of both sexes were said to be still unbaptized, but many of the young people frequently mentioned their Catholic beliefs. Even some men who did not attend church contributed thatch and labor to the church buildings at Poi. Nevertheless, when the Catholic priest (a German) paid a surprise visit to the village, he was almost ignored by adults, who neither greeted him nor interrupted what they were doing. Children sent to the Catholic school on the mainland rarely attended, and little was done to compel them. The Kapo people feared divine punishment if they worked on holy days, but apart from the catechist, showed few signs of interest in the church except when they derided SDA beliefs. By 1986, however, the catechist was expecting one of his sons to be ordained as a priest and said that the occasion would be celebrated with the building of a handsome new church, of permanent materials, within Kapo — an endeavor that suggested considerable commitment to the church on the part of Kapo residents.

In 1968 and 1969 I lived in Somalani, identified by some government officers and missionaries as SDA but by most as mixed. Two middle-aged men, and their families, were particularly strong SDAs, as were a majority of the children and young, just-married, men. Antagonisms between Catholics and SDAs, even full brothers, ran high. The Catholic church had been blown down in a storm just before I came and was not rebuilt during my stays, although a catechist was stationed in the village. There was also an SDA school, first with a Kove and then with a Mussau teacher. Religious services were held regularly and apart from the men just mentioned, attracted mostly children. School hardly met at all while I was there, and people talked of complaining to the mission about the teacher's neglect of his duties. A number of Somalani boys were attending the SDA school in Silovuti. Because Silovuti fees were much higher than those at Catholic schools, and because the students also had to bring such equipment as axes and knives, parents complained about the economic demands but made an effort to supply them. They said they were yielding to the children's desire for a good education, but the Catholic parents tended to deride SDA prohibitions, particularly of foods which they had grown up prizing. Again, I was present when both the Catholic priest and the head of the mission at Silovuti visited Somalani on different occasions, and again saw them virtually ignored except by children.[6]

Despite the quarrels, doctrinal differences for many adults of both sexes tended to be overridden by adherence to the cargo cult. Eventually the cultists, constantly trying to bully me into saying that its doctrines were true, made me decide to move in hopes of finding less fervor elsewhere, and in 1971 I shifted to Nukakau, which has continued to serve as my base. It is also a mixed Catholic-SDA village, and contains many cargo cultists, but they do not make my life so unpleasant.

During my first visits, in 1971-3, Nukakau had a Mussau missionary running a school but complaining endlessly that he got no support from parents. Eventually he withdrew and was not replaced, even when a long-time SDA teacher who had been stationed elsewhere came home. Nukakau also contained two former Catholic catechists, one of whom had left his job because of dissatisfaction with low pay (a common complaint by SDA teachers as well) and one of whom was too ill with tuberculosis to work. After the death of the latter his son, who had not been trained as a catechist, began with the permission of the church to hold Sunday services when he was in the village.[7] These were attended mostly by women and children from the two connected wards which were identified as mostly Catholic, as opposed to the predominantly SDA ones at the other end of the village. Almost none of the older men came, even when the Catholic priest from Sasavoru arrived to conduct a Christmas service in 1986. At that time posts had been cut, and sites selected, for the construction of churches for both denominations, but nothing more had been done. Relations between the two denominations were free of any of the obvious tensions I had found in Somalani. Although I know that some of these tensions still existed elsewhere in Kove (as when the Catholic premier of West New Britain, from Kapo, was blamed by SDA adherents from villages close to Silovuti for having influenced the timber project to choose that site), my impression was that most people were disillusioned with both churches, which had failed to deliver the new way of life that they had expected. They often commented to the effect that, "The churches have been here for many years, and nothing has come to us."

Their expectations have to be viewed in the context of the cargo cult, which began just after World War II. The Allied return to New Britain, which was occupied by the Japanese for $2^1/_2$ years, was led by Americans who pushed east from a landing at Cape Gloucester. The Kove encounter with American technology, abundant goods which were freely shared, and friendliness differed greatly from their experience of Australians and Germans. The attempts of the Australians to re-assert pre-war authority over the people were a factor in producing a strong contrast between what is remembered of Americans and what was observed of other Europeans, especially Australians. Even Kove born after the war glorify Americans. As a fieldworker, I profited from this attitude but also found it a handicap when I refused to confirm that I had been sent by the "King of America" to describe and help alleviate Kove sufferings, such as living in thatch houses and having to work for a living. Their hope derived from a belief that American superiority to other nations resulted from the fact that a Kove supernatural being, long identified with the Christian God, had been rejected by their ancestors but welcomed by the Americans, whom he rewarded (see below).

As regards ordinary church membership, which overlapped with adherence to the teachings of the cargo cult, my impression was that most Kove were considerably less devout than church members in many other Melanesian societies. Although Father Bischof, the first priest in Kove, is still spoken of with respect, partly because of his mastery of the language, and one woman said that she liked the first Tolai priest (Father ToPaivu) because she did not fear him as she did the Germans, priests were often criticized, and men both expressed suspicion of their motives and boasted of standing up to them. A catechist told me that sorcery had driven away one priest, made ill by the older men he criticized and struck.[8] The official headman (*luluai*) of Poi village, where the Catholic mission was located, had several wives, and although one said that she feared that she and her husband would suffer for defying the edicts of the church, her husband never heeded her or the priests.[9] Polygyny is still widespread, regardless of church affiliation. With the SDAS, there is an enormous difference between Kove and what Ross found in Malaita, where church members have abandoned all traditional customs, from song and dance to bridewealth to raising pigs for traditional feasts (Ross 1978:177, 195-196). Kove SDAs give up none of these things — they simply do not eat pork at the feasts, and sometimes express a preference for receiving cash rather than shell money in the affinal exchanges. I did conclude that more women than men were fairly devout, certainly as regards attendance at Catholic services, but I do not know the reason. It may reflect the greater sophistication of the men, more likely to have learned in their travels how few Europeans are devout Christians, as well as the particular male pride in being "big-headed."

No one, however, is so big-headed as to disclaim belief in God. Because God came from Kove, to do so would be to reject their own culture. Furthermore a number of them make it clear that the God is one who enforces at least some edicts that have nothing to do with traditional Kove culture. When a case of infanticide (of an illegitimate child, who would have been killed in the past) was reported in 1986, two hearers spontaneously exclaimed, "God will punish her!" Neither of these took part in any church activities. Several people told me that the many sickly or defective children of a brother and sister were God's punishment for their having collaborated in killing her illegitimate child many years earlier. But the things that offend this God are also thought by some to be failure to stick to either church. A woman whose son was crippled by a fall from a tree suggested that God was punishing him for having twice shifted his church affiliation, and when a young woman (who called herself a Catholic) died in childbirth, several women suggested that God was punishing her for going to the gardens on both Saturday and Sunday. (I have heard it suggested that Baha'ism could not be a "real religion" because it has no day of rest.) Of course the assumption that God punishes non-observance of a day of rest could be correlated with the fact that many who say that they do not belong to a church add they do believe in the Ten Commandments (see below).

To sum up, the Kove population can be divided into the following broad categories. First, a few old people are (or were in the 1960s) said never to have been baptized into any church.[10] My data do not indicate that they really cling wholeheartedly to fully traditional religious beliefs, however. Second, a considerable number of people claim not to belong to any church now. (Often they said that after I had made the same claim about myself, in response to their questions.) Many of these said that they previously "followed" one or more of the local denominations, but became disillusioned by the failure of these to fulfil expectations about major changes in their life-style. Some of the younger members of this category seem never to have belonged to a church. It is the members of the second category who go on to volunteer that they do believe in God, and often they mention support for the Ten Commandments as well. Some of them also express worry about being punished by God for working on holy days, as during the Christmas period and on weekends.[11]

A third category, or set of categories, contains those who upon questioning immediately identify themselves as belonging to a particular denomination, but whose membership seems almost nominal. In the case of the handful who call themselves Baha'i, the only apparent consequence is the opportunity to attend conferences; those I know do not observe any of the distinctive practices or prohibitions of the religion, such as fasting during Ramadan. I do not think they realize that Baha'i are not Christians.[12] "Catholics" in this category may abstain from garden work on Sunday, but they do not attend services even within their own village. "Nominal" SDAs are likely both to avoid garden work on the Sabbath (Saturday) and to abstain from eating pork (which they are taught is disease-laden). They may observe some of the other tabus, as on smoking, chewing betelnut, drinking alcohol, and eating shellfish, but almost none of them observe the full range of dietary prohibitions. Furthermore, they do not attend services, and they do engage in other village activities on the Sabbath. Finally, there are the devout, who regularly attend services, contribute labor and money to church activities, discuss and often defend the teachings of the church, and observe a considerable number of its tenets.[13] SDAs in this category are likely to follow almost all of the dietary prohibitions (perhaps all of them, if they did not convert as adults), and are reluctant even to cook or travel on the Sabbath. Catholics observe the holy days, have their children baptized, and usually send them to Catholic schools.

Cargoists are, however, found in all of these categories, including that of the most devout Christians. Those who profess not to believe in the cult are particularly, but not exclusively, the younger, better educated, most widely traveled (and probably consequently, usually male), but I have learned to mistrust expressions of disbelief. Often those who sound most sceptical either ask questions, spread rumors, tell the cargo myth or respectfully listen when others tell it, in ways that belie earlier statements.[14] I do not mean to imply that all Kove accept cult teachings, but a reference (not uncommon) to "King Mopi's bullshit" is not enough to indicate that the speaker has rejected all the associated ideology.

GOD AND CARGOISM

Because of disruption to government records and the suspension of patrols caused by the war, it is impossible to know just when cult activitiy began and what it included. The Kove only agree that the leader was taught the major part of the myth by an American army officer met in New Britain during the war. Cult members seem never to have engaged in dramatic behavior such as destroying gardens or constructing wharves. The patrol reports that I have seen mention the cult leader but say nothing about the content of the cult. One written in 1954 said that it "seemed to have lapsed," and in 1971 I was assured (erroneously) by a patrol officer that no vestige remained. The earlier activities did include the collection of "taxes" by the leader, who said he would use them to buy off the authorities who were blocking Kove access to their God. In addition, he presented petitions to missionaries, government officers, and at least one visiting UN mission team (in my presence, in 1968). By the time I started fieldwork, the Kove no longer contributed money, but they listened respectfully when the leader visited their villages. He was reported to spend much of his time in Rabaul, until 1966 the government seat for all of New Britain. My impression of the interview with him conducted by the District Commissioner in 1965 was that the administration was worried about the pro-American and so anti-Australian aspects of the cult. These aspects were particularly conspicuous during my stay, because they were expressed in antagonism to any plans put forward by the Australian administration, as for the introduction of local government councils and the leasing of land for commercial enterprises. The widespread Kove assumption was that the Australians intended them harm by these innovations, which must have some hidden purpose, but even those who were not so suspicious asserted that they did not want to engage in activities which would bring such meager rewards. If only the Australians would stop blocking their access to God, they would receive benefits which far outweighed anything the Australians offered.

Precisely because I am an American, I was constantly both told and asked about the cult. My knowledge of it is based on the following information. First, I was repeatedly told the "Moro myth" (often alternatively entitled the 'story of God') by Kove of all ages, with or without a section of the myth relating to America. The tellers included, on different occasions, both the cult leader, nicknamed Mopi, and his second-in-command, nicknamed Moro. The latter also lent me an incomplete text of the myth, written in two hands, which I copied. Through the kindness of the District Office in Rabaul, I was also given a tape-recording of the interview with Mopi, during which he recited a version of the myth. In addition, I recorded various shorter stories relating to 'God' and to the original Kove settlement, Vokumu, 'God's place', from which all the present-day villages derived, most having been founded by migrants from Vokumu who are called 'God's men'. Finally, I heard numerous references to places and phenomena associated with 'God'. If that word was used, I always asked for the Kove version. (All Kove interlard vernacular speech with words and phrases from Pidgin English (*Tok Pisin*), and frequently used the word *Got* 'God' even in speaking Kove.)

The epigraph to this paper points to a major feature of the world view of many present-day Kove. Even prior to World War ll, and up to the present, they not only use 'God' to translate the name of a traditional supernatural being, but identify him with the God of the missionaries. Confusingly, however, 'God' can designate either of two traditional beings, Moro and Araghasi.[15] Some people give one name, some the other, and a few vacillate as to which is the proper designation. The being most commonly identified as God is the same Moro described by Dorothy Counts (1978) in her discussion of Christianity in Kaliai. The Kove are the easternmost society in a distinctive culture area characterized, among other shared features, by a shared art style and ceremonies, which extends westward through the Kaliai (Lusi), Bariai (Kabana), and Kilenge (the area that includes Cape Gloucester), and on to the Siassi Islands off the western end of New Britain. In German times, Kove traveled to Bariai and Kilenge and brought back many ceremonies and ritual practices that originated in the other societies. (Two breakaway Kove villages are actually located within Bariai territory.) Of the two abridged segments of the Moro myth that she gives, Counts says (1978:384): "Moro I is the Kilenge version of a widespread myth whose variants are found at least from the Siassi Islands to the interior of Kaliai." The one she calls Moro II is the section that in Kove is associated with the cargo cult.[16] The central part of the Moro 1 story concerns a pair of brothers, Moro and Akiukiu or Asipel,[17] whose father was killed by their maternal uncle in a dispute over the division of a pig. The boys are given their father's liver[18] as ostensibly the pig's liver, and, not knowing of his father's death, Moro eats it and is transformed into a snake-man, who retains a human head and torso but is a snake from the waist down. The Kove traditonally felt extreme revulsion at the sight of snakes and snake-like creatures such as eels, as many of them still do,[19] and therefore consider it natural that such a creature would hide his shame and be rejected by anyone who saw him, apart from his closest kin. Moro is indeed accepted by his mother, who carries him coiled in a basket on her head, and by his little brother. Moro and his family wander around northwest New Britain, and he demonstrates his ability to produce food, including both domestic and wild animals, and housing, by supernatural means. Eventually he acquires several wives, one of them Kove, who work for but never see him, until one, overcome with curiosity, sneaks into the house in which he is hidden and realizes that she has married a monster. Sometimes, but not always, this is the Kove wife. Enraged, Moro kills her with a blow of his tail, and abandons New Britain from a point in Kilenge, leaving behind his grief-stricken mother, who turns into a rock still visible in the sea there. His brother goes with him.

Some versions contain additional episodes in which Moro and his brother wander around New Britain and the Siassi Islands, eventually leaving each region, after quarrels with people who are rude to or repelled by Moro, or who disobey his instructions. Each episode ends with his announcing that as a consequence they are forever denied benefits such as being able to travel by the power of machines (see Counts 1978:351).

For the cargo cult, however, the most important part of the non-traditional version of the myth has the brothers traveling to America, where they find the people living exactly like the Kove, in houses thatched with leaves and with tools of wood, stone, and shell. The first person encountered is a boy who instead of being repelled by the snake tail, kisses it. In gratitude Moro settles in America and gives Americans benefits which explain why the country supposedly outdoes all others, such as schools, machine-powered ships, advanced weapons, good houses of permanent materials, and food far superior to that they once raised. More importantly, Americans obtain everything they need without doing any physical labor. Finally, Moro proclaims that after death, if the proper ritual is carried out, the dead will return to life. Then, still embarrassed by his snake body and tail, he retires to a place just behind America. All this is part of the myth as most people tell it. The versions given by Mopi and the human Moro not only begin with Biblical references (see below) but have Moro announcing that from now on his name will be God and that of his brother, Jesus. Moro is said eventually to have tried to send his brother back to New Britain to give people the Ten Commandments and, in time, other benefits, but on the way he encounters people of other nations, including the English and the Germans, and is crucified by the Germans. (He rises again after three days.) These wanderings are lengthy and need not concern us here; they serve primarily to account for how other countries received benefits that were denied to the Kove, but also demonstrate God's continuing interest in the Kove themselves. Mopi originally claimed to have been told all this by an American officer, John Mopi,[20] whose name he took, although in the version recorded in 1965, the source was said to be John F. Kennedy, about whom the Kove still talk and ask questions. (The SDA history textbook devotes considerable attention to him.)

In addition to the episodes of the myth, a number of features in the Kove area are still associated with Moro's name. These include a series of large artificial rectilinear mounds in the central part of the region, said to be where Moro planted taro, whch accordingly grows particularly well in the plots between the mounds. Another feature is a tree which rises out of a depression whch is free of undergrowth. In the 1960s, visitors from Kaliai scraped off some of the bark and planted it with taro, and reported particularly good crops, but many Kove are afraid to touch it. Recently, an old woman told me that because crops once grew so well in a particular spot, it was referred to as 'Moro's hill' ('God's hill' in Pidgin), with the implication that he must somehow have blessed it, even though the small island on which it stood was not thought to have been occupied during Moro's time in New Britain. I was also told that "in the past" people said that during the dark of the moon, Moro was seeing it, but this may reflect a misunderstanding of schoolteachers telling the Kove that the sun shines in America when it is night in New Britain (a phenomenon I was frequently asked about).

Although Moro is certainly the man being identified as God, he has a rival in the being whose name is usually given as Araghasi. Araghasi was initially a deity who first sat alone on a mountain in the interior of New Britain, then created land because his legs were tired from hanging down without support, and then created human beings for company. (In Mopi's version he first created Adam and Eve.) The human beings, who are the Kove, settled in the single village of Vokumu, or in a pair of adjacent villages, at a spot near the center of present-day Kove territory which is marked by heavy deposits of shells. One common story has Araghasi hiding himself from men but seducing the women of the village as they go inland to draw water, and displaying his feats by carving depictions of their vulvas on a tree. Eventually discovered, he is chased away. In this and in other versions in which he leaves the Kove, he is sometimes given no destination, but in others he goes to Bariai and becomes the father of Moro. Other stories are told of Araghasi, as that he taught the Kove how to make good permanent canoes instead of the rafts they had been using earlier. He always leaves after a dispute of some sort, and is not represented as retaining any subsequent interest in Kove.

The confusion between Araghasi and Moro is enormous. Because both names are rendered as God, the confusion tends to emerge only when the curious outsider asks for the Kove translation of that word. In the Pidgin written and taped versions of the cargo myth as told by Mopi, both the unnamed creator of humanity, who becomes Moro's father, and Moro himself are called God, and many other Kove follow the same practice, without apparently ever meaning to suggest that there were two Gods. On the other hand, some use the name Moro rather than Araghasi for the creator and/or the being who interacted with the inhabitants of Vokumu. Exactly when and how the confusion arose cannot be unraveled now, nor can the effects of the cargo myth. What does seem precontact is that the Kove were created within their present territory by some supernatural being; unlike the neighboring Kaliai, they have no myth of foreign origin or migration. That the Kove continued to interact with that being, or some other anthropomorphic supernatural with special powers and knowledge, while they were living at Vokumu, seems also to have been part of precontact belief. There is little evidence that other people were thought to have been created at the same time, and several stories tell of the first encounters between the Kove and people living elsewhere in West New Britain, all of whom were initially considered non-human.

More cannot be said; many Kove do not give the creator a name, referring to him just as 'the man who created us' (Pidgin *man i mekim kamap yumi* using the inclusive form of the pronoun, so that the hearer is among those involved). As noted, some call the being associated with Vokumu, Moro. The Moro myth proper seems separate from those that center on Vokumu and its hinterland, at least always starting outside Kove territory.

As Dorothy Counts points out, it is found throughout the culture area (and see also Riesenfeld 1950:273-4).[21] When and why Moro became for most people their sole name for the Christian God is impossible to say; it may have been a result of the cargo myth, which had been stressing that identification for over 20 years when I began my fieldwork. But regardless of this confusion, it is clear that the Kove consider God/Moro to have been the creator of all human beings; the cargo myth explains that he eventually divided the land into different islands containing different nations. Furthermore, regardless of which story is told, it seems always to be assumed that God left Kove (or New Britain) just a short time before the breakup of Vokumu, 'God's place'. Often the same quarrel (over the division of some fish) which usually explains the general dispersal is given as the reason for God's supposedly earlier departure. Since each Kove lineage derives from a paternal ancestor, 'God's man', who left Vokumu to found his own settlement, the number of generations to the descendants makes clear that it is not long since Vokumu was abandoned, and so since God went from them.[22] Men[23] in their forties count a maximum of six generations between themselves and the founder of their patrilineages, and assuming that the Kove always married as early as they do now, the dispersal would have been less than 200 years ago.[24] For the older Kove who accept the points just noted, all of human history must have been compressed into that period. When they asked why their technology was inferior to ours, they would not accept explanations that involved lengthy cultural evolution and the diffusion of inventions. Admittedly they frequently asked how many generations we could reckon, and acted disconcerted or upset at my answers, though one or two suggested that they themselves, lacking writing, might have forgotten the names of some ancestors. I suspect that the concern with counting generations only dated from the visit of the Land Titles Commissioner in 1965, during which he collected many genealogies, but the belief that God had not long left them was found among those who did not have such precise genealogical knowledge.

Eventually I learned that often the questions about when schools were invented and why the Kove lacked ships and cars were not designed to elicit explanations other than confirmation of the cult doctrine or related theories. Even those who seemed genuinely curious rarely seemed to accept what I said, judging from how frequently the same person repeated the same questions. One reason for incredulity was that they knew, both from schools and from what other Europeans had told them, that our ancestors once used stone tools and that Europeans first came to New Britain in sailing ships (the latter fact also being enshrined in a legend of the introduction of tobacco). Their own traditional history was so short that even without the identification of their supernaturals with God, they would have found a much longer period difficult to imagine. But they rejected the possibility that European technology was the result of human invention and labor for other reasons as well. One, of course, was that they never saw Europeans making such things, or indeed performing physical labor of any sort. Some had, however, visited factories in other parts of the country, and conceded that perhaps people could make such things as "biscuits" (crackers and cookies).

The machinery encountered during World War II was another matter; troop carriers and bombers were clearly beyond human capacity. Furthermore, Kove self-esteem has maintained itself in the face of the colonial situation, including missionaries who tell them that their behavior is animal-like and their ignorance abysmal. Despite frequent comments that their dark skin is "dirty" and inferior, Kove often insist that in intelligence and ability (as in warfare) they are at least the equals of any other human beings, and superior to most. They argue that if human beings could have invented such things as writing, their ancestors would have done so. Since they did not, obviously supernatural intervention was involved. Even in 1986, after I had explained what paper is, a man commented that he thought only God could have thought of manufacturing it. The same self-esteem explains Kove resentment that they should be denied the luxuries that they either see others enjoy or imagine that they do. Of all the Kove who told me the Moro myth, only one blamed, and indeed cursed, the ancestors for rejecting Moro and so depriving their descendants. The rest blame the foreigners, particularly Germans and Australians, who according to cult teachings have intervened when their God tried to share his benefits with his own people, either through missionaries or otherwise. (The usual assumption is that the government forbade well-disposed outsiders to share their knowledge, and Mopi's myth says as much.) Kove reactions have ranged from antagonism to the frustrating outsiders to hope that new arrivals will be more forthcoming and helpful. Both disillusion about the missions who have long been present "but have given us nothing good," and willingness to try new ones, are often explained in precisely these terms.

GHOSTS OF THE DEAD

In contrast to beliefs about the nature, deeds, and especially the Kove origins of God, which are shared regardless of an individual's religious affiliation (or lack of it), beliefs about ghosts do vary with mission teachings. (Here I am not concerned with official doctrines but with my interpretation of Kove understandings of them.) The cargo cult, on the other hand, does not have an "official" view on ghosts. Instead, because of its insistence that the dead may return to life, the cult encourages an interpretation of what happens after death that differs from that of the missions. Visions seen in dreams and sickness are taken by cultists as evidence not of a glimpse of heaven or of a different land of spirits, but as proof that the dead have come to life again and are living elsewhere, as in Australia or America. All of these new assumptions are interwoven with traditional beliefs, and the picture is further complicated by individual experience and by stories that circulate purporting to represent the experiences of others.

As in many other Papua New Guinea societies, traditional beliefs about the destination of ghosts seem to have been complex. Each lineage had its traditional hole, often in the sea, into which its ghosts went at death, but there was also a land of the dead inside a mountain farther west. In addition, however, recognizable ghosts often appeared in the bush, in gardens, and particularly after dark, in the village. Sometimes a men's house, which contained the graves of both sexes, was thought to be haunted. Ghosts regularly appeared in dreams, and at the funeral might possess one of the mourners and announce the cause of death. Apart from the bereaved, who might hope only to see the dead person again, contact with ghosts was actively sought for three reasons. First, if no one was possessed at the wake, a seance might be held to which the dead person, accompanied by other ghosts, was summoned to reveal the cause of death and the name of the killer. In addition many men also summoned the ghosts of close male kin to help with hunting or fishing. Finally, a few curers did the same when they went in dreams to rescue souls of village members captured by non-human spirits. Often eyelashes and fingernail cuttings were taken from the corpse and used to maintain contact with the person. Sought encounters were advantageous, and unsought ones might be, as ghosts passed on useful information or protected a sick person from other ghosts, but on the whole ghosts were feared. Apart from wishing to lure the sick to join them, they often behaved unreasonably, punishing people for unavoidable offenses such as not giving the dead person a payment for a marriage that occurred after the death. (One family of my acquaintance was apparently unique in that their ancestor, born in the late 19th Century, argued that there are no true ghosts, only harmless apparitions (Pidgin *piksa* 'picture'), because he could not believe that people with whom one was friendly in life would become malevolent after death. Whatever the behavior ascribed to ghosts they retained their individual identities, being recognizable by appearance, including footprints, and voice. The afterlife seems to have been essentially the same as life before death, in villages under the sea or inside the mountain, involving neither reward nor punishment for behavior in life.

One of the greatest differences between the two main missions has been in attitudes towards ghosts. The official Catholic doctrine is reported as being that nothing recognizable remains to be encountered, because the spirit or the breath (Pidgin *win*), which is equated both with life and the soul, goes straight to God, while the body decays. At the same time many Catholics say that if God is angry with someone, he does not receive the spirit at once. Both protracted dying and reported sightings of a ghost soon after death may be taken as evidence of God's punishment. An example was the ghost of a man whom God is said to have killed by making him fall from a tree he was climbing on a holy day; afterwards his distinctive six-toed footprint was seen, and taken as proof that he was still being punished. When sightings of a particular ghost are reported much later, at least some Catholics state firmly that such things do not exist, because the priest has told them so. By contrast, the SDAs deny not the existence but the nature of apparent ghosts, which are said to be manifestations of the devil. I once, however, heard an avowed Catholic (with SDA children) invoke this idea to discredit the claim of another woman to have been possessed by the first woman's dead husband at the funeral of another man. The main reason seems to have been her dislike of the fact that others kept claiming to have had contact with this ghost (usually in dreams) whereas she, despite her longing to see her dead husband again, had not.

Many reports and conversations made it clear that Christian doctrines concerning ghosts are invoked sporadically by the same individuals who sometimes either express indigenous beliefs or actually report encounters. Apart from statements by members of the family mentioned above, I most often heard the non-existence of ghosts insisted on by the recently bereaved who had actually sought such an encounter, as by visiting the grave, and had failed to see or hear anything. Such people frequently suggested that others who reported encounters with ghosts had lied. Denial of the existence of ghosts was also commonplace among those accused of sorcery in seances and their close kin. On the other hand, one of the most fervent SDAs told me that he had always disbelieved in the return of the dead until, during a seance, he held the bamboo tube to which ghosts were summoned so that they could lead men holding it to the sorcerer responsible for a death. Convinced that the tube was moving independently of the men holding it (as some asserted it did not), he changed his mind. An example of the more usual uncertainties was shown in the behavior of an elderly widow whose dead husband (my adoptive father) had been one of the family of traditional skeptics. I had frequently heard her echo her husband's assertion that there are no ghosts, but when I returned to Nukakau after her husband's death, she first suggested that dogs had barked on the night following my arrival because his ghost had come from its grave on another island to see me. When we went to visit the grave, she both spoke directly to him about my presence, and asked all three of the men buried together there to send us fish. On this and other occasions when she spoke of seeing or hearing ghosts, it was noteworthy that she did not seem to fear them, whereas her eldest daughter reported fainting from fear when she thought she saw a ghost at a distance. In traditional theory, ghosts are not actually dangerous to healthy adults, although children are extremely vulnerable to ghostly attack and so are the ill, but people who encounter them unexpectedly are usually terrified. While Christian teaching may have affected the frequency and interpretation of reported encounters, most remain unwelcome.

Nevertheless, for those who do not regard ghosts as manifestations of the devil, the sight of them is also reassuring because it demonstrates that the person does not simply disappear at death. People generally agree that ghosts appear much less often than in the past, and that the reason is the presence of the missions. At the same time, the doctrine that the spirit goes to God does not offer the same assurance of the retention of identity as did traditional beliefs. My evidence comes from the large number of people who say how dreadful they find the thought that the dead "just rot." In the past they were perfectly aware that bodies decayed, since traditional mortuary rites involved exhuming the mandible after the flesh was gone. But the fact that ghosts so often appeared looking as they did in real life (though sometimes younger or healthier than at the time of death) implied that there was more to the body, and to the associated identity, than what lay in the grave. Ghosts were and are so corporeal that they can often be touched, as well as taking physical action ranging from manipulating the bamboo used in divination to grasping fish and wild pigs to impeding a sleeper's breathing by sitting on his chest. Even those who argued that reported ghosts were only incorporeal apparitions did not consider them anonymous; personal characteristics remained.

Admittedly some Christians do assume that the spirits of the dead maintain their identity. One Catholic woman argued that the failure of her mother's ghost to appear at a seance might mean that at death she had immediately joined the spirit of her husband, dead many years before. A man in his 30s said that his greatest regret at his wife's death was that it would be so long before he could see her again. For most Kove, however, the loss of contact with the dead in modern times seems to be associated with the assumption that identity is lost as well. Presumably their interpretation of Christian teachings has produced this impression.

It would be misleading to suggest that many Kove hold consistent attitudes about ghosts and other spirits. Part of the uncertainty probably reflects the varying precontact theories mentioned earlier, but confusion has certainly been increased by different teachings from missionaries and from the cargo cultists, as well as from increased contact with other outsiders who have their own theories. In Nukakau, a prominent source of new interpretations was the government medical orderly, a man from elsewhere in New Britain who supplemented his injections with magical procedures including sending his soul in dreams to encounter other spirits, and who, though a Catholic, had some idiosyncratic ideas about ghosts.

Apart from having heard a variety of theories from other people, many individuals also have an even more powerful source of confusion. These are dreams and experiences, as in delirium, that often run counter to theories held in the abstract, but that are uniquely convincing to the individual. It is often reported that the person was not dreaming (dreams not being regarded as wholly trustworthy): "I was awake, and the ghost came to me." One Kapo woman was insane for a considerable period, during which she prayed on the beach, claimed to see Christ in the setting sun, and produced illegible "writings." She attributed the episode to possession by the ghost of her dead husband, who did not want her to remarry; her proof was that she was as strong as a man during that period. After recovering, she claimed to have retained exceptional ability as a curer. A Nukakau man, a member of the skeptical family, first said that he was convinced that ghosts did not exist because he saw and heard nothing when he spent the night after his father's death at the grave. Later, however, he told of having been sent back to the grave by the medical orderly, who diagnosed his sickness as having been caused by his dead father's anger at the son's marital problems. He took a strand of shell money to the grave to buy off the ghost, but was so terrified at hearing a rustle "from the grave" that he fled without offering it. A Nukakau woman who similarly insisted that ghosts do not exist because her attempts to contact her husband immediately after his death were fruitless, went on to tell of a childhood encounter with two ghosts outside the Catholic mission station, and seemed to be lending considerable credence to recent stories about ghosts until reminded by a younger companion, a non-Kove married in, that "there are no ghosts." A Somalani man told me of the time he was so ill that he "died" but was sent back to his body by a bright presence in a glass house. En route to the house he recognized the spirit of a living sorcerer walking along a stony road, much inferior to that on which his spirit walked, and when he revived he was able to be cured by sending a payment to buy off that particular sorcerer. The experience gave him two new pieces of information apart from his ideas about the being that sent him back: that the soul does not leave and re-enter the body through the toes, as tradition had it, and that sorcerers would be punished in the afterlife. He consequently resolved not to practice sorcery himself. Like all those just described, including the medical orderly, he identified himself as a Catholic. Such conflicting ideas are found just as often among those who profess membership in a particular church as among the cultists and the self-proclaimed agnostics.

Similarly, I was just as often asked the central question by Christians as by the others. In its briefest form, the question was, "What happens after death?"; the fuller version went on to ask whether we just rot or return to life. I had originally thought the question reflected a desire for me to adjudicate between the conflicting theories of Catholics and SDAs, but soon learned that for the most fervent cultists, it was simply a desire for confirmation of the cult teachings on reincarnation, while for others, it betrayed a similar hope. My usual reply was originally, "We don't know; some churches say one thing and some another, but the dead haven't returned to tell us." A few people accepted this (not bothering to point out that as far as they were concerned, some of the dead had returned), but most persisted. I found that I needed to say explicitly that the dead would not come back to life after a short period. The cultists rejected my statement, accusing me either of lying or of being too young to know the truth (occasionally my sex was offered as an excuse for my ignorance) (cf. Smith, Chap. 8). A number of them offered contrary evidence: that Kove had visited 'Sini' (presumably Sydney) or even America and seen their dead living in those places; that one overseas traveler (the leader of a second cargo cult) had seen on the dock in London a woman who had died at sea and whose body had been disposed of there; that a Japanese soldier who died and was buried during their retreat before the Americans reappeared a day later; than a New Tribes missionary missionary had told a villager (non-Kove) that he was the reincarnation of her dead son, showing a scar on his arm as proof; and of course that the reason I was living there was that I was originally a Kove (why else would I come to such an uncomfortable place?). Intense interest was aroused by photographs of people in traditional dress in a mission publication; they were said to be specific Kove individuals who had died before contact, and the pictures were proof that they were alive somewhere else. (The book turned out to be a celebration of the centennial of the Catholic mission in the Bismarck Archipelago, and the photographs were taken outside Kove, but the Kove had ignored such details as differences in ornaments.) On the other hand, some of the more devout Christians, although they surprised me by still asking the question, tended to accept my statement that the body just decayed with the assertion that yes, the Bible said the same ("dust to dust" often being cited).

For people who had not been persuaded by personal experience or by the reports of others of the existence of ghosts of the dead, Christianity has undoubtedly been the reason for disbelief. Whether they are Catholics attributing sightings to imagination or lies, or SDAs saying that these are manifestations of the devil, all agree in announcing that there are no true ghosts because of what the "church" (or missionary, or Bible) has told us. Because ghosts, even if benevolently disposed, are frightening, it certainly brings some comfort to think that they do not exist at all. The many contradictory statements I have heard from individuals have, however, persuaded me that few if any Kove who claim to have accepted mission teachings are fully convinced on this matter.

GENERAL ATTITUDES

It was noteworthy that apart from the difference of opinion about ghosts, even devout Christians seemed to be unaware of the differences between Catholics and SDAs regarding such matters as purgatory and resurrection. Instead, they focused on certain differences that affected everyday life, notably the different days of rest and the SDA prohibitions on foods, tobacco, and so on. As noted, I found even catechists, much less lay people, totally unaware of Catholic attitudes towards birth control. A consequence of the failure to understand doctrinal differences was that, at least in Nukakau in the 1980s, a "Christian" burial service might be conducted by anyone who was available, regardless of the affiliation of the dead person; in one case, members of both churches conducted the service. Such events were less an indication of ecumenism in general (Armstrong, Chap.12) than the assumption that as regards what happens at death, the two churches agreed. There is also in fact agreement between Catholics and SDAs as regards the importance of the Ten Commandments, and it is probably significant that many people who say that they do not belong to any church — or, if they claim affiliation, acknowledge that they ignore many of the denomination's prohibitions — still say that they believe in these, and often assumed that I did. The Commandments are also central to the cargo cult; in Mopi's version of the myth, God/Moro gives them first to America, then via his emissary Akiuki-u/Jesus to other countries such as England. Just why the Ten Commandments are so important I cannot say without knowing more about how Christianity is taught. It may be relevant that when I heard a priest preach the first sermon ever heard by recently contacted Sengseng, it was devoted to the Ten Commandments. This was the priest who had earlier been stationed in Kove.

As I noted, all the Kove with whom I discussed the matter claim to believe in God. SDA missionaries assert that university students tend to become atheists, and because I taught at a university, the Kove often made a point of insisting to me that God must exist in order to have created the world. But for many of them, God is neither omnipotent or ubiquitous. Furthermore, he is not in heaven but on earth, like the traditional supernaturals with whom he is confused (see Lawrence and Meggitt 1965:9). The problem is to gain access to him.

Most Kove hope that foreigners who have obviously profited from such access, as their standard of living indicates, will provide it to the Kove. Not only do people join churches in hopes of learning the secret of how to get immediate benefits from God, but they interpret Christian paraphernalia and teaching devices as proof of their own beliefs. Kove claim to have seen at a Catholic mission a depiction of Araghasi being cut open for the removal of his liver (a picture of the Sacred Heart?), and movies depicting the life of Christ are, not surprisingly, taken as evidence of the recency of the events shown. The markers left by recent map survey teams on mountains associated with Araghasi and with the Moro myth were interpreted as proof that outsiders recognized the special significance of these places, and the surveyors are reported as having made many comments about evidence of spirit associations with places in the bush. Not only I, but virtually every foreigner, including members of the pre-Independence visiting United Nations teams to whom Mopi presented petitions, was seen as a possible emissary to God.

In addition, significance was read into events that might seem trivial to others. For example, a reported monstrous birth in Kilenge of "God's image," a child with "the body of a snake," was discussed with great interest, especially when the body was said to have been put in a box and shipped away. One Nukakau man expressed the wish that his wife, then pregnant, would bear such a child, who would eventually benefit him. A cartoon in one of my magazines, showing the Loch Ness monster with a human head, aroused such interest that I regretted having let people see it. Kove also mentioned seeing a Chinese or Japanese picture of a creature with a snake body and human head,[25] as further evidence that foreigners knew of Moro and lied in denying that they had benefited from contact with him. Mention by Japanese soldiers of belief in reincarnation was further evidence that they at least had learned how to avoid the annihilation of death.

As the preceding examples show, mission teachngs are only one element in the new world view the Kove have attempted to forge in recent decades. Increased contact with people from other parts of New Britain, and from New Guineans who have their own version of the Moro myth, has also contributed (see Chowning 1969). Such contacts are a main source of stories about people who have returned from the dead. They constantly circulate, and fuel the sort of hopes that made the Kove, from 1968 on, constantly suggest that I was "really" there to impart 'good information about the dead'. This is what they also want from the missions, but the Kove idea of 'good information' is diametrically opposed to the message of Christianity. The failure to receive that information, as Kove statements make clear, explains both change of affiliation on the part of many adults and disillusion about the churches in general. In discussing missions on Malaita, Ross (1978:178) tentatively assigned different personality types to adherents of different missions. His suggestions make perfect sense as regards the ways in which Catholics and Seventh Day Adventist missionaries present their churches, but not as regards the Kove who choose to adhere to one or the other. According to Ross, SDAs would score higher on self-confidence, and low on dependency, compared with Catholics, but all Kove strike outsiders as high in self-confidence and low in dependency. Because God (and, for the cultists, Jesus) came from Kove, people can regard themselves as Christian without actually belonging to a specific denomination. If they do choose to adhere to one, the reason seems to be related to individual experience combined with hope that eventually this doctrine will turn out to yield the expected benefits. But even without church teachings, the Kove seem to have persuaded themselves that God once was uniquely theirs.

Judging from my reading and my knowledge of cargo cults elsewhere in New Britain, the Kove one is not remarkable in most of its doctrines. Furthermore, as other contributors to this volume have shown, the Christian God is closely associated with the local scene elsewhere (see Kaplan and Smith, Chaps. 7 and 8). But in Kove, by contrast with Kragur, it is not suggested that traditional customs are compatible with Christianity. Rather, because their own God gave to other countries not only their religions but the enormous benefits that followed from performance of the ritual associated with these, Kove cultists naturally feel that they are entitled to the same benefits. The problem, of course, is to get access to the ritual. Some keep hoping that the churches will in time yield it, while others try for direct access to God. Not surprisingly, in view of what they expect to achieve from such access, many people prefer to work for it rather than to waste their time on local government councils (finally accepted only in 1977), cash crops, or schooling for children. These latter may bring small increases in income, but count for little compared with the abolition of physical labor and eternal life amidst earthly pleasures. The result is that every new mission group that comes to Kove, especially if it contains Americans (as most do), is greeted with expectations that it cannot possibly gratify. It will be a long time, if ever, before most Kove become persuaded that a hard life on earth, with compensation in heaven,[26] is preferable to idleness and plenty on earth, and no heaven.

NOTES

My research in Kove was supported by the Australian National University between 1966 and 1969, by the University of Papua New Guinea between 1971 and 1976, and by Victoria University of Wellington in 1983 and 1986-7. I made a brief visit in 1978 on behalf of the Papua New Guinea Department of Environment and Conservation.

I am of course indebted to Lawrence and Meggitt (1965) for the title of the paper.

1. I have worked in three other societies: Lakalai and Sengseng in West New Britain and Molima in the Milne Bay Province, interspersing return visits to them with my work in Kove. The principal missions in both Lakalai and Molima are United Church (formerly Methodist) and Roman Catholic, and in Sengseng only Roman Catholic. Both of the other West New Britain societies had been much affected by cargo cults.
2. On one occasion, I was threatened with a court case for 'laughing at our religion' when I was seen smiling as a Catholic woman told me of some of the Seventh Day Adventist prohibitions. I never asked people how they reconciled church membership with belief in cult teachings.
3. They are not aware of the origins of the names but I often found that I was expected to be a Catholic because I have a "Catholic name."
4. A main reason for change has been resentment at being beaten by teachers. In addition, the poor village schools mean that many of those attending mission boarding schools are well-grown adolescents, often betrothed, before they have completed their primary education, and may be expelled for what is viewed as sexual misconduct.
5. At that time the Catholic priest was one I had known in Lakalai, where he had become so angry at members of our team who were living in a wholly Catholic village that he forbade the local Catholics to talk to them. I did not want to risk being in a Catholic village if he recognized me and resented my former associations.
6. This particular priest was considered by some to be foolish if not senile, and may have been disregarded — as he was in Kapo — for that reason, but I do not know why the SDA minister and his companions were not received with more enthusiasm.
7. Kove affinal exchanges often oblige people to spend many months away from home.
8. I had met this priest when he was working with the Sengseng. He was notably given to

berating people.

9. Apart from my being told by the Kapo catechist that I would go to hell because I was not a Catholic, this was a unique example of someone's expressing worry about what might happen after death. Most Kove seemed unconcerned about hell (unlike the Methodists I had known in Lakalai and Molima) but feared that God would punish them during life, as by turning an ax against someone who went to the gardens on a day of rest, or by killing. One Catholic woman from another village said that God had sent wild pigs to devastate the Nukakau gardens to punish the people for not building a church.
10. In 1987 I attended the funeral of an old man who was assumed to be Catholic, but the fact that no one, including his son, knew a Christian name for him raised questions about whether he had been baptized.
11. One self-proclaimed skeptic who often provided me with fish told me that he had observed that he was never successful when fishing on Saturday or Sunday, and so had stopped doing so.
12. For example, one Baha'i told me that he felt uneasy about wearing a waistcloth imprinted with a picture of Christ, because it might offend 'our Big Man' (a term used for both God and Christ).
13. Judging from their own accounts, no Kove seems to observe prohibitions on pre-marital sex, and many married men (and some women) engage in affairs, but women married "with a ring" in the Catholic church often call on the priest to help them prevent a divorce or the husband's acquisition of additional wives.
14. For example, the extremely devout Catholic catechist mentioned in the text asked typical cult questions about the origin of schools. A former policeman who told me he did not believe in cargo cults because the Administration condemned them showed a completely different attitude when the cult leader arrived.
15. To begin with, I should note that one of my co-workers in Lakalai recorded (in the mid-1950s) that prior to World War II the Kove "participated in a series of movements concerned not only with the dead but also with other traditional spirits including a miraculous stone" (Valentine 1958:403). While his information may be correct, I never heard of any pre-war movements from the Kove, apart from their participation in the Lakalai one just at the beginning of the war. The notes from Valentine's informants about the "miraculous stone" indicate confusion about two different stones the Kove told me about, neither of which was tied to the post-war cult. It might also be argued that the post-war movement was not really a cargo cult, because of the absence of obviously religious ritual (c.f. Lawrence 1987), but I am calling it one because of the associated ideology.
16. A major problem as regards the "traditional" content of the Kove version of Moro 1, which differs only in details from that recorded by Counts, is that all Kove have probably heard the cult version. Perhaps unjustifiably, I have assumed that the story as most often told, which differs from that given by the cult leaders, is traditional up to the point at which Moro leaves New Britain or one of the Siassi Islands. There is no obvious foreign content in these versions, and it seems likely that the original (pre-cult) myth simply ended with his departure, with no mention of his ultimate destination. The one aspect that is unclear, and that differs from one teller to another, concerns the extent of his miraculous powers.
17. The latter name is non-Kove in shape; Kove words do not end in consonants. It is recorded in non-Kove versions of the myth.
18. Not the heart, as in the version recorded by Counts.
19. In recent years the fear of representations has been reduced as many Kove have included snakes in the wood carvings they make to sell to tourists.

20. Possibly from the name of John Murphy, a well-known Australian government officer.
21. Riesenfeld cites a variant of the myth in which there is a second being with a snake body in addition to Moro, and in which Akiukiu is Moro's son. The snake-men are creators and "introduced the present social organization, and all natural phenomena." The bibliographical reference he gives is incorrect, so I have not been able to learn more about that version.
22. No one suggested that Vokumu might have been inhabited for a long time after God's departure, even though the heavy accumulation of shells on the beach there was taken as evidence of a lengthy occupation.
23. Women tended to have excellent knowledge of relatively recent kin ties, but perhaps because of patrilineality, the authorities on distant ancestors were all male.
24. C14 dates from excavations within Nukakau, supposedly settled from Vokumu, support the recency of its settlement; the mounds mentioned above were older.
25. Valentine (1958:422) says that this was a "Hindu picture" from a magazine.
26. This was precisely what the head of the SDA mission at Silovuti told me that he wanted for church members.

4

KEEPING THE *LO* UNDER A MELANESIAN MESSIAH: AN ANALYSIS OF THE POMIO *KIVUNG*, EAST NEW BRITAIN

Garry Trompf

INTRODUCTION

As has been made increasingly apparent in scholarly literature, the so-called "cargo cults" constitute but one recognizable form among a whole range of new religious movements in Melanesia (May 1982; Loeliger and Trompf 1985: x-xvii). Whether the earlier emphasis on the region's cargo cultism was due to an implicit allance between anthropology and colonialism, whereby "native peoples" could be shown to be quite unready to govern affairs for having the wildest dreams about sudden riches, is still a matter for debate. What is now beyond doubt in the present context, however, is that there is a small host of discrete Melanesian religious movements for which concern to acquire European-style goods is of little importance. Even among movements warranting the general epithet "cargo cultist" there are very considerable differences — in the kinds of expectations shared about the coming of cargo, the amount of goods anticipated, and the degree to which expectations provide the key rationale for the newly developed group's existence or momentum. Thus alongside those groups expecting the sudden and presaged arrival of supernaturally-generated Western-type goods (cf. Christiansen 1969; Lawrence 1964; Steinbauer 1979), one now finds independent churches (Tuza 1961, 1975; Trompf 1983), spirit(istic or charismatic-looking) activities (Barr 1983; Flannery 1983 - 1984; Kale 1985), sects (Boutilier *et al.* 1978), special religious "interest groups" (Yagas 1985), neo-traditionalist movements (Davenport and Coker 1967), and various other related phenomena. And under the broad heading of cargo cultism lie social forms as divergently classed as "millenarian movements or cults" (e.g., Sharp 1976; Talmon 1966:181-2), "messianisms" (Lanternari 1962, 1963:161-190), "churches" (Trompf 1982:54-7, 59-60, 66-9), "salvation movements" (Schoorl 1978), "protest movements" (Bodrogi 1951), "proto- or micro-nationalisms" (May 1982; Walter 1983), "nativisms" or "traditionalisms" (Linton 1943), and just plain "independent religious movements" (Mair 1958).

This chapter concerns a movement in East New Britain, Papua New Guinea, known as the Pomio *Kivung*, an organization raising many questions relevant to the ongoing processes of social scientific categorization. It has developed since 1964 among the Mengen and neighboring peoples in the Pomio sub-province, to the south of the better known Tolai and Baining culture complexes. Mengen territory proper, which consists of scattered villages holding almost six thousand persons, occupies approximately 190 square miles, mainly on the eastern side of the Nakanai Mountains. Its coastline runs from the Torlu River to Owen Point, including Jacquinot Bay, and it is bordered by Sulka country to the north and the Melkoi to the south, both these groups speaking dialectically related (Austronesian) tongues to that of the Mengen. A non-Austronesian group, the Kol, traditionally inhabited an inland enclave to the west, although during the colonial period Kol immigrants established five coastal villages on Waterfall Bay in the Mengen area (Chowning 1977; M.Panoff 1969a: 1-3; Rath 1980a). At present the Catholic Church is highly visible in the region, with two very large churches at Malmal and Pomio, and twelve community schools throughout the Malmal parish (Catholic Directory 1982:113). To the south of Malmal Mission the Papua New Guinea government has erected a new administrative complex and secondary school.

The Mengen (Maenge) have shared many traditional features of life with surrounding peoples, including a lithic technology, the practice of shifting horticulture, and the limited domestication of pigs. As was typical for New Britain, clan clusters maintained themselves in separate hamlets, each related to the other through a complex history of exchange, marriage, alliance, conflict, and migration. In East New Britain land and property were typically passed down matrilineally, while leadership lay in the hands of managers, better known for their cultivation of personal power and mystery than their organization of magnificent feasts and complicated exchanges, and holding power through skill rather than as hereditary chiefs (A. Epstein 1969:88-109; Chowning 1974; Hesse and Aerts 1982:42). M.Panoff 1969c:2224; Rath in press:29, 198; cf. Valentine 1963:3-7;

The *Kivung* movement originated from Ablingi island off the southern coast of West New Britain, some 35 miles east of Kandrian. The direction of its influence was to the northeast, and it not only affected cultures in and around the Kandrian area but reached beyond Pomio to the Tolai and Baining regions as well (Chowning and Goodale 1965:266-72; Chowning *et al.* 1971:61-3, 80-82). In what follows, however, the special manifestations of the movement in the Pomio sub-province form the center of our attention. It has been among the Mengen especially that the movement has had its greatest impact, such that it remains one of the most impressive and durable independent religious movements in Papua New Guinea today. With researches into the traditional Mengen religion in mind (cf. F. Panoff 1969, 1970a-b; M. Panoff 1968, 1969b), and the historical background also in view, this chapter considers the emergence of this movement as a distinctive type of local Christianity — one without a church, or one for which the term church seems inappropriate.

The organization called the *Kivung* (New Guinea Pidgin: 'Movement') has dominated the affairs of the Mengen people for twenty-five years. This organization is rare among indigenously-founded "new religious movements" of Melanesia for still possessing national political representation. It is the only such movement with a "cargo cult" face, in fact, which has both a national and provincial parliamentary membership (Trompf 1981:21, and in press). Of equal significance, the *Kivung* leadership has consistently attempted to generate and sustain a totally alternative order to separated and uncoordinated "systems of social management" offered by Custom, Mission and Administration. It is the purpose of this paper to show that what has resulted from the Mengen experiments is nonetheless a special indigenous expression of Christianity, despite the movement's own distinctness and its vigorous rejection of select Christian beliefs and structures which came with missionary activity and Western intrusion. My assessment of this Pomio case is based primarily on the *Kivung* members' stated reasons for rejecting that order of things which they have sought to avoid or relinquish, and on the degree to which resentment is expressed against that order. There has been a growing scholarly interest in the way cargo cultists handle problems to do with reciprocity, and it is a special concern of this piece to plot the growth of a spirit of reprisal against outside interferences together with the quest for a dramatically new order of reciprocal relationships (cf. Trompf 1989a and in press on further methodological orientations).

EARLY CARGO CULTS

The relative size of the Mengen region *vis-à-vis* Tolai country in the Gazelle peninsula is important for our consideration from the start, if only because a sense of being "backward" and "less improved" — given the changes in this neighboring region — has steadily congealed into prevalent anti-Tolai resentment. Both the go-ahead Tolai and their Baining neighbors have had a much longer and more profitable history of interactions with expatriates (A.L. Epstein 1969:8-34; T.S. Epstein 1968:34-53; Jaspers 1981), whereas for the Mengen dealings with the whites which were more than superficial came relatively late. After blackbirding at the end of last century (Panoff 1969c:2223), an unwelcome German expedition in 1909 (Vogel 1911:235), the establishment of two plantations which also acted as recruiting stations for laboring further afield before the First World War, and sporadic Australian Government patrolling in the late twenties (Panoff 1969d), the harbingers of Christianity arrived. With two native catechists having laid the foundations in the east of the Mengen area by 1925 (Laufer 1955:41-2), Father Culhane of the Sacred Heart Order came to found the mission at Malmal on Jacquinot Bay in 1931 (a station but a few kilometres from Malmal village, destined to become the "headquarters" of the so-called *Kivung*). The only substantial material changes of these earlier times came during the War, when, as the result of an ANGAU camp being established and American warships hiding in the bay's deeper waters, a series of roads and bridges were built around parts of the bay, with Pomio Patrol Post being set up on the northern side by October 1943.[1] In comparison to the many plantations, road system, and town planning on the Gazelle, these developments were miniscule, and wartime conditions were followed by much less spectacular change.

It is small wonder that cargo cults in the area reflect frustration with the obvious unevenness of change in east New Britain, along with hopes for radical shifts in the Mengen's favour. The cargo cults which preceded the present Pomio *Kivung* expressed a clear desire for dramatic reversal, one which would adversely affect the Australians or the current *mastas* (including what few well-endowed government officials, planters, and Catholic Fathers there were in the area, along with the many more outsiders who were reported by recruited laborers to be in Rabaul). In July 1959, for example, a worried Assistant District Commissioner at Pomio wrote of beliefs at Malmal that the long deceased and renowned Golpak of Sali, who was first appointed by the Australians as local paramount *luluai* (or local supervisor) in 1928 and crucial for the area's pacification, would rise from the dead. He would bring cargo and wrest control over the Mengen from the current overlords. On his arrival "the Australians will not be welcome, but the Americans will be arriving to give assistance to the people;" and in the following month Jacquinot Bay villagers were paying local organizers a 5 shilling "tax to America," on the supposition a ship would be arriving to take them off to an exceedingly better world (Pomio sub-district Files [hereafter PF]:1959a).

This pro-Americanism, which was later to influence the Tolai *Kivung Lavurua* to the north (Tirpaia 1975), and which anticipates the well-known Johnson Cult of New Ireland (Longgar 1975), was perhaps among the last glimmers of hope for the Mengen that the time of rapid changes associated with U.S. presence would return. From 1960 onwards, moments of heightened suspense tended to devolve more around the careful ritual performance of certain specific duties — the weeding of cemeteries (which was already encouraged by the Mission), the maintenance of village cleanliness and roads (upon which the Government insisted) and, more significantly for the future, the preserving of Thursday as a sacred day (a plantation-worker notion brought forward by two returned laborers who had worked on the Gazelle in the mid-fifties) (PF:1959b,c). By this time Mengen villagers were becoming comfortable with talk of the new God, who was patently more encompassing than their old mountain deity Maglila. They had in their tradition a myth about two brothers called Nutu, who were somewhat like "sons" of Maglila, with one who could be likened to Satan for being bad, and the other (the younger of the two) to Jesus, being good and having "created the first people" (Oral Testimony [hereafter OT]: I. Pakulu 1981). But if the enlargement of the picture of God and the linkage between the popular young *Nutu Ewalo* and Jesus made the shift to Christianity attractive, there was certainly a tension surrounding the ancestors, so that any new movement of dissent was sure to accentuate them among other differences between the two religions.

These concerns and ideas were not at first tied up with any open anti-expatriate sentiments. They appear, rather, to be attempts to find the right actions for a new reciprocity, one to open up the flow of new goods; yet a consistent thread in these outbreaks as they have been documented is an expected intervention of the dead, and this hope was bound to be turned into a principle of protest against the most influential whites in the district — the missionaries. The 1960-61 cult emphasizing the specialness of Thursday, for example, which attracted eastern Pomio villages, took the ancestors to be bearers of cargo, whether from a ship or from the cemetery, and it was they who would make it possible that villagers would "be like Masters and will not have to work." Thursday was the ancestors' day, then, and the local organizers attempted to discourage people from attending church on Sundays (PF 1959c:2).

Activities in the "Thursday cult" paralleled the intense and crescendo dancing which analysts have already traced "in the exaggerated *Kongar* (or pig-kill) of the Mur "Madness," in the Koreri movements, and the frenzy of the Filo cult (Fergie 1981:93-95; Kamma 1972; Trompf 1989b). Thursday was to be the day of the cargo's arrival, but the three leaders of this cult were not prepared to say which particular one. In consequence, dancing began regularly on Wednesday nights and went on rigorously to the morning. Usu, one of the leaders, who had been temporarily imprisoned for circulating false rumors about the future, was once found dancing naked with the third member of this petty triumvirate, a man named, Hanon, both of them claiming that "their skin felt very hungry for cargo" and would be "very pleased" when it arrived. These activists put pressure on neighboring villagers to abandon their ideas about forming a recently mooted cooperative society, for "if they did not believe the talk that cargo would arrive soon, (they) would lose out, (and) the cargo would only come to Maso and Meninga" (=Mengen) (PF 1959c: 7-8).

This kind of threat held over local people who wavered about joining the cult or were critical of it is a familiar side to the story of cargo cults in general, as is the desperate effort to persuade the ancestors to intervene through dance and ritual (cf. Trompf, in press, ch.2). The dead were to return as "soldiers of Jesus," coming out of the cemeteries; and they were to bring a totally different order, removing "the people's ancestral ideas" so that "they can live like whitemen." The logic of this exciting, presaged moment of reciprocity was such, in fact, that the peple were to sacrifice all the new-style goods they already possessed — "tomahawks, knives, *laplaps*, bags and boxes, money and tax receipts." Large bundles of these items were actually thrown into the sea — with the hope of extraordinary rewards from the spirit world to follow (PF 1959c:7-8).

THE EMERGENCE OF THE *KIVUNG*

It is against this background of events in eastern Pomio villages that we can better understand the emergence of the *Kivung* at Malmal and other "satellite" centers to the west. This movement goes back to the year 1963, when one Bernard Balitape of Kraiton village attempted to form an organization in advance and in rumored anticipation of the coming of a hero figure from much further to the west: Michael Koriam Urekit. Not alone in his opinion, Bernard saw in Koriam the promise of cargo. The former's incipient organization, it should be noted, took over certain principles which were distinctly home-grown and which preceded Koriam's influence. He looked to the miraculous sudden involvement of the ancestors, for a start, conceiving them to be the creators of cargo; and like the villagers further up the coast he insisted that Thursday was the sacred day. But for Bernard, Koriam was the teacher of the way by which the secret of the cargo would be unlocked, and he had already endowed the latter with semi-divine qualities before his actual arrival in the vicinity of Malmal itself (PF 1965).[2]

Who was Koriam? Intriguingly not a Mengen, but a very prominent figure in and around Kandrian to the south, and an Ablingi Islander whose earlier, varied experiences in Rabaul, and acquaintance with Paliau Maloat, make up an interesting and separate story to be told elsewhere.[3] What is important for the present analysis is that the influential Koriam campaigned as a black man worthy to stand beside and against any expatriate candidates in the pre-independent parliament of Papua New Guinea. After having served as a *tultul* (or assisting chief local official) before the War, appointed as a member of the New Britain District Advisory Council from 1962, and accepted as an observer at the Legislative Council in Port Moresby, Koriam was widely acclaimed for having special access to the new sources of power (Chowning and Goodale 1965:267). His messages portending change had long been percolating through villages to the east and west of Ablingi. Contending for the elections in 1964, he was welcomed among most Mengen as the (super)man who could satisfy their frustrations and open the road to the new wealth and a new order of life. Strange rumors went before his campaigning — that he received special power to overcome his own serious sickness in Rabaul, for instance, that he was dropped by police into the sea with a stone around his neck yet suddenly arrived ahead at the very airport of his destination itself — and his appearance at virtually all places in the Pomio sub-district was heralded by the slogan *Masta San bai i kam* ('Lord Son/Sun is coming'). This last phrase implied he was Jesus, or a figure like him. Certainly many took him for God's special agent: the idea of him as Son was linked with Vurakit, a veiled Mengen spirit, who (like the morning Star among the Biak) would grant riches and every wish if one happened to be able to catch him (Fore 1981; Kamma 1972; Maden 1977:1-3; Tovalele 1977:124).

Up to this time the Christian God — referred to in Catholic preaching and liturgy under the euphonic name Deo — was evidently left in isolation and unintegrated into the cluster of local deities in the minds of most villagers, who struggled to accommodate one set of beliefs with the other. One spirit power, however, eventually presented itself as a "bridge" — both to the missionaries and the people. This was Nutu (from the myth of the two brothers), who in some villages was a spirit strongly connected with garden fertility and thus prosperity in general. The incorporation of the term Nutu for God into the service sheets of the Mass during the sixties, in fact, probably because Nutu was cognate with similar names used for God down the eastern and southern New Britain coasts (and on to the famous Anut of the Madang area), facilitated the apotheosis of Koriam among the Mengen.[4] For Koriam became quickly confused or identified with Nutu, thus fulfilling the role of cargo herald and divine figure combined.

Mounting adulation for Koriam swamped all traditional tendencies to be cautious about provoking the *mastas*. Carried around on a stretcher, both before and after his first successful campaign, Koriam bore a message about the securing of wealth and the ordering of spiritual (or moral) life. His first insistence was on the creation of a regional fund (just as Paliau had argued), an investment to handle future needs and to bring dramatically increased wealth, and a fund through which membership of the *Kivung* 'Movement' — his Pidgin usage — was recorded and confirmed through payments. In this respect he was not out of tune with the so-called cooperative movement popular at the time, although if he sometimes openly connected himself with this cause, he also thought of himself going "one better." In accord with his concerted effort to get villagers saving money and creating their own institutions came his suggestions about the better organization and upkeep of gardens (a thrust of his policy which strengthened common identification of him with Nutu).

These simple practical teachings, however, were coupled with a general moral message, although one very loosely formulated and somewhat ambiguous. On the one hand, he taught strict adherence to the Ten Commandments, and advocated this as a 'straightening of thought and life' (*stretim tingting*) which he taught was sufficient to indicate one was a Christian. Already implied by these commandments, he indicated, was the abandonment of magic (because it meant appealing to a power other than God's), of sorcery and theft (because the former could be death-dealing and the latter obviously transgressed the Eighth commandment), and also of betel-nut chewing (which would apparently undermine the discipline necessary to keep the new *lo* 'law' as a whole). On the other hand, he deliberately presented this *lo* as squaring well with the more obviously positive traditional values — to do with group loyalty, sharing in a subsistence economy, and the fulfilment of obligations through reciprocity or exchange. Right from the start he intimated the advisability of a system of punishments to guarantee the law's observance (cf. below).

The fact that Koriam was an independent message-bearer made his cause appear to supersede that of the missionaries, who had not yet been able to get through to the people the way this new hero could. In Koriam's initial message, however, there seemed little for missionaries and their loyalists to worry about. After all, the Ten Commandments were extolled by the Church, and in conformity to the Fourth, Koriam made it known that Sunday, as the missions taught, was to be a holy day (OT:F. Baiami, B. Nemka, 1981; Snowden 1982:128; cf. Tovalele 1977:126).

For all Koriam's apparent ingenuousness, however, as a spokesman for improvement on these very basic terms, he nevertheless filled out his message in Pidgin ambiguities which lent themselves to high anticipations of some grand transformation. And he himself was susceptible to being sucked in and made party to the cargoist hopes pinned upon him. If nothing in Koriam's campaigning was contrary to prevailing law and if his moral insistence was so apparently innocuous, there were in fact forces within the Mengen culture area to radicalize whatever anti-expatriatism or spirit of independence was already consequent upon his mobilization of a widespread response. These forces surrounded Bernard Balitape (mentioned above), who in the train of Koriam's startling impact on a people not his own, initiated an organization to consolidate local fervor and aspirations. By 1965 there were "compulsory meetings on every Monday night [to] inform members of all the laws and commandments. No questions raised by members" [*sic*] (PF 1965). The leaders included Bernard as Headman, Miranalali of Malakua as President, and Alois Koki of Malmal (later to become the regional representative in the House) as Vice-President.

Apart from the promulgation of Thursday as a "public holiday," the organization insisted on each interested village laying out what was termed 'Koriam's Garden', a huge plot of eight different plants (mostly food crops, but including decorative and fertility-associated croton bushes), with the plants being set out in orderly fashion around a spotlessly clean *centrum*, known as the 'Ten Commandments'. Morning prayers were to be said collectively by members in the gardens; and guards were appointed to watch them at night, because, in Bernard's cargoist interpretation of Koriam's talk about better food production, the dead were to convey important messages from these special plots. The first laws of the *Kivung* were framed: a fine of one (Australian) shilling if members were absent from *Kivung* gatherings; graded fines to cover wrongdoings of one member against another; a tax for Koriam's travel; a special fund raised 'for Koriam's benefit' (which more or less corresponded to Koriam's own requests); and "a fund raised for dead peple to come back to life again." Substantiated by the use of local Mengen beliefs, Koriam's earlier message had now provided the rationale for a "cultic" religio-political innovation, and it came to be a key tenet of the infant movement that the ancestors would soon return via a specially cleared pathway out of the gardens. As in tradition, so now it was in the *Kivung bilong Koriam* that "a beautiful garden" was one of the "tokens of the gardener's ability to entertain good relations with the other world" (F. Panoff 1969:21).[5]

Bernard's policies, furthermore, turned out to contain a greater element of opposition to the colonial order than his hero's. There developed, in fact, a strong element of reprisal against white interferences in his stance. Cooperation with the Catholic Mission was discouraged (and although attendance at Sunday Masses was not completely debarred, *Kivung* pressure tended to be against it); the Thursday holiday, just as important as Sunday as a time for expounding the Commandments, flew in the face of assumptions government officers held as to the days local Mengens should be found at their employment; and primary teachers saw their schools virtually empty, first on Thursday, then still more frequently on other days, the more Bernard's rejection of all government institutions increased. Partly in response to various pronouncements by Koriam about eliminating the differences between Tolai advantages and the lack of change further south, but especially because of Bernard's training of emissaries to pressure more and more villages to join the *Kivung* and to subscribe to the policies of his "central government," Mengen and Sulko laborers in northern (Tolai) and southern (Hoskins) plantations were asked to return home (especially during 1965-6), and hundreds of would-be members left their former (often isolated mountain) villages to join *Kivung* centers on or nearer the coast.

Not unexpectedly, these developments began disturbing the Administration. Government pressure on Koriam, however, brought him closer to Bernard, whose organizational powers were remarkable, and whose admiration for Koriam soon made the latter appreciate that the place where his ideals could be best realized would be around Jacquinot Bay. It was not so much managerial success that was the sign of "bigmanship" among the Kandrian, Massinga, Mengen, and Sulka cultures, but the possession of a great secret, and both Koriam and Bernard were eminently adept at enshrouding themselves in an aura of mystery or double-talk, and also in acquiring such status they seemed a match for the Europeans (see above, and cf. PF 1966,.1967a-c).

By 1975 the movement had captured the support of 18 out of 37 major Mengen villages, and of the remaining 19, 10 were divided in their allegiance. Of the 25,000(+) inhabitants of the Pomio sub-district, over 8,000 could be counted on as loyal adherents. Rather than to the south, and toward Koriam's birthplace, moreover, growth had been much more to the north, incorporating Sulka and Baining villages along the northeastern coast of New Britain.[6] With the base of cooperation considerably widened, Koriam changed the place of his major residence. He had a large dwelling built near Malmal, which he favored while not in parliament at Port Moresby (as the recurrently successful candidate) until his death in 1978. For almost two years, between Bernard's death in 1976 (significantly on a sacred Thursday) and his own, Koriam found himself vulnerable as the leader of a cult he had not strictly speaking organized into existence. Imputations that he accepted his supporters' claim that he was God (= Nutu), and a court case airing strange *Kivung* views initiated by a competing, yet unsuccessful candidate in the 1977 election campaign, reached the national press, and preceded his death as a Member of Parliament in office the following year (*PNG Post Courier*, 18-21 Oct., 1977). After that, Bernard's brother Alphonse was in prominence for about a year, until Koriam's more hard-headed political successor Alois Koki and the ultra-secretive "religious frontman" Kolman Molu edged the movement towards greater respectability. Whereas Alphonse had once engineered the building of an airstrip to receive cargo (near Malakur), threatening the life of the local Papuan schoolteacher in the bargain should he interfere or report anything, Koki and Kilman tended to concentrate on the collection and left it up to the *tumbuna* 'ancestors' as to when they should return.[7]

THE *LO* OF THE *KIVUNG*

Over the two decades of the *Kivung*'s heyday, the leaders' strategies included manifest and basically consistent themes of reprisal, even acting out retribution (as non-cooperation) against outside control. The movement expressed disaffection with colonial overlordship. Koriam the campaigner was from the beginning an embodiment of *kanaka* 'native' leadership in place of expatriate interference, and he himself maintained that the Commandments his supporters should practise would take away the necessity of (outsider, often Tolai) police. As early as 1964, possibly with some knowledge of Paliau's activities, he created the Mengen local council (*Kaunsal Tumbuna* 'Ancestral Council'), and with the 11 *Kivung* representatives dominating over the 8 remaining members, kept possible local opposition to a minimum. The movement, moreover, at first responding to Koriam's recognition of unredressed imbalances between the Gazelle and people to the south, soon developed a strongly anti-Tolai stance, and under Koki and Kolman it has settled down to be a political lobby group, both in Port Moresby and in the new provincial legislature at Rabaul, in favor of a separate Pomio province. We must understand, of course, that the option to take up a successful armed revolt was not open as a realistic course of action, nor was it acceptable in the light of new values, such as peaceableness, or the government-enforced prohibition to kill. On the other hand, the impetus to "get back" at the "imposed" authorities with an independent organization welled up from what the *Kivung* members never questioned, a (justified) sense of recrimination, because they suffered unwanted interference and lack of autonomy.

With Papua New Guinea's independence in 1975, the emphasis has shifted away from the need for a quite alternative form of government (under Koriam's rules) toward repeated affirmation that the Ten Commandments should be carefully obeyed, because all the *gavman* 'states' of the world, including the national one, are based on these rules of God (OT: Kolman Molu, 1981). A group of younger politically-minded *Kivung* adherents, indeed, dubbing themselves the *Pomio Tru Grup,* have recently sought to extract the movement from old cargoist taints, and to window-dress it for outsiders as a political force with the highest moral ideals (Bailoenakia and Kloimanrea, 1983:171-76, *Papua New Guinea National Gazette* 1981).

As for more distinctly religious matters, steadying disillusionment with the Mission (partly connected with 6 changes in parish priests at Malmal Mission since 1962, just before the *Kivung*'s advent), has congealed into a special "neo-Jewish" separatism. Various members familiar with expatriate epithets seek to disown the term "cult," because the *Kivung* is a "total way," as much to do with subsistence activities as with special rituals, for a start; and it is perhaps sensible to take their cue and simply characterize it as a special "new religious movement." It is not strictly speaking an independent church (its leaders not seeking this status), although the stress on the Old Testament Commandments (the Latinate capital numerals I-X painted prominently on eight foot high village entrance posts) is reminiscent of African ecclesiastical independencies with a strongly Hebraist touch (Turner 1967:1-7).[8] *Kivung* protagonists uphold a firm reliance on the ancestors (and on Nutu = the now deceased Koriam [= Jesus] as the crucial vehicle of contact with them), and the cleaned cemeteries are overshadowed by 8 foot high poles which have "Koriam/Nutu" inscribed at the top and the relevant ancestors listed below (see Plate 1). This is a neo-traditionalist element, for in fact the ancestors were those spirits receiving the most prayerful and ritual attention in pre-contact times. But we have to recognize that preoccupation with the dead has produced elements smacking noticeably of "cargo cultism." Right through the *Kivung*'s history, the ancestors figure as the prospective cargo-bearers, and evening drumming and offerings to them are above all the outward, distinctly religious signalling of a rejection (if not sometime noisy flouting) of Catholicism.

In keeping with this negative, more retributive side to things, we find the institution of *lo* by *Kivung* leaders imposes a heavy social pressure on those wavering over their allegiance, or on those who want to defect (the usual reason for dropping out being the lack of tangible results). The Ten Commandments have been specially interpreted to reinforce a centralized control. Not only is the Fourth understood to refer to Thursday as well as Sunday, but the Fifth (concerning the honoring of one's parents) is related back to the good Mengen *kastam* of the *tumbuna* ancestors and to the need for good *gavman* (as also are 6-8), while the Tenth (concerning covetousness) is stretched to cover sinning "in the head" before acting.

PLATE 1: VILLAGE BOUNDARY MARKER, WITH THE SIGN OF THE TEN COMMANDMENTS, PAMALMAL VILLAGE, EAST NEW BRITAIN (1981)

Confessions of sin have been demanded in evening rituals in the presence of the ancestors since the late sixties, and roughly graded fines extracted by leaders from those ready to confess have been ritually paid to the dead for remission. These financial impositions, as well as taxes for Koriam and the fund (see above), were laid on villagers by Bernard much more rigorously than Koriam earlier proposed, as the sub-district officials of the colonial government came to recognize by 1968. Failure of villagers to comply, admittedly, was rarely sanctioned by dire threat of punishment, whether human or divine, yet judgments were delivered with the portentous phrase perhaps best translated 'I advise you...' (Mengen: *potong*), implying that otherwise there would be bad consequences, which could include not only fines, ostracism from the *Kivung*, or God's punition, but a reporting to the (outside) government and thus jailing (PF 1968, OT:Baiami).

The legal stringencies and the demands for a willingness to give, as one might expect, were integrally tied in to the retributive principle that blessings would not flow unless the new rules were obeyed. *Lo*, significantly, denoted more than negative requital, but also the breaking in of the new time of the cargo ('*lo bai bruk*'), which was a time set in advance in cycles (e.g., 1964, 1968-9, 1971-2) and thus in some accord with the rhythm of traditional festal occasions, when masks such as the *urasena* were worn at initiations, or at the honoring of those with blackened teeth.[9] In 1971, indeed, at at time when hopes of cargo ran high, Koriam was feted to a large and enthusiastic "life-cycle" ceremony. All such activity, it seems, amounted to new commitment to the old belief in the efficacy of positive reciprocity with the dead. Virtually every night, and especially on Sundays and Thursdays, gifts of food and money, along with confessions, were regularly given to the ancestors. By the mid-seventies, each member village possessed a cult house for this purpose, linked both to the cemetery and so-called Paradise gardens by specially known tracks; and by the late seventies, each village erected a colorfully decorated store-house, in which the *Kivung*'s collections could be safely deposited before they were added to the central fund (Plate 2) (OT:Longi, Naingis 1977:2; cf.Panoff 1968:275-61).

PLATE 2: *KIVUNG* MONEY HOUSE, PALMALAL VILLAGE, EAST NEW BRITAIN (1981)

ELEMENTS OF POSITIVE RECIPROCITY

All these local collections were distinctly cultic and sacrificial, as forms of reciprocity, since most villagers expected the likelihood of the physical return of their ancestors. While not actually bringing the cargo with them, the dead would come back in response to these human gifts, and would, by a mere *wish*, be able to bring tinned food-stuffs, boats, and houses of permanent building materials into sudden realization. So confident were they in these powers that some envisioned the rapid appearance in and around Malmal of a city as big as they imagined New York to be.

By contrast, though, the central fund, which has steadily grown over the last two decades, reflects greater realism in Western terms, if not a (paradoxical) eagerness to participate in the wider world of *bisnis*. Interestingly, the *Kivung* turned out earlier on to be a competitor against what outsiders might reckon to be a viable economic proposition, namely a cooperative society, opted for by various non-*Kivung* villages in 1964. However, the slow demise of the cooperative down to 1979 (when its organizers drank themselves and their concern into a collapse!), boosted the chances of an added local financial backing of the *Kivung* fund. By 1977 the movement's money had reached the K100,000 mark, and by 1982 over K244,000 was in a Rabaul Bank (with K33,000 invested in Government

Security Bonds) (OT: F. Sinaimo, F. Koimanrea). Although Bernard had appropriated a good deal of money for his own purposes (a misdemeanor which, along with alleged sexual liberties unbecoming in an upholder of the Commandments, produced some serious defections), the growing fund after his death came to symbolize a sound economic stability for the future, and an achievement to be proud of which sat alongside of and was in no way contradictory to the members' longings for a supernatural intervention (Tovalele 1977:132).

In the earlier days of the *Kivung*, members were already given a sense of participation in the whiteman's money-making fashions through the issuing of bank pass-books (upon Koriam's request to the Commonwealth Bank in Rabaul, 1966), and these tended to be treated as "passports to the Cargo" (OT:L.G. Balena 1981, cf. also *PNG Post-Courier* 30 Oct., 1972). But by 1978 *Kivung* members were persuaded by Alois Koki (currently custodian of the fund) to embark upon what must stand as the grandest piece of participative reciprocity in the history of all the cargo movements to have emerged thus far: the generous donation of K6,000 to the Papua New Guinea highlands famine relief, and K4,000 to the Brisbane flood victims, in Australia. The by-now-independent nation was advertising the sorry plight of those whose crops had been destroyed by mountain frosts; while devastation along the river front of Brisbane, city of the former ruling power, received a good deal of photographic coverage in the PNG press. The use of the money in this way, considering so little of it flows back to the subscribers themselves, apparently "betokens the leaders' desire to enter into reciprocity with powers which have large financial resources," and which may hopefully choose in return to bestow their benison upon the *Kivung* (cf.PF 1979, Trompf 1984a:44). In 1974, the group's leaders had been unsuccessful in trying to persuade government officials to put up as much as K26,000 toward a new (and first) high school in the Pomio area, but the Government did not want the possibility of a continued cult involvement, so the 1978 gifts mentioned above seem to find *Kivung* fishing for a still bigger catch. Predictably, *Kivung* members did not appreciate pressure from the new East New Britain Provincial Government to dig into its *own* fund to help provide succor for the earthquake victims of 1985, some of whom were in the Pomio area itself (National Broadcasting Corporation newscast, August 3, 1985).

The rationale of the Pomio movement, therefore, lies in its special combination of reprisal and concession toward agencies of change, or toward the abetters of the new set of circumstances facing the Mengen. What the movement has become has been largely determined by the leadership's recurrently reinforced discrimination between pressures and developments to be rejected and those to be accommodated. On the one hand, we find a spirit of independence and the creation a "a [general] altercation" (Desroche 1979:36), the *Kivung* being accepted by its adherents as a countervailing statement over and against the supposedly superior non-local forces of *Gavman, Misian, na Bisnis.* On the other hand, there remains the paradoxical mixture of dependence on the traditional spirits (as the media of transformative redemption from deprivation and loss of face) with an eagerness to test possible means of prosperity-bringing interchange with those very foreign sources of power associated with dissatisfaction in the first place. The question is, however, assuming we do possess criteria for deciding whether social phenomena are Christian or not, how are we to characterize the Christian elements of the *Kivung* more specifically?

A CHRISTIAN CARGO CULT

As already mentioned there is a strong "Hebraist" character about the *Kivung*'s ideological position. The critical importance placed on the Ten Commandments as the basis for social ordering and sanctioning might persuade one that we have here a neo-Jewish movement. We are not to forget that there are varieties of so-called Jewish Christianity (Daniélou 1964) and the *Kivung* might be valuable viewed under this rubric. On the other hand, the keeping of the Commandments within the *Kivung* members' frame of reference is quite inseparable from the maintaining of *lo* in the broader sense they have in mind, and we would be mistaken to suppose, first, that their emphasis on the Decalogue is an index to a general interest in Hebrew law, or second, that they conceive Biblical Law to be more an antidote to *kastam* than a fulfilment of it. There has been, as one might expect, a collective *Kivung* "forgetfulness" of all that is 'unworthy' (*no gut tru*) about the 'ancestral ways' (*pasin bilong tumbuna*) as they applied before the coming of the Mission. But the Decalogue has become the vehicle for revalorizing all that is considered best in tradition, engendering a neo-tradition in which the introduced, more universal, ethical values and *tabus* have fulfilled custom, and drawn out of it what is more than parochial and capable of cementing a new, preferred cross-tribal order (Trompf 1986:20-21).

Ritual collections and preparations for the ancestors' returns, then, are included under *lo* in a broader sense, as are other teachings and prescriptions which are dependent on pre-Christian myth and regulation. Without the catalystic effect of the "Ten Rules," perhaps, and without the Christian ethos which was borne with them by the missionary message, (neo-) traditionalism would be the obvious denotation to cover the case. As it is, though, there is a suffusion of so much that is associated with the *neue Zeit* (Tomasetti 1976:139-92) that the *Kivung* presents more like an alternative *sios* 'church' than a movement whose members are bent on digging in their traditionalist heels. The *persona* of the experiment, to illustrate, is significantly different from that of Moro Movement on Guadalcana, Solomon Islands, in which the majority of supporters try to prove that they can re-live the *kastam* that the British and the missionaries had tried to undermine (Davenport and Coker 1967; Trompf 1983:68-69). The *Kivung* protagonists like to contend that they are achieving what the Mission and government officials wanted to but could not properly fulfill: peace, for a special example, both in relations between the organization's members and in the plain absence of need for police in the district. They achieved this, moreover, through establishing a "total way" as against the separated forces of control called *Misian, Gavman, na Kastam,* a point in their own defence members like to make which has its parallels among the voices of independent churches (e.g. Trompf, in press).[10]

The *Kivung,* on the other hand, only has a limited number of points in common with "independent churches" (cf.esp. Barrett 1968; Sundkler 1961[1948]; Turner 1967), and I have refrained from listing it among the 15 or so I surveyed in recent years (Trompf 1983:51-72). Its followers have not pushed the image of an alternative church competing with other denominations, as with the Paliau Movement (= Baluan Christian United Church), Peli (now = Niu Apostolic), *Wok bilong Yali,* Nagriamel (= The Nagriamel Federation Independent United Royal Church), and so on. Actual use of the term *sios* would only compromise the reestablished totality they seek to maintain. The Church or Mission, indeed, is being rejected for failing to provide an unfragmented unity. It is actually being paid back by setting up a *wok* 'work', movement which can be acclaimed as superior, and it is being quite consciously hoisted on its own petard through the appropriation of the Commandments as the regulative basis of *Kivung* and ideally all village life. Rejection of Mission and Church, mind you, varies from outspokenness to indifference. As we saw, members are not debarred from going to church, only discouraged. If they attend Mass at Palmalmal Church, incidentally, they will find the very same Latinate figures (I-X) proclaiming the Decalogue on the wooden church pillars. But they will be reminded in the heart of the *Kivung* cult itself that, as the movement's drums beat on into the darkness during Saturday and Sunday nights, the truth does not lie with the mission Fathers.

We have been reflecting on the neo-Jewish and law-keeping side to things, but has not the Pomio *Kivung* its Jesus figure? Has not Christ been Melanesianized into the new Son/Sun, the "black Messiah," the late Koriam Urekit? Is this not sufficient reason to be talking about Melanesian

Christianity in connection with the movement? While admitting there remains the vexing question as to whether this particular messianism is "really" or "properly" or "strictly speaking" Christian or not,[11] yet setting this issue aside as inappropriate for this study, the motif of messiahship in *Kivung* discourse and practice certainly has to be taken seriously as an indigenous expression of Christianity. In the cultic activities, certainly, all worshipful concentration is on Koriam, who is lord of the ancestors, those about to return with the power of the cargo. Thus an incipient local Christology has grown up through the glorification of the organization's founder, but without the accompanying emergence and explicit group identification of a new *sios*, a new 'church'.

This specially limited set of developments, according to which a new organization's members claim to be Christian but nonetheless stop short of establishing a church, can be paralleled elsewhere, more particularly on Manam Island, with the heroicization of Irakau (Burridge 1960:3-13, 1969:59-61; Maburau 1985:15-16). Messianism in itself, of course, or the acclamation of some divinely appointed Savior-Figure, is not intrinsically Christian (Lanternari 1962:52-67), and any movement which, for other reasons would not normally be reckoned Christian, cannot be re-read as such simply because the structure of a Jesus figure "returns" to the system (as, for instance, with Shi'ite imamology, cf. Corbin 1964; Trompf 1980:9-10; Trompf and Kasaminie 1981:191-2). But both the leaders and the rank and file of the *Kivung* assert that all their concerns, ritual and worshipful ones included, are Christian, in spite of the institutional church's criticisms and acts of excommunication to the contrary. They have dissociated their Christianity from its supposed European origins and institutional trappings, and derived inspiration for a preferred new form of social cooperation from both select Christian elements and traditional principles of positive reciprocity. Indeed, as the younger, very idealistic and better educated protagonists for the *Kivung* contend, the movement's achievements exceed those of Church or Mission followers because the latter "have forgotten Christian principles" (Bailoenakia and Koimanrea 1983:184,c.185).

The unique ambivalence plotted here — i.e., the consolidation of a collectively expressed choice to snub the colonial (and post-colonial) order but deal with it in selective ways, and to turn one's back on the Mission and the introduced institution of the church yet espouse the Christian road at the same time — is of particular interest in the study of Melanesian Christianity, and has required a special kind of analysis. I have chosen to identify the grounds for altercation, "schism," and retributive energies in the *Kivung*'s case, and attempted to demonstrate how these have been expressed ideologically — as well as tempered in accordance with other considerations — precisely because it is the phenomenology of differentiation which provides the key to a group's identity. Out of this means of self-identification the new membership perceives more strikingly what it has (and considers should have) left behind, including what is disliked about the allegedly relinquished order.

With the *Kivung*, however, the degree of reprisal against the Catholic Mission, and the amount of dislocation involved in establishing an effective alternative organization, has been relatively slight by comparative standards (cf. Trompf, in press). In other words, there has been a subtle withdrawal, and not the confrontation we find with movements which confront police or tear-gas (the Hahalis Welfare Society, for instance, or the Paliau Movement in the guise of Makasol, cf. Rimoldi 1971:156-71; *PNG Post-Courier*, 30 May 1983). There have been no physical conflicts and few highly voluble outbursts between parties competing for control in the district. The quietness and element of passive/pacifistic resistance in the *Kivung*'s case has made for its greater success and for the absence of political repression (even though some Tolai representatives of the present East New Britain Provincial Assembly would certainly prefer to see it "put down"). This ostensible "peaceableness," indeed, if perhaps coupled with traditionalist-looking secretiveness, shows the extent to which the movement participates in the pacification ethos of Christianity in a Melanesian setting. But matters are not so simple because in a special sense so-called "cargo cultism" also participates in this ethos. Through the expectation of some dramatic act of reversal and transformation brought about by the spirit powers on behalf of "the faithful," cargo cults have often take a leaf out of Christianity's book by projecting eschatological solutions — the longed-for retribution against unwanted elements, the establishment of the True Law, and the perfection of reciprocity — into the hands of other-than-ordinary-human agencies, who make violent resistance unnecessary because they will soon arrive in their invincibility (Trompf 1989a). That element certainly remains strong in the Pomio *Kivung*, and thus all in all it presents itself as a Melanesian Christian cargo cult, which would be my considered definition of it.

NOTES

1. See Brigg and Brigg (1967) on military affairs (and the 3,000 allied troops around the bay). For some of these matters I also rely on my own fieldnotes, 1981 (including consultation of the files at the Pomio sub-district office and with Fr. James Corbally, MSC, considering the destruction by fire of the Malmal Catholic Mission records).
2. I have not yet found substantiation of P. Tovalele's claim that it was Koriam, not Bernard, who advocated the specialness of Thursday. Cf. Tovalele (1977:126). Koriam,

however, appears to have reinforced Bernard's advocacy of Thursday locally.

3. Paliau, incidentally, is renowned in New Guinea for creating the first indigenous church and local government council, as well as being the object of much cargo cultist expectation on the Admiralty or Manus Group (cf. esp. Mead 1956, 1964:192-234; Schwartz 1968a).
4. For background, P.W. Culhane (1939:9, 1954:1-3) and the later service of Misa (Ms.). Also OT: Daniel Roth (Summer Institute of Linguistics) and Leo Longi, 1981; and cf. C. Patre (1977:2-4) on Nutu as a special deity of fertility.
5. See PF, 1965 (whence quotations), cf. also 1967a:1-4; M. Naingis (1977:plate C); Tovalele (1977:126) for variations on the lay-out of gardens. I have not yet been able to establish which particular legend was central. For possibilities M. Panoff (1969c:2225) and Maden (1977) also typed legends told by Kolman Molo (present religious leader of the *Kivung*) deposited in the Pomio sub-district files, the first entitled *"Sampela tok bilong,"* 'cargo to come'. The important go-between bringing Koriam and Bernard closer together, incidentally, was Peter Pagun (OT:1981).
6. The role of traditional marriage (including property and trade) links between villages, in a matrilineal, virilocal society very similar in structure to that of the Tolai, was crucial for this widening allegiance. For the figures I rely on the parish patrol findings of Fr. Pius Osa, M.S.C. from 1981 (with kind permission); Naingis (1977:plate 1), cf. National Census (1981). That the movement also affected the south, see e.g., Chowning (1974:175), and cf. Trompf and L. Longi, fieldnotes, 1981.
7. OT:Tex Siro (Rigo, the Papuan concerned, was at Tauran Community School, Gazelle Pennesula during the time of the interview in 1981); Kolman Molu, 1981; Francis Koimanrea, 1982. For an earlier firing of millennial-looking hopes of transformation, centered on a coming bridge and ship in 1966, see Tovalele 1977:128.
8. The changes in parish priests occurred in 1962, 1967, 1970, 1975, 1978 (twice), and 1986. The priest in charge during the beginnings of the *Kivung* was the American Fr. William Burrows, M.S.C., later to emerge in the U.S.A. as a brilliant young radical ecclesiologist. Cf. "Baptismal Register, C.M. Malmal" (Baptismal Register Ms.).
9. The ethnography of the *urasena* is incomplete and is currently being documented by Longi.
10. Another problematic for his analysis is a related one: the decision as to whether the greatest influence for change is exogenous or endogenous (see van Baal 1979:614).
11. The answers to these questions do not come with ease, because there are no set or consensus-grounded rules for concluding that an organization is Christian simply because it has a comparable structure to the worship of Christ as "God-Human." Harold Turner once put it to me (pers. comm. 1982), and at the time I thought rather too forcefully, that no organization could be called a Christian church if it lacked a Christology (or doctrine of Christ). I felt threatened by the possibility that some of the movements I had put in the category of Melanesian independent churches did not satisfy this criticism, because some of them (and I think especially of Wok bilong Yali and Hahala) honour black Messiahs who are alternative to Jesus (Yali in the former case, Mattanachil in the latter) (Trompf 1983:56, 67-8). I salved my conscience, however, when I reflected that, with these two examples, Jesus is recognized as the Messiah for the whites but not for the blacks, and in that sense conventional Christology retains a footing, however weak. With the Pomio *Kivung*, however, this messianic duality does not appear to be manifest in discourse, and lies only latently behind the alternation of certain members' attendance between *Kivung* and church gatherings.

   Focussing on the messianic element here, incidently, does not mean I consider it the only criterion important for deciding whether a movement is Christian or not. Obviously crucial for our present analysis, though, is the gauging of the extent to which

Koriam, as Messiah type, substitutes for Jesus in *Kivung* faith, hope, and ethical expectations.

CHRISTIANITY, CARGO CULTISM, AND THE CONCEPT OF THE SPIRIT IN MISIMAN COSMOLOGY

Martha Macintyre

Ever since the phenomenon of "Vailala Madness" was documented by F.E. Williams (1976) the problems of cultural incongruence between Papuan religious cosmologies and those introduced by colonizers have attracted anthropological attention. Chiliastic and millenarian elements of cargo cults provided a rich source of material for analyses of syncretic and incorporative responses to missionary evangelism and colonial administration (Burridge 1960; Worsley 1968). More recently, studies of indigenous Christianity in the Pacific region (Boutilier, Hughes and Tiffany 1978; Whiteman 1983) have restructured the debate with respect to the persistence and independent historical development of Christian adherence. Missiologists and anthropologists have attempted to redefine and elaborate the old problems of syncretism in terms that at once acknowledge the historical specificity of Pacific Christianity and its cultural integrity (Berde 1974; Trompf 1984b).

This paper examines religious beliefs in a southern Massim society: Misima in Milne Bay Province. In the 1980s, with the consolidation of the United Church as a national institution, Papua New Guinea Christianity cannot be interpreted as a mere imposition, nor can the various cultic forms it takes be seen as ephemeral responses to cultural contradictions or misunderstandings. My concern is with the integration of beliefs about spirits, as these beliefs are expressed in ideologies of the relationship between the living and the dead; in the natural and supernatural domains; and in the concept of the person. I shall explore these subjects by examining a persistent millenarian movement called *losevasevan.*

Misima is an island in Milne Bay Province, Papua New Guinea. It is situated about 115 miles off the southeast tip of Papua New Guinea. A mountainous volcanic island, it is one of the largest in the Louisiade Archipelago. Misima is part of the Massim and there are broad cultural similarities with other societies in the region, particularly those of the Louisiades (Leach and Leach 1983). In particular, the cultural importance of mortuary ceremonies is common to all these societies.

Misimans are now almost all members of the United Church and many attribute their commitments to education and to the changes in their economy to the progressive teachings of successive missionaries. The churches and schools centrally located and well-maintained in almost every village, testify to the force of these introduced institutions in contemporary Misiman society. The United Church is the only denomination based on Misima. There are a few Roman Catholics, mostly migrants from the Sudest area where there is a mission. Their spiritual or pastoral needs are met by visits from the priest stationed at Nimowa. On Misima each village has a "missionary" or pastor who leads the congregation and the church has organized women's fellowship and youth groups. Until recently, the mission organized community schools and many older Misimans are literate in their own language because of mission schooling. The church is an important institution in every Misiman village. It is a focus for communal gatherings of a social or recreational nature as well as for worship. Even Misimans who do not regularly attend church services profess belief in a Christian God and ideals of public and private morality are derived from Christian doctrine. Misimans were instructed by Methodists who were strict sabbatarians and even today people do not work on Sundays.

On Misima, we find a society which has been subjected to the comings and goings of Europeans for over a century. In the late nineteenth century, Misimans witnessed their first gold rush, as hundreds of white men swarmed over the island in their search for the precious metal (Nelson 1976). At about the same time the first Methodist missionaries set about converting the people, who within the Louisiades were renowned as sorcerers especially skilled in a "spirit-stealing" magic that was inevitably and irrevocably lethal. The success of the missionaries was probably not instantaneous, but as yet no thorough historical account of their endeavors exists. My own assessment is drawn from fragmentary oral testimony and the visible strength of the contemporary church.

Today on Misima, beliefs about sorcery appear undiminished, in spite of a century of Christian opposition.[1] Moreover, ideas about sorcery, witchcraft, and magical forces co-exist with beliefs in Christianity and a peculiarly persistent cargo cult called *Losevasevan* 'to make, or do, spirits'. It is the co-existence of divergent, sometimes mutually exclusive, cosmologies that is the subject of this paper.

Initially, when I began inquiring about Misiman beliefs, I was intrigued by the existence of one of the longest running cargo-cults in a region where missions have had great success. Misima is a Christian society, to the extent that while only about half the people regularly attend church services, in census interviews conducted in three villages all but one man identified themselves as practising Christians. A stated belief in God, annual attendance at Christmas services, and contribution to *Mulolo*, the "gift-offering" competition held each year between all congregations, were deemed the true, minimally determining characteristics of the Christian. Methodism is not a veneer, it is a pervasive and institutionalized belief system on Misima. Moral rectitude, political probity, and a firm faith in God's purposes are spoken of as Christian virtues that can be observed in individual social behavior. As an observer from a predominantly secular culture, I was struck by the integration of religious ideals and practices into political and social spheres. Many public gatherings begin with prayers, inter-village competitive exchange is conducted under the auspices of the church (Gregory 1980), and men and women who hold office in the church are politically prominent. The yearly and weekly cycles are defined by seasonal horticultural activities and by church services. Whilst the stringent sabbatarianism of the first sixty years of the mission has declined, Sunday remains a day of rest and the social activities — family visits, picnics, hymn singing — are those prescribed by white missionaries intent on diverting people from pagan pursuits. The Christian festivals of Easter, *Mulolo*, and Christmas are observed by all villagers. At the same time, adherence to the cargo cult, *Losevasevan*, is widespread in almost all villages, and membership of church and cult is often convergent. In 1985, I estimated that about one third of the population were (in varying degrees) adherents to the *Losevasevan* movement.

Before I explore the relationship between the two institutions and their cosmologies, I shall briefly describe the *Losevasevan* movement. Perhaps too, I ought to explain that insofar as the organized movement has a name it is 'Cargo Cult'. *Losevasevan* refers to the activities or practices of the cultists — but Misiman people themselves refer to the institution as 'cargo cult', using the English words, even when they are speaking Misiman. Given the pejorative implications of the term in anthropological discourse I shall refer to it as a social/religious movement and call it *Losevasevan*.[2]

The *Losevasevan* movement is not confined to the island of Misima itself and there is evidence in patrol reports for the past forty years that the people who live on the neighboring islands of Motorina, Kimuta, and Bagaman are more ardent in their commitment to it (Patrol Reports, Bwagaoia 1954-85). It began on Misima in the village of Eiaus in the late 1930s. The instigator was a man called Buliga who, like many of his counterparts in Melanesia, was a charismatic orator who preached a doctrine of autonomy, stressing the necessity for all Papuans to adopt particular European practices at the same time requiring his followers to wear only traditional garments and ornaments. Unlike other leaders such as Paliau and

Yali, Buliga appears to have been only an observer of European ways. He never worked for Europeans, neither on plantations nor in the goldmines. He was, in his own social context, a leader of his lineage and a member of the clan Manilobu (which contemporary reports suggest was dominant at that time in the villages where *Losevasevan* sprang up).

Initially his injunctions followed lines familiar to all who have read the "cargo cult" literature. He exhorted all adherents to follow variations of the hygiene regulations that government patrols had been attempting to enforce on their visits since the mid-1920s. In his natal village, Siagara, he required people to dig latrines, sweep the village, wash regularly, and burn rubbish. At the same time, he insisted that traditional clothing be worn. He claimed divine inspiration through dreams and told people the central myth of Kimbauwa/Jehovah that constituted the inspiration for his proselytizing activities.

The myth itself appears to have changed little over the years, as Whiting's version, collected in 1974 is substantially the same as one collected twenty years earlier. It has elements of an origin myth of autochthony in which there are two brothers, one good and one an evil man who becomes the leader of all witches. The evil one's name is Taumudulele and he is a prominent mythic figure throughout the southern Massim region. The second, Mwasai, was a great warrior leader whose qualities as a fighter and leader were so divergent that he was called Mosenakulikuli when he fought and Gwamalala ('mouth goes in two directions'?) when he was being a just and good lineage leader.

Having established his domain on Misima, Gwamalala set sail for Sudest and went up on the mountain, which is called Rio or Lio and is regarded as a source of magical knowledge in some southern Massim communities. On Rio he took out his *baubau* (the traditional pipe used for smoking, before Europeans introduced black tobacco — by 1930 this would have been an archaic object) and from it he shook out many things — shell valuables, axe blades, pig's tusks, lime pots, and spatulae. Indeed, on Rio he became the master of all valuables known to the Papuans. He was then renamed Kimbauwa. As Kimbauwa he sailed north to New Ireland and New Britain, then on to Samoa, Tonga, and Fiji. At each place he took control of the forces of regeneration over all things valuable to those people.

Finally he sailed to the land of whitemen. There he was called Jehovah. He created things they value — money, tea, sugar, flour, steel, boats, and prefabricated houses. He gave out sweetened tea to all and so gained many followers. As Jehovah he has remained in the land of white people, but someday he will return to his place of origin, bringing with him abundant wealth. At this time Misimans will turn white and all Europeans will turn black — with attendant reversals of fortune.

I have abbreviated the story but the elements are clearly similar to other "cargo" myths insofar as they explain current reality, account for obvious inequities, and offer hope for a future in which there will be no poverty and no work. Jehovah's virtues are quite explicitly those of the *guyau* 'lineage leader', whose magical control over wealth and food production, combined with his extraordinary generosity, make him the supreme and just leader of all humanity. What is perhaps more noteworthy in this indigenous theory, derived from traditional values, is the absence of culpability and sin. Kimbauwa/Jehovah does not leave Misima because of any offence to him. His own values are not questioned. Yet in many respects he conforms to the archetype of Massim mythology, characterized by Michael Young as "The Resentful Hero," the supernatural being who, when crossed or rebuffed, stalks huffily out of the society of mere mortals, taking with him his unending supplies of food or wealth or other good things (Young 1983:70-74).

I shall return to this theme later, but foreshadow my interest in the context of the Kimbauwa/Jehovah myth. Within the myth there is no expression of the idea that Misimans somehow earned the disfavor of Kimbauwa and were therefore abandoned by him. The implication is that for quite simple, material reasons the land of the Europeans is more comfortable. There is an emphatic technical bias in the myth that is even more marked in the cult practice. Clean villages, latrines, regular bathing, and the adoption of particular names or titles are the activities that mark off the adherents who prepare Misima for the millenial return. But these people do not constitute an elect who will be the exclusive beneficiaries of the superabundance of wealth and food. The task is to lure back Kimbauwa/Jehovah by displaying to him the vast improvements made in Misiman living standards since his departure. In this way, the *Losevasevan* movement, like other "cargo cults" was organized as a means of gaining control over forces of change in ways that would benefit Misimans rather than the intruding whites. It was a genuine "self-help movement" (Gerritson, May and Walter 1981). Buliga was a visionary who wanted to lead people into the new order — but all Misimans would eventually enjoy the material changes brought about by Jehovah's return.

The idea of placating and enticing Jehovah back to Misima probably owes as much to established beliefs in the continuity of interaction between the living and the dead as it does to Methodism's chiliastic teachings on the necessity to prepare for God's kingdom on earth. Indeed, I shall argue that it is the point of convergence of these ideals that provides the pivot for the sets of beliefs that otherwise seem not merely incongruent, but contradictory.

Almost all recent studies of indigenous Christian movements have stressed the ways in which converts subsume elements of the new cosmology into familiar or traditional frames of reference (Comaroff 1985; Whiteman 1983). Equally, there is a tendency to convert known categories so that they accommodate innovations (Turner 1983:1-3).

From the beginning, the land of Europeans was associated with the place where departed ancestors lived. Insofar as it is possible to reconstruct pre-colonial religious beliefs, Misimans envisaged life beyond death as free of care, work, and pain. The name of the paradisial place was Tuma, (as it is in several other Massim cultures) and it was simultaneously visible and accessible, and yet not subject to the mortal, earthly constraints of time and space. Tuma was a vast underground cave, accessible at the eastern tip of Misima. The spirits of the dead moved between the world of the living and that of Tuma. As a place of abundance, it became identified with Australia. Similarly, as in many other Melanesian cultures, white skin was identified with spirits, so incoming white people were assumed to have special association with ancestral spirits. As leader, Buliga had privileged access to the world of Kimbauwa/Jehovah and the departed spirits of other Misimans. He communicated their desires for social and economic transformation to his fellow villagers and gradually gained their support. In the period immediately preceding the Japanese invasion of the region and the defence by the Allied Forces, Buliga's movement gained momentum. In 1942 he prophesied the millenium and banned the planting of gardens. Seed yams rotted and several villages were without food.

Unfortunately this disaster coincided with the panic evacuation of all whites as news of Japanese advances reached Misima. Hundreds of immigrant mine laborers from Orokaiva, Fergusson Island, and Goodenough Island were abandoned to fend for themselves. The only remaining white men were two disreputable (and usually drunken) miners who proceeded to commandeer all stores, and to tear the little township of Bwagaoia apart in their rum-inspired conviction that the departed miners had left gold caches behind. In this chaos, with hunger stalking the island in the forms of abandoned mine workers, no harvest, and no cargo boats bringing rations — people turned against Buliga.

To cut a long story short, in his desperate flight from disillusioned supporters and ANGAU officers, Buliga went from Misima to outlying islands and back again. On Motorina he and some of his followers murdered a patrol officer and some of the search party. For these crimes he and eight men were captured and sentenced to death. Buliga was found hanged in his cell — probably by his fellow prisoners, who hoped to avert their own punishment.

Subsequent investigations suggest that the behavior of the patrol officers and other Europeans on Misima at the time may explain the murders on Motorina. Nothing in the *Losevasevan* movement before or since, reveals it as a political movement advocating violent insurrection.[3] The mythic reversal of black and white, while clearly revealing resentment of colonial domination, does not appear to have had any political manifestations. Indeed, this magical solution might be interpreted as an expression of the desires to *avoid* confrontation and to achieve political ends without overt conflict. However, there can be no doubt that Buliga wished to identify himself and his movement with both Church and State, and that in organizational terms his aim was not only to emulate, but to gain complete control of the powers their agents wielded on Misima.

This brief description of the origins of *Losevasevan* and the historical reasons for its notoriety is meant only as a background. In the forty-odd years following, the movement has continued to flourish and it has retained the organizational form that was developed by Buliga. At various times the administration has investigated its activities and considered charging leaders. The waxing and waning of interest probably has more to do with the whims of the administration than with the dynamics of the movement over time. However, there do appear to be periods of efflorescence and increased activity over the years, and it is the events that generated such upsurges that provide insights into the complexity of Misiman cosmology.

Losevasevan means 'to make, or to do spirits' and it involves activities that are common to many spiritualist cults. Buliga's support was dramatically increased one day when he (and others) observed a large boat on the horizon shortly after he had conducted a "service" involving invocations to Kimbauwa/Jehovah and the ancestral spirits. As he pleaded with them to return, people saw a small boat being lowered and those in the boat paddling towards them. Just as they were about to land they turned and vanished from sight. This event, the summoning of spirits, became a central feature of the movement. Indeed, I contend that *Losevasevan*'s relative longevity is attributable to its spiritualism rather than its blatant material millenarianism. While such an assertion is fundamentally untestable, I base my contention on the fact that informants invariably stressed "communion with the spirits" as the purpose of the cult, and that efflorescences have occured after particular people have claimed personal encounters with visible *sevasevan* or spirit possession.

So, to dispense with that query that posed itself as "Why in a community that is so overtly and devoutly Christian, do we have a very long running 'cargo cult?'": Their coexistence is not problematic, for the "cargo cult" elements are secondary and sporadic. The *Losevasevan* movement is better understood as a spiritualist movement in which good and devout Christians participate with only mild misgivings as to the inherent contradiction between beliefs in Misiman *sevasevan* and Christian souls. But there is a contradiction and it is this that absorbed my interest and attention as I tried to understand Misiman beliefs about themselves, their lives, and their deaths.

CONCEPTUALIZATION OF PERSON, SOUL, AND SPIRIT

The contradiction which I consider crucial is that between the ideas of continuity, life after death, and the ancestral spirits as they are conceptualized and manifest in *Losevasevan* activities, and the particular body/soul distinction that was taught by Wesleyan missionaries. This is not simply a "lack of fit" between one set of ideas and another, it entails oppositional conceptualizations of morality, of mental and physical health, and explanatory models of human action.

The ideas about spirits, ancestors, and life beyond the grave that are expressed in the *Losevasevan* movement draw on a persistent cosmology that undoubtedly informed the pre-colonial religious system. I shall not here attempt an historic reconstruction of traditional Misiman religion (although I think that such an enterprise is both possible and worthwhile) but shall outline some of the continuities in beliefs as they are expressed in contemporary ideas about health and illness, and in the *Losevasevan* movement.

I am not suggesting that there is some functional necessity for *Losevasevan* activities and beliefs. My interest is in the movement as an historically specific manifestation of a tension, a fundamental disquiet generated by enforced changes. It is in this case a disquiet that derives from this equally fundamental contradiction between the Western views of body and soul/spirit that missionaries introduced, and a more complex, multifaceted concept of the person that permeates Misiman culture.

Rather than relinquishing those aspects of personal and collective integration that are inherent in ideas about the elements of a person, Misimans have sustained their complex notion of the person by constructing an alternative, subcultural religion, the *Losevasevan* movement. The cosmology implicit in their spiritualist activities entails continuities with the precolonial religion, but these have been reformulated so that they constitute an innovative response that is in opposition to the "mission" concept of person and spirit. The relationship between *Losevasevan* and indigenous Christianity is thus both complementary and oppositional. It is complementary to the extent that both *Losevasevan* and Christianity are responses to the cultural interventions of the colonial period. It is oppositional insofar as the Church, as a formal institution is not only critical of Losevasean ideologies, but publicly aligned with State attempts to suppress cultic movements.

As Mauss observed, "Our own notion of the human person is still basically a Christian one" (Mauss in Carrithers, Collins and Lukes 1985:19) with clear distinctions between the divine and the human. Indeed, the sort of Wesleyan Protestantism that provided the basis for Misiman indigenous theology stressed the neat Cartesian dichotomies of human/divine, body/soul, and proposed a "method" of integrating individual faith and its imperatives within an institutionalized framework — the Methodist Church — in ways that assume a separation of individual person from society. The idea of the person is not merely explicit in Western culture but has whole intellectual disciplines devoted to its cultural elaboration. In other cultures the category "person" is less clearly defined (see Marsella, De Vos and Hsu 1985). In Massim cultures the category of the person has blurred boundaries, often merging with ideas of regeneration and reproduction of qualities, attributes, and identity that are collective rather than individual (see, for example, Weiner 1976:15, 21, 230).

Misiman, like several other Massim languages, has a word for "human being" — *gamagal.* Humans are distinct from other creatures — *bwasumu.* It was in the context of learning about etiologies of disease that I gathered information about human attributes and this paper will undoubtedly reflect this orientation; however, a Misiman theology student, writing about the Misiman concept of Man, isolates the same elements as those I now discuss (Namunu 1983:2-30).

1. *Tuan* — Body; flesh and bones; sensate, physical being. Contemporary ideas about the body draw on both Western and traditional biological knowledge. People continue to believe that conception occurs only after repeated acts of sexual intercourse, and that blood and semen coagulate to form the foetus which is comprised of elements derived from the male and the female parents. In keeping with their ideas of matrilineally defined social identity, Misimans believe that in essence, procreation is determined by the female. The contribution of the father is viewed as sustenance and is acknowledged in important mortuary prestations of sago cooked in coconut milk which is seen as "payment for the umbilical cord." Traditional tabus on shaving and cutting hair continue to be kept in the belief that this prevents weakening of the umbilicus before birth. Ideas of infection are regularly conflated with notions of "dirt" and "matter out of place" so that bacterial or viral transmission of disease often appear indistinguishable from either willful

infliction by use of "dirt" (i.e., human hair, nail parings, etc.) or breaches of tabu whereby inappropriate substances are brought into dangerous proximity. Illnesses brought about by breaches of tabu are often seen as matters of simple physical interaction — comparable with, for example, the effects of dirt and flies on an open wound. Thus, the illness of a baby that occurs if the parents break the tabu on sex during lactation is attributable to the effect of semen in the mother's body — it spoils the milk. The lack of correspondence between our materialist explanations and those of Misimans should not be mistaken as evidence of an entirely non-materialist view of bodily processes and ailments. Rather, there is in the Misiman view an entirely different conceptualization of the "natural laws" pertaining to substances and their interactions. Moreover, while people seemed always to attribute major illness or death to sorcery, minor cuts or bruises were often dismissed as the result of ignorance, stupidity, or juvenile risk-taking.

When dealing with things physical Misimans are pragmatic people whose view of the human body includes ideas of the frailty of the very young and the aged; very complicated ideas about sustenance, physical growth, and well-being; notions about the circulation and properties of blood (which owe much to health education about malaria as well as traditional beliefs about blood), and views on parasitology. But physical vulnerability and the mortality of the human body are essential elements in the Misiman concept of the person. No doubt the missionaries encountered only assent when they first taught of the transience of mortal, bodily existence. For the Misimans, who practiced secondary burial of skulls, the rapid decomposition of the body at death was something quite familiar. However, the bones of ancestors endured — and in their physical continuity became a material reminder of those less substantial, but more important aspects of the person that were immortal.

2. *Yawal* or *Yana* — breath; life; alive. These terms for 'breath' are metaphors for life itself. As the person breathes, so he or she is alive and part of the everyday world of mortals. A person's capacity for life is, however, closely connected to another element which, in English, is less readily distinguished from the idea of breath as "vitality." This element is termed *gasisi.*
3. *Gasisi* — Energy; vigor; 'life-force'. This concept is important insofar as individuals vary in the degree or amount of vigor they have, and it is the term applied to explain the influence or impact of one person on another. Sorcery directed at a person's *gasisi* not only weakens him or her physically, but diminishes that person's

capacity to interact socially, to control and influence others. Just as we speak of energy as if it is concrete and measurable, so Misimans refer to *gasisi* as if it is something substantial; however I am convinced that the term refers to an abstract, insubstantial element and that to interpret it literally would be to misrepresent a conventional metaphor (cf. Keesing 1987:167-68).

4. *Nuatu* — mind; will; capacity for thought and intention. This term now incorporates the Western concept of the "brain" and is one which has definitely altered over time. In normal everyday speech it refers only to abstract, mental processes. One elderly informant suggested to me that in former days, before Europeans taught people about brains, Misimans believed that the heart was the seat of thought — however, as our conversation was in Tubetube (another Massim language) where the etymology of the term is clearly descriptive (heart is *nuapou*', literally, 'thought egg') I cannot affirm this. He did suggest however, that consciousness was not deemed to have anything to do with the brain/mind, but was a sensory capacity of the body, usually explained with reference to the eyes. The eyes can be afflicted by sorcery in a variety of ways, many of which involve what we would consider "altered states of consciousness." Spirits or ghosts do not have bodies, therefore they have no variation in consciousness — most especially, they do not need to sleep. What is most important however, is that spirits continue to think, to consider the lives of their mortal kin, and to harbor intentions — both good and evil. So, while spirits are not sentient (because they lack bodies and all the qualities and capacities entailed) they are willful, and are capable of wishing harm, vengeance, and illness on the living. They are also able to exert benign influences, protecting people from harm, and can magically bestow abundant wealth on people. It is these attributes which are the focus for the continuing relationship between spirits and living humans.
5. *Ati/Ate* — emotion; compassion; the ability to imagine and thereby identify with other human beings; by association with the idea of individual response it approximates the concept "personality" in English. The word is from the Proto-oceanic word meaning "liver" and until recently referred to that organ as well as the abstract meanings. Largely because of mission teachings that located emotional response in the heart, the majority of Misimans now think of *ati* as meaning the heart. The same shift in meaning has occurred in Dobuan and Ware languages in the Massim region.[4] Although the spirits of the dead do not have physical hearts (or

livers!), they retain the incorporeal qualities linked to that organ and may feel anger, joy, or compassion for living relatives.

6. *Kakanun* — shadow; reflection; image; insubstantial representation of the person. This element is one that has no real counterpart in European thought insofar as the qualities that inhere in the shadow or image are conceptualized as *essential* to the real form they represent. Thus, if a sorcerer performs magic on a person's reflection (in water) or shadow then the *tuan* 'body' will be affected. It is as if the *kakanun* constitutes the essence or supernatural reality of the physical person. Witches can malevolently steal shadows and burn them so that the person experiences a raging fever and dies. Witches can also steal the images of people and assume their appearance in order to commit nefarious deeds in the guise of another person. Spirits, on the other hand, have no essential relationship with their appearance as mortals. They can magically assume the forms of animals, fire-flies, or adopt some shape that they had when alive. Thus a recently deceased elderly woman may visit in ghostly form, taking on the appearance of "herself" as a young woman. Clearly then the *kakanun* is an element which, while representing the *tuan* during life, continues beyond the grave and is an attribute of immortals as well as living people.
7. *Kilewa, Yaluyaluwa* — Spirit, and now, the Christian 'soul'. The spirit exists within the body from the time of quickening in the womb. The spirit and its qualities seem invariably to be linked with the *ati* 'personality' and *nuatu* 'mind' inasmuch as individual attributes of compassion, knowledge, wisdom, and particularly, moral principles are spoken of as aspects of the spirit or soul. The *yaluyaluwa* is immortal and leaves the body at death, to journey to the world of spirits (or now, to the Christian heaven). However, sorcerers and witches are able to make their spirits leave their bodies even during life.

When referring to spirits in their life beyond the grave, people generally use the term *sevasevan.* The precise meaning of the word in its pre-colonial context can only be a matter of speculation. In contemporary usage it means 'souls', in the sense of the spirit forms of people who were once individual human beings. It also connotes 'ghost' in the sense that it is used to refer to any incorporeal manifestation of a spirit — as perceived by mortals.

Sevasevan are above all, ancestral spirits. In view of the pre-colonial practices involving secondary burial and successive mortuary feasts honoring the dead, it is clear that ancestral spirits loomed large in the world of pre-Christian Misimans. The spirits of the unavenged dead, or those whose bodies had been consumed by enemies, or those who had been killed by drowning when flying witches broke canoes — such spirits could not rest easily in Tuma. Instead they returned to the villages of living relatives and there urged them to take revenge or incur their supernatural wrath. Sometimes ancestral spirits appeared in dreams, to offer advice or to warn a loved one of danger. Occasionally a *sevasevan* entered the body of a person whom he/she had loved dearly in life, occasioning fits that resulted in death — so that the *sevasevan* removed the spirit to Tuma. More often the *sevasevan* simply assumed temporary control over a person and he or she had convulsions or behaved in bizarre ways characteristic of spirit possession. Even today, fits caused by epilepsy and fevers are often considered to be instances of spirit possession.

But when Europeans came to Misima, many of the feasts were modified to exclude pagan elements that were abhorrent to missionaries and administrators. Formerly, when the skull was disintered to be placed in the matrilineage cave, a large feast was given to propitiate the ancestors and commit the spirit of the recently deceased to their care. Every year, when the large sea worms appeared (about November) people would prepare the distributory feast called *helagi yauyau* to specifically honor the *sevasevan* of all ancestors.

Secondary burial was banned by government administrators on the grounds of the health risks associated with shallow graves in villages and contact with decomposed flesh. But Christian missionaries were even more zealous and the abandonment of various practices associated with *sevasevan* must be attributed to their untiring efforts.[5] Skull preservation and the rituals that expressly honored the dead by gift-offerings were repressed as idolatry. As skulls of enemies taken in battle were taken as trophies and some skulls were used as valuables in exchanges (see also Whiting 1975), the missionaries also conflated all uses of skulls as evidence of cannibalism.

On Misima, as elsewhere in Melanesia, mission evangelism often proceeded in directions indicated by mutual misunderstandings. But for many years now, Misimans have managed their own churches and preached their own sermons. And while the Church as an institution vehemently opposes the *Losevasevan* movement (in similar terms to those of its European-dominated predecessor), there is abundant evidence for overlapping adherence to cult and church.

Publicly, *Losevasevan* and the United Church are disassociated because of church disapproval. There is a cult house where members of *Losevasevan* meet, and both the place and the 'services' are regarded as sacrilegious by local ministers. The cult leaders have always stressed commitment to Christianity and religious worship. They do not view their activities as pagan or oppositional to either church or state.

The *Losevasevan* movement was revived by a nephew of Buliga in the 1950s and he has remained leader to this day. Now all the leading members are men who at some time worked for the Australian administration and at least two have been elected as local councillors. While many speak English, few have much formal education. These men are in many respects conservatives who are dissatisfied with the lack of economic development in the area. Apparent anti-European elements in the political rhetoric are in reality assertions of an ideology of local autonomy. Leaders have never advocated political insurrection. Rather, they have exhorted their followers to be good Christians and to participate in government-sponsored projects, such as local copra production in the 1950s, and the co-operative societies established in the 1960s. The leader now owns a small tradestore. Others have been involved in various development projects.

The cult hierarchy is modelled on that of the state. The leader is the Prime Minister; there is a Governor-General, a General, public servants, and others bearing titles of rank that appear to be neologisms, having no meaning in the local language or in English. This style of organization first emerged about the time that Papua New Guinea achieved political independence. Prior to that, the officers had included a king, resident magistrates, and other officers associated with colonial administration. Membership is a relatively simple matter, requiring payments of amounts of money, between K1 and K5, and attendance at seance-like meetings where the leaders calls forth ancestral spirits (*sevasevan*) to speak with particular descendants in the meeting house. People give money in the belief that 'dividends' will be paid and that, eventually, all contributions will be returned a thousandfold. Some adherents are given tobacco or other goods by the leader who claims that these gifts have been brought by the spirits.

In 1973 the District Officer in Charge reported that the cult had established a hamlet at Boma, inland from Siagara. A two-storey building, vaguely reminiscent of the District Officer's house at Bwagaoia, was built as a meeting-house. Over the years, Boma has become a small settlement for cultists and recently people have begun to make gardens around the hamlet. There were rumors in 1985 that the gardens were being made in preparation for feasts to be held when the ancestors returned in 1986 in large ships filled with money and European goods. Boma is patrolled by guards who exclude non-members from meetings.

The cult is really more concerned with the relaying of messages from the spirits of departed ancestors than it is with millenarian economic transformation. At various times over the years, members have reported seeing ghosts or spirits of departed relatives, and on each occasion there has been an efflorescence of activity that has brought the cult to the attention of district authorities. For most of the adherents who were prepared to discuss their membership with me, the spiritualist element was primary. While they paid their membership fees, they viewed the 'cargo business' more as a lottery than an investment. Many members have become disenchanted as years pass without any sign of their 'dividends'.

All meetings are conducted in darkness. The leader goes upstairs in the meeting house and attracts the spirit with sounds of coins, engine noises, and verbal invocations. The 'spirits' sometimes appear and can be dimly seen, wearing white clothing and eating food offerings that have been brought for them. Usually they present themselves as voices in the dark and occasionally a 'spirit' will proffer a hand to be touched. Their usual messages consist of exhortations to lead a good life followed by a whispered request for more money.

There are very explicit statements concerning the spirits that support a "relative deprivation" explanation for the origins of the cult. As the spirits left Misima to dwell in a more congenial world, in which there is a superabundance of luxury goods, so they have to be coaxed back. One recurring theme in information I collected was that the spirits would be lured back by money and gold — evidence that modern Misimans were diligent workers and capable of managing the wealth that the spirits control. A mysterious white woman, dressed in a nurse's uniform, seems to be the prophet of this millenial return. Another element in the practices and beliefs is the use of codes to record or convey information. These codes are very simple, being numerical and alphabetical transformations, probably based on the codes used for stock records in European tradestores. Secret messages in the forms of songs or rhymes are conveyed to a select few in the cult. These follow patterns of traditional magical spells, being short invocatory rhymes in mostly unintelligible words. Adherents memorize these communications from the spirits in the belief that, at a later date, the meanings will be revealed to them. Like magic spells, these words are thought to be instruments of power over the material and supernatural worlds. At various times in the past *Losevasevan* has appealed to people who were unhappy with the lack of material benefits coming as a result of taxpaying and gift offerings to the United Church. However, most members are regular church attenders who give more money to the church than to the cult, and there is no pressure on members to avoid taxpaying or to resist government authority. Equally, there are many people who do not belong to the cult, who express cynical disillusionment with the government, its agents on Misima, and the organization or perceived financial mismanagement of the local United Church. While several educated Misimans represented the cult to me as a hotbed of political insurrection and criminal activity, I found little evidence to this effect. In the past, European administrators held this view.

Local administrators continue to object to the cult mainly because they perceive it as a threat to their authority and they regard the leaders as immoral. They view the collection of moneys as criminal fraud and at various times in the recent past have considered charging leaders with spreading false rumors. In recent years, a new form of communication with the 'spirits' has become a feature of cult meetings — there are reports that female members have been required to submit to their sexual advances. While such practices could be described as rape by fraud, it does appear that the women concerned were willing partners and are not forced to have sexual intercourse. Many people in the community are grossly offended by the sexual licentiousness allegedly occurring at Boma and their disapproval led to a decline in attendance at meetings.

I do not think that this marks the beginning of the end of this durable cult. One of the major reasons for the persistence of *Losevasevan* is undoubtedly its incorporative, *inclusive* tendencies. The church in Milne Bay Province has always been exclusive and, with respect to other Christian denominations, sectarian. *Losevasevan* leaders have promoted economic development, public health measures, education — indeed they have consistently endorsed policies they consider progressive. The Church has similarly identified itself with the forces of economic and political advancement, but required of converts that they repudiate beliefs and practices branded as paganism or sorcery. As many of the powers they drew upon came from the realm of the *sevasevan*, the magic that wrought good and evil being passed down ancestral lines — so the demand of repudiation meant the impossible — the denial of a whole cosmology.

People might have abandoned practices, but as I have argued, they have retained their view of the nature of spirits and other supernatural forces. Patterns of illness and death continued as they had before missionaries arrived — constantly testifying to the power of ancestral spirits, sorcerers, and witches. Moreover, the Wesleyan missionaries unwittingly perpetuated involvement with *sevasevan* by endorsing those mortuary ceremonies which they perceived as revering the departed. The early missionaries in the Louisiade Region encouraged customs which they thought gave expression to the higher sensitivities of peoples whom they otherwise considered "savage" or devoid of compassion. Having by 1891, when they first moved to Misima, become familiar with various Massim mortuary rituals, they were prepared to promote syncretic practices on a very small scale. The Misimans had focused much more on spirit placation and rituals dealing with secondary burial than had their western neighbors on

Tubetube and Normanby islands, and so the missionaries insisted that they adopt aspects of the mortuary rituals of these other groups (Whiting 1975:175).[6]

There was a convergence between traditional ideas about *sevasevan* and Methodist teachings about the community of saints in heaven. Similarly, as preaching and teaching were in the vernacular, the Christian distinction between body and soul or spirit were readily translated into the familiar *tuan/yaluyaluwa.* In perpetuating crucial ideas about the nature of humankind, the mission generated subtle contradictions which it then failed to confront or analyze.

Like many Christian missionaries, their attacks on aspects of traditional belief were often crude and uncompromising. Sorcery was viewed as the work of the devil, sorcerers denounced as evil charlatans. Ideas about, for example, *kakanun* 'shadow' were hastily dismissed as primitive misunderstandings about effects of light that produce shadows and reflections. In so reducing the meaning of *kakanun,* the missionaries cut themselves off from important insights into Misiman views of the real/unreal, or essential/vestigial elements of being. In the same way, *sevasevan* were dismissed as "ghosts" and fantastical apparitions that were mere figments of the savage imagination. But simultaneously, the idea was constantly invoked that the human spirit endured beyond the grave, living in a world free of care, work, sickness, and death. The mission endorsed those mortuary ceremonies which were expressly concerned with restructuring social relations between ancestors and their living descendents.

These ceremonies constitute the most dramatic social events in all Massim cultures and they are the focus for major exchanges of pigs, yams, and valuables of various sorts. The Misiman rites are substantially similar to those of Panaeati described by Berde (1974) in his Ph.D. dissertation "Melanesians as Methodists" and the notions of spirit/soul(ghost)/life force are common to most southern Massim societies. In the Louisiade Archipelago, where the *Losevasevan* movement has been strong for half a century, the spirits of the dead are the focus of several major rites. From one perspective (and that favored by those early missionaries who sought to intervene), the rites and exchanges reconstruct social and economic relations between those whose relationship has been jeopardized by a death (specifically, but not exclusively, affines). At the same time, several prestations that are *apparently* the exclusive concern of the living, entailing transmission of land rights or property, are also placatory of a deceased, and so the give and take between the living is a mediation between the ancestors and those who survive.

On Misima there are many prestations which can be examined in these terms, but I shall limit myself to a single one, *powon. Powon* is probably best translated as 'compensation'. It is the term for a variety of prestations but in the context of a death, it is usually a very valuable shell necklace given to an affinal lineage as a token of grief and an expression of innocence against anticipated accusations of sorcery. It is really *required* of affines in order to avert blame for the death. While analytically such prestations can be seen as enchained in a series of affinal exchanges that begin with marriage, it is important to recognize that the symbolism of *powon* is that of mediation between life and death. Failure to give adequate *powon* at death may thus incur the wrath of the deceased's spirit as well as his or her living relatives.

This cursory look at *powon* is presented here as an example of the way in which the traditional ideas concerning the person are sustained within exchange institutions concerned with death. When we examine the effects of *breaches* of mortuary tabus or obligatory prestations we find that they are similarly viewed as offensive to the deceased as well as his or her remaining relatives. Which brings me back to the central theme of this chapter, which is the perpetuation and persistence of concepts of the person. If offended, the spirit, or *sevasevan*, can *feel* hurt or anger, that is, it retains human responses associated with *ati* 'personality'. Thus offended, the spirit may inflict injury or otherwise disturb the well-being of living relatives. On the other hand, if the living have consistently maintained a loving, reverential relationships with the spirit and provided abundant mortuary gifts, then that spirit may comfort, reward, or protect the living because he/she is gratified by such actions.

Spirits can warn people of impending harm, in dreams, or by appearing as a recognizable figure (assuming their own *kakanun* 'reflection' or adopting another's) can converse and console a grieving relative. Sometimes the spirit might reward beloved kin by helping them in exchanges, in fishing or sailing, or in other productive enterprises. But whatever the terms of the continued relationship, the point is that it does not cease. Furthermore, it remains negotiable — so the living can make amends to the departed by giving lavish feasts of honor.

So, central to my argument is the continuity of an ideology of social integrity that incorporates a spirit into the world of the living — not simply as someone beloved and remembered, but as a force to be reckoned with in everyday interactions. Spirits have allegiances, lineage identity, and continue to experience emotions that motivate moral, purposive actions. The distinctions between the ancestors and their mortal descendants are effectively very different from the spirit/body distinction that dominates Christian thought. As *sevasevan*, spirits move *between* the paradisial world of ancestors where living is easy and the world of mortals, where life is hard, brief, and marked by sickness and need.

Christianity did not seriously challenge the world view that incorporated spirits and mortal beings in a single tangible world. Even now, after almost a century of Christian influence, those things that enshrine and protect indigenous conceptualizations of the person as a social being have persisted as if unassailed.

The criticisms of the cult by pastors and others within the Church have tended to be directed at specific practices or claims by cult adherents, not at the deeper existential elements that inform beliefs about spirits. They are often in the form of accusations about deceit, fraud, or unChristian behavior that do not explicitly question the epistemological foundations of *Losevasevan.* It is my contention that in encouraging mortuary rituals that centered on and symbolized the transformation of a living person to an immortal ancestor, the missions inadvertently sustained an ideology of social integration that encompassed the living and the dead. The attempts at suppression of these with the practice of Methodism (now United Church) has not generated tensions that are overt, precisely because the *Losevasevan* movement has developed in ways that enable communication with spirits to continue.

But it is not simply a matter of continuity. Just as the world of Misima has been changed and people there have had to confront or accommodate institutions brought in by Europeans, so through *Losevasevan* Misimans have been enabled to subtly reframe their spiritual worlds and to redefine their relations with ancestral spirits.

The economic and social millenialism of the movement may well have emerged at certain historical conjunctures. I have not been concerned here with the *origins* of the cargo cult, but with its persistence. It persists as a *spiritualist* movement, in tandem with Christian beliefs. But it entails none of the moral judgments in which the benefits of the afterlife are reserved for the redeemed. Rather it rests on ideals of social interaction and enchained indebtedness established in the mortuary ritual complex that dominates Misiman political economy. The mortuary ceremonies, in turn, are structured around an ideology of social identity that is preserved in language, in beliefs about sorcery, magic, illness, and the supernatural ordering of production and reproduction.

In this paper I have embarked on a project which I hope will eventually involve an examination of the ways in which Misiman ideas of spirituality are enacted and reconstructed in an indigenous Christian world view. I do not see Misiman Christianity as a veneer, indeed many of the people I met there I consider to be devout and sincere Christians whose religious adherence imbues their whole existence. But in teasing out some of the strands of these complicated and enmeshed ideologies I have highlighted the ways in which contradictions can be virtually ignored in one context because they are seen to be resolved in others. It is not a clear cut case of "Sunday Christians, Monday sorcerers" (Kahn 1983) for there are subtle mergings and conflations. *Losevasevan* appears to be a product of, or response to, European intervention. I have argued that it is also the vehicle for the perpetuation of indigenous (and pre-colonial) ideologies of person and social universe. At the same time, Christianity confronts and incorporates those cultural norms as it seeks to alter their moral framework. Having here begun the analytical task of distinguishing elements, the major project remains: for we have to examine and explain not simply the persistence of particular conceptualizations and beliefs, but their coexistence as dynamic, but often contradictory cultural forces.

NOTES

Material for this paper was collected in 1986 while I was undertaking a social impact study for the Institute for Applied Social and Economic Research into a proposed goldmine on the island. I have also utilized two unpublished dissertations on Misiman society and culture (Namunu 1983; Whiting 1975).

1. On Tubetube, some hundred miles west of Misima, where the traditional belief system was very similar, beliefs in sorcery have not only diminished but have altered considerably under the prolonged and concerted efforts of mission and medical officers to banish them.
2. There are two accounts of the cult, one detailed ethnographic study by Susan Whiting (1975), in her M.A. thesis; the other, by M. Hess (1982).
3. The political directions of the Losevasevan movement are discussed in more detail in R. Gerritson & M. Macintyre (1985), Volume 1.
4. Whiting (1975) translates *ati* as 'liver' in the mid-1970s and assures me that most elderly people rejected the reference of the heart completely, personal conversation. This was not the case when I was there in 1985 and Simeon Numunu translates the word as 'heart'.
5. For a more detailed discussion of the (often harsh) methods employed by missionaries in this region see Macintyre (1983:280-288).
6. Familiarity with Tubetube and Duau (specifically Bunama) mortuary rites allows me to assert that, in spite of the Misiman tradition that their current rituals are all "borrowed" from Tubetube/Duan — the ritual sequence has only structural similarities with those of the South West Massim and it seems that only a few practices were incorporated. A more accurate interpretation seems to me to be that having successfully stopped secondary burial, dancers carrying skulls in bags, and exchanges of skulls for valuables on Tubetube, missionaries were simply requiring that the Misimans change likewise. The pre-colonial mortuary ceremonies on Tubetube and Misima appear to have been remarkably similar.

6

FATHERS, ALIENS, AND BROTHERS: BUILDING A SOCIAL WORLD IN LOBODA VILLAGE CHURCH SERVICES

Carl E. Thune

INTRODUCTION

Given the tenor of life in Loboda village on Normanby Island, Papua New Guinea, the local branch of the United Church might seem to be a puzzle. In a world in which large scale co-operation is difficult to achieve, the church is only slightly less successful than the government in inducing most adults to devote a day each week to its material maintenance and another morning each week to attending its services. In a world in which self-willed, discrete, and independent individualism is taken seriously, the church induces most adults not only to attend Sunday morning services but to pay at least superficial attention to its other activities. And, in a world founded on egalitarianism, the church presents a message reflecting hierarchical relations between human and non-human beings. Even more surprisingly, these relations parallel equally hierarchical relations between humans having greater and lesser access to an absolute truth existing apart from social relations between specific individuals.

However, if we look at the content of Loboda village church services, viewing them as centered around a literary exploration of the fundamentals, possibilities, and impossibilities of the social world, local acceptance of the church appears less problematic. Indeed, the organizational uniqueness of the institutional church is overshadowed by the fact that its services indirectly address the same kinds of concerns spoken to by literature of traditional genres.

This paper will embed the literature of the Loboda village church service within the larger Loboda village literary universe. In particular, it will explore the assumptions about the social world that underlie prayers and sermons. I will argue that the literature of church services, like Loboda village literature associated with other alien social universes such as the colonial and contract labor worlds, is "about" building expansive social relations.

ORAL LITERATURE OF EVERYDAY LIFE

Two assumptions underlie my approach to Loboda village church services. First, I take the elements composing each church service to constitute a coherent body of literature that can be addressed, by combining the analytic techniques derived from anthropology and literary criticism. And, second, I take these church services, despite their Western origin, to be a part of the Loboda village cultural world. If they make sense to Loboda villagers, it is because they address villagers' concerns that almost certainly long predate the appearance of Christianity in Papua New Guinea.

Unlike the anthropologist's oral histories, myths, and folktales, the content of much of a church service is largely spontaneously improvised rather than strictly derived from an inherited and codified oral tradition. And, unlike the literary critics' written texts, most prayers and sermons are unwritten and ephemeral. Yet, like the literary critic's discrete and self-contained written literature, church services can be profitably treated as texts that can be illuminated by explaining their formal structure and critical assumptions; and, like the anthropologist's oral literature, Loboda Village church services must be understood as texts having a complex relation to the structural dynamics and problematics of the social and cultural world of which they are a part.

My interpretation is based on limited discussion of these services with Loboda villagers. But it is also based on seeing them as a part of the overall corpus of Loboda Village oral literature including myths, folktales, and oral histories. Finally, it is based on viewing them in terms of themes and issues within Loboda Village social organization that appear over and over as Loboda villagers discuss the mundane concerns of everyday life.

LOBODA VILLAGE AND THE HISTORY OF THE LOBODA VILLAGE CHURCH

The church service discussed in this paper was held in Loboda Village, a community of about 325 people located on Normanby Island in the Milne Bay Province of Papua New Guinea. Loboda Village social organization is centered around small, discrete matrilineages. Internal relations among those of a single matrilineage are strong and solidary, being based on a shared identity. External relations with members of different matrilineages, including affinal and paternal relations, are necessary though tentative, fragile, and conceptually problematic to villagers because they threaten the integrity of the matrilineage which is the one truly natural unit of the social world (Fortune 1963; Roheim 1950; Thune 1980). With few exceptions, external relations are between equals both at the individual and at the matrilineage levels. In order to maintain this equality, all formal prestations are formally repaid by equivalent prestations so a final, egalitarian balance of the participating parties is achieved (Thune Ms. *b*).

From a broader perspective, external relations between those of different matrilineages provide a model for the complementary joining of those of alien social worlds. Hence, external relations of opposition between those of different matrilineages are paralleled by wider external relations between those of alien geographical or cultural universes. Conversely, the internal relations within a matrilineage provide a model of more broadly defined internal relations that reflect what the Lobodan people take to be geographical, historical, cultural, or social unities.

However, while this sketch suggests Loboda village social life is built around a rigid matrilineality, for many purposes, individuals, as self-willed, autonomous, independent equals, are the basis of social life. As people describe why specific individuals perform specific actions, they mediate the social world grounded in and generated from matrilineality through their discrete and independent minds and their relations to other specific individuals with equally discrete and independent minds.

Predictably, given the significance of internal relations and boundaries, the construction and exploration of relations transcending these boundaries is of major importance within traditional literature (Thune 1980). Similar concerns are also visible in such contact literature as the story of the founding of the first mission on Dobu Island (Thune Ms. *a*), autobiographical stories of contract labor (Thune 1987), and stories of World War II (Thune in press). In the following pages I will argue that the acceptance of such introduced forms as prayers and sermons is in part the result of villagers finding within them new perspectives on these same concerns.

After the Rev. W. E. Bromilow founded the Methodist mission[1] on Dobu Island in 1890, he sent missionaries, in most cases South Pacific Islanders, to other islands of the southeast Papua. Indeed, while Bromilow's party included a number of European ministers, missionaries, and "sisters," the bulk of the day-to-day missionization was performed by South Pacific Islanders who were less expensive to maintain and who, at least from a European perspective, were better able to blend into the village social world (Wetherell 1978).

Loboda villagers take pride in the fact that the first missionary to be resident on Normanby Island was sent to their village.[2] However, older villagers point to the difficulties early missionaries had in making convertions and emphasize the missionaries' lack of acceptance, especially by the more powerful members of the community. For example, one of these missionaries is reported to have been killed by sorcery after having chastised a local sorcerer for working on Sunday.

While there was a mission presence in Loboda village during the early 1890s, it probably did not successfully integrate itself into village life until at least the 1920s or 1930s.[3] Certainly by the 1950s and 1960s the mission was well established in the village, not only conducting specifically church-related activities but providing a variety of social services including education and medical care. Older villagers recall this period as the time of the mission's greatest importance to villagers both in terms of its role in village life and in terms of the interest villagers brought to it.

More recently the government has assumed responsibility for providing many of the social services formerly offered by the church. And, today, villagers, more aware that the church is not simply another extension of the government with all of the latter's coercive powers, are less willing to devote significant amounts of time and money to its maintenance. But, perhaps most importantly, as the church has become localized, its attraction of providing a powerful tie to a wider world of people, knowledge, plants, manufacturing techniques, and customs has declined. Whereas even twenty years ago, villagers could count on the church to provide them with contacts with a variety of people from Europe, Australia, the South Pacific, and other parts of Papua New Guinea, today the village pastor is a Normanby Island man, and even most of those based at the United Church headquarters in Baluwada and Salamo are Papua New Guineans. The church in many ways has ceased to be an alien presence with all the attractions of exoticism and social expansion that that implies. Perhaps another contribution to erasing the church's earlier exoticism is its mundane everyday familiarity to those who have known it all their lives.

The village pastor is the local representative of the United Church. As the Loboda language term, *misinari*, suggests, he is heir to the position of the village-based South Seas missionaries established by Bromilow during the early years of the Dobu Island Mission. Village pastors receive a year or more of training at one of the nearby United Church centers.

Village pastors are usually not from the village they serve and, in many cases, are not fully fluent in the local language. However, while being outsiders and representatives of a more distant institutional church, they are responsible for managing the local church including organizing services, maintaining church facilities and finances, and organizing such church-related activities as hymn singing sessions, women's groups, and children's Sunday Schools. However, while the pastor has formal responsibility, much of the day-to-day work is performed by local villagers who for all practical purposes are responsible for the success of the local church.

The normal Loboda Village church service is based on the model originally introduced in the early years of the Methodist Mission. It consists of a hymn, followed by a more or less spontaneously composed prayer, the Lord's Prayer, a Bible reading, a formal sermon centering around an exegesis of the Bible reading, and a final closing hymn and brief prayer. This structure may be elaborated with responsive readings, additional hymns, a second sermon, and additional prayers. Although services are usually organized by the resident village pastor, lay participation is encouraged. Less experienced members of the congregation may present the prayer and lead hymns; more experienced members may present the sermon, and, even occasionally, assume overall organizational responsibility for the service.

As will become clear, varying degrees of improvisation are allowed in different sections of the service. The Lord's prayer, for example, can only be recited. By contrast, the sermon, while beginning with the chosen Bible reading, is composed freely. Hence the sermon allows the greatest freedom for the expression of Christian themes in local terms, and, conversely, for the expression of local concerns in Christian terms.

This paper will focus upon texts drawn from a single service presented in the Loboda Church by Wailasi, a student at the small Dawada Bible School.[4] While it is shorter and more concise than most services, it is similar to them in structure and overall content.[5] My translations are deliberately "naive," intended to capture the difficulties and ambiguities in the language used in the service rather than to convert it into a conventional English theological vocabulary. In many cases, use of what might seem to be an obvious English theological term would obscure the critical redefinition of borrowed concepts in more locally meaningful terms. And, it would suggest the term was a part of a larger set of English conceptual and theological vocabulary rather than a part of a very different set of Loboda vocabulary and concepts for individual motivation and social relations.

THE OPENING PRAYER: THE CONSTRUCTION OF TRANSACTIONAL HIERARCHY

Loboda Village church services begin with a short prayer. Within the service this prayer represents a first step in defining the relation of the human world to the world of God and Jesus. Wailasi's prayer is typical. Although it is constructed from formulaic phrases, the prayer is presented more or less spontaneously. Within a structure derived from an alien convention, there is room for considerable improvisation. This allows him to transform an alien form so it addresses and makes sense of local concerns.

Our big man [leader, '*inapwana*] and our big [old, important] father [*tama*]. You are the maker of the ground and the sky [heaven]. This morning we feel your air [breath, euphemistically, life] is with us. And your spirit [shade, *yaluwaluwa*] is here with us.

At this time we praise you and call you our big man [*'esa'esa*]. We praise [*tupu*] you and we call you our big man because you stay [live, exist, are] so very far away. And, so, for that reason, we praise you and call you our big man.

So, our father, at this time we also pray [*sida*] to you for our mistakes [errors, sins, *to'umalina*] in years past and months past. If our eyes have behaved wrongly [*gesi*] or our legs have stepped wrongly or our minds [thoughts, consciousness] have thought bad, wrong thoughts, God, we pray to you to wash away our mistakes with the blood of your child, Jesus Christ.

God, we are praying. And, also, we thank you for your gifts [love, concern, *oboboma*] from which we eat and drink. So, at this time we thank you. And we thank you very much for your child [*natu*], Jesus Christ. Because of his birth and his death you called to us and as a result we understand [comprehend, know] things.

So, we should do whatever is your will [*nuwana*, mind, intelligence, desire]. Because of the earth and the things on it we say "Thank you very much." God, all kinds of things are [exist] here [on earth], so many that we cannot count them and we cannot name them.

You are the first and the last. And so, because of all the things, we pray to you, our big man. Jesus Christ is his name.

Amen.

The opening prayer is built around images of dependency of people on God and Jesus. In contrast to traditional appeals to other beings for assistance or co-operation such as occur in magical spells, the prayer is spoken by people who are essentially subordinate to beings who occupy a superior position. Prayer, more than any other Loboda Village speech form, is built upon a vocabulary of asymmetrical social relations that is unmodified by any of the irony within which traditional expressions of humility or subordination traditionally were and in almost all cases still are cloaked.[6]

Some of the words of this vocabulary, such as *'esa'esa*, 'big man' and *'inapwana*, 'big man' or 'distinguished elder'[7] are never used today to describe living people no matter how respected or powerful they may be in terms of rhetorical power, knowledge, or transactional skill,. Occasionally, one or two major figures of the past are described using the Loboda language cognate, *kinapwana*. However, *'esa'esa* and *'inapwana* or *kinapwana* are rarely used even to describe individuals of the local past. More frequently, though even then only rarely, they may be used to describe individuals of Dobu Island and east Fergusson Island during the early contact period who acquired a fame and renown that was known as far away as Loboda.

Thus, *'esa'esa* and *'inapwana* would be used to refer to individuals whose influence, power, and fame transcends their matrilineage to extend across an entire hamlet cluster, village, or district. They represent a social possibility built upon a radical expansion of individual fame, influence, and power within a geographical rather than matrilineal field. As such, they are recognized as threatening to the matrilineal order. And, as a result, people are both unwilling to claim such a position and unwilling to attribute such a position to others who might be able to exercise power over them.

Other words used in the prayer point to activities that, being implied by asymmetrical relations, are rarely seen in normal, everyday life. *Sida,* 'pray', 'request', 'implore', or "beseech" and *tupu,* "praise," are almost never used because they define a relation in which one individual adopts or occupies a distinctly subordinate position vis-a-vis another. More importantly, the implication is that this subordination is permanent with no possibility of reversal as the result of the movement of sentiments, goods, or services in the opposite direction.[8] Thus, these words are used to refer to an ahistorical, structurally frozen relation that is not affected by actions within the social world.

Similarly, the phrase *'alokagutoki imu oboboma'o,* 'we thank you for your gifts', is used to make clear the role of the speaker and congregation as recipients who are not expected to reciprocate. While, in fact people use the Loboda cognate word *kagutoki,* 'thank' or 'acknowledge' when they receive prestations as a part of formal transactional activities, the word implies a voluntarism in the other's gift or service. More commonly, *kagutoki* is used to acknowledge a relatively informal, freely-given gift between two individuals who do not explicitly represent larger social groups for the purposes of the interaction. Like 'pray' and 'praise', *kagutoki* moves the relationship out of the social arena into a more personal domain.

Oboboma, the critical term of the phrase *'alokagutoki imu oboboma'o,* which I have translated as 'gifts' can also be translated as 'love', 'concern', or 'personal interest and support'. It reflects the fact that 'love', 'concern', and 'interest and support' are physically visible in freely presented gifts.[9]

In other words, *oboboma* as sentimental, as a physical instantiation of the sentimental, and as a personalized, internally driven action, is grounded in an non-social world both generating and representing the structural precursors of the social world. It does not so much build or represent the social world itself as generate prior forms — friendship, relations which may lead to marriage, and, as we will see, paternity — which makes that world possible.

Kinapwana and *'esa'esa,* 'big men', as gift givers are distant from everyday village life. Notable, when Wailasi says, *'a'wa'ese'eseyo manuna 'oyo 'umiya tue wawawae,* "we call you our 'big man' because you are so far away" he is speaking of a conceptual rather than strictly physical distance.

The important point is that not only is 'prayer' and 'praise' directed towards those who are more powerful but this relative efficacy is built on a permanent complementarity of position that is independent of the historical vagaries of everyday social life. Those to whom one directs 'prayer' or 'praise' are able to act on asymmetrically defined social goals that may involve others but that are independent of and unaffected by the interests of these others. Thus, the intentions, desires, and goals of such beings are not and cannot be negotiated to be aligned with those who pray to or praise them. In this sense, their intentions, goals, and desires are not of the social world at all.

Against this background, Wailasi uses words like *to'umalina,* 'bad', 'mistake', or 'error' and *gesi,* 'wrongly', 'incorrectly', or 'mistakenly'. Rev. W. E. Bromilow, as he attempted to create a Dobu language theological vocabulary, clearly intended to expand the word *to'umalina* to include the Christian concept of sin (cf. Bromilow 1929). However, despite this intention, the local understanding of *to'umalina* does not have the English word's association with an absolute and universalizing law. Rather, words like *to'umalina* and *gesi* are less about actions of an independent and discrete person than about that person's relation or desired relation of humility to and dependency upon God. These words, then, point to a definition of a specific relation to God that implies or requires His tolerance and acceptance.

Socially decontextualized power of the kind attributed to God in the prayer, for example, or sorcerers or bigmen in traditional society, represents a serious social problem for Loboda villagers. On the one hand, as threatening to and uncontrolled by the social world, it potentially undercuts the integrity of that world. On the other hand, it offers the possibility of expanding the scope and complexity of the social world if it can be contained and controlled to serve social ends. In many ways, the most important implicit thrust of the service and especially the sermon deals with containing and controlling the power described in the prayer so it supports rather than undercuts the social order.

The one context in which the language of permanently asymmetrical relations can legitimately be used is when speaking to or of one's *tama-,* 'father'. A 'father', most restrictively, is the man who is publicly credited with responsibility for impregnating one's mother. Everything else being equal, such a narrowly construed 'father' is likely to be (or, at least, have been) one's natural mother's husband. However, the word *tama* also includes the husbands of the one's mother's sisters, the brothers of one's father, and the brothers of one's mother's sister's husband (Thune 1980). In its most generic sense, a 'father' is simply a male affinal relative of roughly the first ascending generation.

While one would never term a 'father' *'inapwana* or *'esa'esa* or 'praise' him, occasionally people use the word *-sida* to describe their "requests" for assistance or material goods from their 'father'. These requests at once reflect the fact that the item or service requested is not automatically due the requestor, that, if received, it will not be formally repaid, and that, by requesting it on these terms, the requestor is explicitly acknowledging a dependant position.

At the same time, *-sida* reflects an appeal to a generalized sentimental, feeling, interest, and concern, *nuwakikita,* that a father should have for his children. Such a feeling, even of a father for his child, is by no means taken to be inevitable. Rather it is the result of a voluntary decision on his part. Indeed, a child's indebtedness to his or her 'father' derives as much from this voluntary sentimental interest as from his actual actions, gifts, and services.

Almost necessarily built within the paternal relation are complementary differences in power, social and personal efficacy, and dependency. Indeed, paternity is the only legitimate, permanently asymmetrical relation in traditional village life.[10]

The paternal relation, alternately viewed in terms of sentimental interest and transactional indebtedness, is problematic for Loboda villagers. It, at once, is a structurally prototypical relation with the world beyond the matrilineage and one in which an asymmetrical indebtedness deriving from paternal concern and labor provided during childhood can never be repaid. If balance is the structural goal of any transactional relation, it is the one relation in which balance is not only impossible but meaningless.

In many ways, Wailasi's prayer, read from a Loboda perspective, is about the hope of building a relation to a powerful, apparently uncontrollable God. As with all external relations involving beings, whether human or non-human, claiming a supernatural position, the effort is to define an expectation of, if not balanced, at least recognizable reciprocity. To the extent that the prayer represents a transformation of an asocial power and implied asocial indebtedness into paternal concern and independence, a degree of transactional structure is built into the relation. In other words, the use of the language of paternity within the prayer represents a movement away from differences in power that cannot be incorporated or encompassed toward a sentimental interest and dependency which is not socially destructive.

More abstractly, the entire church service is "about" relations with beings occupying difficult and ambiguous conceptual categories. God, like all fathers in Loboda, is a being with whom one has an external relation, one from whom one expects the kind of sentimental concern automatically a part of internal relations, and one apparently requiring an explicit deference, submission, and subordination. This is to say that God, like a father, is presented as occupying a boundary position, the closest of all external relations, and, as such, is in many ways a bundle of contradictions.

Underlying this attempt is a visible and important complicity of Wailasi, the speaker, and the congregation. This is not simply the complicity of a complementary opposition of a now unified party against a more powerful alien party. Loboda villagers routinely deal with aliens but they do not thereby create a unity of all villagers juxtaposed against an opposed body of all aliens. Rather, the effort is normally to fragment the alien world in order to discover within it minimal units of the same scale as natural, minimal social units within the village. *Kula* voyagers, for example, never speak of visiting Dobu Island but of visiting a specific hamlet of a trader or even a specific trader. Similarly, contract labor stories fragment the European world until they identify specific Europeans with whom the storyteller can establish close relations.

Uniquely within the prayer, rather than fragmenting a universe of more powerful beings in order to generate units that correspond to a natural fragmentation of the village world, Wailasi unifies the congregation in order to approach a unified non-human world. Perhaps this must be most accurately read as a marker of the extremity of the problem which God as an alien, as a powerful figure, and as a father poses. In the prayer, God, reformed as a paternal figure becomes more intelligible. Nevertheless, His sheer power almost inevitably forces Him to exist against a unified, depersonalized Loboda Village social world.

It is important to recognize that portrayal of God through a model of paternity is overdetermined. Given God's position as a powerful figure dispensing gifts but not demanding a clear reciprocation, other roles, while perhaps imaginable, would not make sense given Loboda village presuppositions about the social world. Hence, an individual's relation to his or her mother, mother's brother, or other matrilineage mate, because it is between those who are formally identical, is always between equals. It should be clear, then, that whatever its historical origins, attributing paternity to God is a very different thing for Loboda villagers than might be defining God as a "mother" or a "mother's brother."

THE LORD'S PRAYER: LAW, MIND, AND UNEMBEDDED SOCIAL EFFICACY

In contrast to the opening prayer's reflection of subordination and indebtedness of speaker and congregation to God and Jesus, the Lord's Prayer portrays God and Jesus as beings existing in and of themselves, having independent, non-situationally based social efficacy, power, and strength. Hence, there is an extreme subordination of speaker and congregation to God that cannot be easily encompassed using the traditional language of paternity. The asymmetry is absolute and radical, lacking the ambiguity that is paternity. God, in the Lord's Prayer, is portrayed as much more aggressive, assertive, powerful, and threatening than He is in the opening prayer.

The following literal translation of the Dobu language text reflects the Lord's Prayer's original relatively loose translation into Dobu.

> Our Father in heaven, we obey Your name, Your law [desire, rule, decision, *'ebeloina*] will come. We should [would] do Your will [desire, *nuwanuwa*] like those who live in the sky [those who live in 'heaven', angels]. You give us our food this day. Do not payback [*'eisa*] us for our bad deeds [crimes, mistakes, *to'umalina*]. And we will not payback other people for their bad deeds. You prevent [*wasegigi*] our errors and stop us from doing bad deeds. You are our lawgiver [source of law, restrictions, external demands, ruler, *'ebeloina*]. You are our strong man [*waiwai*]. You are our big man [*'esa'esa*]. It will never be finished.
>
> Amen.

Unlike the opening prayer, in the Lord's Prayer judgmental words are not only present but have an importance they would never have in the world outside the church. Words reflective of sentimental concern or interest are altogether absent.

The judgmental connotations of the word *to'umalina,* 'bad deed', a word which first appeared in the opening prayer, are much more prominent in the Lord's Prayer. People are rarely described with this word. *To'umalina* is generally reserved for reference to physical objects where it means 'bad', 'broken', 'tattered', 'exhausted', or otherwise 'defective'. When used to describe physical objects *to'umalina* has a relatively neutral connotation.

On the infrequent occasions when *to'umalina* is used to describe people, it suggests serious defects in their social presence and serious disorder in their relation to the speaker. In other words, it is a relative, positional rather than absolute term. If used to describe a member of one's own matrilineage, its use reflects a dramatic internal division within the lineage, pointing either to the deliberate and chosen disengagement of the speaker from the remainder of a disagreeable matrilineage or to the collective rejection of the person so described by his or her lineage. When used to describe those of other matrilineages, it may suggest that a person has violated their normal, usually affinally based, external relations and obligations to the speaker.

More commonly, *to'umalina* is used to describe an individual who has single-handedly constructed an "unnatural" association, typically with the speaker, that does not have a basis in the matrilineal social order. Hence, the word may be used to describe suspected sorcerers who, for purely idiosyncratic reasons, typically threaten those to whom they have neither an immediate matrilineal nor matrilineally-derived connection. However, the important point is that judgmental words like *to'umalina* are not applied to those with whom one has an even minimal positive and legitimate social relation.

Thus, actual use of the word *to'umalina* is less indicative of a problematic individual than of a problematic social relation. Probably never in "conventional" life would a person seriously describe themselves as *to'umalina* if for no other reason than that the term tends to imply a social relationship between two people.[11] The unusual character of the use of the word in the Lord's Prayer is heightened because that is the only context in which it is seriously used to describe not one person but a group of people in relation to another being.

'Eisa, 'payback', 'revenge', or 'payment', similarly reflects a difficult ambiguity in the relation between the congregation and God. While the word suggests a transactional relation, this is a relation founded on power and violence rather than equality. Unlike a normal transactional payment, *maisa*, such as occurs, for example, during affinally-centered feasting, this kind of 'payback' underscores an alienating distance rather than an oppositional solidarity. This, in turn, is based on the fact that the violent 'payback' is uncontrolled and unnegotiated, rather than generatively creative. At least as people describe 'payback' killings of the pre-contact period there is no sense that these, however provoked, yielded anything other than absolute, unbridgeable social distance.

The word *'ebeloina*, 'source or origin of a rule, restriction, or prohibition' is conceptually related to *to'umalina* and *'eisa*. It and its root, *loina*, 'law', 'rule', 'restriction', or 'prohibition', are rarely used outside of church or government related contexts. *Loina* suggests an attempt at the imposition of control by one person over another. But, more than this, it suggests that a being is making a claim to an absolute authority existing apart from specific social relations. 'Law', in contrast to the 'power' or 'social efficacy' discussed in the previous section is not based in social obligations derived from a transactional history.

Occasionally *loina* is used to describe a matrilineage elder's decisions regarding behavior of younger matrilineage members. More frequently, it is used to describe a ruling or decision that is independent of any single matrilineage. Such a rule would be intended to apply to a geographical domain such as an entire hamlet cluster. Nevertheless, the most common use of the word is to refer to government decisions or rules, that, as absolutes, exist apart from situationally specific social relations.

But *loina* also suggests a rule or prohibition has its origin within a specific individual. Indeed, in many cases a better translation of *loina* would be 'desire', 'will', or 'ruling' to emphasize its active creation and propagation by a willful individual. Unlike *loina*, more generic prohibitions that cannot be tied to a specific source are usually termed *bubuna*, 'custom' or 'habit' (cf. Thune 1980, Ms. *b*).

Not only are *loina* derived from a specific individuals but they develop from within the *nuwa*, 'mind' or 'consciousness', of that individual. Hence, from the Loboda villagers' perspective, there is an important connection between God's 'desire' or 'will', *nuwa* and the 'laws', *loina*, that He propagates. Like the *loina* that exist apart from the social situation in which it is applied, 'will' or 'desire' derives from within an individual unmotivated and uncontrolled by the external social situation of which he or she is a part.

The 'mind' or 'consciousness' of an individual is a point of opacity beyond which interpretation cannot pass. It is not only uncontrollable by external forces but is literally not understandable. In other words, use of the word *loina* not only places the origin of a decision within a single person but makes it clear that the content of that ruling is derived from internal sources rather than from a larger external situation of which that person is a part.

Finally, note that unlike the earlier use in Wailasi's opening prayer of *to'umalina*, 'bad deed', in the Lord's prayer the word is contextualized by the word *loina*. Here *to'umalina* is here much closer to an absolute concept of sin. And, indeed, far more than in the opening prayer, *to'umalina* does not serve to tie speaker and congregation to God as much as separate them from him.

The critical terms of the Lord's Prayer are tightly interrelated. *To'umalina*, 'errors' or 'mistakes', can only be defined by the presence of *nuwa*, 'desire' or 'will' on the part of an *'ebeloina*, an autonomous decision maker, who has a *nuwa*, 'mind' or 'consciousness' existing independent of the social world. To 'prevent', *wasigigi*, another's activities requires not only this 'will' or 'desire' but the willingness to act even should no legitimate, matrilineally-based reason exist to do so. It reflects a willingness to act in disregard of one's corporate self, driven only by one's internal, mental self. And, indeed, this is precisely the character of a 'big man', *'esa'esa.*

Indeed, in many ways, the following representation would be accurate:

> The God of the Opening Prayer : The God of the Lords Prayer :: A Village Father : A Village *'Esa'esa*

This extreme language of power and efficacy would rarely if ever be heard within everyday village life. In other words, a clear equation of the matrilineal, the legitimate, and the comprehensible is the logical backdrop against which the Lord's Prayer and other parts of the church service exist. Ironically, the only other type of intelligent beings familiar to the village world who would be attributed such an asocial existence and efficacy are *barahu* 'sorcerers' representatives of the colonial world. Like God, sorcerers and representatives of the colonial world exist independently of their matrilineal relatives being driven by unintelligible internal forces and ideas.

The opening prayer portrays an asymmetrical social world having a structure that, though not currently visible in the village world, at least is within the realm of its possible configurations. More importantly, it is a structure which can be interpreted, domesticated, accessed, and controlled using the model of paternity.

By contrast, the social world of the Lord's Prayer is one in which power is not socially embedded, because it exists in and of itself, rather than as instantiated within routine, balanced transactional social relations.[12] The problem that the Lord's prayer poses is one of the minimal relationship. Put slightly differently, it is the problem of what is the presumed power of prayer, given the fact that here it apparently only exists within a minimal non-transactionally generated social world. In many ways, Wailasi's subsequent sermon addresses these problems by presenting an alternative model for founding relations with God that attempts to sidestep the entire issue of relative power.

THE EXEGETICAL SERMON AND THE CREATION OF CONGREGATIONAL SOLIDARITY

The core of each church service is a 'sermon', *guguya,* that is an exploration or exegesis of a text from the *Buki Tabu,* the translation of the Bible into the Dobu language completed in the late 1920's (Bromilow 1929). In dramatic contrast to the two prayers, Wailasi's sermon is implicitly about a solidary internal relation based on essential identity and sympathetic concern rather than an divisive external relation based on equally essential differences and violent or oppressive opposition. The loose, improvisational quality of the sermon allows Wailasi indirectly to redefine the congregation's relation to God and Jesus thereby expanding the social world to include rather than simply remain opposed to the divine.

As the translator, Rev. W. E. Bromilow, noted, translation of the Bible was a painful and difficult process requiring considerable extension of the Dobu language to incorporate alien psychological, theological, and ethical concepts. While all Loboda villagers are relatively fluent in Dobu, the translation was into a dialect of Dobu not widely spoken even at the time. This, together with difficulties in the translation itself, changes in the Dobu language with the passage of time, and the theological obscurities of the text, means villagers have considerable difficulty reading and making sense of most Bible readings.[13]

My translation of the reading from John 20:11-17 used in Wailasi's sermon is based on a transcription of the text as it was read from the *Buki Tabu* during the service. Several important "mis-readings" of the Dobu language text occurred at the time of its reading, most notably a brief shift from third person to first person ("But I [*sic*] didn't know it was Jesus").

> And Mary went to the grave and stood and was crying. So she was crying and she bent over and went into the grave and she saw two angels wearing white clothes. Previously Jesus's body was lying there. And one [angel] sat where his head had been and one where his feet had been. And they asked her, "Woman, why are you crying?" She said, "They took my big man and I don't know where they put him." When she had spoken she looked behind her and saw Jesus standing. But I [*sic*] didn't know it was Jesus. Jesus said to her, "Woman, why are you crying. For whom are you looking." She thought that he was a gardener. So she said, "If you took my big man from here and you put him somewhere, tell me and I will take him." Jesus said to her, "Mary." She looked behind and said in the Hebrew language, "Rabbi." Here we say "teacher." Jesus said, "Don't touch me or I won't go up to my father. And you should go to my brothers and tell them, 'I am going to my father and your father, to my God and your God.'"

This is Wailasi's sermon that followed his Bible reading.

> In Chapter 20, verse 17 Jesus said to her, "Don't touch me or I won't go up to my father. And, go to my brothers and tell them that I am going up to my father and your father, to my God and your God."

The book here is the story of how Jesus stood up again. John wrote the good story about how Jesus stood up again. We have read the whole book about Jesus' standing up, from verse 11 to 17.

And Jesus stood up again from the grave in order that he could go up to his father. Mary was looking for Jesus and wanting to see her child. Mary wanted to touch him. He said, "Don't touch me or I won't go up to my father and your father, to my God and your God." Then he said, "You go and you tell my brothers I won't be able to go up to my father and your father, to my God and your God." This is our major explanation.

We don't need to go on reading for a very long time. You all know the story of Jesus's standing up again. So our point derives from verse 17. Because Jesus said "father," we say "father" to God. That verse says, "Jesus said to her, 'Don't touch me or I won't go up to my father. And you tell my brothers I am going up to my father and your father, to my God and your God.'" Our point derives from that phrase. Jesus said "father" so we say "father" to God. Within this point we find his thought.

My father's life is finished. If some time I came from Miauwa hamlet cluster and Abelamo is staying in his hamlet and if Abelamo takes his basket and his knife and goes up [the mountain] to his father at Wegala hamlet, if he goes to his father, then I might call out "Abelamo, where are you going?" "I am going up to our father." If my father is dead and Abelamo says "our father" to his father then we will say "our father" to Elaisa [Abelamo's father].

Jesus said to them, Mary and his brothers and sisters "I will go up to my father and your father, to my God and your God."

I have no father but Abelamo says 'our father' so I would say "our father" to his father, Maigain [Elaisa, Abelamo's father].

I have no sister but if I think of a woman living at Baweheliheli named Susana, and if I have no sister and my mother and father are dead and I said "sister" to Susana, we would say "our father" to Tomas [Susana's father].

And this is the meaning of our point, the thing we should think about.

So Jesus said, "I will not be going up to my father. Don't touch me or I won't be going up to my father." He said, "You should tell my brothers that I am going up to your father and my father, to my God and your God."

This is our point, Jesus said, "our father" so we say "our father" to God. If I didn't have a father and Abelamo or Susana said "our father" to her father, we would say father to her father. And so because this phrase appeared we know [understand] about Jesus's birth and Jesus's death.

In the old days the Jews divided the people. They took their way [laws, custom] from their ancestors and they divided the people so they alone had their God because they were clean. And we, ourselves, as outsiders, therefore had no God.

And, at the time Jesus died and stood up again this phrase appeared. In verse 17 it says, "I go up to my father and your father, my God and your God." So our point emerges from that verse. Jesus says, "father" so we say "our father" to God. As a result of Jesus's death and his standing up again, the outsiders, and the Christians, and the Jews became a single group and we call one another brother and sister. Because Jesus said "father" to his father we should say "father" to God.

As our second saying, he said, "Don't touch me. Don't touch me." If there is a rule [restriction], we cannot touch the thing restricted. If we touch it, there anger will develop. If there is a restriction, we cannot touch it. We cannot touch that thing because it is clean and we, ourselves, are dirty. And so, because Jesus was born and stood up again, his body was clean, not dirty.

So Mary didn't touch him because he said, "I will not be going up to my father." So he said our second phrase, "Don't touch me."

Mary gave birth to her child, Jesus on earth. She gave birth but she couldn't. His mother gave birth to him but she couldn't touch him.

If we think about any woman who has given birth, the child is the source of restrictions of his/her mother and father. We [as parents] cannot touch them. Later when they come out of the house to the ground we can touch them [the infants].[14] We can't touch them because we are unclean. The rule that we cannot touch them comes from our ancestors.

Perhaps this was because Jesus was clean and not dirty. So he stood up again and because his mother might touch him, he said, "Don't touch me because I will not go up to my father."

Our two words are, "My father and your father, my father and your father." Jesus said, "My father and your father." Now we speak like the Jews of their God. As a result of Jesus's death, he took us and he took the Jews and the outsiders, and he took all of us Christians. And so Jesus cried, "I won't go up to my father and your father."

Formerly the Jews had their God alone or perhaps Jesus alone had God. And as a result of Jesus's death he said, "I will not be going to my father and your father."

Our third phase is "my God and your God." Long ago God was only the Jew's God. But because Jesus was born and he died and he stood up again he said, "I won't be going up to my God and your God."

So he said to Mary, "Don't touch me or I won't be going up to my father." Because Jesus said "father" we say father to God. In the old days we couldn't say "father" because he was only the Jews' God. But because Jesus was born and Jesus died and stood up again, he said, "You tell my brothers and sisters and perhaps Christians that I am going up to my God and your God."

Our verse says Jesus told her "If you touch me I will not be going up to my father. And you should go to my brothers and tell them I am going up to my father and your father, to my God and your God." Because he said "father" we can say "father" to God.

Our church service is finished.

Like other Loboda Village preachers, Wailasi does not really explain or explicate the Bible reading in his sermon, at least in the Western sense. Indeed, the reading seems, in many ways, an opaque field containing a wealth of ideas, concepts, relationships, and activities that, on the one hand are minimally intelligible but that, on the other, are both provocative and unintelligible in their reference to problematic issues with which Loboda villagers are concerned. At most, they are only repeated and thereby emphasized.

Hence, while Loboda Village sermons tend to focus upon points in the Biblical text that might seem to be relatively straightforward to a naive Westerner, these are points that simply do not make local sense. Certainly villagers have trouble dealing with such alien concepts as rabbis, Hebrews, sheep, and frankincense. But these are relatively concrete concepts that can be left poorly understood without raising issues of serious local concern.

Rather, sermons dwell upon an underlying social world described in the Bible reading that is both incoherent and, nevertheless, apparently central to the message of the text. Sermons focus upon these points of incoherence and attempt to redefine them so they make sense in terms of local presuppositions about the nature of the social world.

Guguya is the Loboda and Dobu word used to refer to a sermon. In "traditional" contexts, it occasionally is used to refer to formal 'advice' or a 'lecture' normally given only by a matrilineage elder to younger members of his matrilineage. Such advice is based on an underlying unity of speaker and listeners that obligates a reasonable listener to pay attention to a respected speaker. As such, it is not surprising that traditional *guguya* convey "social knowledge" about how to build a social persona and social relations with those beyond the matrilineal world. Hence, the content of such a *guguya* frequently would be inappropriate were it offered by a non-matrilineage mate.

In most cases, an individual offering a *guguya* would be a *tau sinabwana*, a knowledgeable and experienced, often distinguished older man of one's own matrilineage with whom the listener had a close, respectful relation. An *'esa'esa* or *kinapwana*, 'big man', given his focus upon the larger, extra-matrilineal world would not normally be expected to present a *guguya*. And, a *guguya* is quite different from the less formally and structurally defined 'advice' that a father would offer to his children.

Within the church service, the *guguya*, is built upon a similar unity, here of church leader and congregation. Complementing and structuring this internal unity is an external opposition to God as 'father'. However, whereas in the prayers, with their stress on asymmetries of power and authority, the emphasis is on the juxtaposition of the congregation to God, within the sermon the focus is upon an internal relation uniting the congregation, Wailasi, and Mary. Note that Wailasi assumes that the Mary (Mary Magdalene) who spoke to Jesus after his return is the Mary who is his mother.

Thus, a major underlying theme of the sermon is the contrast of maternal and paternal relations. In simplest terms, Mary, taken to be Jesus's mother, is rejected and distanced in favor of a solidary alliance with God, Jesus's father. At once, Jesus tells his mother that he cannot be touched by her and that he is going to go up to his father.

In Loboda village a son's rejection of his mother, no matter what the circumstances, represents a social pathology of an extreme order. Within the entire corpus of traditional Loboda literature, no matter how fragmented internal relations may become, this fragmentation never is represented by the rejection of a non-threatening mother in favor of an alien, explicitly powerful father.

The fact that Jesus was presumably dead or at least had temporarily returned from the world of the dead only makes his rejection of his mother more incongruous, strange, and rhetorically powerful. While the most visible and dramatic mourning for the dead is performed by affines, everyone recognizes that the most authentic mourning is by a mother for her child or by a child for his or her mother. Whatever the discordances of everyday life, it is inconceivable that a child, at death might, reject a mother in favor of his or her father. Indeed, the identity of a child and mother after death is such that there is an ideal, even if generally not practiced, of being buried in one's previous deceased mother's grave. Certainly, a major "goal" of mortuary related activity is to sever a person's association with his or her father and solidify it with his or her mother (Thune Ms. *b*).

The full conceptual difficulty of this maternal rejection is reflected by

Wailasi's comparison of it to the care taken by outsiders to avoid touching a newborn child. Notably, despite Wailasi's example, there is no problem with a mother touching her child. Loboda villagers do not phrase such an avoidance as the result of the application of a personalized "rule" or "law" but of reasonable, sensible decision-making based on clear, well understood more or less "natural" forces of the world. Underlying Wailasi's example is the suggestion that there is, apparently, a reasonable and sensible basis for this alienation of Jesus from his mother, even though, given the matrilineal structure of the human universe, the basis of this reasonableness and sensibility is, and remains, opaque to speaker and congregation. Thus, his example suggests a point of logical incoherence that cannot be explained and, indeed, cannot even be explored.

Certainly Jesus emerges as the pivotal figure within the sermon, both generating the congregation's internal unity and its external location vis-a-vis God. Like other pivotal figures in Loboda literature, he is an ambiguous figure condensing within himself a bundle of contradictions.

All the same, the relation between God and Jesus exists as a backdrop behind the much more important relation between the congregation and Mary. Mary, far more than Jesus, is the protagonist within the sermon for it is her presence, rather than Jesus's actions, which drive the sermon forward. And, more importantly, Mary rather than Jesus provides the key to the resolution of the unintelligible distance between the congregation and God. Mary does not provide a mediation between God and the congregation as is the case in Western Christianity but a focus to highlight the unbridgeable distance between them.

Wailasi's shift from use of the third to use of the first person to refer to Mary in the Bible reading reflects his and his congregations's identity with her rather than Jesus. Slipping into a brief use of the first person pronoun in this way is an important Loboda village rhetorical device that foregrounds the identity of speaker and leading character at dramatic highpoints of a story. Indirectly it is a marker of the overwhelming dramatic significance of an event within a text.

Thus Wailasi uses the invocation of an internal relation among the congregation, himself, and Mary as a way to step back from the inexplicable external paternal relation between Jesus and God. Jesus's rejection of natural matrilineal alliance and acceptance of paternal incorporation indirectly invokes an expanded world of internal relations. It is this internal relation between villagers and Jesus, all of whom share a collective relation to "our father," rather than the abnormal alliance of Jesus and God that is the core of the sermon's message.

Invocation of paternity, "My father and your father," must be read as an expression of an external relation on the part of Jesus to God that can be paralleled by equally external relations between villagers and God. Paradoxically, then Jesus's invocation of paternity and rejection of maternity provides a way of foregrounding the external relations between God and Jesus in order to point to an equally external relation between God and Jesus, Mary, and Loboda villagers.

The alienation inherent in paternity is indirectly reflected by Wailasi's examples as he, personifying Abelamo and Susana, speaks with the conceit that their father is dead. The example, then, seems to suggest that a constructed paternity is possible only with the death of a true father. Again, why this should be so is not and apparently cannot be explained or explored. However, this failure of explanation is a second point of logical incoherence in the sermon. At the most, the suggestion is that underlying Jesus's tie to God is a link just as tenuous as the actual paternal relations of Abelamo and Susana to their supposedly deceased fathers and their constructed paternal relations to their adoptive fathers. As in Wailasi's previous example, this example seems to point to a message quite different from that which would be required to make the text truly intelligible.

Jesus, then, is a pivotal figure, affirming indirectly by his created, unnatural alliance with God his more fundamental internal relation to the village world. He is very much like a person whose unnatural created tie to his or her spouse, if improperly stressed simply extracts the person from his or her matrilineage altogether and allies him with his or her spouse's matrilineage. If properly controlled, such a tie has the effect of reinforcing the internal relations linking the pivotal person to the remainder of his matrilineage.

But, as with affinal feasting, the pivotal person — the individual providing an affinal link to another matrilineage — is often invisible if not altogether absent. During marriage-related feasting the structurally pivotal marital couple is often conspicuously absent; during affinally-related mortuary feasting, the deceased and his or her spouse are similarly absent. Instead, the visible role is provided not by an individual with divided loyalties but by an individual who embodies the internal universe within himself or herself. In village feasting, this is usually an older man, who can personify within himself the matrilineage as an undivided, unambiguous, uncompromised whole.

Jesus, precisely because he is pivotal and ambiguous, torn as he is between the maternal and the paternal, does not provide a point for constructing an internal solidarity. Mary, embodying no such tensely constructed ambiguities, provides precisely their articulating center.

CONCLUSION: THE TRANSFORMATION OF HIERARCHY AND THE EXPANSION OF THE SOCIAL WORLD

Each section of Wailasi's church service reflects a different perspective on social relations with the more powerful alien. The opening prayer addresses the possibility of domesticating social asymmetry to build vertical relations through the use of an image of paternity. The Lord's Prayer focuses on the social impossibility though occasional forced reality of asymmetrical relations between those separated by unbridgeable differences in power. And, the sermon focuses on the use of constructed internal relations to generate social expansion and to provide an indirect, external relation to the more problematic, distant alien. Each section provides a frame within which are viewed the issues highlighted by the others.

The church service when viewed within the context of traditional Loboda Village literature is notable for its focus upon hierarchy. Hierarchy is a social possibility that was probably less of an immediate problem during the pre-contact period from which most traditional literature derives than it is today. Traditional literature tends to be "about" internal egalitarian relations and derivative, most frequently, affinally-based, external though equally egalitarian relations. It looks at the difficulties of forming necessary but unnatural associations with equals of the wider world. And, it looks at the potential fragmentation of the internal, matrilineally-centered world that these associations can engender. In other words, traditional literature explores the potentials for and dangers of expanding the social world in order to access the power and social efficacy of others of roughly the same status as the main protagonist.

The more recently developed literature of contact with the non-traditional world certainly still concerns internal and external relations. However, in this literature internal and external relations are used as a model for understanding associations between those having different statuses, wealth, or power. Stories of the arrival of the first missionary, of contract labor experiences, and of World War II experiences address problems of comprehending, encompassing, and domesticating hierarchy by redefining it using a traditional language of internal identities and external differences. These stories center around the transformation of the initially alien and more powerful into the metaphorically egalitarian fraternal or the hierarchical paternal. That is, it uses the fraternal and the paternal models to suggest approaches for accessing the more wealthy and powerful to expand dramatically the social world. However, because external and internal relations in these stories do not support but tend to undercut one another, this social expansion is fragile and, in most cases, only temporary.

Wailasi's sermon adopts a different strategy. Here, rather than trying to define a direct relation to God, Wailasi identifies an internal relation of shared identity with Mary, that, by its presence, suggests an indirect relation to God. Rather than acknowledging and accepting hierarchy through the language of paternity as he does in the first prayer or acknowledging hierarchy but classing it as altogether uncontrollable and asocial as he does in the Lord's Prayer, in his sermon he transcends the issue of hierarchy altogether. This strategy of social expansion through internal identity structurally places God in something of an affinal position — as the son's father of the congregation's intimate, Mary — that while external is by definition between equals. Note that no such dramatic social expansion and accompanying escape from hierarchy is visible in the prayers that are focused on hierarchical rather than egalitarian relations.

This is not to suggest that Loboda villagers assume that God is an actual equal any more than they assume any other more powerful human or non-human being with whom they form an egalitarian association is an actual equal. Rather they seek to define an egalitarian association to God precisely so they can access His greater power and efficacy.

Notably, the service's radical social expansiveness is initially generated by the presence of an "other," God, who is uncontrollable and unintelligible. Thus, an underlying but central effort of the service is the definition of a point of incoherence in the external world that, by being redefined, can yield a larger social world. The problematic God of the opening prayer constructed using a vocabulary of paternity is transformed in the Lord's Prayer into an absolute, uncontrolled power, but only in order to produce an unencompassable "other." The presence of that "other" implies more direct solidarity among the congregation and the preacher and implicitly between the congregation and Mary. This unity in the face of the socially incoherent and incomprehensible provides a means of indirectly accessing the power of God who, being asocial, uncontrolled and absolute cannot be accessed directly.

NOTES

This paper is based on field research conducted in Loboda village on Normanby Island in the Milne Bay Province of Papua New Guinea from September 1975 to May 1977. It was supported by the National Institute of Mental Health (Grant # 1 F31 MOH5340). I gratefully acknowledge the help and support I received from Bunsa Taukwaelo, Toni Lemunaiya, and Alipi Gibson and all of the other Loboda villagers with whom I lived and worked. John Barker and Susan Montague provided detailed editorial comments on earlier drafts of this paper.

1. Since the independence of Papua New Guinea, the churches founded by the Methodist Mission have become a part of the United Church.
2. This may or may not have actually been the case. Bromilow also established a mission station of Ubuya Island off the coast of western Normanby shortly after the Dobu Island mission was founded. Loboda villagers are probably correct in asserting that theirs was the first Normanby Island village-centered mission.
3. During this period the mission began to sponsor local schools and health services and appears to have played an important role in the "pacification" of the region. However, probably the most important accomplishment of the mission during this period was the introduction of new food sources, including new varieties of bananas, coconuts, yams, and taro from the South Pacific as well as some western plants, and handicrafts such as techniques for mat and basket making. At least by the 1920s, a small number of young men and women began attending school at the more formal, mission-sponsored schools on Dobu Island and the mission center of Salamo on Fergusson Island.
4. Wailasi is a young Loboda village man who, at the time of his sermon, had spent approximately six months at the Dawada Bible School. The Dawada Bible School is a small school of some half a dozen students. It offers a basic training in theology and church practice for students who return to their villages. Many will become deacons or other important figures in their local congregations. Village pastors receive more training at the major church centers at either Baruwada on Normanby Island or Salamo on the adjacent Fergusson Island.
5. Wailasi presented the service in Dobu, the lingua franca of the church in the d'Entrecasteaux Islands and the language of the only completely translated Bible available in the region. While written church literature used in the service — the Bible, the Lord's prayer, hymns, and responsive readings — is always in Dobu, frequently prayers and sermons given by villagers are in the Loboda language. In any case, all villagers speak both Loboda and Dobu, although as noted below, the Dobu version of the Bible is difficult for even native speakers of Dobu to understand.

   Much of the church-centered vocabulary, even if perhaps originally constructed in the Dobu language by early missionaries, has entered into the Loboda language. Hence, for the purposes of this paper, while the differences between the Dobu and Loboda languages are recognized and well understood, they are not significant.
6. Roheim (1950) argues that certain Normanby expressions of humility and inferiority were in fact implicit but clearly recognized claims to power and importance. Notably such expressions of inferiority were only made during celebrations of major achievement.
7. This prayer and the following sermon were given in the Dobu language which is a close relative of Loboda. *'Esa'esa* and *'inapwana* are Dobu words which are recognizable to all Loboda speakers. *Kinapwana* is the Loboda cognate of the Dobu *'inapwana.* There is no Loboda cognate of *'esa'esa* though occasionally the Dobu word is used. In the Trobriand language *'esa'esa* means 'rich man' probably reflecting the fact that a major Trobriand Island organizing figure can accumulate much more wealth than is possible on Normanby Island. While *'esa'esa, 'inapwana,* and most other words discussed in this paper were originally a part of the Dobu language, they are all recognized and even occasionally used in Loboda Village today. Many have Loboda cognates.
8. See Thune (1980) for a discussion of alternating and non-alternating asymmetrical patterns of transactional indebtedness.
9. The more abstract Trobriand language meaning of *oboboma* as 'something which keeps the social world running successfully and coherently' captures the implication of the concept. I am indebted to Susan Montague for a Trobriand exegesis of *oboboma.* While the Trobriand and Loboda languages are not mutually intelligible they share a signifi-

cant number of cognates. More importantly, many of the concepts underlying the local understanding of the world are common to both the Trobriand and Loboda languages. While I do not know if Loboda villagers could provide a similar exegesis, the underlying concept is similar if not identical to the Trobriand exegesis Montague found.

10. Elsewhere, for example in relations between affines or siblings, asymmetrical relationships are rigorously avoided. Indeed, any public claim of asymmetries in affinal or sibling relationship is likely to be associated with serious social difficulties frequently resulting in the collapse of the relationship.
11. Conceivably *to'umalina* might have been used reflectively in the ironic, self-abasing rhetoric of men shouting up to Yabowaine following major successes. However, as Roheim makes clear, such speech was deliberately ironic and certainly not to be taken as literal (Roheim 1950).
12. This kind of absolute power of desocialized wills is very similar to the isolated, not bodily encapsulated "minds" which Montague has described in her treatment of Trobriand Island theories of the relation of mind and body (Montague, personal communication).
13. Even though contemporary United Church linguists recognize the severe inadequacies of the translation, it continues to be used throughout the southeast d'Entrecasteaux Island region.
14. Immediately following childbirth, a mother and her newborn baby remain in their house for several weeks to a month respecting a variety of prohibitions restricting contact with the everyday world. These restrictions are generally explained as intended to prevent mother and child from becoming chilled during a period in which they are weak and fragile (cf. Fortune 1963; Thune 1980).

7

CHRISTIANITY, PEOPLE OF THE LAND, AND CHIEFS IN FIJI

Martha Kaplan

"Erau sa veivolekati nai tovo vakavanua kei nai tovo vakalotu."
(The traditional ways of the Fijians and the ways of Christianity are close to one another.)

— Epeli Rokowaqa (1935)

INTRODUCTION

This paper explores ways in which Fijians have made "the *lotu*" (Christianity) part of their system of meaning. I analyze and contrast the Christianity of the people of a particular village, the village of Drauniivi, with other versions of Fijian Christianity, especially as they have been revealed during the 1987 coups, the recent upheaval in Fiji's national politics. I seek to show how a Fijian cultural logic underlies the different ways in which Fijians have apprehended and encompassed a foreign god.

A century ago, the people of Drauniivi[1] and neighboring peoples of the northern (Ra) and interior hill (Colo) provinces of Viti Levu island were notorious in colonial and missionary eyes for activities deemed "heathen" and "rebellious," while in contrast the coastal and eastern peoples of Fiji had largely converted to Christianity by 1854. Most important was the rise to prominence of Navosavakadua of Drauniivi village, a hereditary Fijian *bete* 'oracle-priest' who espoused a syncretist doctrine, known in the colonial record as the "*tuka* movement." Nowadays, however, like their eastern coastal neighbors, the people of the hill and northern provinces are largely Methodist and all are Christians. In Drauniivi, among the descendants of Navosavakadua, Christianity and the Christian god have a central place in ritual and communal life. This paper will explore the basis of this change in the relation of introduced Christian forms and the indigenous Fijian system of meaning in Drauniivi and will compare it to other forms of Fijian Christianity.

My argument is not that Drauniivi is a "typical" Fijian village from which to generalize. Quite the contrary, I will argue that study of Drauniivi reveals a particular permutation of the relations between Christianity and indigenous cultural principles quite different from that of eastern, chiefly Fiji. Though far from typical, an examination of Drauniivi's Christianity reveals a central Fijian cultural logic, involving a basic relationship between "land people" and "chiefs," as it has developed historically in a particular case. Emphasizing the "land" side of this cultural logic, the Christianity of Drauniivi provides a particularly apt comparison with another permutation, expressed by the leader of the recent Fiji coup, which stresses the relationship of Christianity and "chiefs."

The concept of cultural logic orienting this analysis is developed from recent anthropological interest in "structure and history" (especially Hooper and Huntsman *et al.* 1985; Sahlins 1981, 1985). How are we to understand Pacific societies as simultaneously cultural and historical? Interest in the reconstruction and reanalysis of indigenous Pacific systems (e.g. J. Smith 1974; Valeri 1985) has intersected with increasing study of change in the Pacific with concern to understand change as indigenously motivated (e.g. Sahlins 1985), as arising in the context of contact, missionization and colonial situations (e.g. Dening 1980; Boutilier, Hughes and Tiffany 1978), and as the transformation of Pacific "societies" into post-colonial "nations." The reconstruction of nineteenth century indigenous Pacific cultural systems contributes significantly to our understanding of present day social life. Such reconstructions may emphasize systematicity at the expense of indigenous variation and indigenous historical change in precontact societies. But they are crucial to the understanding of the new systems of meaning wrought in mission colonial and post-colonial contexts, for many Pacific peoples remain distinctively and varyingly Pacific, rather than "Westernized." With these issues in mind, "Fijian cultural logic" is used here to denote aspects of Fijian culture (such as the "land" - "chiefs" opposition that is found in polity relations, ritual structure, and chiefly installation) that are enduringly and particularly Fijian, yet simultaneously variable and historical.

To study Fijian Christianity I therefore consider the structure and history of colonial and post-colonial Fiji. The colonial and mission history is approached as the institutionalization of Fijian and British constructions of each other (what Sahlins [(1981)] has called "structures of the conjuncture"). With attention to these institutionalizations[2] Fiji's colonial history can be analyzed to shed light on how Christianity has come to be considered "Fijian custom" by present-day Fijians.[3]

The paper begins with a historical prelude tracing the different reception of Christianity by different Fijian groups. I discuss the "land" - "chiefs" relationship, and mission and colonial arrivals, and present an interpretation of Navosavakadua's syncretist movement as an encompassment of a foreign god by the people of the land. Next, in an ethnographic section, I discuss contemporary Drauniivi Christianity as a "religion of the land." In the third and concluding sections I trace an alternate permutation of Fijian cultural logic and Christianity, in which it is claimed that a special relationship to Jehovah authorizes the political paramountcy of Fijian chiefs and of indigenous Fijians more generally in multi-ethnic postcolonial Fiji.

HISTORICAL PRELUDE: FIJIAN DIVISIONS AND THE ENCOUNTER WITH THE *LOTU*[4]

Within the Fiji group in the nineteenth century were a number of confederacies and smaller polities engaged in constant warfare. In the eastern islands and on the coast of Viti Levu were kingdoms ruled by high chiefs, polities with subject groups, and networks of allies. In the interior and north of Viti Levu and Vanua Levu islands were smaller polities not necessarily linked with the greater coastal kingdoms. The relation of the various interior groups and the more hierarchically organized coastal kingdoms, can be understood in terms of a Fijian cultural logic of an opposition of "land" (interior) and "sea" (coast). These cultural categories were not only geographical, but also implied autochthony versus foreignness, and "ownership" of land versus rule over it (see e.g. Hocart 1929:43 ff.; Quain 1948:3; Sahlins 1985:73-103). Key to the relationship is the proximity of the interior and northern peoples of Viti Levu to the Kauvadra range, home of the deity Degei, ancestor deity to both the inland and coastal peoples. Throughout the nineteenth century, in encounters with Europeans, coastal kingdoms would claim to rule over northern and inland peoples, claims which the northern and inland peoples would deny, asserting, in the case of Navosavakadua of Drauniivi, ritual preeminence over other Fijians deriving from their prior relationship to gods of the Kauvadra range.

Tongan teachers, Fijians converted in Tonga, and British Wesleyan missionaries brought Christianity to the coastal and eastern kingdoms of Fiji, from 1830 to 1854, where large-scale Fijian conversion followed the conversion of high chiefs. In 1854, Cakobau, paramount chief of the major confederacy of Bau converted, thereby placing himself in a relationship with the powerful Christian god, and gaining the military assistance of the Christian King of Tonga. Cakobau's conversion to Christianity and his relations with other Europeans, who came to Fiji in increasing numbers in succeeding decades, created and helped to sustain his claim to sovereignty over all of the Fiji group. This claim was instrumental in the annexation of Fiji by Britain in 1874, a colonization represented at the time, and construed by the British and many Fijians since then, as the free cession of the islands by Cakobau and other high Chiefs to Queen Victoria.

With the acceptance of the *lotu* (Christianity) in the coastal and eastern kingdoms the god-houses of major deities were destroyed and churches constructed in their places. But in the 1860s and 1870s in the interior, local warfare prevented the consistent presence of Fijian teachers or European missionaries. Missionaries, like settlers and the colonial Europeans came to categorize Fijians during this period, as either "Christian" or "heathen." "Heathenism" became a political category, denoting the people of the interior, the less hierarchical, hinterland dwellers. The Fijian distinction between coastal and interior people was adapted by Europeans, as they experienced a different reception from the northern and interior people. This categorization was reinforced by the 1867 death and cannibalization of missionary Thomas Baker as he ventured into the interior. It took Bauan armed expeditions (in 1868 and 1873) and, after cession, a British colonial punitive expedition (in 1876) to bring the various fiercely autonomous peoples of the area into submission. Conquest by Bauans and Europeans required, in Fijian perception, submission to the Christian deity.

By the 1880s outright warfare had ceased among the hill and northern peoples but the European perception of the areas as recalcitrant continued. Both colonial rulers and Wesleyan missionaries charted with concern the successes of Catholic and Seventh Day Adventist missionaries and teachers in the interior. More importantly, religious and colonial observers alike noted with alarm the influence of Navosavakadua in the hill and northern provinces, seeing in his syncretic doctrine both heathenism and anti-colonial revolt.

Navosavakadua[5] was a hereditary oracle-priest, who had a particularly effective oracular relationship with the gods of the Kauvadra range. He was renowned for his divinations and miracles. He preached that the Twins, banished grandsons of Degei (the great ancestral deity of the Kauvadra range) would return to Fiji to assert the power of the old gods of the land. According to some accounts, he claimed that Jehovah and Jesus were really the Twins and that the Europeans were trying to deceive the Fijians. He renamed places in the landscape from the Kauvadra hills to the coast, identifying them as Biblical sites. He foretold that the people would imminently rule the chiefs and that Europeans would be driven from the land. Navosavakadua's direct influence extended along the network of relationships of a small confederacy of northern and hill groups. His renown traveled further into the coastal kingdoms as well. In the colonial view, his influence threatened a return to warfare and cannibal sacrifice. In 1885, he was deported to the island of Rotuma, where he died in 1897. In 1891, his kin group and other followers who lived in the village of Drauniivi were deported to Kadavu, a smaller island in the Fiji group, for fifteen years. The colonial authorities explicitly intended the example of Kadavu, a long-Christian Fijian kingdom, to provide a model and stimulus to the people of Drauniivi to conform with colonial expectation.

In order to understand Navosavakadua in his own time, we must understand him and his followers as "people of the land." They were custodians of the gods of the Kauvadra range; they were known to the coastal people as savage authocthonous warriors. They conceived of themselves as the original peoples of Fiji, superseded politically but not ritually by the high chiefs of the great coastal polities. Like many other interior and northern groups, Navosavakadua's people considered themselves to be politically autonomous, linked to larger polities as noble allies, not subjects. They were faced with the encroachment of eastern coastal people and Europeans, empowered by a foreign deity, Jehovah. I argue that they conceived the situation in terms of ritual relations between "land" people and stranger chiefs, and that Navosavakadua's intention was to ritually encompass the foreign god. Navosavakadua's apprehension of Europeans and his project in response was motivated in the potentialities of Fijian cultural logic.

In nineteenth century Fiji, the relation of land and chiefly people was not simply one of opposition (Hocart 1969, and especially Sahlins 1985:73-103). Fijian polities (from villages to great confederations) headed by divine chiefs, the installation of these chiefs, and the structure of Fijian rituals, were organized on the basis of relationships between land and chiefly people, the two opposed sides interacting to create a synthesis. The divine chief was a primary example of such a synthesis. In origin myths, installation rituals, and the various ritual and political activities of nineteenth century Fijian life, the land side encompassed the (culturally conceived) stranger king, as Sahlins has shown in an analysis of origin myths and installation rituals:

> Initially a stranger and something of a terror the king is absorbed and domesticated by the indigenous people, a process that passes by way of his symbolic death and consequent rebirth as a local god. (1985:73)

In addition to installing chiefs, "land" people served as priests and warriors in nineteenth century Fijian war-culture. Hereditary priests were the interpreters of gods of war. *Bati* warriors although autonomous noble allies, fought for chiefs in the chiefly wars. Particularly in the hill countries, warrior priests, empowered and made invulnerable by the gods of the land, led battles. Other ritual experts invoked the gods to enter warriors, and conducted sacrifices. Nowadays, although a century of colonial and post-colonial factors also shape the meaning of chiefship, it is still the case in many Fijian polities (from villages to larger confederations) that the hereditarily delineated group of people of the land side install the chiefs who will rule them. When his dangerous aspects have been "domesticated" or "encompassed" the chief, as synthesis, represents the polity as a whole.[6]

As a hereditary priest, in an area strongly linked to the Kauvadra range, Navosavakadua was a quintessential representative of "land people." Within his own polity, he was of the installing group. At another level the people of his polity stood in a relation of asserted autonomy to incursions by local coastal chiefs, Bauan envoys, and Europeans. In claiming Jesus and Jehovah to be Fijian deities, and in conflating Biblical events and landmarks with the myths and mythical landscape of the Kauvadra range, he brought to bear against the coastal chiefs, the new white men, and their god, an attempt to ritually encompass them, by claiming Jehovah and Jesus as already Fijian, as gods of the land. Navosavakadua did not succeed in maintaining his own freedom, nor the political autonomy of his people, nor could he prolong the central ritual practices of worship of the old gods. But his assertion of Christianity as autochthonous, motivated in the cultural logic of the encompassment of the foreign by the land, lives on in the place of Christianity in the meaningful system of his descendants and followers, as we see below.

ETHNOGRAPHY OF CHRISTIANITY IN DRAUNIIVI

Drauniivi village today is a settlement of over 250 people[7] perched between the King's Road (which circles the perimeter of northern Viti Levu island) and the coastal mangrove swamps. On their return from deportation, Navosavakadua's kin and followers were resettled on this site rather than inland. Their former lands, alienated in the 1860s, are now a government-owned cattle ranch and farm. Knowing of the people of Drauniivi village only from the colonial record of their participation in the "superstitious" and "fanatic" *tuka* cult, I was most interested to encounter their large Methodist church, serene Sunday services, ladies' Thursday worship, prayer meetings, and Sunday school. As in almost every Fijian village, the church is positioned facing onto the *rara* 'central village green', the ritual center of the village, where in the old days the *bure kalou* 'god's house' would have stood.

The church is presided over by a *Vakatawa* 'pastor'. Not formally a minister (*Talatala*), he has had course of training at the Methodist college in the capital city. Other church officials include the *Tui Rara*, who keeps order among the children during the service, the Sunday school teacher and assistant teachers, the choir director, and a number of *Dau Vunau* 'preachers' who are village members (both men and women) who occasionally give the sermon or read the lesson. Once every few months the *Talatala* 'ordained minister' of the circuit comes to preach, and at least twice a year he or another visiting dignitary officiates at a Communion service, and baptizes the children recently born in the village. As in most Fijian Methodist churches, services follow a set pattern of psalm recital, prayers, hymns, Bible readings, sermons, announcements, and collection. Village hierarchy, kinship, and gender divisions are mirrored in church seating and are the basis of assignments for responsibility in church-related tasks. Visitors to the village, who will have made separate ritual presentations to the chief and elders, also are welcomed and introduce themselves to the assembled community during the Sunday service and later take their leave in a similar fashion. Church services are the only ritual events in the village that begin on time. This is made possible by a series of warnings, beat on the big village *lali* 'drum' to summon worshippers.

Soon after I arrived, however, I began to learn that the people of Drauniivi, and related groups nearby and inland, believe themselves to have a special and originating relationship with Jehovah. A member of the household I lived with, himself a pillar of the church, told me that many of the places mentioned in the Bible, including the site where Moses parted the Red Sea, were located in the lands stretching from the Kauvadra range to the sea, a mere walk from the village. Stories about Navosavakadua, well known by all in the village,[8] revealed that he is nowadays considered to have received his *mana* from Jehovah, and to have done miracles, "like Jesus." Exploring this information with informants, an important contrast became apparent. In conversations with Fijians in the capital city about religion and in studying accounts of ceremonies marking anniversaries of important moments in the founding of the Fijian Methodist Church, I had identified a distinction made by some Fijians, between a "time of darkness" of cannibalism and heathenism, and a "time of light" ushered in by the arrival of Christian missionaries. In this village and surrounding areas, however, people do not conceive of their Christian history in that form. Nor, it may be added, do they describe Christianity as a doctrine imposed on them in the process of their subjugation to other Fijians and Europeans, as a doctrine which contradicts or supplants Fijian cosmological forms. Instead, they now conceive their knowledge of Jehovah as predating the arrival of European missionaries in Fiji, and they consider Christianity to be *vakavanua* 'in the way of the land', i.e. a part of Fijian custom. Even their ancestor Navosavakadua is now portrayed as a Christian. This reading of Methodism needs to be explored in the context of the Fijian cultural logic of land and chiefs.

Methodism in Drauniivi can be understood as the fulfillment of Navosavakadua's project: as an encompassment of a foreign god by the people of the land. Both insofar as Christianity serves as an ethical system for Fijians (as it does, partially) and more importantly as part of their cosmological system, Jehovah is now in many crucial ways (though not all) a god of the land. In Drauniivi, people relate to God through a social and cosmological hierarchy, communally, and differentially. Christianity in Drauniivi does not generally entail an individualistic world view, nor a belief in a natural state of sin and individual achievement of grace through a personal relationship with God; nor does it entail the universalism that this belief would imply. One consequence is that Christianity helps maintain older convictions of local autonomy and autochthony. Another consequence is that in Drauniivi, explicitly Christian principles of sharing, generosity, and kindliness are identified as Fijian custom and are simultaneously conceived to be limited to the Fijian community. By examining a myth that explains the relationship between Jehovah, the people of Drauniivi, other Fijians and the rest of the world, and then considering in turn the concept of *loloma* 'kindly love' and the current interpretation of Navosavakadua as Christian figure, I will discuss the place of Christianity in the system of meaning of the people of Drauniivi.

Jehovah the highest god

The collective or communal nature of Fijian society is rooted in the Fijian theory of the divinity of chiefs and founding ancestors. As Hocart (1950, 1970) has shown, the basic Fijian social groups (*mataqali*) are constituted not as kinship groups (real or fictive) but as ritual communities which replicate hereditarily the nature of their founding ancestors. The ancestor gods are therefore differentiating, and *mataqali*, founded by them, consist of specific kinds of people of differing hereditary natures. There are three different *mataqali* in Drauniivi: chiefs, supporting warrior allies, and installers of the chief.[9] In each case the group's standing is simultaneously ritual and political. Nowadays, the sacred aspect of the group is grounded in the leader or the group itself, rather than in active sacrifice to or veneration of the ancestor deity. These groups, implicitly sacred, are the foundation of Fijian social life.[10]

Now, Jehovah is meant, in Western Christianity, to be a universally accessible deity. How then can Fijians relate to Him? Either, perhaps, by rejecting group ties and conceiving themselves as individual sinners coming to him, which seems to be the pattern in some urban communities in Fiji, or perhaps by rejecting Jehovah as irrelevant and inappropriate for worship as some Fijian intellectuals have done. In this village, however, a different alternative has been developed: it is claimed that Jehovah defines Fijians too, as a group hereditarily and ritually distinct from and preeminent among others in the world.

If Jehovah is a differentiating god for the people of this village, He is at once more powerful but less claimable than the old gods of their land. If He is to be claimed by them, as Fijian and particular to Drauniivi, then the rest of the world remains to be explained. Moreover, Jehovah's relation to the old gods, and the social groups which represent them, must be clarified as well. Certainly the Christian God is the highest God, often referred to by Fijians as the true God, Creator, or Savior, but also sometimes as *na kalou cecere* which may be translated as 'the highest god', implying what is indeed the case, that older deities remain in the cosmology of Fijians (in Drauniivi, and throughout Fiji as well).

Here is a version of the story that forges the link between the Christian God, the people of Drauniivi village, the ancestor gods of other Fijian polities, and the other peoples of the world.

> Concerning the origin of the three ritual kinship groups.
>
> God just spoke and He made the world. I have heard it is written in the Bible that He made it, with His hands. But I know that God just spoke. "In the beginning the word lived, and they were together, God and the word, and the word was God" [he is paraphrasing John 1:1]. By the word only did God make things, the world, the heavens, men, and every single thing.
>
> When He had made the world He then divided the land in two. One half was the dry land, and one was the water. When it had been created, then He made a stone, and it had three names, which Jehovah gave it. The first was Stone of Time, the second was Brain, and the third was Degei.... Our three ancestors, they were descended from this rock. First a man and a woman were born from the rock. They married and then three children were born. The eldest was Lekaninabuya.... Their standing was that of gods. God just spoke and made them, they were descendants of the stone.
>
> Then the eldest got married, he was our *kalou vu* 'ancestor god'. He was married and then three children were born. God just said, "Get

> married." He took a lady, he just spoke, and then the three founders of the groups were born. The first was Bulibulivanua, [founder of the installing people's group]. The second was Saumaimuri [founder of the warrior allies group] The third was Lewanavanua [founder of the chiefly group]....
>
> It is written in the Bible that it was Adam and Eve, but in the ancient words we were descended, we all, the people of the world including you [the anthropologist] and everyone else, no matter from what country, we are all born from the Stone. We of the three *mataqali* groups here, we were born (the children of Lekaninabuya), then Degei, the youngest of the three (younger brother of Lekaninabuya) got married. He married one hundred women. Then these hundred women had children. Then the ancestor gods were divided into many parts. These children of Degei were ancestor gods. They then went to all the different places [in Fiji], they went to your land too [the anthropologist's]....

Although my informant[11] was too polite to press the point, the story is elaborated in other versions, to stress the fact that the Drauniivi people are descendants of the first son of the first man and woman to be born of the stone that Jehovah made. The rest of the world, including the coastal chiefly groups of Fiji and all the different peoples overseas, are the descendants of the younger brother of their ancestor. In a logic found elsewhere in Polynesia, the elder brother retains ritual precedence over the younger brother, even when the upstart younger brother may eventually oust him or succeed him. Or, put in specifically Fijian terms, the autocthonous land people, closest to the Kauvadra range represent the older brothers and they must install the outsider chief who represents the younger brother. This cultural logic is seen in the part of the story of the three *mataqali* groups of Drauniivi in particular, in which the older brothers eventually cede the chiefship to their younger brother. Thus the Drauniivi people claim as interior land people, to have a closer more autocthonous relation to Jehovah and to the Fijian ancestor gods, than the Europeans and Fijians from other coastal kingdoms who have dominated them politically since colonial times.[12]

In Drauniivi, the combination of Christian and older Fijian deities is oriented by the Fijian cultural logic of encompassment of the foreign by the land. Although this myth does not represent the nature of the Christian god as similar to that of a founding ancestor god (He creates, He does not beget), it expresses a claim to a relationship with Him that is particular and prior. The relationship thus conceived is made through the ancestor gods, who are the founders of the ritual kinship groups. As a founding myth, it is an expression of group — not individual — relations with God. To conceive God as having made the stone of origin deep in the Nakauvadra mountains is to conceive Him as having established the deepest "land" principles of Fijian tradition.

Loloma and Christian Grace

The myth related above makes explicit meanings and relations found in many other aspects of social life in Drauniivi, from the ritual-political relations of the chiefly, installing, and ally groups to the relation of the Christian God and ancestral deities in the peopling of the world. The cultural logic that orients this myth, and in particular the special relation of Christianity and Fijians it claims, is also manifest in the concept of *loloma.*

Loloma is generally glossed as 'kindly love' or 'gift' (Capell 1971). When I first began fieldwork it was the aspect of Fijian life that the Fijian family with whom I lived and other friends in Drauniivi were most concerned to communicate. "Look," they said to me, "when we Fijians eat, if we see anyone walk by, a stranger, a friend, a relative, we must call out to them 'Come and eat' or 'Come drink tea'. We know that Europeans who live in the world of money do not do this, but we must do it. This is the meaning of *loloma.*" *Loloma* is an indigenous characterization of the whole Fijian system of generalized reciprocity (Sahlins 1972), a system not just economic but ritual, political, and social as well. What does this have to do with Christianity? *Loloma* is also the word the missionaries used to translate the concept of "grace."

On the one hand, therefore, *loloma* is associated with Jesus, the kindly and interceding aspect of the Christian God. There is a tremendous sentimental force to the Fijian understanding of Jesus, who gave himself as a *soro* 'sacrificial offering' to God on humanity's behalf.[13] This self-sacrifice takes meaning and reverberates within the cultural impetus to give and to share which has been described above. And it is explicitly conceived nowadays as a defining characteristic of Fijians, as central to their very nature.

Expressing this belief, an older informant recounted the story of how the Twins rebelled against their ancestor Degei. (Degei here stands for the entirety of the elder Fijian gods.) A war was fought at Nakauvadra mountain, and eventually the grandsons were defeated. They got into a canoe and piled it high with all the gifts and attributes that God had given humanity. They took wealth and wisdom and technological know how. They took all these valuables in their canoe and they drifted to foreign lands, including England and America. They married women of these lands and founded lines of descendants. The gifts that they brought were responsible for the successes of England and America. The only thing they left behind in Fiji was *loloma.* A teen-aged sibling in the Fijian household where I lived made the same point even more specifically. He asked me, "Marica, what god do you (Americans) worship in America?" I answered that different Americans have different religions including Methodism, Catholicism, Judaism, there are even some Muslims and Hindus. "I think you worship money," he said. "The Indians [Fiji's ethnic group of South Asian descent] worship money, and live in the world of business. You Americans live in the world of business and so I think you must worship money. We Fijians worship *na kalou dina* 'the true god', (i.e., the Christian God) and we have *loloma,* but we have no business."

In the myth of the Twins, Fiji, and the Nakauvadra range are again claimed as the origin point of the world. The myth affirms both the precedence of grandfather (Degei) over young upstart grandsons (the ancestors of the Europeans) and the Fijian Christian attribute of *loloma* over all the knowledge, power, privilege, and money of the Europeans who have ruled Fiji. In both statements, *loloma* as it is now used in this village conflates redemption through Christ with the ritual, social, and economic system of Fijians. Essentially it is an argument that by being Fijian the people of Drauniivi achieve (a locally defined) Christian grace.

Navosavakadua as a Christian ancestor

The revaluation of Navosavakadua as empowered by the Christian God both requires and supports the belief in a special relationship between the people of Drauniivi and the Christian God. Important in this synthesis is the Biblical passage John 1:1 "In the beginning was the word (*na vosa*) and the word was with God and the word was God."[14] This passage is used frequently in Drauniivi, especially as a text for sermons. The current construction of Navosavakadua, as prophet and martyr, takes many of its themes from the Biblical story of Jesus Christ. No one confuses him with Jesus, nor is Jesus forgotten in Drauniivi. Rather, Jesus' suffering on behalf of mankind, and Navosavakadua's persecution at the hands of the colonial government are likened, and Navosavakadua is seen, like Jesus, as the bearer of great *mana.* It is not surprising to find that, as with the concept of *loloma,* a translational equation of *mana* with Christ's miracle-working in the Bible has led to a revaluation both of the Fijian concept as it is applied to "traditional" aspects of Fijian ritual and to the introduced conception of Christ's powers.

The most vivid example of the blending of explicit reference to Navosavakadua with specifically Christian ritual I saw was at the first all-village fundraising festival of December 1984. Christmas day was chosen as an auspicious date, and non-resident relatives of the people of the village were invited to come to bring donations of money, to contribute to a competitive fundraising between the village ritual-kin divisions. The money raised in this *soli* 'fundraising festival' was then to be used for projects to benefit the whole village. (*Solis,* at the provincial, district, and village level, and within village divisions, are the principle way in which Fijians amass money for collective use, exemplifying continued Fijian discomfort with alienated labor, and "business" customs more generally.) A *meke* 'dance' was performed by village women to an old chant about Navosavakadua, to honor and welcome the relatives who came to donate to the festival. Ironically, the morning church services, on that Christmas day, were poorly attended, due to the preparations for the festivities. The day itself, however, as a whole, incorporated *na siga ni sucu* (Christmas, literally 'the day of the birth') as an integral part of self-presentation and celebration by the people of Drauniivi.

Nonetheless, the proposition that Navosavakadua was empowered by the Christian God is not without contradictions. It requires the argument that the colonial authorities "made a mistake" in judging him heathen and deporting their ancestors, an argument made explicitly by some in Drauniivi, but not by all. (Indeed nowadays the later colonial era is cited by some as a golden age of discipline, respect, and proper observance of the customs of the land.) While Jehovah has entered explicitly into local myths, references to Navosavakadua in church services are more covert. For example, although John 1:1 is cited, overt discussions of the ancestor do not occur in sermons. They do not occur in *tikina* 'district' council meetings (which begin with Christian prayer) either, nor in other spheres whose content and form have been fixed since colonial days. Indeed these spheres contain no explicit discussion of any sort of ancestor-deities, or non-Biblical deities, no matter how pressing a topic such things might be in the village gossip and discussion around *yaqona* 'kava' bowls late at night. Colonial disapproval is immanent in these spheres and to raise Navosavakadua to explicit discussion would be to raise the potential contradiction.

Navosavakadua is both an ancestor and a deity in the village of Drauniivi. His descendants see him as an extraordinary ancestor, but also as one with them, of the same heredity and nature. As they have constructed their relationship to the Christian God as one of encompassment, so they have simultaneously reconstructed Navosavakadua and themselves as part of a world in which Jehovah made the stone from which their ancestor gods sprang. This encompassment was, in fact, Navosavakadua's own project. The "*tuka* movement" was the attempt, in Fijian ritual terms of the time, to control and encompass a ritually and politically threatening stranger god. When Methodist and colonial forms were imposed on the people of Drauniivi, they apprehended and accepted these forms and the Christian God according to a Fijian cultural logic and generated this Fijian-Christian system in which the Methodist *lotu* is a 'way of the land'.

CHRISTIANITY AND THE NATION OF FIJI

Thus far, I have sought to show how Christianity has been encompassed, as a "way of the land" in Drauniivi village. I have focussed on Christianity as it has been apprehended by and incorporated into the cultural system of meaning of a particular group of Fijians. This has been presented as an example, following the older Fijian ritual system, of the domestication of a foreign god into a god of the land. In this section I will consider another version of Fijian Christianity apparent in the wider context of Fiji as a present-day multi-ethnic "nation," by looking at two other statements of the relation of Christianity and being Fijian, occasioned by the recent military coup.[15]

A vision of the relationship of chiefs and people, of Fijians and Fiji Indians, and the constitution of that relationship by God, is given in a speech by Colonel Sitiveni Rabuka, leader of the May 14 military coup.

> There is only one reason for this coup, that is my apprehension that the time might come when the rule of our land and our soil might be taken and that in such future times our descendants might therefore be impoverished. We people of Fiji have been well off, because of the religion of our living God.
>
> If we welcome the enlightenment of this religion of God and we believe it, we must accept everything that comes to pass in his world.
>
> When first God's religion came to our land the chiefs of that time were strong and they were strong and successful in war then.
>
> God decreed that those true chiefs of the land of that time should convert to Christianity.
>
> These true chiefs welcomed the religion then, and it was fortunate that they did, we nowadays have received its blessings. We are enlightened thereby, our land was developed thereby and we have learned much nowadays.
>
> If we approve of and welcome this, let us welcome the fact that these chiefs were the source of our blessedness. Their descendants who are leading nowadays, they are blessed because their ancestors who have passed on before them welcomed Christianity.
>
> The basis of our blessedness is their having accepted our God's religion, His name, His salvation, and His light. It is right thereby that we see everything that comes to us as something blessed, including development in the work we do, and the coming here of the Indians

was a thing of blessedness to our land. Everything has happened because of the acceptance of the religion by our true chiefs who have led us from those days to the present.

It is thus right that we use all of these blessings, to employ them for our use, but let us not lose the paramountcy of [national political] leadership of the true chiefs of the land.

Let not our thoughts thereby be led astray so that we say to ourselves, since we have studied we can be chiefs. It's wrong, if we study we are wise, if we are chiefs, we are chiefs; they the chiefs are chiefs only from God, as the Apostle Paul says....

I also ask if possible that we spread the word to our relatives the Indians that its not our intention that they should be thrown out of our land. I confirm that they are gifts of God to us, that they may be partners in life in our land, and especially in life in the way of money, this is a blessing to us, their coming to work our land and lease it, as the path of our blessing, because of the money they give us as lease money. This is God's blessing to us.... (*Nai Lalakai*, 16 July 1987)[16]

Rabuka's stated concern to preserve Fijian land and leadership against "foreigners" is in many ways similar to the aspects of the "religion of the land" held by Navosavakadua's descendants in Drauniivi. Like the Drauniivi villagers, he distinguishes between Fijians and Indians in part by noting the Indians' "life in the way of money" as opposed to the Christian Fijian life of *loloma* 'kindly love'. Also similar is his ultimate attribution to Jehovah of the founding relations which he seeks to uphold ("if we believe in this religion of God we must accept everything that comes to pass in His world"). But quite unlike the "land Christianity" of Drauniivi, Rabuka's vision of the Fijian social order constituted by Jehovah involves Jehovah's empowerment passing through the ruling chiefs who converted ("these true chiefs welcomed the religion then... the basis of our blessedness is their acceptance of our God's religion"). In contrast in Drauniivi it is believed that Jehovah empowered their ancestor gods, the politically superseded but ritually prior ancestor deities of the Kauvadra range. Citing St. Paul, Rabuka argues that Jehovah, not the people of the land, installed and empowered the ruling chiefs. These chiefs are not syntheses of land and sea, they are not reborn as gods of the land, but rather, are purely empowered by the foreign God (note, God was still foreign, as this constituting act took place at contact with Europeans). This vision of chiefly hierarchy reflects and informs the growth from colonial days to the present of an aristocratic class in Fiji who have exercised power in post-colonial national politics of the last two decades. It is a permutation of the "land" - "chiefs" cultural logic that has come into existence in the colonial and postcolonial era, the development of which I will now briefly trace.

A systematic change has taken place as a culturally linked but politically fragmented network of warring polities became "Fiji," first a colony and then in 1970 a "nation."[17] Christianity has been of fundamental importance in this transformation. The change is from a cultural system based on the principles of "land" and "chiefs" existing in a diachronic and synthetic relationship to each other, to a more rigid, centralized, and reified hierarchical system, existing at the new "national" level of Fiji. This new cultural system is only one of many possibilities potential in the earlier Fijian cultural logic, and it came into being in the encounter with colonial and missionizing Europeans, and in the encounter with Fiji's other ethnic group, South Asian Indians, who came to Fiji as indentured labourers on British plantations. One major arena in which this reification was both accomplished and expressed was land tenure. Scholars have noted that models of Fijian kinship groups and land tenure used in practice by colonial administrators and accepted early in this century by some anthropologists were actually reifications of much more fluid and diverse entitities and practices (e.g., Clammer 1975; France 1969). Carrying their points further, and with reference to recent thoughts on "the invention of tradition" (Cohn 1981; Hobsbawm and Ranger 1983), I will suggest how the "chiefs empowered by Jehovah" came to rule Fiji at the national level.

Fiji's indigenous cosmological systems had no one central deity, but a multiplicity of deities, who could be overcome, dispossessed, and recreated in the ongoing course of ritual political events such as warfare between ritual polities. The current position of Jehovah, however, as the unalterable head of the hierarchy of Fijian deities brings to the system a new type of hierarchy, and fixes it. The centrality of Jehovah parallels, and indeed enabled, the centralization of power in the hands of Europeans and coastal high chiefs in Fiji, which began in the mid-nineteenth century with the coinciding projects of Europeans and Cakobau of Bau. Through this change, the nineteenth century Fijian "stranger chief," who must be ritually reborn as a child of land and sea, has become a hereditarily determined chief. Currently, the codification of polities and genealogies of rulership resulting from colonial projects such as the British land tenure commissions enable present day officials of the Lands Commission to arbitrate succession disputes. The emphasis on descent and primogeniture rather than conquest, arbitrated from a central source, creates a "class" of chiefs. It is not a coincidence that the Lands Commission records are frequently referred to by Fijians as "the Fijian Bible." They have taken on a connotation of ultimate authority that first came to Fiji in Christian teachings about the Bible.

Simultaneously, the category of *vanua* 'land' has developed a new general meaning as "tradition," similar to what in other Pacific nations is being called *kastom.* Formerly the "land" side was defined in relationships such as that between installing people and chiefs, and between people of the interior and people of the coast. Now "land" is used by Fijians by Fijians to describe the relation between a Fijian "race" generally and their Indian compatriots.[18] Within this reified notion of "the way of the land," Christianity has become part of the distinguishing identity of Fijians. On the one hand, this creates a commonality of Fijian interest, where once separate ancestor gods meant separate natures entirely, as in Rabuka's claims on behalf of the "*taukei*" 'people of the land' in general. On the other hand, as in Drauniivi, as I have shown, sometimes interested divisions within Fijian communities claim closer relations to Jehovah to express separation or autonomy.

In the multi-ethnic context of Fiji, many Fijians have a notion of themselves not only as indigenous "owners of the land" but also as closer to Jehovah ("the true God") than others. Among leaders and staff of the Methodist church (at the national level and at the village level as well) there has been concern to promote an ideology of cultural pluralism and religious tolerance. Thus for example, a number of Fijian leaders of the Methodist Church in Fiji condemned the coup.[19] One wrote to condemn it and to condemn the coup-leaders' scare tactics about Indian domination as racism, and compared it to Nazism:

> Racism is a heresy against God whether it is Nazi Germany, South Africa, or Fiji. The Church must never condone it. Silence in the face of injustice is sinful.
>
> This is the question which we as Christians in Fiji must come to terms with. Every time we shrug when we hear of another midnight raid, the cries of terrorised women and children, and a squad of military making their presence felt without any regard of human decency, then somewhere in Fiji another potential [Klaus] Barbie is getting a start in life, only in a climate of hatred and injustice and terror do such people arise. For anyone claiming to follow the Christ of the Gospels, to identify with such behaviour is an insult to the rest of the Christian community who condemn it. (*Fiji Sun,* July 9, 1987)

However, in other contexts, the configuration of Christianity within a newly reified "Fijian custom" is all too frequently expressed as intolerance towards Hindu and Muslim fellow citizens, and this combines with the political interests of the new chiefly class whom Rabuka claimed to represent through the coup. In Rabuka's new reified form, relations between the "land," now meaning Fijians in general, and the rest, primarily the

Indians, are not synthetic but hierarchical. The dominant positions of Fijian chiefs are considered to be fixed and divinely sanctioned, following from the place of Jehovah in the Christian system as he constructs it.

CONCLUSION

In conclusion, I have sought to show how the concept of cultural logic can contribute to an understanding of Fijians as simultaneously cultural and historical. I have focused on two very different sorts of Fijian Christianity, which inform very different social and political projects, at two distinct moments in Fiji's history. In greatest detail I have delineated the "religion of the land" that is Christianity in Drauniivi village, largely wrought by the project of Navosavakadua. Drauniivi Christianity is both atypical and fundamentally revealing. Understood through the explication of the Fijian principles of "land" and "chiefs" as principles of a dynamic cultural logic, we find that in Drauniivi Jehovah has been encompassed as a god of people of the land. Further, in analyzing the project of coup leader Colonel Rabuka who claims Christianity as an outside force empowering high chiefs (or stranger kings), I have shown how the "lands" - "chiefs" principles recur in a different permutation, in a widely held alternate vision of the relation of chiefs, people, and the Christian God, which is now shaping the fate of Fiji as national "imagined community."

Seeking to show how a concept of cultural logic can link the study of culture and history, I argue that the Fijian cultural logic of land and chiefs enduringly shapes social life in Fiji and variably shapes that social life, through differing indigenous emphases and through plural articulations with colonial, missionary, and now post-colonial introductions. Perhaps most interesting in the study of structure and history in Fiji is the way in which the ritual and the political remain entwined for Fijians.[20] Like the divine kingship of the British Empire (upholding "good order under God and the Queen," as Colonial Governor J.B. Thurston lectured the people of Drauniivi in 1891), Fiji's colonial and post-colonial orthodoxy have been founded on Lotu, Matanitu, and Vanua ("religion," "government" [chiefly government] and "people" [or "land"]). Not just orthodoxy but also both challenges to it and radical action to preserve it have taken their meaning and made claims to moral force because of this inseparability of the ritual and political. From Navosavakadua's movement of people of the land, claiming Jehovah as an indigenous god, to Rabuka's cataclysmic linking of Fijian nationalism, chiefly custom, and Jehovah as powerful stranger, radical agency on the part of Fijians has drawn its power from the power of gods. An ironic historical contrast has emerged, for the incipient warfare of Navosavakadua's movement was suppressed by the colonial and Christian chiefly orthodoxy, resulting in a local and quiescent conception of ritual authority based on a special relationship with Jehovah. In contrast, in Rabuka's case, the chiefly conversions of which the missionary and colonial British so approved have been used to justify military overthrow of Fiji's democracy and constitution, and severance of relations with the British crown and commonwealth.

By considering "the *lotu*" in Fiji in the context of Fijian systems of meaning of past and present, I have hoped to show the analytic usefulness of a concept of cultural logic. The goal has not been to trace enduring stasis, but rather, to understand the differing place of Christianity in the now post-colonial system of meaning of different groups of Fijians, and to understand their difference in Fijian terms as those of chiefs and people of the land. Through attention to the indigenous Fijian ritual-political system and to the history of the colonial and missionary interaction, I have hoped to show as well the contribution of a historical perspective to the analysis of current systems of meaning.

NOTES

This paper is based on fieldwork in Ra Province, Viti Levu, Fiji and on archival research and residence in Suva, Fiji, in 1984-85. I thank the Fiji Government for research permission, and I thank the National Archives of Fiji, the Methodist Church in Fiji, and the Catholic Church for access to records. I acknowledge research funding from the National Science Foundation and the U.S. Department of Education Fulbright-Hays program. I thank friends and informants in both village and city, and I thank John D. Kelly for many readings.

1. Reference to the people of Drauniivi village and their kin and allies of present and past as the "Drauniivi people" rather than by their *yavusa* 'kin group and polity' name is for convenience to readers who may have encountered the *tuka* movement in the works of Burridge (1969) or Worsley (1968) or in the various historical accounts of Fiji.
2. Which need to be analyzed both as colonial constructions of Fijian orthodoxy (as "invention of tradition" in Hobsbawm and Ranger's [1983] phrase) and as Fijian cultural encompassments of the foreign.
3. Christianity is thus analyzed in relation to the "land" — "chiefs" cultural logic, rather than as it is defined nowadays by the aims and goals of the leaders of the Fijian Methodist Church, or in the past was defined by British missionaries (for these perspectives, see Calvert 1983; Garrett 1982; Thornley 1979).
4. This narrative interprets historical records available in the various collections of mission and governmental papers held at the Fiji National Archives in Suva, which I have consulted, including the Cakobau Government papers, Colonial Secretary's Office Minute Papers series, and records of the Methodist Mission in Fiji. Other collections consulted include the British Colonial Office series (consulted in microfilm in Canberra), Methodist Mission papers held at the Mitchell Library, Sydney, and the Archives of the Catholic Mission, Suva, Fiji. Relevant published histories include Derrick (1950), Macnaught (1971, 1982), Routledge (1985), and Scarr (1984).

5. Colonial and mission records on Navosavakadua are to be found in the Colonial Secretary's Office, Methodist Mission, and Colonial Office series noted earlier, see also Brewster (1922). I have collected accounts of Navosavakadua from his descendants. See also *Nai Lalakai*, March - July, 1984. For a detailed analysis of Navosvakadua's *tuka* movement as a movement of "land" people see Kaplan (1988a).
6. The cultural logic of the land - chief relationship of encompassment itself allows for permutations and differences between polities and over time. In the north and the interior polities were chiefly led, but of much smaller scale relative to the nineteenth century coastal kingdoms. These "less hierarchical" northern and hill polities may be better understood as polities in which the "land" side has been more dominant. Leadership by warrior priests, and the rise of "inspired" leaders such as Navosavakadua are one example of the possible dominance of the "land" side in "political" as well as "ritual" matters. Nowadays it is still possible for installing people to manipulate events within a particular polity, for example by refusing to install a new chief.
7. Forty-two "households" in the 1976 census.
8. The distribution of knowledge about Navosavakadua follows Fijian principles as to the "ownership" of knowledge. The name Navosavakadua is known throughout the islands, but the Drauniivi man is sometimes confused (e.g. by several Fijians I talked to in Suva) with another prophet-leader of the 1910s and 20s. In Drauniivi in particular, the stories of his miracles, are known by everyone, from older people to school children, and no one I talked to ever claimed to disbelieve them, nor to doubt that his *mana* was ultimately Christian. Other Fijians do doubt this, as is clear from a debate carried out in letters to the Fijian-language newspaper *Nai Lalakai*, following the publication of some stories about Navosavakadua sent in by a man from the village. (This publication may have influenced the consistency with which stories are known in the village, but even teenagers know other stories, heard from their elders, that were not published.) More complex stories about Navosavakadua, including his kin affiliations and detailed exegesis on his *mana* are known and told by older people in the village, in particular people in his kin group. Extended narratives about ancestor gods, the Kauvadra range, and about Navosavakadua are the specialty of certain persons, generally older men, who include custodians of knowledge passed down by previous village leaders, representatives to Lands Commission inquiries or Provincial Councils or their heirs, and those who are knowledgeable about the ancestors because they are in communication with them.
9. This is a simplified presentation of a more complicated series of divisions and statuses. For further details see Kaplan (1988a).
10. As a consequence the local concept of sin (e.g., committing adultery, stealing) involves entire *mataqali* lines, since improper behaviour can result in the illness or misfortune of one's relatives. This is not to suggest that the supernatural (in the form of Jehovah, or other gods) serves merely as a form of social control, or that religion merely validates social relations. Rather, *mataqali* and relations between them are simultaneously "religious" and "social."
11. A village leader and leader of the installing *mataqali*, a man in his fifties.
12. This sort of claim with regard to Christianity and autochthony is found elsewhere in the north and interior. In particular, in Kavula, another northern polity with a syncretic tradition noted in the colonial record, it is currently claimed by members of one group that Jesus is buried in their sacred ancestral origin mound.
13. Nowadays a *soro* is a sacrificial offering acknowledging repentance. In nineteenth century Fijian war culture, it was a sacrificial offering signifying submission in defeat.
14. The significance of this passage lies in part in the context of the efficacy of words,

formulas, and names in indigenous Fijian ritual. One essential aspect of Fijian ritual is simply the elaborate naming and invocation of the deities and *mataqali* of the participants, and the detailed and formal description of their relationship and the transaction or interaction which is taking place. *Navosavakadua* 'he who speaks but once and is thereby effective' and *Vosamana* 'he who speaks and is thereby effective' are appellations that were given to deities and priests in early nineteenth century Fiji. The title was also used by Fijians to refer to the colonial Supreme Court Judge referring to his prerogative of final decision making (Brewster 1922:239). I do not know whether Navosavakadua and his followers were familiar with the Biblical passage when he was given the appellation, or whether the conflation with the Biblical passage developed later.

15. The May 14, 1987 army coup overthrew the coalition government led by Dr. Timoci Bavadra, a non-chiefly Fijian, head of the Fiji Labour party which in conjunction with the predominantly Fiji Indian National Federation Party had unseated the Fijian chiefly-led Alliance Party, in power since Independence in 1970. Rabuka later led a second coup on September 25 and soon thereafter proclaimed Fiji a Republic, separated from the British Commonwealth (for fuller analyses of these events see Kaplan 1988b; Lal 1988).
16. This is a partial text of a speech given by Col. Rabuka to a group of Nadroga people in early July 1987 explaining his motives for leading the coup. The translation is mine. At the time this article is being written, it seems that his appeals have legitimized the coup in most Fijians' eyes. However, the coup will alter many aspects of Fijian society, and I do not necessarily expect that Rabuka's rhetoric will remain constant, nor that the particular post-colonial permutation of the relation of God, chiefs, and people which he appeals to here will remain constant (see Kaplan 1988b; Lal 1988).
17. For a discussion of the analytic status of "nation" see Anderson (1983).
18. In Fiji "race" is the term generally used for ethnic group, thus indigenous Fijians, Fiji Indians, and local Europeans are "races."
19. See Lal (1988) for a discussion of different positions taken by Fijian Methodist leaders.
20. This is not to suggest that I consider "politics" to be universally or fundamentally separate from "ritual," but only to contrast this Fijian vision of political order (based in the cultural logic I have outlined) with those political orders which propose a sustained separation of (indigenously defined categories of) "church" and "state."

8

CATHOLICISM, CAPITALIST INCORPORATION, AND RESISTANCE IN KRAGUR VILLAGE

Michael French Smith

INTRODUCTION

A visitor to Kragur village, in Papua New Guinea's East Sepik Province, is likely to come away with the impression that it is very Catholic. The principal leader of Catholic religious life commands respect and attention. Although attendance at daily evening prayer sessions in the center of the village is often sparse, almost everyone turns out for Sunday services held in a well-kept, bush-materials church. Villagers themselves will tell you that the people of Kragur are particularly devout in their Catholicism. As evidence, they can point to the statue of the Virgin that they erected in 1976 at the highest point on the main trail across this steep volcanic island. They can also point out that several Kragur men have worked in other parts of Papua New Guinea as catechists for the Society of the Divine Word, that one village man is a Marist brother, and that another is one of Papua New Guinea's few indigenous Catholic priests.

Catholicism has played a major role in villagers' encounter with the new world of money, wage labor, commodity production, and great disparities of wealth and power that has engaged them ever more deeply in the few decades since first European contact. While the Catholic mission was the earliest sustained emissary of the capitalist world to Kragur, it is difficult to define the role of Catholicism in the process of incorporation in any simple way. As Comaroff and Comaroff (1986:1) note, to phrase the question of the missionary role in colonization in such terms as "'Whose side was the missionary really on?'" is to risk oversimplifying a complex issue. I would agree with Beckett (1978:209) that "Christianity in the South Seas must, in the final analysis, be understood in terms of colonization." But it would be a mistake to reduce the significance of Christianity to its role in furthering indigenous peoples' incorporation into the spreading capitalist political economy. Comaroff (1985:152) notes that viewing missionaries as "mere 'colonial agents'" fails to "discriminate between intended and unintended outcomes or to distinguish subtle motives from structural effects." Catholicism in Kragur has furthered capitalist incorporation by fostering a romanticized view of the basis of European wealth and power that contributes to the transformation of indigenous temporal orientations and the legitimation of forms of equality characteristic of the colonial and post-colonial social orders. But Catholicism has also contributed to cultural currents that call into question capitalist values and express deep discontent with domination by Europeans and an emerging indigenous elite. Neither missionaries nor villagers have had full control or consciousness of the political and economic significance of their involvement with Catholicism. This indeterminacy is a common feature of Christian missionary endeavors, a feature scholars have traced to inherent ambiguity in both the conceptual and the explicitly political realms.

Comaroff and Comaroff (1986) describe how the activities of Protestant missionaries among the Tshidi people of South Africa both laid a conceptual basis for capitalist incorporation and contributed to the rise of expressions of resistance to and discontent with the colonial and post-colonial political and economic orders. The Comaroffs stress the importance of the equivocal nature of the missionary role in the explicitly political sphere, the realm of "explicit power relations," but they also imply the significance of the varied implicit messages conveyed by the mission. In particular, they stress the contrast between the Protestant values conveyed by much of mission practice and the "charter for liberation" that literate Tshidi found in the scriptures (1986:15-16).

In examining the Kragur case I focus on the ambiguity of the mission contribution in the conceptual realm. The role of the Catholic mission in the Sepik in the realm of "explicit power relations" certainly appears to have been relatively limited and straightforward compared to that of the Protestants in South Africa as described by the Comaroffs.[1] I also focus on ambiguity in the conceptual sphere because it was readily visible from my vantage point in the village — in the talk of villagers in public gatherings, while gardening or fishing, or gathered around cooking fires — and in itself it clarifies a great deal about the role of Catholicism in contemporary Kragur. Finally, multiple, sometimes contradictory, messages are perhaps a more universal feature of Christian missionary enterprises than ambiguity in the explicitly political sphere.

Ambiguity and indeterminacy are nothing unique to Catholicism or even Christianity in general. As Gary Marx (1967:104) notes in his discussion of the role of religion in Black protest movements in the United States, Christianity is like most ideologies, whether religious or secular, in that it "contains many themes, which, if not in contradiction, are certainly in tension with one another." Stokes (1975) analysis of Afrikaner Calvinism makes a similar point, focusing on the role of historical circumstances in determining which themes are emphasized. He argues that the historically specific features of Afrikaner life resulted in their Calvinism becoming a force for collectivist economic conservatism rather than the individualistic entrepreneurial activity Calvinism inspired in Europe. Like other ideologies, Calvinism encompassed extremely diverse and often inchoate potentials. The nature of particular historical circumstances determined which of these was realized.

More germane to the Kragur case — and other cases of European Christianity's encounter with non-capitalist peoples — is the tension within European Christian missions between the task of creating Europeans and that of creating Christians (Burridge 1978:21) and the tension between what is often the missions' interest in accommodating their clients to the new political and economic order, and Christianity's concern with and imagery of liberation from worldly oppression. As Webb (1986:119), following Theissen (1978), points out, a similar tension has informed Christianity since its beginnings. He writes of early Christianity that:

> [The] new faith was not free of the exclusiveness and even dogmatism characteristic of many Iron Age missionary religions... the church unfortunately did carry over — from the clash of parties in ancient Palestine and from its early struggles to survive — an element of narrow ethnocentrism and self-righteousness, reworked into an often bigoted, mean-spirited, and obscurantist role for the guardians of orthodoxy. Yet the ancient nativistic and peasant orientation of Yahwism, freed of its ties to a specific ethnicity by the activity of Jesus and his followers, ensured that however narrow-minded the new cult might at times be, one of its most enduring prejudices would be a bias (at least latent) in favor of those on the bottom of the social order.

Catholic missionaries brought European attitudes and habits to Kragur as well as the teachings of Christianity. Kragur villagers have noted the difference between the Christian ideals espoused by some European mission personnel and the impersonal *quid pro quo* world of European daily life. And among contemporary representatives of European Catholicism on Kairiru — brothers, nuns, priests — one can find a broad range of feelings concerning the compatibility of indigenous culture with the aims of Christianity and the necessity of living like a European in order to live like a Christian. As will be discussed in the following section, this lack of consistency has also been manifest over time, as the attitude of the mission toward indigenous practices has become more tolerant. Added to all this ambiguity is the fact that the messages, both implicit and explicit, that Catholicism has brought to Kragur have fallen on active minds, operating in a specific, changing historical context.

I begin examination of the Kragur case with a description of the geographic and social setting. Next I sketch the history of Catholicism on Kairiru, and discuss the circumstances that have led to its special importance in Kragur and the nature of villagers' belief and involvement in Catholicism. I then discuss Catholicism's contribution to the transformation of temporal orientations and the legitimation of new forms of inequality and its contribution to cultural counter currents that extol non-capitalist virtues and express discontent with new forms of inequality. In my conclusion I consider the political significance of these phenomena. While at present it seems unlikely that these counter currents will give rise to explicitly political resistance to capitalist incorporation, recognizing them reminds us of the complexity of the Christian missionary role in colonization and is an antidote to one-dimensional history which credits only those historical possibilities that emerge dominant.

THE SETTING: ISLAND AND VILLAGE

Kairiru island is about 4 miles long and 3.5 miles wide at its widest point. It lies about 12 miles as the crow flies northwest of Wewak, the administrative center of the East Sepik Province. To reach Kairiru by boat, however, one must circle the island of Muschu, which in stormy weather is often obscured by Kairiru's more imposing profile, becoming almost invisible from the mainland. Some 15 to 20 villages, depending on how one aggregates named and populated locales, are scattered around Kairiru's periphery. Most are accessible only on foot or by sea. The only road on Kairiru is the single-lane dirt track on the south coast that links St. John's and St. Xavier's. The former is a small Catholic seminary for young indigenous men training for religious vocations and the latter is a Catholic boarding high school for men. Both serve the Sepik mainland as well as Kairiru and other Sepik islands. When I last visited Kairiru in 1981, both schools were staffed largely — although not exclusively — by Whites, many of them members of Catholic orders.

In the past, Kairiru islanders made trading expeditions to other Sepik islands and points on the mainland coast by outrigger sail canoe. Today, however, most travel is to and from Wewak. A few small power boats, owned by islanders, and the St. Xavier's boat — which makes regular trips to Wewak, weather permitting — supply transportation. The quickest way to reach Kragur, on the island's rugged north coast, is by boat. But during the monsoon season, from roughly late November to April, rough seas often make it impossible to land on Kragur's narrow, rocky beach. Then, one can take a boat to the south coast and hike over the mountain on a precipitous trail that climbs about 2,000 feet and plunges the same distance down again, bringing one to Kragur, perched on a cliff between the forest and the sea. Kragur people often cross the mountain to the south coast and some travel periodically to Wewak. Few outsiders, however, make the journey to Kragur from Wewak, St. John's, or St. Xavier's.

Kragur's approximately 200 residents live in houses made of bush materials, set on posts from two to four feet above the ground. The village site climbs from the cliff to the forest in irregular terraces, walled with the island's plentiful volcanic rocks. The village is divided into nine named residential divisions called *koyeng* in the Kairiru language. The backbones of these units are male household heads descended from common male ancestors. A few men reside in the *koyeng* of their wives or mothers. Both men and women, however, maintain an identification with their natal *koyeng* as well as their *koyeng* of residence. In addition to *koyeng* divisions, there is also a tripartite division of the population that in the past was part of the structure of men's cult activities and marriage exchange. The two largest of these divisions, Seksik and Lupelap, are the most prominent, giving the appearance of a *de facto* moiety system. While this division does not now seem to play a significant role in regulating marriages, and the men's cult is gone, the Seksik/Lupelap division shows up in such contemporary contexts as membership in the village's two accounts with the Copra Marketing Board in Wewak.

Some *koyeng* enjoy more prestige and influence than others. One very important basis of *koyeng* standing is possession of rights to important magical knowledge for such purposes as aiding subsistence efforts and controlling the weather. Such rights are vested in individuals, but they are generally passed from generation to generation along patrilineal lines so they are strongly identified with particular *koyeng*. The authority of traditional leaders — known in the Kairiru language as *ramat walap* 'big men' — is based in large part on their possession of rights to vital magical knowledge.

In the 1950s the Australian administration of what was then the Trust Territory of Papua and New Guinea created the Local Government Council system. Kragur joined in 1961 and since then the village has also had an elected village leader, or councillor, known in Melanesian Pidgin as the *kaunsil*. The *kaunsil* represents Kragur in an area-wide Local

Government Council organization that levys a head tax and conducts public works. In the village, the *kaunsil* is responsible for organizing communal work on such tasks as maintaining trails near the village and cleaning the village grounds. The various *ramat walap*, however, still hold sway when it comes to such fundamental questions as food and health, for Kragur villagers still produce most of their own food and most believe in the magical power of the *ramat walap* to aid or hinder their efforts.

Taro, sweet potatoes, yams, and sago palms are the primary crops in Kragur. Villagers also fish and, less frequently, hunt wild pigs and a variety of smaller game. They occasionally supplement their diet with canned mackeral and rice purchased from tiny village stores. In recent years there have at times been as many as three of these, and one has been in continuous operation for a number of years. Established with funds collected from groups of villagers, then managed by individuals, they occupy small bush-materials buildings or partitioned corners of houses. They do most of their business in rice and canned mackeral, although they often stock such other items as kerosine for lamps, newspaper for rolling cigarettes from home-grown tobacco, soap, sugar, flashlight batteries, and navy biscuits.

In general, however, Kragur people do not use or consume many things that they do not produce themselves. All families do own aluminum cooking pots, some metal tools, and perhaps a kerosine lamp and sheets or blankets for bedding. Everyone also has a few items of European clothing. Like their other mass-produced possessions, villagers' clothing is faded and worn.

Kragur people have very little money to spend on such things as canned mackeral, rice, or clothing. Per capital annual income in 1980 was equivalent to about 25 U.S. dollars. Most of this came from copra production. Several other business ventures — for example, market gardens, a charter cargo and passenger boat, a piggery — have been begun, but as of 1981 no such businesses had endured (Smith 1989). Prospects of significantly increasing income from copra or other cash crops are small because of unstable prices, the limited and generally unsuitable land available on Kragur's rugged mountainside, and the lack of economical transport to mainland markets.

Fortunately, resident villagers do not have to rely for money solely on their own scant earnings. Many villagers, primarily men, leave Kairiru to work for money, and remittances from migrant kin help resident villagers cope with their children's school fees, the Local Government Council tax, and other unavoidable needs for cash. The scale of such migration is impressive. In 1976 there was a resident population of just over 200; but from 90 to 100 villagers over the age of 20 were gone. A few were in secondary or tertiary schools, but most had left to work for money or to be with spouses working for money. Some leave only temporarily, but others are gone for many years and appear to have taken up permanent residence elsewhere. Many migrants are in the prime of life and this has left the village with an hour-glass age distribution; from 80 to 90 percent of the residents are either younger than 20 or older than 40.

The difficulty of acquiring money is a source of great concern to most villagers. But the rhythms of daily life in the village are still predominantly those of a community in which people produce the majority of their own subsistence and in which the distribution of goods and services beyond the household is largely determined by mechanisms of delayed reciprocity — informal sharing of food among kin, pooling of labor to build each others' houses or canoes, and the more formal prestations that mark marriages, funerary observances, and other significant social occasions. With the exception of rare purchases from the village stores, very little money changes hands within Kragur.

MISSION CONTACT AND CATHOLIC INVOLVEMENT

Catholicism dominated the early history of Kairiru island's and Kragur villagers' encounters with the European world. In 1896, German missionaries of the Society of the Divine Word arrived on mainland New Guinea about 200 miles southeast of Kairiru in what is now Madang. Later that year they set up headquarters on Tumleo island, an offshore island west of Kairiru. A mission vessel's visit to Kragur sometime between 1900 and 1910 was probably the first direct European contact with the village. Either on that first visit or soon thereafter a handful of village men were recruited to work for the mission on Tumleo. These men and others recruited by the mission thereafter were exposed to religious training as well as wage labor, so the ground had already been prepared when the first indigenous catechists began their work on Kairiru. The first catechist established a church at Surai village, about 2 hours walk west of Kragur, in the 1920s. Not long after, a catechist came to live in Kragur itself, and by around 1930 Kragur had abandoned the men's cult as a gesture of allegiance to the new religion.

In 1935 the Bishop moved his headquarters from Tumleo to a site on Kairiru's southwest coast, attracted by a good harbor and an abundant supply of fresh water. During the 1930s, priests began visiting Kragur periodically and villagers sometimes hiked over the island to attend Mass at the mission headquarters. In 1938 several priests travelled to the island's north coast to conduct a mass baptism of converts from Kragur and neighboring villages. In 1939 a catechist training school — St. Xavier's — was built on the southwest coast of Kairiru. The Bishop eventually moved back to the mainland, but St. John's now occupies the former site of his headquarters. St. Xavier's eventually became a high school offering a secular curriculum but staffed in large part by members of Catholic orders. St. Xavier's and St. John's remain a strong Catholic presence on Kairiru and a major source of contact with European institutions for Kairiru islanders.

The Catholicism that has been presented to villagers by the mission has not, however, been unchanging. As I discuss at greater length elsewhere (Smith 1980, 1988), today's Catholicism is different from that which once successfully pressed villagers to abandon the men's cult and staged mass baptisms. Villagers have noticed that religious observance is no longer compulsory for students at St. Xavier's, and that the mission's militant campaigning against all indigenous magico-religious practices has given way to tolerance and even encouragement not to abandon what is "good" in pre-contact religious customs. Much of what they have observed has been part of a trend in the Catholic Church as a whole toward less emphasis on religious rites, artifacts, and individual conversion, and more emphasis on integrating Catholicism into community life, a trend made manifest in the Vatican II Ecumenical Council of 1962-65 (cf. Arbuckle 1978; Armstrong, chapter 12).

Although Catholic institutions have not engaged in commercial ventures of any size on Kairiru, they have played an important role in introducing Kragur to capitalist institutions. Kragur has long been a source of migrant wage labor, and distant mission plantations were Kragur villagers' first employers. For most of the history of schooling on Kairiru, Catholic institutions have dominated the scene, eventually opening for a few the way from the village to white collar or professional employment. Kragur's intense, though complex involvement with Catholicism, however, is in part the result of its isolation from greater opportunity to participate in the cash economy or other aspects of the larger post-contact society. As noted earlier, there is little land on Kairiru suitable for cash cropping; the northern side of the island is particularly steep and rocky. There has not been enough commercial activity — copra, coffee, or cacao growing — to stimulate the development of regular transport to and from the mainland. North coast villages are extremely difficult to reach by sea during the monsoon season and Kragur itself lacks a good harbor. Kragur people have seized upon Catholicism in part because of the relative absence of other means of involvement in the rapidly changing world beyond the village and the island.

Why Kragur among all Kairiru or all north coast villages has laid special claim to leadership in Catholicism is an additional question. An alleged appearance of God in Kragur prior to mission contact may have lent a special resonance to first encounters between missionaries and villagers; and if Kragur was one of the island's larger villages in the past as it is today, this also may have attracted mission attention. It is undoubtedly important that the village is the home of an extremely vigorous proponent of Catholicism, active since the 1950s, though his career has itself been shaped by Kragur's special circumstances (Smith 1978:349-360). What Schwartz terms a characteristically Melanesian pattern of "competitive innovation" (1976:112) has probably played a major role in Kragur's involvement in Catholicism. Such involvement currently provides Kragur a source of distinction among other villages in a social system marked by competitive striving for prestige.

The result of this complex of historical, geographic, and cultural factors is that Kragur stands out as an exceptionally Catholic village in the eyes of others as well as in its own. Beneath the surface, however, the picture is more tangled, for villagers have not simply abandoned existing forms of magico-religious belief and practice in favor of those provided by the mission. Syncretic formulations abound. Some speak of the Christian deity, God, as a metaphorical way of referring to deceased ancestors, while others speculate that when they appeal to deceased ancestors it is really God who hears their entreaties. A few conceive of God as resembling the dangerous nature spirit — *masalai,* in Melanesian Pidgin — with the head of a man and the body of a snake said to inhabit the lake at the top of the mountain. Quite a number freely admit that they find such ideas as God, sin, heaven, and hell rather puzzling, though this does not deter them from taking part in Catholic religious observances (cf. Thune, chapter 6). It is not uncommon for villagers to treat Catholicism as primarily an instrumental alternative and to appeal to God or the Virgin Mary in addition to appealing to deceased ancestors or using indigenous magical procedures. Purists claim, however, that to achieve the best results it is best not to mix Catholic and indigenous practices.

Despite the heterodoxy of many villagers' views, their degree of interest and public participation in Catholic endeavors has brought notice from European mission personnel. A few single out Kragur for special mention. One priest on the mainland describes Kragur as "a real stronghold of Catholicism" populated by "people who have real faith" (cf. Smith 1978:90-91). My own introduction to Kragur came about because the brothers at St. Xavier's had special esteem for the village and suggested I visit there during my search for a fieldwork site. Many Kragur people are aware of their reputation and take pride in it: "We're number one in the eyes of the mission" says one older man. Yet even among those who note the village's reputation with pleasure, one also finds suspicion of European-dominated Catholic institutions. For some who have pinned millenarian hopes to their Catholicism, repeated disappointment has aroused the suspicion that the mission has withheld from them Catholicism's true knowledge and power. They turn a jaundiced eye on official Catholicism, while they cling to the hope of discovering the true doctrines that will lift them from the bottom of the social heap (cf. Chowning, chapter 3).

Nevertheless, Catholicism in some form is ubiquitous in daily life in the village, from the frequent services and prayer sessions to its use in curing illness and as an adjunct to traditional subsistence magic. All villagers have been drawn into a degree of participation in Catholic institutions, whether in Catholic schools and on mission plantations or simply in the regimen of Catholic observances organized by local leaders and the occasional visiting priest. In addition, many villagers find broad continuities between Catholic and more familiar practices; for example, some note the similarity of confession to the indigenous practice of publicly revealing anger in curing illness and sometimes speak of the latter, in Pidgin, as confession.[2] As will be discussed below, a powerful theme that unites disparate individual approaches is that of the similarities between mission teachings of Christian charity and brotherhood and contemporary versions of autochthonous norms. As the predominant religion of the European colonial powers as seen from Kragur, Catholicism has commanded enduring interest. The variety of syncretic formulations and the alternative of seeing Catholicism as distinct from the European dominated mission institutions has made it possible for villagers to consider themselves Catholics, and pride themselves on it, despite the lack of firm agreement on all that this entails (cf. Smith 1988). But what this engagement with Catholicism means in terms of incorporation into the new political economy is a complex issue.

TIME, WORK, AND ACQUIESCENCE TO INEQUALITY

By far the most striking way in which the Catholic mission has contributed to restructuring the conceptual universe of Kragur villages is by calling into question the moral adequacy of indigenous forms of social order and harmony. In doing so it advances the transformation of indigenous temporal orientations and lends legitimacy to new forms of inequality.

At least some mission personnel have consciously sought these ends. For example, in 1921, in a letter to the Australian Administrator of what was then the Mandated Territory of New Guinea, Father Andreas Puff, Prefect Apostolic of the Society of the Divine Word mission, wrote that "the missions have the obligation to help the native tame his wild nature, overcome idleness, and learn order and obedience" (Wiltgen 1969:358). As the Comaroffs (1986:2) point out, such "colonization... of indigenous modes of perception and practice" need not rely on brute force, but can be accomplished through teaching "the unassuming 'arts of civilization'"(*ibid.*:12). But while capitalism is well-established as the dominant political economy of the surrounding world, for many Kragur villagers its associated European customs have still not become unthinking routine. It is therefore significant that Kragur people have made their own contribution to forming perceptions of European moral superiority and indigenous moral inadequacy that smooth the way for deeper engagement with the new order.

Such perceptions are especially likely to come to light when villagers consider the subject of European work and wealth. It is not uncommon for villagers to assert that Europeans are wealthier because they are more harmonious and cooperative than Papua New Guineans and to point to the way that Europeans work as a prime example. As one Kragur man puts it, "It isn't right the way we work. You [Europeans or Whites] work together, but we work individually." The indigenous culture and social organization do contribute to the difficulties of instituting long-term, community-wide cooperation in Kragur. These difficulties are probably most pronounced in efforts to gain a foothold in the cash economy through community business ventures (Smith 1989). But villagers have a tendency to exaggerate their own such problems and to romanticize the European way of working, including the characteristic temporal regularity and coordination of European labor processes — their uniform pace, the closely coordinated tasks, and workers' ready adherence to schedules.

I have argued elsewhere (Smith 1984) that what many villagers find admirable in the European way of working is not simply its temporal coordination and regularity, but what they perceive as the spontaneous cooperative spirit that makes European coordination and regularity possible. This helps explain villagers' admiration for the European way of working, even though most know that when Papua New Guineans work *for* Europeans, coordination and regularity are the products of hierarchical control.

Perceptions of spontaneous European cooperation and regularity have arisen from the juxtaposition of indigenous conceptions of the relationship of social harmony to material well-being and the prominence of Catholicism in villagers' experience of the European world. In the indigenous view, success in many productive endeavors — such as hunting, fishing, and gardening — depends as much on avoiding social conflict as on technical skills or the amount of labor invested. One could say of Kragur views of work, as Schwimmer (1979:301) says of Orokaiva gardening, that: "Time is... a highly inappropriate measure of useful activity..." Similarly, much serious illness is thought to be caused by deceased forebears who mete out illness to those who have angered their living descendants, whether the living will it or not. Healthy people, productive gardens, good fishing and hunting are evidence that a village is free from rankling disputes and unexpressed anger. There is, then, indigenous precedent for viewing material prowess as a manifestation of a morally commendable state of good social relations. Catholicism's apparent importance in the European way of life as seen from Kragur has exacerbated that tendency. Some villagers, especially younger villagers, seem to have developed an admiration for the purely secular and instrumental efficiency of the European style of work. But the prominence of Catholicism, with its emphasis on ritual action and morality, in the European encounter appears to have helped foster among others the impression that European material prowess has a primarily moral and magico-religious basis. Further, it has helped foster the impression that this has something to do with characteristically time-conscious industrial modes of labor.

Catholic missionaries' teachings of Christian brotherhood, cessation of warfare and sorcery, and so on were inextricably mixed with inculcation of new habits of punctuality and temporal regularity in work on mission plantations and schooling in Catholic schools. Punctuality and regularity in ritual observance was not the least of the concerns of early missionaries and it is a prime concern of present day village Catholic leaders (cf. Barker, chapter 9). A Melanesian Pidgin version of the *Prayer Book and Hymnal for Catholic Natives of New Guinea* (Anonymous 1968), which I came across in Kragur, lists failure to pray regularly and to be punctual at Mass as sins one should reveal to the confessor. Village Catholic leaders often publicly harangue those who come late, or not at all, to daily prayer meetings and weekly services. Although full collective participation was important in some aspects of indigenous magico-religious practice, the Catholic demand for methodical temporal precision and regularity in ritual action has no precedent. Given substantial indigenous precedent for associating material well-being with social harmony, Catholicism's close association with new temporal patterns seems to have led many villagers to see the time consciousness characteristic of European work organization as at least in part a manifestation of a novel form of social harmony and a magico-religiously effective ingredient in the materially successful form of European cooperation.[3] One can construct nearly the full chain of reasoning from villagers' own statements, if allowed to draw freely from different persons and contexts; but the perceptions I describe here are probably less the product of conscious reflection than of the habitual application of taken-for-granted assumptions.

To use E.P. Thompson's (1967:85) language, many Kragur villagers are still fighting against time rather than about it, but Western industrial temporal perspectives are making inroads. Catholicism's role in lending European modes of time-reckoning and time-conscious activity organization the aura of forms of ritual action facilitates that process, motivating villagers to acquire European temporal concepts, fostering emulation of European forms of activity organization, and encouraging changes in the temporal structure of daily life that provide a context in which European temporal concepts and values are more plausible and compelling (Smith 1982a:516, 1984:133). Acquisition of western industrial temporal perspectives is a key dimension of the process of capitalist incorporation. It prepares villagers to accommodate to the rhythm of wage labor, and the further compartmentalization of the highly "polychronic" (Hall 1983) indigenous activity stream. Perhaps more important, it sets the stage for transformation of labor into a commodity with a monetary value, and the conceptual differentiation of a category of "work" appropriate to commoditized labor. As Comaroff puts it: "If labor is to be reducible to a compensation independent of the value it generates, then time becomes its irreducible measure; for time itself is then equatable with money... During the process of proletarianization, the impartial clock prizes labor free from its embeddedness in undifferentiated social practice, setting apart 'work' from 'leisure'..." (1985:142; cf. Thompson 1967).

The association between moral superiority and success in the new economic order to which prevalent views of European work and temporal conduct contribute also facilitates the process of capitalist incorporation. Pre-colonial Kragur society was not without hierarchy and inequality. But in the new world villagers are entering they are already encountering new and more pronounced forms of inequality; from the gross disparities between European wealth and rural New Guinean poverty, to the differences between village people and the emerging urban indigenous elite, to new distinctions arising among villagers themselves (Smith 1985). The stability of the new order depends in large part on people's acceptance of these new divisions. Believing or even suspecting that European wealth and attendant political power is based on moral superiority has undoubtedly lent European dominance some legitimacy in villagers' eyes, as is suggested by the pointed criticism that villagers often level at their own work habits when comparing them with those of Europeans. "We're not ready yet," says one middle-aged man, "We can't do anything right" (cf. Smith 1984:128-130).

I have argued elsewhere (Smith 1985) that new indigenous elites — lacking sufficient resources to satisfy expectations born of independence and lacking the foreigners' mystique — may find it more difficult to legitimate their power and privilege than did the colonial rulers. Kragur villagers' assumption of the moral basis of European dominance may not transfer readily to other Papua New Guineans. Yet the association between virtue and success in the new socioeconomic system that has been forged could provide a precedent for a moral justification of new post-colonial forms of inequality. A few Kragur young people are attaining significant success in the world beyond the village, but in the years to come most will probably become members of a poor peasantry or an urban proletariat. Believing or suspecting that success in the new order is somehow the product of virtue could lead them to regard their position in the new class hierarchy as their just reward.[4]

Increasing experience of market relations and wage labor and the diminishing importance of Catholicism relative to other secular and religious institutions in their environment are probably making it harder for villagers to romanticize the European way of life and ignore the element of coercion in European-style cooperation. I have been more impressed, however, with the persistance of romanticized views than with their attenuation.

I have emphasized the role that villagers themselves have played in creating perceptions that precipitate them uncomprehendingly into deeper entanglement with the new order. I do not wish to imply, however, that their involvement with Catholicism made this in any way inevitable. Whatever one may think of the results, this is a product of the same exercise of autonomy within structured circumstances that has also led villagers to use Catholicism in fashioning a new positive identity and in expressing their discontent with their lot in the new world, topics I turn to next.

CATHOLICISM AND CONTEMPORARY IDENTITY

The job of securing villagers' acquiescence to the new order is far from done. A significant case in point is the way in which Catholicism has lent itself to efforts to create a positive contemporary identity that bolsters individual and community integrity in the face of the new order's assaults. Villagers create and maintain this identity in part by claiming an historical relationship to the Catholic deity, God, independent of their relationship to the mission, and by claiming the continuity of Catholicism with indigenous values.

When villagers says things like "Our ancestors were close to God," they may mean this quite literally. The story of God's appearance to a Kragur man, Masos, years before the arrival of the first missionaries is well known in the village (cf. Kaplan, chapter 7). Sometime around the turn of the century, Masos — a respected leader before his meeting with God — was at the place called Sumulau, where one of Kairiru's many streams passes close to the village. He was sharpening his stone knife on a large boulder while his small granddaughter (the mother of the current Catholic leader) played in the water, when suddenly he found that his hands were stuck fast to the rock. Afraid that this was the work of a *masalai,* or dangerous nature spirit, he sent his granddaughter running back to the village to tell people to bring gifts for the spirit. But when she returned — accompanied by men bringing bananas, coconuts, and shell rings — they found Masos already free. He told them that while he waited for his granddaughter's return he had heard a voice speaking to him saying that the being's name was God and that it lived above in the sky. God had given him a set of instructions to convey to the other people of the village and had told him that he wished to bless Kragur that it might prosper. Following God's instructions Masos told the villagers that they must sweep well inside their houses and burn all old and decaying bark mats, fiber skirts, and string bags and put on clean new skirts and bark-cloth loincloths. A few who told me this story added that God also instructed them not to fight or steal among themselves, and not to kill strangers who came to the village but to give them food and a place to sleep and treat them well.

Masos was dead by the time the first catechists arrived in Kragur, but when they did, as villagers told me, Kragur people were able to say "Yes, we already know about God and his teachings." It is said that many of those who had greeted Masos' story skeptically became convinced he had spoken the truth when they heard the missionaries also speak of God. This independent relationship to God is an important part of the religious consciousness of Kragur people. The leader of contemporary village Catholicism expresses few of the ambivalent attitudes toward the mission that simmer below the surface of many villagers' outward devotion; yet even he pointed out to me that I should be familiar with the Masos story so that I did not think that in his preaching he was simply parroting the mission.[5]

Some see God's appearance in Kragur as recognition of an admirable moral tradition that extends into the past well before the time of Masos. Today, villagers speak in Pidgin of the "gutpela pasin bilong Kragur;" that is, Kragur's good way. To simplify a more complex phenomenon (Smith 1978:77-101, 332-361), this is Kragur people's claimed exceptional hospitality, generosity, and cooperativeness. The interesting point about this idea of Kragur's special moral qualities is that it links Catholicism with indigenous notions of virtuous behavior. *Pasin i wankain* — that is, the customs or moral codes are the same — say villagers when comparing Catholicism and its teachings of Christian charity and brotherhood with what they claim as an indigenous emphasis on generosity and hospitality (cf. Flinn, chapter 11; Kaplan, chapter 7). They assert that they are good Catholics because they have long tradition of living in terms of a similar moral code.

For example, in 1975-76 villagers refused to allow me to pay them money for food and various services, including building my house, preferring instead to enter into gift-giving relationships. They explained that this was consistent with Catholicism — noting that missionaries had preached to them that excessive concern with money was sinful — and that to give things away without thought of reward, to *givim nating* in Pidgin, was also a custom with deep indigenous roots (cf. Trompf, chapter 4). Some villagers told me that they knew that Whites made their visitors — even members of their own families — pay money for food and shelter, and that many Papua New Guineans were also falling under the influence of that unfortunate custom. These views, of course, are a romanticization of indigenous practice and an exaggeration of European practice. And like Kragur villagers' intense involvement in Catholicism, emphasis on this dimension of the mission's message is also to some extent an adaptation to Kragur's isolation from ready opportunity to participate in the cash economy.[6] But none of this invalidates the essential message: to be a good Catholic is to behave in a way that is consistent with contemporary versions of the ideals of a non-market economy of gift-giving and delayed reciprocity.[7]

I could multiply examples, but the point is that villagers have used Catholicism to create a way of feeling good about themselves in a world in which many of the traditional bases of positive identity have been destroyed. Comparison with European wealth and political power, for example, has radically devalued traditional scales of material wealth and political accomplishment. A claim to an independent historical relationship to the Catholic deity allows villagers to associate themselves with Catholicism without sacrificing a claim to autonomy or seeming to devalue the pre-colonial past. Weaving together the claim to being exceptionally good Catholics with an interpretation of Catholicism that finds in it continuity with ideals rooted in pre-capitalist society gives those ideals contemporary significance, helping to keep them alive and helping those who still find them compelling to do so with less ambivalence (cf. Armstrong, chapter 12).

Villagers' contemporary identity is, however, subject to modification. I doubt that there has ever been unanimity among villagers concerning the exact parameters of Kragur's moral uniqueness. For example, toward the end of my first stay in Kragur, when I had come to know them better, some of the younger men told me that they would gladly have accepted wages for building my house, but their elders had forbidden it. This may reflect political struggle between the old and the young. That is, younger men may have felt that work for wages would give them more freedom from the authority of their elders, who would take the lead in a more traditional endeavor. Such differences between old and young are also in part the product of the young's greater experience of an outside world increasingly more preoccupied with buying and selling than with praying and confessing. Time and change have affected the attitudes of older villagers too. To a few, the coming of national independence in 1975 seems to have called for rethinking established customs. In 1976, complaining of her relatives' frequent requests for the home-grown tobacco hanging in the rafters of her house, one older woman explained to me, "We're Papua New Guinea now. They should pay for my tobacco!" But, while some villagers are modifying the identity fashioned in the decades since European contact, few if any are rejecting it outright. One young man's formulation illustrates the direction modification is taking. He says:

> We young people should do as the Australians do... when someone comes to the village we can't just give things to him. He should pay rent and things like that... We Kragur people are good people, we're generous and helpful... I think the people in my village are good people, but they're a little mixed up too.

He has not relinquished the claim to special virtues that link the past and the present, but he is redefining those virtues to be more compatible with the larger political economy (cf. Smith 1982b).

CARGO AND DISCONTENT

Although romanticized perceptions of the basis of European wealth and power lend legitimacy to new forms of inequality, the legitimacy of post-colonial elites is provisional (Smith 1985); undercurrents of discontent with European domination have long coexisted with outward acceptance of European political and economic primacy. Millenarian hopes of deliverance from poverty and powerlessness relative to European and other elites have been percolating in Kragur at least since prior to World War II (Smith 1978:258-282). The influence of Catholicism has been neither a necessary nor a sufficient condition for the growth of such millenarian hopes. But given the radical devaluation of indigenous standards of material wealth following European contact, the importance of Catholicism — carrying Christianity's messianic message — during the colonial period, and indigenous conceptions of the magico-religious roots of prosperity, Catholicism's deep implication in millenarian ideas and cargo cult practices is not surprising.

Some Kragur villagers are aware of two of the most widespread and enduring cargo cults in Papua New Guinea, the Yali movement and the Peli Association, the latter of which is centered in the East Sepik Province. I know of only two instances, however, of large scale, overt cargo cult involvement by Kragur villagers. One of these, just prior to World War II, was allegedly based in another north coast village, but a few young men from Kragur are said to have taken part in the marching and drilling on the pattern of European soldiers that was a major part of cult ritual. The other instance took place in Kragur and peaked in the early 1970s. Only one of the two largest of the tripartite divisions is said to have become deeply involved in the cult, suggesting that cult participation had more to do with social and political allegiances than ideological differences (cf. Schwartz 1968b:27). Failure to produce results contributed to the decline in public interest in the cult; but so also did accusations of sorcery against one of the cult leaders. The principal cult ritual was communal prayer in the village burial grounds. The burial grounds themselves are artifacts of Catholicism for in the past the dead were buried beneath the houses of their living kin. Villagers offered prayers of two kinds: Catholic prayer — specifically, the rosary — and what one villager calls "our own prayer" — that is, petitioning deceased kin.

During my research in Kragur many villagers were loath to discuss past cargo cult activities. A handful, however, often spoke eagerly to me, in private, of their ideas about European wealth, Papua New Guinean poverty, and the Europeans' religion, Catholicism. Some of the cult lore they recounted — allegorical tales of riches and supernatural power — had no explicitly Catholic content. But they also told tales of the miraculous powers of bishops and priests that hold out the promise of sudden transformation of villagers' lot (cf. Huber 1987:120; 1988).

Such stories are not consistent in tone. One village man, for example, told me that some European priests know how to get money from the dead, and not only have withheld the secret, but have used it to solicit money from the dead ancestors of indigenous Papua New Guineans, money that should rightfully belong to the Papua New Guineans themselves. Some even suggest that the emerging indigenous elite may know more than it is telling. One Kragur man told me, "You [Whites] understand how money comes and goes, but we don't understand...." He then wondered aloud whether Michael Somare, the Prime Minister at the time, also understood but for some reason hadn't yet revealed the secret to the masses.[8] Another, however, told how priests on Tumleo had first taught the indigenous people how to successfully petition their dead kin for wealth, but later deprived them of that power after the people began behaving lewdly and riotously, breaking the mission's rules of conduct. While stories of deceitful priests and secretive national leaders cast poor Papua New Guineans as victims of injustice, the story of Tumleo casts them as having brought their fate upon themselves. So also do the parallels some villagers draw between Kairiru myths and the Christian myths of Adam and Eve and Cain and Abel, finding therein explanations for their ancestors' loss of the esoteric knowledge supposed to underly European wealth.

I do not think, however, that one could neatly sort those who have been involved with cargo cults by their views on the origin of the present state of things — that is, whether it is the result of blatant injustice or a fall from grace. Some seem to harbor both hope of fully justified deliverance and a nagging fear that they are getting only what they deserve. Among all who still cling to the cult lore, however, there is the hope of somehow achieving parity with those who look down on them from higher social strata, upsetting the existing social order, confirming their shaken self-worth, or regaining grace. Although cargo cult belief and speculation in Kragur is informed by both doubts about the worth of indigenous ways and anger at perceived injustice, it serves in all cases as an expression of profound discontent with the present order and a reservoir of hopes — albeit fantastic hopes — that it can be changed.

There was no organized, collective cargo cult activity in Kragur during either of my stays there, in 1975-76 or 1981. A few villagers, however, were still trying to find the secrets hidden in the cult lore. What looks like orthodox Catholicism in Kragur also at times has a cult-like intensity, and some have clearly attached extravagant hopes to their dogged regimen of ritual observance — for example, in the Legion of Mary, which is now defunct but which was active in the East Sepik Province for a number of years.[9]

AMBIGUITY AND HISTORICAL POSSIBILITIES

The introduction of Catholicism in Kragur has been inseparable from political and economic colonization. It is easy to see missionization as primarily a part of the process of transforming Papua New Guineans into participants in a new kind of political economy. Certainly Catholicism has furthered this transformation in Kragur by acting as the thin wedge of European colonial power and aiding in the transformation of indigenous temporal perspectives and the legitimation of new forms of inequality. But, as I have pointed out, Catholicism has also contributed to Kragur villagers' attempts to affirm indigenous non-capitalist values, and the growth of millenarian expressions of discontent with the post-contact order. Two major factors account for Catholicism's equivocal role in the long process of incorporation. The first of these is the varied potential meanings to be found in mission practice and precept, a variety that reflects the tension in Christianity itself concerning the relationship of becoming like the Europeans to becoming Christians. Christianity carries messages of millenarian deliverance from all human social orders and teaches moral ideals that are easy to see as contradicting the mores of daily life in a modern capitalist economy. But Christianity came to Kragur, as it has come to many other peoples, in an institutional package decidedly the product of the European social and cultural order.

Second, even had Catholicism spoken with a clearer voice, its message would have been subject to interpretation, since villagers have sought to understand it in terms of their own experience and cultural categories. The most obvious example of this is the variety of ways in which Kragur people have sought to make sense of God. Villagers' contribution to integrating Catholicism with their own experience has also, as discussed earlier, extended to their efforts to discern its relationship to both the indigenous gift economy and European material prowess. The equivocal and inconstant nature of the Catholicism presented to villagers has given an added dimension to the necessary task of forging culturally relevant interpretations. Thus, these interpretations partake of Catholicism's ambivalence toward the European world, as well as villagers' own. Hence, one finds villagers using elements of Catholicism to extol non-capitalist virtues and register deep discontent with the new order at the same time that other dimensions of mission Catholicism are contributing to the formation of perceptions that further capitalist incorporation.

The political significance of all this is another question. Time and change may well weaken the tendency to romanticize European forms of work and cooperation. Nevertheless, at present, Catholicism clearly continues to further Kragur people's accommodation to and acceptance of the new political economy that encompasses them. But what about the counter currents it feeds? Have they any actual or potential political significance?

When working for wages far from the village, Kragur people confront the new capitalist political economy at close quarters; and in the village they do not escape pressures to alter their way of life — for example, to devote more time to cash-cropping or to participate in new political institutions. Villagers also face such immediate demands of the new order as those transmitted through the village councillor that they adapt their pattern of activities to a regular weekly schedule and submit to greater regimentation on days designated for council work. As I have discussed at greater length elsewhere (Smith 1982a), villagers sometimes react strongly to the councillor's attempts to impose greater temporal order on their activities. In the face of harangues to respond quickly to the summons of the village bell or to cooperate more readily with the councillor's plans for communal work on inter-village trail maintenance or other projects, villagers often grumble and practice passive noncooperation; and occasionally someone erupts in shouts of protest that they are men, not dogs or pigs, and need no one to tell them how to work. Catholicism does not figure in these acts of overt protest and resistance.

The counter currents in which Catholicism figures prominently are more subtle. One could even argue that, although on the surface they seem to push against the grain of the new political economy, they have little concrete political significance and may even smooth the way for the gradual transformation of villagers' way of life. While the contemporary identity villagers have forged using elements of Catholicism does give new life to old values, it concedes the dominance of capitalist market relations in such spheres as cash cropping and migrant wage labor. The identity is real and potent, but it is compartmentalized (cf. Barker, chapter 9). This view of the situation is reminiscent of Laitin's model of hegemony and culture, elaborated in his study of Yoruba politics and religion. Laitin argues that within multicultural societies a particular cultural "subsystem" may exercise hegemony in the political sphere, defining the political order — and, one could say here, the economic order — in its own terms. Other "subsystems" can coexist, but they "do not necessarily threaten the political order" (1986:181). It could even be argued that the existence of a counter-capitalist identity, in a parallel but separate world, serves capitalist incorporation by channeling expression of a competing value system in a way that poses no direct threat to the larger order of wage labor and commercial transactions.

Concerning the political significance of cargo cults, it can be argued, of course, that an obsession with supernatural deliverance impedes the development of more sophisticated political consciousness and distracts people from effective secular political activity. In discussions of poverty and inequality with Kragur villagers I sometimes found it frustrating when talk of the magico-religious roots of European wealth and speculation on the reasons for cult failures displaced talk of secular political and economic issues. Similarly, cargo cults have been described as divisive (Schwartz 1968b:42) rather than as stirrings of nationalist unity (Worsely 1968). Cult activities in Kragur have at times aggravated intra-village factionalism (cf. Smith 1989).

To leave matters here, however, would be to dismiss these cultural counter currents too lightly. As the Comaroff's (1986:261) note, "The *real-politik* of oppression dictates that resistance be expressed in domains seemingly apolitical, and the dynamics of resistance among oppressed people... have shown that the connection between seemingly unworldly powers and movements and the politics of liberation is subtle and various, denying simple dichotomization in terms of resistance and compliance." Like the messages the Catholic mission has brought to Kragur, the phenomena they have helped shape also display multiple possibilities, the expression of which will be governed by changing historical circumstances.[10] Certainly the role of cargo cults in the development of secular political action is complex (Schwartz 1968b:43), and does not lend itself to simple blanket judgments. Similarly, villagers' contemporary identity, fused from tradition and Catholicism, displays contradictory potentials. As noted earlier, however, changing circumstances appear to be leading toward a narrower definition of Kragur's special moral qualities, one that cedes even more spheres of life to capitalist market relations.

Laitin argues that "hegemony can create a dominant subsystem; it cannot create a congruent and harmonious social system" (183). And within the larger society there may exist "noncongruent... cultural subsystems that hold within themselves the sources for counterhegemony (183)." At this time, it is admittedly difficult to imagine the counter currents to capitalist incorporation described here as sources of serious challenges to capitalist hegemony. But it is best to keep an open mind, if for no other reason than to give due recognition to the complexity and indeterminacy of the role of Christianity in the colonial encounter. In addition, one can anticipate a need to recall such counter currents when trying to understand the course of events. Fernand Braudel writes that "victorious events come about as the result of many possibilities," and that "for one possibility which is actually realized, innumerable others have drowned," often leaving little trace. But, Braudel argues, "it is necessary to give them their place because the losing movements are forces which have at every moment affected the final outcome" (quoted in Gutman

1973:580).[11] One cannot understand contemporary Kragur Catholicism without recognizing these counter currents. We must wait and see what traces they will leave.

NOTES

This discussion is based on fieldwork conducted in Kragur village in 1975-76 and briefly in 1981. The latter was funded in part by a grant from the Institute for Intercultural Studies, Inc.

1. Whereas the Protestant missionaries in South Africa described by the Comaroffs (1986) became deeply embroiled in attempts to shape institutional political arrangements — for example, forming alliances with chiefs and lobbying Great Britain for support of their political visions — my impression is that the Catholic mission in the Sepik has been primarily concerned with achieving a *modus vivendi* with prevailing secular powers. This is apparent, for example, in the Society of the Divine Word's relations with first German then Australian governments in the mission's first three decades in the Sepik. In these early years of the colonial period the SVD did find itself at odds with the German New Guinea Company and the German colonial government over the issue of land on which to establish plantations and mission stations. The mission, however, argued its case by stressing the lack of conflict between its goals and those of secular commercial and political institutions. In a letter to a member of the German Reichstag in 1900, Father Eberhard Limbrock, the first SVD Prefect Apostolic in what was then German New Guinea appealed for assistance in acquiring more land for mission plantations, arguing that "through cultivation the land will become healthier and more productive, the people will learn how to work and have order in their lives, and businessmen will acquire a continually expanding field for their activity and thereby greater profits" (quoted in Wiltgen 1969:337). Following the establishment of the Mandated Territory of New Guinea under Australian rule in the aftermath of the World War I, Father Limbrock's successor, Father Andreas Puff, made the case for continuation of the mission's work — in particular its plantations — to the Territory's first administrator in similar terms: "...like every colonist and business firm, the mission has a natural right to regular productive work... the missionaries work for charity and for the benefit of the country, and so their work should not be less esteemed than that of businessmen" (quoted in Wiltgen 1969:358; cf. Huber 1988).
2. The dead are said to make people sick to retaliate against those who have angered the deads' living kin. In curing, male villagers (who also, it is said, speak on behalf of their female kin) publicly voice their various complaints about the behavior of the patient until it is felt that the most plausible causal grievance has been located. Some form of restitution or reconciliation is then arranged.
3. Thompson (1967) and Rodgers (1978) each describe the significant contribution religious institutions made to the growth of industrial capitalism in Europe and North America by promulgating new work habits and temporal values. Under the influence of Weber (1958 [1920]), we often think of Protestantism as the religious impetus behind the rationalization of activity patterns characteristic of capitalism. It is well to remember, however, that Catholic monasticism played a major role in the development of "the earnest regulation of time-sequences" and "the orderly punctual life" in the West (Mumford 1963 [1934]:13-18). Comaroff and Comaroff (1986:12) contrast Cath-

olic evangelism in 17th century Mexico — which "relied heavily on collective ritual and dramatic spectacle... often incorporating local populations in a depiction of their own subjection" — with Protestant missions which "taught the unassuming 'arts of civilization'... whose mundane logic worked upon the processes that most forcefully shaped the self and 'natural' reality." The Catholic mission in the Sepik, however, also placed great emphasis on the latter endeavor. From the standpoint of Kragur villagers I suspect all Whites or Europeans look rather "Protestant" in their never-ending concern with time, order, and material efficiency.

4. Sennett and Cobb (1972) describe working class belief in the association between material success and individual moral adequacy in the United States and note its function in legitimating class divisions maintained by structural limits on social mobility.
5. Accounts of such pre-missionary encounters with God apparently are common in Papua New Guinea. Some Kragur villagers, in fact, told me that the inhabitants of nearby Walis island also claimed that God had visited them before the first missionaries arrived. See also Chowning (chapter 3), Trompf (chapter 4) and Kaplan (chapter 7).
6. This hasn't entirely escaped the notice of some villagers. On one occasion an older Kragur man was telling me of how the people of a mainland village he knew weren't good people because they thought only of money. He concluded, however, that "Kragur people are just the same, only they don't have a way to get to the market. If they did, they'd be the same way."
7. Villagers seem to be untroubled by the fact that delayed reciprocity is not exactly the same as ideal Christian charity, which expects no return. While it is clear that it is delayed reciprocity, not bottomless charity, that rules in practice, villagers often speak of the indigenous norm as though it were actually analogous to the Christian ideal.
8. Villagers sometimes asked me questions about money. When one cult aficionado found my explanation of the origin and value of money unsatisfactory, rather than calling me a liar he politely suggested: "You're still young, they haven't told you yet" (cf. Chowning, chapter 3).
9. The contemporary identity villagers have constructed also can give off an aroma of ritual. A few villagers give the impression that by systematically minimizing involvement in monetary relations they hope to show themselves worthy of the supernatural favor that would reveal the secret of wealth on a greater scale.
10. Piven and Cloward (1982:143) make a related point in a study of the containment of class conflict in the United States. They write, "social control is never complete, and never enduring. The very mechanisms that effect such control at one historical moment generate the possibilities for political mobilization at another."
11. Comaroff (1985:261) makes a related point, arguing that "if we confine our historical scrutiny to the zero-sum heroics of revolution successfully achieved, we discount the vast proportion of human social action which is played out, perforce, on a more humble scale."

9

MISSION STATION AND VILLAGE: RELIGIOUS PRACTICE AND REPRESENTATIONS IN MAISIN SOCIETY

John Barker

With few exceptions Melanesians have adopted Christianity remarkably quickly. Students usually attribute this to Melanesian "pragmatism:" for example, the desire to acquire superior technology, knowledge and power from Europeans, or to end local hostilities (Forman 1982:89ff; Hogbin 1958). Studies of conversion, however, dwell on moments of transformation and disruption, on initial conversions and outbreaks of "cargoism." What light can an analytic focus on pragmatism and practice shed on the neglected topic of long-term accommodations to Christianity? If Melanesians initially preferred mission practice over Christian theology, how is this preference reflected in the emerging "practical religions" of Christian communities? And what are the implications of a reshaping of the practical world for Melanesian understandings of themselves, of Christianity, and of the larger world from whence Christianity came?

In this chapter I examine the practical environments of an Anglican mission station and the surrounding village of Uiaku on southwestern Collingwood Bay in Oro Province, Papua New Guinea. I suggest that: (1) the mission station and village form distinct and incongruent practical environments; (2) both environments persist with support from the Maisin, who move easily between them; (3) the environments therefore should be regarded as complimentary aspects of one society; (4) the biculturalism of Maisin society complements wider hegemonic structures in Papua New Guinea; and (5) Maisin talk about the relation between the station and the village reveals on another level their attempts to reconcile their cultural identity with their involvement in the dominant political and economic system of Papua New Guinea.

The analysis has four stages. First, I examine how mission practices hastened the Maisins' entry into the colonial system. Following this, I describe Uiaku society in the 1980s, focusing on the practical dichotomy between village and station activities and their associated values and orientations. I turn in the third section to Maisin representations of the station-village relation. I identify and discuss three permutations — an exchange relationship, the station as model for the village, and the village as model for the station. The concluding discussion focuses on two questions arising from the analysis: how Maisin biculturalism is sustained, and possible directions in the station-village relationship.

THE MISSION STATION

Mission stations spearheaded Christian expansion in the nineteenth and twentieth centuries. Stations served as base camps for the evangelization of the pagan countryside, housing European missionaries, their indigenous assistants and native boarders, and providing support services: stores, plantations, and workshops; senior schools, teacher colleges, and theological schools; clinics and hospitals. Stations also served as boot camps for new Christians: places where novices could receive an intensive introduction to Christianity away from pagan influences (Beidelman 1982; Fountain 1969,1971).

Most students of mission stations stress their importance as instruments of acculturation. Guenther (1977:457), for example, describes them as "sample communities" — "condensed replicas or versions of the society which they represent." Such communities intensify certain Western values, institutions and contradictions. Comaroff and Comaroff (1986) argue that while missions in southern Africa differed in their notions of Christianity and attitudes to Western industrial society, their practical labors drew upon a common set of largely unconscious orientations and values drawn from their European background. Africans living at and near stations gained practical acquaintance with the ideological premises of the mission (and colonial) system by rearranging their lives according to the mission clock, by adopting the division of labor of the mission farm, and by accepting the authority of the written word. Stations, then, were the scene of a "subtle colonialization" in which Africans internalized habits of everyday life compatible with the impinging colonial order (Comaroff and Comaroff 1986:2).

Yet mission stations were not just instruments of change, they were also social systems in their own right (Beidelman 1982; Tippett 1967). Often stations dissolved into the surrounding Christianized societies once the missionaries departed. In a few cases, however, like Metlakatla in British Columbia and some "industrial" stations of the south Pacific, they became Christian communities (Barnett 1942; Heise 1967; Wetherell 1973). Although stations received their initial support from metropolitan churches, they depended upon local support to survive. Over time, some stations were reshaped by their supporters. Etherington (1976) and

Strayer (1978), for example, show how African refugees who settled at mission stations gradually assumed leadership of the emerging communities, forming a "new African culture" at once indigenous and Western (Strayer 1978:159). Burridge (1973:206) describes another permutation in which Aborigines in northwestern Australia incorporated mission stations into their nomadic social patterns of "walkabout." Indigenous peoples have thus sometimes developed mission stations into new communities and innovative forms of social organization. While the mission station at Uiaku has been an acculturative force, we shall see that it has also provided the seeds for a new kind of society.

The Anglican Mission in Uiaku Village

Anglican missionaries arrived in Papua in 1891. After establishing a base on the high plateau of Dogura, overlooking Bartle Bay, the mission gradually expanded along the northeastern coast of Papua, from East Cape to the (then) German border. The philosophy of the mission was a peculiar mixture of Anglo-Catholic conservatism and highly romanticized views of indigenous village societies. Hostile to the secular trends in European industrial society, many mission spokesmen thought they saw in Papua village life the simple values of medieval Christendom (Barker 1979:133-37, Wetherell 1977:127-30). Some argued that the church and the Papuans had a natural affinity for one another. In the words of Henry Newton, the church in Papua "is not to be a body distinct from the native life, but rather one that permeates the whole by its influence. The Mission has not come... to change native life into a parody of European or Australian civilization" (Newton 1914:251).

Culturally tolerant in philosophy, the Anglicans resembled other European missionaries in practice (Barker 1987).[1] Few of them investigated the Papuan customs they admired in the abstract. Anglican policy instead stressed conventional church teachings on the liturgy, Bible, sacraments and marriage; church discipline; and education in the "3 R's" and basic health care. A range of commonsense orientations to the world grounded these policies in routine mission practices. Some missionaries realized that mission stations could be useful vehicles for transmitting such basic orientations into native life. For example, one priest suggested in 1929:

> All the regulations and rules of the station should be formed with one clear purpose in view — the fostering of a *christian habit of life* (*sic*). In this scheme, insistence on punctuality and alert obedience (the spirit of 'work when you work' — 'Do it heartily' etc.) would naturally have a special emphasis (Gill 1929, original emphasis).

Anglican stations were modest by Papuan standards. Short on money and staff, the mission depended on villagers for building materials, labor, and food.[2] Nevertheless, the stations served as examples of Western society for the isolated Papuans of the northeast coast. In the church and classroom, villagers learned their first crucial lessons concerning the ways of the Europeans and thus entered the colonial order.

The Maisin villages lay only 80 kilometers to the west of Dogura and received periodic visits from the missionaries through the 1890s. In 1899, the mission built a regional station at Wanigela on the west side of Collingwood Bay. Two years later, Percy John Money, the lay missionary in charge at Wanigela, purchased a block of land near the center of the largest Maisin village of Uiaku, and began constructing the station. He used bush materials for most of the buildings and hired Maisin laborers, but he clearly had Western designs in mind in laying out the mission complex. The station grounds were rectangular, marked off from the surrounding village by a fence. Around the perimeter, Money built a church, classroom, houses for the station teachers, and a house for himself. Photographs taken at the time reveal that the original station varied little in design from that of the 1980s. In form as well as function, the station was an alien social system implanted in the heart of a traditional community.

Non-Europeans manned Uiaku station for most of its history: at first Vanuatu and Solomon Islands teachers and later Papuans from older parts of the mission.[3] The teachers carried on the routine work of the mission, teaching and preaching on the station and in the villages. The district missionary made the 12 kilometer trek from Wanigela at least once a month to administer Communion, marriages, and baptisms, deal with disciplinary problems, and inspect the teachers' work. The Melanesian missionaries muted the incongruities between station and village in several ways. First, the Melanesian teachers shared many cultural traits with the Maisin, including a profound respect for magic and sorcery. They also became deeply involved in local exchange networks. Further, the white missionaries did not trust the Melanesians with station boarders, so children continued to spend most of their time when out of church and school with their own people. The poverty of the mission further muted the incongruities. The teachers received support from the mission and so had to depend upon the sympathy of villagers for garden land, for food, and for labor in maintaining station buildings. The station began as an alien institution, but it was not imposed upon the Maisin in any simple sense; without the support of the villagers, the station community would never have survived.

The mission made slow but steady progress. Teachers reported steady attendance at the church and in the classroom during the first decade. The first baptisms took place in 1911 and by 1920 the majority of the younger population of Uiaku had become Christians (Barker 1985a:107). The new Christians lived amongst their pagan neighbors with few signs of tension. The missionaries at Wanigela often wondered about the sincerity of Maisin conversions. Mission log books from the early period contain a litany of complaints: Christians attending pagan death rituals, divorcing legally married spouses, or, even worse, taking second wives. Indigenous rituals and attitudes towards marriage did gradually change, but Christian teachings were often minor factors (Barker 1985a:325-32). Evidently, Maisin Christians did not feel that what they learned on the station required a sharp break with established village ways.

But Maisin did understand that their support of the mission entailed a radical change in relations with the outside world. At the time of European contact, the Maisin were the most feared raiders on Collingwood Bay. In early 1901, government police brutally "pacified" Uiaku by shooting dead three men (Monckton 1922). With this demonstration of strength, leading men became village constables responsible to the Resident Magistrate at Tufi, the government station sixty kilometers to the north. In succeeding years, both missionaries and government officers were careful to maintain distinctions in their work among the natives, but it is clear that they regarded each other as useful allies. Indeed, William MacGregor, the first Administrator, originally invited the Anglicans into Papua to complement government efforts at controlling and "civilizing" the natives (Barker 1979:33-34). The Anglicans assisted in expanding the hegemony[4] of the colonial regime in two ways. First, they helped to create a pliant work force for the emerging industries of the Territory. Second, they helped to internalize and legitimate the colonial administrative system by introducing village-level organizations based on Western models.

As I noted earlier, the Anglicans romantically wished the Papuans to remain villagers living in Christianized traditional societies. Yet the mission provided the means for many Maisin to make the transition from the village into the colonial economic system. An ability to read and write simple English and to perform calculations became important over time as clerical and then administrative positions opened to Papuans. But at least as important as the content of education, was the form of instruction in the village schools and churches. Maisin students and catechists were exposed to a novel system of authority, one based upon absolute principles rather than reciprocity: the authority of the teacher to order rote learning and to inflict punishments more or less at will, the rigid schedule of classes and services, the division of people into different Standards (grades), and so forth. Prior to the Second World War, the station provided boys with a preview of the discipline they would experience on plantations and in mining operations and, for a few, in the mission or government services. Following the War, the Anglican church established one of the first highschools in Papua. Maisin boys attended the early classes and were well placed when important government and business positions opened up for indigenous people in the period of decolonialization in the 1960s and 1970s. By 1982 a third of the Maisin population had permanently migrated to urban areas of the country, most taking well-paying positions of doctors, dentists, civil servants, businessmen, and teachers (Barker 1985a:128-31). Remittances in cash and store goods had become an essential part of the local economy. Most of the migrants, like the remaining villagers, kept their connections to the Anglican church. Indeed, six Maisin from Uiaku had become priests.

While assisting the Maisin to enter the Territorial economy, the mission also brought the institutions of the hegemonic order into the village. The Maisin, like most other Papuans, recognized no formal positions of leadership at the time of contact. Their villages were multinucleated settlements, made up of several localized patriclans. Polities above the level of hamlets were unstable, fluctuating according to the skills of influential men and contingencies that made some groups allies and others enemies. This system was unsuitable for indirect rule, and so the colonial authorities developed village-level authorities and polities, at first constables and later councils. The mission introduced the basics of the new political order into Uiaku. The church and school provided the important first lesson by serving all villagers regardless of their kinship affiliations and alliances. In the early 1920s, the mission organized the first village-level council in Uiaku to handle church affairs. The government followed soon after with its own council, made up entirely of young Christians. These early councils had limited impact. But following the Second World War the Maisin enthusiastically embraced village-level organizations. They became involved in a series of attempts to establish successful cooperatives in the area and to raise funds to build a permanent church at Uiaku (Barker 1985a:131-40). New village committees handled school matters, developed local artifacts for trade, and promoted women and youth activities. These village organizations belonged to larger regional and national bodies. By 1982, they had become the major political arena in Uiaku (Barker 1986).

The Maisin today are unequivocally Anglicans. Several generations of children have gone through the village school and have been baptized in the church. Meanwhile, the Anglican Mission has become an independent and almost entirely localized national church. The Maisin have had their own priest since 1962, and the parish is self-supporting. Since the early

1970s, the government and villagers have shared responsibility for education. The station, long supported by Maisin taxes and labor, has ceased to be a foreign institution. As we have seen, it has been a crucial agent in adapting the local community to the national order. Yet it has not been absorbed into village society as the early Anglican missionaries expected. Nor has the village society taken on the cultural qualities of the station. A large measure of the original incongruity between the station and the village remains. No longer external and impinging, this incongruence forms an important dynamic in modern Maisin society.

THE STATION AND THE VILLAGE IN UIAKU

In the early 1980s, the "ethnographic present," about 1200 rural Maisin lived in four communities along southwestern Collingwood Bay. The villagers are far from markets and, although they depend upon remittances from employed relatives for school fees, taxes, and some commodities, they meet most of their material wants by subsistence gardening, fishing, hunting and gathering, and by utilizing local bush materials. Each community has a church and the two largest, Uiaku and Airara, also have village schools offering education up to Standard six. Villagers continue to refer to the area surrounding churches and schools as 'mission stations'. And they usually call the national clergy and teachers 'missionaries' (using the English term).[5] My observations and analysis here are confined to Uiaku, but much of what I say here holds true for the other communities as well.

After some eighty years of association, the village and mission station in Uiaku are aspects of a single society. Yet they retain much of their original incongruence. The village connotes received traditions for Maisin while the station represents the values and aspirations of the outside European world. The contrast between the village and the station recapitulates in concrete form a basic tension in Maisin historical and social experience.

To say that the village connotes tradition is not to imply that there have been no important changes in village society or even that villagers are unaware of such changes. There is little if anything in village life that has not been touched by its integration into the larger society of Papua New Guinea, from the clothes worn, to the design of houses, to language.[6] Yet in its basic orientations, the village speaks to Maisin of "custom." Village life is oriented primarily by kinship and affinal relationships, by ceremonial exchange obligations incurred through the life cycle, and by the cycle of subsistence activities and informal exchanges. Introduced elements are important and influential, but the people tend to place them in a matrix of relationships and practices which they attribute to their ancestral past (Barker 1985a).

The station has also changed in important ways. There are now two distinct kinds of 'missionary' — clergymen and teachers — where before teacher-evangelists combined both roles; villagers play a larger participatory role in setting policy in the church and school than before; and the station has come to form the main venue of political activities for the villages and the region. Yet villagers are not entirely anachronistic when they refer to the church and school as the 'mission station'. The station stands apart from the village not only physically, but also in its symbolic orientations which are clearly Western. The continuing incongruities between the station and the village freeze the two localities into archetypical opposites: the "modern" versus the "traditional," the "Western" versus the "native," and the "Christian" versus the "pagan." From a historical viewpoint, the station and village are intertwined components of a single society. When viewed ethnographically, however, they reveal distinct practical orientations that suggest they are best understood as sub-cultures.

There are clear spatial dimensions to the demarcation between station and village life (cf. Comaroff and Comaroff 1986). Like other Maisin settlements, Uiaku is composed of a series of hamlets along the coast. Most of the hamlets are contiguous, their boundaries marked to the knowledgeable by a tree or stream bed. Three hamlets, which I was told are more "traditional," form separate units off the main village path. Each hamlet is made up of a cluster of houses occupied by members of one or two patriclans. Villagers keep the area around their houses entirely free of grass. The houses unevenly surround a cleared area which, in some of the higher ranking clans, forms a plaza in which feasts and dances may be held. Village patterns, then, reflect kinship and to some extent inherited rank.

The station forms a large rectangular block of land located between two hamlets near the physical center of Uiaku. Station buildings include the school, the church, houses for clergy and teachers, and a shelter for meetings. The house for the priest is especially large, as he is expected to host many non-Maisin visitors to the village. Although made primarily of local materials, and built by local people, the station buildings follow urban models.[7] They are arranged around the edges of the station, connected by broad straight avenues. Low stick fences and crotons, maintained by the school children, complete the image of orderly neatness. A large grassy field takes up the center of the station and serves as a site for school assemblies and for community sports. The spatial organization of the station reflects its specialized functions and public nature.

The spatial regulation of the station is complemented by strict temporal regularity. Each day is divided by the ringing of a bell placed near the church. There is a bell for Matins, to call children to school, for the Angelus, to dismiss school, to announce church services, and to celebrate Evensong. No such regimen is observed in the village, where activities proceed according to cycles based upon subsistence needs, exchange obligations, and personal whim. As I discovered while waiting hours for village meetings first to convene and then to disperse, a sense of time scarcity is far less developed in village affairs than on the station (cf. Smith, chapter 8).

Daily activities mark another dimension of incongruence between village and station. Maisin spend most of their time engaged in labor intensive but non-specialized subsistence activities outside of the village. There are some cooperative endeavors such as beginning a garden and building a house, but mostly men and women work on their own and in domestic groups. Infants enjoy a similar autonomy. They wander around the village and in the garden, usually under the supervision of older siblings. Children learn mostly by watching and imitating their elders. Public gatherings in the village are irregular, centered around life transitions, such as marriages and puberty, and crises, including major accidents, sickness, and deaths, which are usually attributed to sorcery. Such gatherings are always arranged on kin and affinal lines and frequently involve exchanges. Individuals and work groups sometimes call on ancestral spirits to help in some endeavor such as catching pigs or chasing away the spirit of a recently deceased person. And people say that spirits and ghosts attack individuals, at which time the stricken person may seek one of the local healers (Barker 1989). There is no public worship or propitiation of spirits.

The teachers and clergy, on the other hand, instruct students and the congregation in the classroom and in the church, activities which require a high degree of specialized training. Children are discouraged from playing on the mission station; the only recreation that takes place there is organized team sports after school and on Sunday afternoons. Scheduled public events, usually connected to some aspect of the church year, are also organized on the station by teams coming from different parts of the community — no clan or kinship divisions are recognized. And, of course, interactions with the divine take the form of public Christian worship at regular times. The priest conducts a relatively ornate (High Church) service that is disciplined and somber — there are no surprise intrusions by God. The incongruence in the activities of station and village goes further, because neither in the Uiaku school nor in the church has there been much effort to accommodate the local culture. Both schooling and church services today are conducted almost entirely in

English.[8] In neither case is much village input expected or sought. By the same token, the Maisin regard the mission staff, including the priest, as strangers who have no business poking their heads into village affairs unless invited to do so.

There are also significant differences in the economies of the station and village. The villagers received occasional gifts of cash from working relatives or through the exchange network in the village, but they rely primarily on subsistence activities for their survival. The situation is reversed for the staff, who rely upon money for much of their food, but supplement it with food from their own gardens and with gifts from the villagers.

The village and station differ, finally, in their forms of authority. Influence in the village finds its basis in notions of seniority, personal power, and reciprocity. In village gatherings, the senior members of the high ranked clans are formally respected by other villagers and allowed to speak first. Actual influence in village affairs, however, is more or less earned through a man's or woman's ability to gather and distribute food, money and goods, and to speak well for their factions. Like other Melanesians, Maisin have nary a good word for people who appear to them to be greedy, secretive, bossy, overly rich, or in some other way non-reciprocal. Such people are seen as prime targets for sorcerers, and may well be sorcerers themselves. Leadership in the village, then, is situational and contingent — so much so that it is often hard to distinguish between the leaders and the led. The political process involves much gossip and much negotiation.

The priest and teachers are obvious figures of authority within the confines of the classroom and the church. Their authority to speak and advise is non-reciprocal and originates from outside of the village. Similarly the station is formally governed according to explicit rules set down by the church constitution and by the Department of Education, and subject to only limited negotiation with the villagers.

The village and station, therefore, differ along several important dimensions: spatial and temporal relations, activities, economics, and assumptions about authority. We would seem to be dealing with two cultural systems.

Villagers often speak of the station and village as two distinct societies inhabited, respectively, by foreign 'missionaries' and village people. One friend advised me to take pity on the poor 'missionaries':

> They are station people. They follow the time and they do their things on time. As a village man, I eat breakfast when I want. Or I make my garden or go fishing. It is not like [the] mission staff. They cannot just

> run off. That is the greatest difference. If the station people use their money unwisely they have to pray that people will help them. We in the village just need to look for food and anything we can collect will do. For the mission staff, it can be hopeless (recorded in 1983, in English).

This perspective celebrates the power of the villagers over the station staff, but it is misleading in two respects. First, it ignores that the village has become increasingly oriented towards the cash economy in recent decades and, because of this, increasingly dependent on the station as a point of entry into the national education system and to jobs. Second, it ignores the reality that not only the staff but villagers spent a not inconsiderable part of their lives engaged in station activities and submitting themselves to station discipline. My friend, for example, attended the village school in his youth, went to high school and the church teachers' college, and then became a 'missionary' teacher in another village before returning to care for his ailing father. Along with his village activities, he spent some time each month collecting stewardship funds in the village in support of church work. Maisin can oppose the station and the village as cultural patterns but they can hardly reject one for the other. To do so would mean rejecting part of themselves.

REPRESENTATIONS OF THE VILLAGE AND STATION

The village and the mission station in Uiaku exist in an ambiguous relationship. They are mutually dependent aspects of Maisin existence, domains of a single society, and yet they concretely represent opposed and exclusive practical environments. This potential exclusiveness is continually overcome in numerous small ways: teachers make gardens and enter local exchange networks, for example, and villagers rebuild their houses to conform to station styles. Maisin sustain and for the most part seem comfortable with their biculturalism. Yet at times they speak of the station and village in ways that highlight the potential tension between an indigenous tradition and an introduced modernity. The ways Maisin speak of the relation between the mission station and the village, and between 'missionaries' and 'villagers', are of special interest for they reveal how the people are attempting to reconcile their cultural sense of themselves with the demands and opportunities they are experiencing and seeing on the periphery of the world system. In this section I shall report on how villagers represented this relationship in general discussion during community meetings and in a series of structured interviews I conducted on Christian ideas and practices in 1983.

Missionaries and Villagers as Exchange Partners

The Maisin most commonly contrast themselves with other socio-linguistic groups along Collingwood Bay and with their own 'missionaries', the teachers and clergy living on the station. They tend to picture missionaries and villagers as living very different types of lives, but nevertheless morally linked through enduring exchange relations (cf. Schwimmer 1973:77-81). An elderly church councillor, for example, explained to me why villagers support mission staff: "They are not from here. They came from another place to help us. So we must also help them.... They are teaching our children, so anything that they need or want for their work or the mission station we must give as payback." Such 'payback' may include food, labor, materials, companionship, and, especially since Uiaku became part of a self-supporting parish in 1975, a relatively large sum of money in clergy wages and church materials as well as school supplies.

My informants were clear that each side had something different to bring to the exchange. An elder in the neighboring village of Sinapa, told me, [The clergy] "perform the service and see sick people. They pray for all and give the Holy Sacrament." In return, as it were, the clergy receive material support from the villagers. As in most Melanesian societies, these exchanges are not simple business arrangements. They are means of creating, manipulating, and monitoring social relationships (cf. Kahn 1986; Weiner 1976). I found that many Maisin rationalized paying stewardship in support of the clergy, attending church, or bringing food to local teachers as types of prestations. At a church council meeting, for example, one man argued:

> If nobody goes to church the priest wastes his time. So you must think that when the priest starts to work to go and attend church first and then come back to do your own work. When the attendance is down it shows that we hate the priest and the deacon. If we want them to stay we must show the sign by attending.

By the same token, 'missionaries' are expected to reciprocate by doing their jobs well, visiting with villagers, and contributing to village events. But many villagers complained that as wages have risen, and the teachers and clergy have become less dependent on local people, the 'missionaries' are not always meeting their reciprocal obligations. One elder told me: "In the old days the teachers always shared their things with the village people. Their wives would always go into the village to cook. Now they only stay on the station." Consequently, villagers are also doing less for the teachers.

For many villagers, particularly those who have lived in Uiaku most of their lives, the ideal relation between 'missionaries' and villagers should be one of balanced reciprocity. They express this state in the term *marawa-wawe,* a word that suggests peace, friendliness, and moral equivalence (Barker 1985b:283). Feasting is a particularly potent index of *marawa-wawe.* Thus several informants stressed feasts taking place on the mission station as representations of the ideal relation of village and station: "On big days like St. Thomas [the annual patronal church festival in Uiaku] all of the people go in and help the missionaries." Traditionally, the intertribal feast marked the culmination of a series of exchanges leading towards balance between the sides, to *marawa-wawe.* The church feast similarly marks an enduring peaceful relationship between mission staff and villagers. But it (potentially) unites all the factions of the village in one exchange — something that never happens in village society. At the same time, the idiom of exchange between village and station confirms and preserves the separation of the two spheres.

Most villagers I interviewed presented an image of the station and village linked in a reciprocal relationship. Yet Maisin leaders rarely mentioned this image in public speeches. Both station and village people most often evoked it when discussing church or school matters, usually to chide one side or the other for not meeting their obligations. This representation was obviously well-known and accepted, and it probably did not require much airing. It appears to have provided a basis for the two more elaborate representations I discuss next. In both of these latter constructions, spokesmen transformed an external relationship between two autonomous and distinctive orders into an internal relationship that defined the whole Maisin community.

The Station as a Model for the Village

As a newcomer to Uiaku in 1981, I was presented with a very different image of Maisin society. My first acquaintances were high school graduates. Mostly in their 20s to mid-40s, they had returned to the village after working for several years in well-paying professions in the towns or in government service in rural areas. Many spoke fluent English. They were now expected by their less educated neighbors to serve the community by supervising local associations and economic projects (cf. Carrier 1980).

When I arrived in Uiaku, many of the villagers were occupied with preparations for St. Thomas Day, the annual patronal feast in the parish. My first language teachers, both high school graduates, were very involved in this event and, I soon discovered, in no less than five village committees. When I asked them about their committee work, they described the village as a well-regulated corporation. They listed ten organizations. Most of these, such as the Local Government Council committee, the Parents and Citizenship committee, and the Uiaku Business Group, belonged to the 'government side' of Uiaku. The Church Council and Mothers' Union were the main organizations on the 'mission side'. 'Village side' activities, not under committee control, included subsistence activities, crafts, customary ceremonies, and exchanges. According to my informants, villagers maintained a rigorous schedule of council and church work days, when the entire community turned out to labor on various community projects and repairs on and off the mission station, interspersed with work days for the Mothers' Union and Youth Club. With Sunday reserved for worship and community sports, there were only two days left when all villagers were free to pursue their own as opposed to the common good.

I soon discovered that this description told me far more about what the educated faction would like Uiaku to be than about what actually took place. My informants' depiction of village organizations resonated with a larger set of public representations embracing the relationship between mission station and village. In these representations, the station figured prominently in two ways. First, educated villagers often explicitly identified themselves with station personnel. For example, when asked about the duties of the clergy, an educated villager who had previously worked as a manager on a government oil palm project told me:

> They should make sure there is Christian living in the community — no fighting. The Church should control the disagreements in the villages. They should try to gather the people as one and bring back those people who have fallen away. They should visit the sick people regularly and find out the needs of the people. Most of all they should educate the people to know the Church, what it is there for, and how it came to be. This means they have to know Christ Himself — to be a witness.

This informant and many others said virtually identical things about the duties of village councillors, church councillors, and Mothers' Union members: in short, about all leaders. Those who have education and possess specialized skills tend to assume management positions in the village organizations, usually with the backing of less well-endowed villagers. These new "managers," however, have limited powers. Villagers imagine the role of their educated members as analogous to the missionaries: those who have education must 'help the village' rather than work for themselves. Young leaders are more than regulators, they are educators. Indeed, this was a role many Maisin fitted me into as well. The leaders also worked the analogy, but placed greater emphasis on the inherent authority of their offices.

The mission station figured in such representations in a second way.

Certain common communal activities on the station, notably church celebrations, served as models of the type of moral order many Maisin said they would like to see in the village. The notion that the station might serve as an exemplar of a better moral order derives in part from mission teaching, but also arises from the desires of villagers to rise above local factionalism, based in part upon clan affiliation, in order to build a stronger community. I recorded several speeches at village meetings in which leaders manipulated church images to build community solidarity, arguing that such solidarity was fundamental to the economic salvation of Uiaku. In the following passage, the village councillor stands up to harangue the villagers about their community duties:

> In the old days on St. Thomas [the church festival] all the people in the village worked together. They hunted and fished and cooked together. These days at St. Thomas only a few people go fishing and hunting, and only a few people cook in the station. In the old days people worked together and helped each other. But now people always argue and do things the way they want to do them. So now if there is work to do one will go and the other will do as he wishes. When your time comes you start arguing or gossiping about other people. When the [Local Government] Council committee announces that there is work to be done, you get your knife and axe and go to the garden. It is always that way. When the Council committee says there is work to be done, you get your fishing nets and go and do whatever you want to do. So you must know who is making it bad. It's you! You are the ones spoiling it. It's you, not the others! It's you who put the Council committee, Youth and Board of Management. You must listen to them! That is the "legislation." You elected them as leaders and they are the ones who will tell you to work (translated from a recording in 1983).

The councillor passionately repeated and emphasized his points for about twenty minutes. Several elders and educated leaders followed, somberly confirming this unhappy picture of a village falling apart and warning of the consequences of 'selfishness'.

I witnessed many such speeches, made primarily by younger educated managers. These representations clearly emphasized the station side of the village-station relationship. One might suspect that the leaders wished to replace the village's egalitarian exchange ethic with the hierarchical singular authority style of the station. This interpretation, I think, would be quite wrong. These men clearly wanted to be seen as new types of leaders, but they were not Western democrats. Their notions of leadership, authority, and work, although based on station images, also embodied village ideals. This point can be illustrated by a careful unpacking of the speech segment reported above.

In painting his dismal picture, the councillor subtly reconstructs and merges traits associated with the village and the station. He directs his ire towards those who do not participate in community projects. In a station idiom, such persons are disobedient, they refuse to obey the 'legislation'. The image also resonates with village-oriented values. As Burridge (1965) and many others have shown, most Melanesians abhor those self-willed individuals who drop out of exchange and kinship obligations. As best, Maisin regard them as 'rubbish' or 'crazy'; at worst, they suspect them as sorcerers. Against such individuals, the councillor presents the image of the patronal church feast, St. Thomas Day. This also resonates with both station and village values. As I noted above, the St. Thomas feast reminds Maisin of the large inter-tribal feasts of the past and provides an important occasion for groups to demonstrate their unity and prowess in providing food and valuables and in performing the old dances. St. Thomas is also a major day in the church calendar, usually marked by a visit from the bishop and a major church service. The ceremonies that take place on the station that day indicate the devotion of the whole community to Christ — their *unity* in Christ. The councillor identifies a successful St. Thomas feast with successful work in general, notably that work carried out by village committees. The overall implication of the speech is the committees and their leaders combine station and village orientations and values. On the one hand, they embody the cooperative ethic of the village feast; and on the other, they represent the authority of 'legislation' and singular authority (exemplified in the person of the missionary-priest-teacher).

The representations discussed in this section express a sentiment that Maisin society should more closely approximate the station. They do so not by dismissing village practices and orientations, but by appropriating them and representing them as embodied in station institutions and structures of authority. What I am suggesting, in other words, is that the managers take the station as a model for Maisin society, thus obviating the distinction between village and station. The result is a picture of Maisin society as a highly rationalized organization sustained by a "traditional" egalitarian and cooperative ethic. Although articulated mostly by an educated minority, it is an image that most Maisin find congenial and plausible. I never heard anyone protest or contradict those who made this kind of argument in public or in private. Indeed, many expressed opinions that this was the way things should be. As the councillor's speech indicates, however, this solution to the opposition of village and station has been hard to make into reality.

Village Traditions as a Model for the Station

I became aware of a third set of representations only towards the end of my fieldwork, as I learned more of Maisin traditions. Village clans, as I noted earlier, possess and embody what Maisin regard as unchanging traditions. Traditions take both oral and material forms. Although all villagers are aware of and respect traditions, only a few elders possess detailed knowledge. But this knowledge is not limited to village matters. It serves as a unifying framework for the village and station domains. Significantly, the most articulate spokesmen of Maisin traditions have been closely associated with the station and the church for many years, often as church councillors and as former 'missionaries' (teacher-evangelists) themselves.

I begin with the oral traditions. In the beginning, most Maisin clans emerged from under the ground at a site in the Musa Basin, about 70 miles to the west of Uiaku (cf. Williams 1930:154). Each clan, in possession of its distinguishing emblems (*kawo*), then fought its way through enemy territory to Collingwood Bay. Maisin elders tell their stories for drama and to back claims to land and influence. There is much disagreement concerning the relative truth of different versions. There is less debate concerning a fundamental opposition drawn in the oral traditions between the two ranks of clans — the *kawo* and the *sabu*.[9] Most elders speak of the higher ranking *kawo* as peace-makers who sought alliances with other tribes through inter-marriage and feasting. They led the *sabu*, 'care of them', and could command their labor for feasts. The *sabu*, on the other hand, are said to have been the chief warriors. Both raiding and feasting were presented as complementary modes of clan interactions; but the legends also indicate that the violence of the *sabu* was tempered by the diplomatic efforts of the *kawo*: hence the superiority of the latter.

Local historians present the story of arrival of the Anglican missionaries in terms of this hierarchical structure. The missionaries take the role of *kawo* while the Maisin are *sabu*. A retired mission teacher in Uiaku told me of his grandfather's meeting with the first missionaries: "When the missionaries... came to this place they made friends with Wanigera [as *sabu* warrior leader]. Before that time there was no peace." In this and other stories, the clans are pictured as being in a continual state of enmity with each other and outside enemies. Like the *kawo* clans, the missionaries mediated between separate and mutually suspicious groups.[10]

Although only a few elders could tell me about the arrival of the missionaries, many villagers pictured 'missionaries' and villagers in their daily relations along the lines of *kawo* and *sabu*. Informants, for example, frequently stressed the clergy's role as peacemakers during times of tension (a role, incidentally, that the present mission staff and its predecessors have avoided according to available evidence). Exploring this relation further, I asked thirty villagers what they saw as the greatest difference between the heathen and Christians. The answers showed little variation. Heathen were said to be quick-tempered, violent, selfish. One villager said: "Their lives are the same. The Christians have a different name. There are wild pigs in the bush and there are village pigs. The village pig is like a Christian; it is looked after by a man who washes and feeds it. The bush pig must find food on its own." *kawo* and missionaries alike were said to 'look after' the *sabu* and villagers, to give them advice and spiritual food, and to domesticate their violent propensities.

Such representations serve to reduce the foreignness of the missionaries. Other comments I recorded suggest that some Maisin also saw Christian teachings reflecting a deeper indigenous tradition. One man in his 40s told me: "Before we were taught that all of the traditions came from the hole [i.e., the original time]. But now we know that they come from God." His point was not that Maisin traditions are wrong, but that the ancestors, being 'ignorant men' (*toton tamata*), possessed only a partial understanding of the truth of things. All of those I interviewed affirmed that God was present in Papua before the mission arrived, even if the ancestors had but a dim awareness of him (cf. Smith, chapter 8). Missionaries brought the truth of the Bible, a truth which, so some informants said, clarified traditions. Consequently, as a Maisin church deacon told me, "If a thing is good, the people will carry on doing it. If it is bad, the missionaries keep on talking and the people give up this thing."

The physical church forms a second point of unity between tradition and Christianity for many Maisin. Father Kingsley Gegeyo, an Anglican priest from Uiaku, pointed out to me:

> ...if anyone came here and spoke against Christianity everyone would fight to protect it. They believe it is the seat of our survival.... It becomes something they value very highly. They take it as the most necessary part of their community and survival. It's not like the government. It doesn't come and punish and order. [The] church is something that belongs to them. And it doesn't hurt them — it gives them a sense of protection.... If someone tried to take the land away from the church they would get very angry. That is [the] physical value of the church: sacred land to them.

This statement touches on themes mentioned by several of my informants. Let me take just the last point, the notion of sacred land. In what sense is the church 'sacred land' for Maisin villagers?

To answer this question we must return to the traditional *kawo* clans and the intertribal feasts for which they were responsible. Such feasts were always held in the clearing of the *kawo* clan's hamlet. In the center of the clearing, the villagers constructed a small house composed of emblematic materials (*kawo*) that were the exclusive property of the host clan. Only the *kawo* leaders could order such houses to be built, and then only for feasts. During the feasts huge piles of taro and other foods were given to guests and the dancing extended over several days. The feast hut (*kawo va*) symbolized the traditions, the cultural identity, and ultimately the power of the clan.

Inter-tribal feasting declined and disappeared completely in the years following pacification. In the past a man proved his mettle in warfare and in exchange activities, but by the 1950's younger men became more concerned with attracting money to their villages. The Church Councils and women's organizations formed a new basis for the local concentration and control of labor in the co-operatives. Indeed, it is clear from informant testimonies that many people then, as today, associated material prosperity with a Christian identity. They identified the quickening of local economic activity with a vigorous local church.

Towards the end of the 1950's the villagers decided to put their energies into building an iron-roofed church, partly in hope that the Mission would give them their own priest and partly to mark their new status as full Christians. They also made a statement in a traditional idiom: "All of the clans brought their emblems and put them around, making a big fence. They said that they were building God's *kawo va* 'feast hut'. God had given the emblems to the people and so they had to give what they had back to God for His *kawo va*." This sacrifice of the symbols of clan identity to the church was an indigenous innovation. The church became "sacred land" in a way analogous to hamlet clearings. But whereas the symbols of ancestral identity appeared only periodically in the hamlets and marked clan boundaries as well as unities, the "*kawo va*" of the mission station is a permanent feature embodying the collective identity of the Maisin and indeed, as is often pointed out in sermons, the whole of Christendom.

The elders who reflect upon the traditions of their clans, and who attempt to construct a historical memory for their communities, often spoke to me along the lines outlined here. They sometimes aired these representations in public meetings where they were listened to with respect. These images, like the other permutations, stress the need for solidarity and cooperation in the village, and take the feast as the central symbol of this ideal. But the village and its customs forms the ultimate foundation. And because of the basis in eternal tradition, such representations imbue the station and Christianity with some of the same timeless "mythic" qualities.

CONCLUSION

To recapitulate: Mission stations were originally established in Maisin villages as bases for teachers and as cultural enclaves in which Christian values could be taught and demonstrated. Secreted within regular station activities were a number of practical orientations which over time hastened the Maisin's integration into the emerging politico-economic hegemony of Papua New Guinea. Although all Maisin are today Christians, and although the mission has become a national church, the station remains a distinct entity within Maisin society. Its distinctness from the surrounding hamlets is signalled in several practical ways: differences in lifestyles, typical activities, temporal and spatial relations, and so on. I suggested that Maisin participate in both environments and thus the station and the village are domains within a single society. Maisin representations of the relationship between station and village recognize the incongruities but attempt to place them within a larger framework. I discussed three distinct sets of representations. The first presents the relation between village and station in terms of exchange, ideally of balanced reciprocity. In the second, the station is used as a "model for" the desired moral order in the village as a whole. And, finally, a third set of representations subsumes the station within Maisin traditions.

The analysis raises several interesting problems of interpretation. By way of a conclusion, I shall briefly address two of these: How is it that the Maisin are able to support a distinctly village culture given their long-term and heavy involvement in the station and, beyond it, the larger economy and society of Papua New Guinea? And, what are the implications of the different village-station permutations for the future of Maisin society?

David Laitin's (1986) recent study of Christians and Muslims among the Yoruba of Nigeria provides an intriguing answer to the first question. Laitin points out that most Yoruba hold two distinct and incongruent cultural identities. They are members of a church or mosque, and they are descended from certain ancestral cities. Although religious affiliation provides abundant potential for political manipulation, the Yoruba consider their religious differences to be without political significance. Instead, they organize themselves in terms of descent from the ancestral cities, although few people still live in these rural centers. Laitin explains the situation in terms of hegemony. When the British established control over Nigeria, they co-opted the rulers of the ancestral cities as proxy "chiefs" in a system of indirect rule. This strategy established the cities as a privileged domain from which political symbols could be generated and disputed. The ruling elite who succeeded the British continue to exploit the same symbols. The religious subcultures are non-hegemonic but pose no challenge because they are not utilized politically. The contradictions between religious and hegemonic values remain tacit. The Yoruba simply are not concerned with them.

Although the Maisin situation is somewhat different, a similar argument can be made. The Maisin participate in two incongruous subcultures, represented locally by the village and the station. In Papua, unlike Nigeria, the colonial administration established "indirect rule" through *introduced* institutions, notably mission and government posts and village councils. For the rural Maisin, the station has over time developed as the privileged locus for the production of political symbols within and between communities and the state. It is part of the hegemonic system. The values and orientations of the village subculture are distinct from the station, but because Maisin do not recognize these differences as politically relevant, the village system does not directly clash with the station system and what it represents. The potential for the political manipulation of the incongruous aspects of the rural situation is there; but it remains tacit and undeveloped.

This line of interpretation can easily be extended to the ways in which Maisin rationalize the relationship between the village and the station. Although each rationalization is distinct, each accords a superior position to the 'mission' and 'missionaries' side of the relation. In the first, the 'missionaries' give knowledge and peace; in the second, they offer a highly bureaucratized model of social organization; and in the third, they provide a sacred center for community. All of these rationalizations recognize the mission station as the locus of political symbols. They are highly compatible. The village subculture provides political symbols in a much more constrained way: in uniting clan against clan in bridewealth or sorcery disputes, for example. But whenever such disputes threaten to get out of hand, leaders inevitably draw again on the hegemonic symbols of village unity centered on the station. I have never heard a Maisin, including the elders who are the most knowledgeable about village traditions, suggest that the station be done away with, replaced by village values. This should not be surprising. The majority of Maisin, after all, have been Christians since the early 1920s.

I saw no indication that Maisin regarded these different interpretations of the relation of station to village as alternative political programmes. People never compared them, and often the same people employed one or another at different times. There was, however, a general correlation between a person's age and experience and the ways he or she saw the village-station relationship. Older and less educated people tended to rationalize the relationship in terms of the morality of exchange and the sacred qualities of identification with the center of the community. Younger and more educated people have clearly internalized more of the hegemonic values associated with the station. But even those heavily involved in promoting government and mission 'side' activities say that there must be a 'village side' as well to perform traditional ceremonies and deal with kinship and exchange obligations. While the society is clearly undergoing progressive secularization, I see no reason to suppose that a distinctly Melanesian village society will disappear in the future. The challenges of the past to the village way of life were in many ways more severe than those of today. The Maisin have successfully developed a bicultural society that allows them to have something of two worlds.

The findings of the present study, like other recent sociological reappraisals of missionary institutions, bears important implications for future research into religious innovation among newly Christian people. At first blush, the Maisin might appear to present a simple case of attempted "Christianization" — the imposition of Western forms of worship upon an indigenous people. The apparent indifference of the people to these forms, and their continued adherence to many old customs and values, would seem to imply that Christianity is but a veneer, a superficial covering over the "real" Maisin culture. On the other hand, one might also see the Maisins' strong support of the church and their heavy involvement in the larger society of Papua New Guinea as an indication that the village subculture is at best a residual "survival," soon to disappear as the Maisin totally acculturate. Yet such interpretations would involve serious misreadings of the mission history of the region and, more importantly, a misconstrual of Maisin attitudes. The Western nature of the local church is precisely what makes it a potent symbol for the Maisin. The Maisin and many other "conventional" Christians of the Third World take their adherence to Christianity and the new ways they see it representing very seriously, but they do so in their own terms (cf. Strathern 1984:33) . As ethnographers we need to give our informants' involvement with Christianity the serious attention that, from the indigenous point of view, it seems to deserve. Otherwise we will continue to produce ethnocentric understandings of indigenous Christianity, even if fashionably critical of "missionization."

NOTES

I am grateful to the Social Sciences and Humanities Research Council of Canada, the Killam Foundation, and the National Geographic Society for supporting research in Papua New Guinea in 1981-83 and 1986. Thanks as well to the staffs of the Anglican Church of Papua New Guinea, the New Guinea Collection at the University of Papua New Guinea and the National Archives of Papua New Guinea for their assistance and permission to use materials in this study. Anne Marie Tietjen, Michael Smith, and Martha Kaplan made incisive comments and criticisms on earlier versions of this paper. My greatest debt as always is to my Maisin research assistants, informants, and friends.

1. Rowley (1965:138) notes that the early missions to Papua and New Guinea shared "a broad but suggestive similarity of technique largely made inevitable by the nature of the task [of evangelization]." Mary Huber (1988) has recently written a book exploring the contradiction between ideological aspirations and practical necessities among Roman Catholic missionaries in the Sepik area. She does not, however, address the significance of such contradictions for emerging indigenous Christianity.
2. The New Guinea Mission of the Anglican Church suffered throughout its history (as the successor church does today) from the rather tepid support it received from the home churches in Australia and England. This lack of financial stability may well have limited the influence of the church as much as the mission bishops' liberal philosophies of evangelization (see Barker 1987; Wetherell 1977).
3. The first Melanesian teachers made their way into the New Guinea mission from the sugar plantations of Queensland. For many years they formed the major part of the mission staff (see Wetherell 1977:chapter 3). An Australian priest made Uiaku his base in 1917. Unable to abide the Maisins' penchant for pigs and drumming, he fled in 1920 (Barker 1987:77-81).
4. Following David Laitin (1986:183), I define hegemony as "the political forging — whether through coercion or elite bargaining — and institutionalization of a pattern of group activity in a state and the concurrent idealization of that schema into a dominant symbolic framework that reigns as common sense."
5. When the government took over schooling in the early 1970s, the people of Airara elected to have the classrooms and teachers' houses built on the outskirts of their village, away from the church. They continue to refer to both the church and the school areas as 'station', however.
6. At contact the Maisin built small enclosed sleeping platforms on high posts, using the verandahs underneath for cooking and socializing. They abandoned these at the urging of government officers in the 1920s and 1930s for the rectangular, windowed houses now commonly found throughout coastal Papua. Maisin switched from tapa cloth to European clothes in the early 1960s and today wear tapa only on ceremonial occasions. The effects of 80 years of village schooling are apparent in the number of loan words from the "church language" of Wedau at Dogura that have been incorporated into the language along with Hiri Motu and more recently English and Tok Pisin. Many of these changes are obvious and recognized by Maisin, who occasionally discuss their relative merits over the old ways. But many, perhaps most, changes are subtle and difficult to identify, particularly when the influences have been other Papua New Guinean people and Melanesian missionaries (cf. Chowning 1969). I would therefore argue that Maisin assumptions about traditions — that they are unchanging and essential — should be understood as an ideology, not as proof of cultural continuity or "reproduction" (cf. Carrier and Carrier 1987).

7. Some Maisin had worked for periods as carpenters and they applied their skills to station buildings although not to their own village dwellings. In 1981-83 the only iron-roofed dwellings in Uiaku were two teachers' houses on the station. In 1986 one villager with much financial support from relatives working in town began to build a semi-permanent house in the village.
8. This has been the case even though a translation of the service into Maisin was prepared in 1920. Part of the problem is that few of the teachers and clergy stationed at Uiaku have had the time to learn Maisin and for many years the Church discouraged establishing clergy among their own people. In 1986, a Maisin priest began to work at Uiaku. Although he delivered his sermons in Maisin, he still spoke the service and the lessons in English, which at least half of the congregation cannot understand. When asked about this situation, Maisin say that as long as they cannot agree on an accurate translation they would rather leave the liturgy and readings in a more respectable "church language."
9. On this point of history, as many others, Maisin were not in complete agreement. Some clan members in Ganjiga maintained in 1986 that the difference between *kawo* and *sabu* clans was limited to ceremonial rank; both types of clans were traditionally violent. This was a minority view. One man in 1983 argued that *sabu* actually ranked higher than *kawo*! I found no one else who suggested this construction.
10. Kahn (1983), Thune (1981), and Young (1977) also report oral traditions in nearby Massim societies which credit missionaries with transforming a Hobbesian state of war "of all against all" to an ambience of brotherly peace.

10

INVENTING THE MORMON TONGAN FAMILY

Tamar Gordon

The Kingdom of Tonga, the only Pacific island nation to have maintained its sovereignty from colonial rule, also has the distinction of being the most successful foreign mission field for the Mormon Church. In its relatively brief history of nearly 100 years in Tonga, The Church of Jesus Christ of Latter Day Saints has been steadily gaining converts at the expense of Tonga's other churches, and has established a costly infrastructure that belies its status as a minority church. According to the 1976 Tongan Census (the last one available from the Government), approximately 9% out of 104,000 Tongans declared Mormon membership with a projected increase to 12% by 1986.[1]

While material considerations form an undeniable motivation for conversion and continued membership, and while the Mormon Church encourages the adoption of a certain model of social life, Tongan Mormonism is by no means a wholesale adoption of an imposed model. Mormonism in Tonga is a religious idiom through which Westernization takes place, but with Tongan logic on Tongan terms.

As in other Polynesian nations, Tongan Christianity is pluralistic, an arena of sectarian cooperation and competition based on diverse systems of meaning, occasional schism, and extensive attrition within multi-denominational kin networks (cf. Boutilier, Hughes, and Tiffany 1978). The various churches that comprise Tongan Christianity — the Free Wesleyan Church dominating — are products of complex historical and structural relations; but all to a greater or lesser degree have been brought within the compass of Tongan culture. The indigenization of Christianity and its appropriation into what Tongans have constructed as their tradition support Burridge's observation that "there is no social order that could be described as specifically Christian" (1978:19). The study of Mormonism in Tonga comes to focus, not on the didactic relation between foreign missionaries and converts, nor on the utilitarian adoption of a monolithic religious model, but on Tongans' negotiation of their religious identity and on the processes of intercultural translation, both within the Tongan Mormon Church and in relation to the dominant religious traditions that it encounters in Tonga.

Why the Mormon system is attractive to some Tongans, and the extent to which this uniquely American religious tradition has become "Tonganized" like other imported institutions, can be glimpsed in Tongan Mormon families. Because a unique symbolic construction of the family is the cornerstone of Mormon doctrines of salvation, the family has long been a major locus of redefinition within which Tongan Mormons must both represent and negotiate meanings vis-à-vis American Mormons and other Tongan Christians. The attainment of high Mormon Church callings, and the opportunities for enhanced social status and economic advancement within Mormon circles are contingent on very visibly embracing certain idealized family structures and practices. Mormon husbands and wives ideally form an exclusive couple and decision-making unit for the nuclear family; together they should work to keep resources within their immediate family rather than sharing them with extended kin. The Mormon model of family stands in opposition to the mainstream Tongan Christian model which interprets the Old and New Testaments to emphasize traditional behavioral conventions, bonds of obligation and resource-sharing among extended kindred, and respect for authority that reinforces hierarchical controls outside of the nuclear family.

Such vast sectarian differences in Tonga can come to be highly socially significant and symbolically charged in certain contexts, but ultimately those differences must be interpreted and calibrated with respect to what all Tongans continually invoke as *anga fakatonga*, 'the Tongan way'. Bott (1981) has characterized Tongan society as a richly optative field of competing principles which are selectively invoked according to social context. Mormon identity rests on notions of social separateness through religious distinctiveness; but Tongan Mormons must also manifest proper Tongan behavior and invoke the appropriate traditional values in order to function in the multi-denominational village settings that necessitate resource sharing with Mormon and non-Mormon kindred, and in order to maintain face with the non-Mormon powers that be. Tongans accomplish this by "inventing" viable representations of the Mormon nuclear family while preserving many core Tongan values relating to kinship, economic cooperation, and status rivalry among family and church groups which make social life possible and meaningful. In its guise as difference, however, the Tongan Mormon family embodies a powerful new discourse and imagery about power, status, and new avenues for temporal success that addresses Tongan expectations and serves Tongan needs in a rapidly changing society.

TONGA TODAY

The Tongan archipelago consists of 136 islands, about 40 of which are inhabited. The Tongan islands form three major groups: Tongatapu, Haa'api, and Vava'u, with additional islands 'Eua at the south and Niuatoputapu and Niuafo'ou at the extreme north. The population numbers around 104,000, almost half of which lives on Tongatapu in and near the capital of Nuku'alofa.

A constitutional monarchy, Tonga is the most conservative and highly stratified of the contemporary Polynesian societies, consisting of three hereditary classes that are linked through extended, cognatic family networks called *kainga*: the Royal family, the chiefly nobility (who "own" and allocate lands), and the commoners. A formal hierarchy of rights and obligations permeates all social relations, from the highest chiefly titleholders down through the unit of immediate family members called *famili*. The rank system continues to preserve a form of the traditional redistributive economy based upon reciprocity, feasting, and prestations among family groups and chiefs, and also ensures disproportionate representation by high-ranking individuals in Parliament and government offices. With Tonga's increasing incorporation into the regional and global economy, however, an emergent class system has become intertwined with the system of hereditary privilege, and educated and wealthy commoners have come to play an important role in the country (cf. Marcus 1980, 1981).

Limited employment opportunities (Walsh 1972), lack of tertiary education, and increasing land shortages (Maude 1973) have led to high rates of emigration to the industrialized countries; the overseas Tongan population probably exceeds that of Tonga. Opportunities for emigration come in the form of government scholarships to study and work abroad and chain migration, both legal and illegal, through extended family networks. It is the rare Tongan family indeed which does not receive regular financial remittances from overseas members.

Tonga's churches can be placed in two broad camps: the mainstream Wesleyan-influenced denominations, and those that promulgate significantly differing doctrines and organizational structures. The former include the Free Wesleyan Church and the two Churches of Tonga. The latter include the Catholic, the Anglican, the Mormon, and the Seventh Day Adventist Churches. Also in the latter group are Evangelical and Pentecostal sects which are subsumed under "All other" and "Unknown" in the Government censuses (see Table 1). Of Tonga's six major churches, the Mormon Church provides the best opportunities for Tongans to live, work, and study abroad. Indeed, it has been characterized to me as *koe matapa ki muli*, 'the door abroad'.

Denomination	1931	1939	1956	1966	1976*
	Percentage of Population				
Free Wesleyan	58	53.9	49.6	49.9	47.3
Free Church of Tonga	16	17.1	17.5	14.3	13.7
Roman Catholic	12	13.6	14.7	16.0	16.1
Church of Tonka *Hou'eiki*	10	10.5	9.9	9.0	8.9
Mormon	—	2.9	5.1	7.1	9.3**
Seventh-Day Adventist	—	.8	1.5	1.8	2.1
Anglican	—	.8	.9	1.0	1.0
All other	4	.1	.3	.8	.9
Unknown	—	.3	.5	.1	.3

* Tongan Government Census of 1976, Nuku'alofa
** Increase to 12% projected in 1986.
Unpublished Tongan Government Census Summary, 1983.

TABLE 1: DENOMINATIONAL AFFLILIATION IN TONGA, 1931-1976 (Source: Korn, 1978; Government of Tonga, 1982)

THE MORMON CHURCH IN TONGA

Tongans typically characterize the coming of Christianity as "the coming of light," supplanting the precontact "nighttime" of warfare, punitive chiefly rule, enforced tribute, and pagan worship. Tonga's religious history has been the subject of diverse and detailed treatments (e.g., Latukefu 1974; Rutherford 1971, 1977; Wood-Ellem 1983). These works span the first years of significant contact via Captain Cook, the establishment of the Wesleyan Mission in 1823, the arrival of the Catholics in 1842, and the political alliances forged between Wesleyan missionaries and the powerful chief, Taufa'ahau, who was to unify Tonga in the framework of a Christian state, and emerge as the first King, George Tupou I. As Wesleyan Methodism developed from a missionary church into an indigenous religion in the hands of Tongan ministers, and as other missionaries arrived, a dominant model of Tongan Christianity emerged with structures and ideologies of authority, cooperation, and support for church that were compatible with Tongan cutural logic. Tonga's churches, including the schismatic Churches of Tonga, became integral to village organization, providing new roles, new arenas for status rivalry and power, and new social ties that cross-cut kinship networks. The village churches also coalesced around new arenas of economic obligation and competition in the yearly round of feasts, conferences and annual donations that played through pre-existing values and structures of kin cooperation and resource-sharing. Religious authority nonetheless remained largely subordinate to chiefly authority in Tonga.

By the time the first Mormon missionaries gained a tenuous foothold in Tonga early in 20th century, the Tongans had already successfully forged a model of Christianity adapted to the familiar practices of Tongan life. The early Mormon missionaries encountered extreme resistance to the establishment of yet another denomination, especially one which would chip away at the membership of the majority church (already depleted by schism) and crowd the mission field of the others.

Mormons had been proselytizing in the Pacific virtually from the inception of the Church, when Joseph Smith sent missionaries to the Sandwich and Society Islands in 1844. Tonga was designated as a district of the Samoan mission and the first two American Mormon missionaries arrived in Tonga from Samoa in 1891.[2] With only sixteen converts after six years, the mission was ordered closed by the First Presidency (the office of the Prophet and his Counselors). Missionaries returned to Vava'u in 1907 to open a school in the port town of Neiafu. The village of Ha'alaufuli requested its own school in 1909. The demand for education and literacy that had proved to be such a drawing card in the early years of the Wesleyan mission was repeating itself. However, there was little popular incentive to join the new church which remained poor and unproven by Tongan standards. Moreover, Mormon doctrine differed significantly from the Protestant teachings. With its intensive in-group focus, its explicit rejection of social obligations to chiefs and economic cooperation among inter-denominational networks of kin, and obedience to a foreign religious authority, the new church radically challenged accepted ideas about political authority, kinship, and religious identity. Local and foreign ministers of all the Tongan churches denounced the Mormons as unChristian and successfully encouraged the nobility and commoners to take steps to ban the newcomers.

The Mormons had established 20 missionaries in Vava'u and on Tongatapu and made a small number of converts when they encountered their first serious opposition. Responding to complaints by various sectors of Tongan society, Great Britain, under whom Tonga was officially a protectorate, refused to issue additional visas to Mormon missionaries from 1917 until 1920. In 1921, the noble Tu'i Vakano, in alliance with the Wesleyan Church, expressed his disapproval of the Mormon presence by denying all land leases and instigating legislation in Tonga reinforcing the ban on visas. Members of the Tongan Parliament in 1922 accused Mormons of heresy and perversion, despite the fact that polygamy had been officially renounced 30 years before.

From 1924, when the Mormon exclusion laws were repealed, to 1951 when Liahona College was completed, the Church grew steadily. During the period of gradual expansion, the Mormon missionaries brought films and slides from Salt Lake City to instruct Tongans about their "other" ethnic identity. The Book of Mormon teaches that Pacific Islanders, along with Indians of the Americas, are descendents of Lost Tribes of Israel who journeyed to the New World and were baptized by Christ himself. This message was heavily emphasized in the talks of Apostle George Albert Smith whose visit to Tonga in 1938 marked Tonga's emergence as an important mission field for the Church. Membership went from 1,000 in 1924 to over 3,000 in 1951 (Britsch 1986:450). During that time, the numerous leadership positions circulated among a group of Tongan families that have continued to dominate the Church in recent years.

The Mormon Mission was effectively shut down during the war years when Americans were recalled throughout the Pacific by the U.S. government. In 1946, the Church published a Tongan language version of the Book of Mormon, instigating a more extensive translation program of the large corpus of Mormon scriptures and manuals. The extent of this program has been unmatched by any other church in Tonga (Britsch 1986).

In 1947 the Mission President acquired plantation lands on eastern Tongatapu and commenced building the school complex which became the spiritual and administrative hub of Mormondom in Tonga: the envisioned "gathering place," or sacred community, of the Tongan saints. Such communities had already been established in Hawaii and New Zealand. It was called Liahona after the mystical compass described in the Book of Mormon used to guide Israelites (the supposed ancestors of the Polynesians) to the New World. The Liahona High School complex was modern and extremely costly by Tongan standards, and its dedication by Queen Salote in 1952 was a major event. Liahona became the prime vehicle in the socialization and conversion of Tongan youth, while providing a self-contained system of employment that is financed by the American church.

Mormon Church leaders throughout the world comprise a lay clergy; all men who have "the priesthood" are eligible to become bishops of local wards, presidents of more inclusive stakes, presidents of missions, and even to be chosen to serve on the Quorum of the Seventy or Twelve Apostles, the highest ecclesiastical bodies under the Prophet. Such religious offices are prerequisites in order to be employed in high administrative positions in the Church such as Regional Director.[3] Women do not possess these avenues of mobility within the Church, as they lack the "spiritual authority" of the priesthood. They can, however, work as teachers and support staff in Mormon schools and administration. I was informed by Tongan staff workers in Mormon administration that their performance as good wives and mothers, and their leadership roles in women's and children's auxiliary groups are taken into account when their husbands are "called" to church positions.

The Church ecclesiastical and administrative hierarchy in Tonga has become increasingly indigenized as Church membership continues to grow. The creation of the first Nuku'alofa Stake in 1968, with its Tongan Stake counselors and bishops (though with an American Stake President) was the first watershed on the way to "full spiritual maturity" for Tonga. Tonga's growing Mormon membership has necessitated the creation of ten more stakes since then, the majority on Tongatapu, all with Tongan leaders. American Mormon leaders still ultimately oversee regional Church affairs and minister finances. With the initiation of a Temporal Affairs Office in the early 1980's under two Tongan Regional Directors, however, Tongan men have gained considerable power to manage the organization and form of Mormon culture in Tonga.

For Tongan members, their Mormon history culminates in the dedication of the Tongan Temple at Liahona in 1983 — the result of a vision experienced by Prophet David O. McKay in 1955 when he visited Tonga. The sacred rituals performed inside Mormon temples ensure the persistence of family ties after death, and are critical for salvation in the celestial afterlife. Tongans no longer have to travel to New Zealand and Hawaii to do "Temple work:" genealogy research, eternal marriage "sealings" and proxy baptisms of the dead.

Active Mormons must demonstrate "worthiness" to enter the Temple in interviews conducted by a bishop. Worthiness includes evidence of faithful tithing, following the ban on smoking, alcohol, non-medicinal drugs, and caffeine drinks, and most importantly, being a good family person. The "Temple recommend" conferred by Church leaders is a mechanism that ensures the greatest commitment and conformity to the culture of the Mormon community. Like the Mormon schools and administrative offices, the Temple has its own Tongan President and other ecclesiastical officers, and employs scores of people in its management and upkeep. The Temple dedication in August, 1983 was a lavish event which mobilized the resources of family networks, Tongan alumni of the Mormon high schools at Liahona and Vava'u and Brigham Young Universities, and the village wards all over Tonga.

By the mid-1970's, the Mormon Church had the fastest growth rate both of converts and infants born to Mormon mothers of all the Tongan churches, including the Catholics (Government of Tonga 1982). The membership rolls have swelled increasingly since the Church leaders started appointing Tongan mission Presidents in the late 1960's. During 1983, for example, 2,261 convert baptisms were performed by the 140 or so Tongan Mormon missionaries who made their rounds.

The Mormon Church today is one of the largest employers in Tonga outside of the Government, and has by far the highest building budget of any Tongan church. The 1983 budget for its two modern American-style high-schools, for example, exceeded what the Tongan Government spent on its education and health systems combined. The Mormon Temporal Affairs Office runs an extensive building program which contracts for, constructs and maintains the modern Mormon chapels found in every Tongan village. Weekly salaries in Church employment ranged in 1982-84 from $16.00 a week for chapel maintenance and plantation workers to $150.00-$200.00 for Liahona High School teachers, to $400.00 for the highest level administrative jobs. By contrast, the average Tongan civil servant during this period was earning $20.00-$40.00 per week. The Church Welfare system also provides a safety net for families in need that ranges from distribution of clothing and extra food to emergency medical care overseas.

Mormon and non-Mormon Tongan families alike depend on remittances from overseas relatives who create networks of chain migration to optimize and diversify their economic base (Marcus 1981). The Mormon Church is highly instrumental in this regard. The Church creates overseas networks for Tongans by providing visas, employment, and scholarships for students to study at the Brigham Young Universities (BYU) in Hawaii and Provo. Once having served a two year "mission" (fulltime service as a Mormon missionary in Tonga or sometimes overseas) and having graduated from BYU (and often just from Liahona High School), Tongans are virtually guaranteed employment and a chance to be called to high ecclesiastical positions in the Church system. Elite Tongans employed by the Church also have opportunities to travel to the U.S.

The Mormon Church thus not only provides avenues for Tongans to go overseas, but brings its system of rewards home, creating an alternative, self-sufficient class system relative to other Tongan sectors, with its own structure of stratification and its own ties of dependency to the mother church. The prosperity of the Mormon Church in Tonga, its American ties, its unseemly flaunting of political authority, its "unChristian" doctrines, and its "unTongan" ethics continually provoke the open antagonism of the non-Mormon political and religious establishment, including

King Taufa'ahau Tupou IV himself.[4] In the words of one Wesleyan minister: "Tonga has become a colony of the Mormons."

PERCEPTIONS OF MORMONISM WITHIN CONVENTIONAL TONGAN CHRISTIANITY

Unlike conventional Tongan Christianity which reinforces traditional family and political practices, Mormon doctrine offers new symbols and an explicit, practical agenda for acculturation to a particular model of Western society. Mainstream Tongan Christianity — the state Free Wesleyan Church and its offshoots, the Churches of Tonga — is embedded in traditional discourses of political authority, kinship, resource-sharing, and social obligation. Respect for rank and political authority can be heard in the language of sermonizing and prayer which makes use of the semantic system reserved for the King and chiefs to address God and Jesus. While this convention also appears in Mormon religious language, the Wesleyans go further in mirroring traditional Tongan oratory by prefacing sermons with the *fakatapu* 'sacred/respectful prologue', acknowledging all secular ranked authority from the national level down to the immediate social grouping.

Such Biblical teachings as "love thy neighbor," "love for the poor" (neighbors and the poor can be contextually considered kin) and "honor thy father and mother" are interpreted as honoring the bonds of obligation and sharing of resources with all categories of kin, both inside and outside the nuclear family. These values are demonstrated in the role behavior of clergy and lay preachers, economic support for churches through the yearly cycle of feasting and fundraising, and unstinting voluntary resource sharing with extended kin. Children are exhorted in Sunday school and in front of the congregation to respect the authority of parents and all adults. Jesus Christ is the embodiment of love; in following his example, Tongans emphasize the lowly, commoner values of humility, respect, and generosity. 'Sharing love' (*fe'ofo'ofani*) enables people to carry out *ngaue malohi* ('strong work', a gloss of the doctrine of works). Manifesting these feelings and conduct causes the inner self to willingly conform to the demands of the social system. The Wesleyan churches have historically administered their own high schools and their own finances, and have served to integrate village and kin networks in the celebration of holidays, ceremonial events, and life crisis rituals within communities. Their powerful ideology of mutual support between kin underlies a moral economy that weaves together the financial survival of families, villages, and the church from the local village chapel to the centralized ministries.

Of the non-Wesleyan/Church of Tonga denominations, the Mormon Church appears to present the greatest challenge to the Tongan Christian model of correct moral relations. Adherents of the other Tongan churches concur on doctrinal and cultural grounds that the Mormons are not true Christians. They charge that the Mormons worship three distinct gods; that they "pray to Joseph Smith" and also "pray to money;" and that they rely on sacred texts other than the Bible. In the popular perception, Mormons don't have to raise money within the community, but depend on handouts from the United States. Tongan Mormons, like their American counterparts acquire bureaucratic, entrepreneurial, domestic, and other practical knowledge in contexts that the rest of Tongan society defines as exclusively religious, like Sunday worship meetings. In contrast, members of Tonga's other churches see Christianity as the guardian of the soul and not of the social sphere, and define religious contexts quite narrowly (cf. Puloka 1979). They thus perceive an unseemly blurring of distinctions between the sacred and the profane in Mormon practices. They note that the Mormons use their chapels to hold dances and organizational meetings, and that they hold social activities on sacred holidays. There is "no spirituality" in the Mormon Church, according to one Seventh Day Adventist minister, because of its seeming lack of ritual in Sunday meetings, its plain-spoken religious discourse stripped of metaphor, and the distinctly bureaucratic and secular look of its clergy.

There are many additional charges. Mormons are too focused on Church programs and activities that leave them little time and interest for traditional socializing, such as kava circles and tapa-beating, and traditional knowledge. The young Tongan Mormon missionaries are inappropriately direct and relentless compared to Wesleyan and Catholic missionaries. It is widely alleged that Mormon Tongans flaunt traditional political authority; that they discharge their obligatory prestations to King and nobility in the spirit of bribery and cynical flattery. This brazenness derives from their obedience to a foreign authority which dispenses a seemingly unlimited cash flow.

Finally, according to Tongan critics, Mormons teach disrespect and the breakdown of family ties by encouraging taboo behavior between brothers and sisters, by baptizing youngsters in defiance of their fathers, and by appearing to pass over economic responsibilities to non-Mormon members of their *kainga* 'extended kin' in favor of their own nuclear families and ward congregation.

American Mormons, who are regularly called to Tonga to serve as administrators and financial advisors to the local stakes and the Church, also form perceptions of Tongan Mormons. To these expatriates, Tongan

Mormons appear to be overly preoccupied with status advancement: they engage in competitive events that drain resources from their families and they too often compartmentalize their spiritual and temporal affairs. They note that some overstep the limits of their ecclesiastical positions for their own purposes and that all too many engage in gossip and teasing to bring their colleagues into line. Such failings, of course, are hardly unique to Tongan Mormons; in the present context, however, the criticisms imply something further — that these Mormons are still a little too Tongan.

Although contradictory, both of the perceptions outlined above have some basis in reality. Mormon doctrine and many of the religion's practices do force a sharp distinction between its adherents and other Tongan Christians. Yet these differences do not extend across all contexts of life. In many practical ways, Tongan Mormons continue to honor conventional values that mark moral kin behavior in the society. Because they must negotiate two sharply divergent identities, Tongan Mormons are vulnerable to charges of foreign corruption, on the one hand, and moral hypocrisy on the other. We can see this process of negotiation at work very clearly in the Mormon construction of the family.

MORMON DOCTRINES OF THE FAMILY

The Mormon theology of mankind's salvation, and of the most efficient and rational practices to prepare for it, is quite divergent from mainstream American Protestantism. Mormons teach that purpose of Adam and Eve's transgression was to establish humanity's tenure on earth in accordance with a predestined plan to enable pre-existent spirit children to "get bodies." The primary purpose in life is thus to create earthly families — the more "tabernacles" to house spirit children the better — and experience the joy of being human. A righteous and purposeful life "anxiously engaged in good works" which includes caring for a family, holding offices in the Mormon church, and converting others, attracts the material "blessings" of health and prosperity (cf. McConkie 1979). The Mormon doctrine of blessings makes particular sense to Tongans because it is consistent with the tenets of mainstream Tongan Christianity which in turn derives from a pre-Christian world-view: God rewards hard work in fulfillment of family and church obligations, and punishes social transgressions with economic hardship, ill health, physical deformity, infertility, and bad luck. To all Tongans, *ngaaki tapuaki,* or the 'blessings' of material prosperity, fecundity, and a strong church community indicate moral superiority.

Mormons believe that, if sufficiently worthy, people return once again to heaven after death and live a celestial existence along with their other family members. There, they themselves beget an infinite number of spirit children and populate another world like that of earth. "Families are forever" is Mormondom's most famous slogan.

The institutional apparatus that enables families to achieve celestial glory includes the Temple and genealogy. Men and women worthy enough to be married in one of the Mormon Temples participate in rituals that "seal" them, and their children, together for "time and eternity." Ancestors who died without the opportunity to join the church may gain salvation in the next world and the opportunity to reproduce celestial families through the efforts of living relatives who may baptize them in proxy. Through such research and rituals, infinite networks of kin become reconstituted and sealed together as Latter-Day Saints.

In the Mormon Church community, the two-generation nuclear family is the basic social building block; it forms the basic unit of spiritual and economic production. It is a moral imperative for nuclear families to strive for self-reliance and self-regulation, while remaining interdependent with other Mormon families in a close-knit, cooperative religious community. The earned privilege of dwelling in heaven with one's family is predicated on a number of culture-bound notions of the family. The Mormon Church's biggest challenge in kin-based societies is 1) the reorienting of family practices toward intimacy, privacy, and exclusive sharing of decision-making between husband and wife; in order to 2) exclude extended, ranked kindred as a significant power over the nuclear family; and thus 3) redirect resources inward, to the nuclear family, and outward, to the Mormon Church community.

The Mormon family is characterized by a division of labor between husband and wife that reflects their divine potentials as men and women. The man is the husband, father, ritual specialist, breadwinner, and ultimate authority figure; the spiritual and temporal fate of the family rests on his worthiness as a priest and as a provider. He is known as the "patriarch" of his household; he has the "authority" to deliver blessings, perform faith healings, and receive divine revelations from the Holy Ghost.

Women are primarily defined through their roles as wives, mothers, homemakers, members, and officers of the Latter Day Saints women's auxiliary organizations such as the Relief Society and Young Women's Mutual Improvement Association, and helpmeets to their husbands (work called "sustaining the priesthood"). Women learn in church about the perfectibility of the family and their service role within it, and they receive lessons in home economics, "cultural refinement," and parenting.

The glorification of Mormon women's and men's roles in the family is the theme of many talks and programs that occur throughout the year.

Mormon leaders stress that the roles of husbands and wives are entirely complementary, and "equal though different;" they are mediated through a discourse of mutual respect and love. Most distinctively in the context of non-western kin-based societies, the relationship between spouses is uniquely privileged and privatized. Their joint decisions about the welfare of their family are, as a Tongan bishop explained to me, "a celestial, sacred thing. It's no one else's concern."

There are a number of contexts in which families are publicly constituted and displayed as Mormon. The first is in church. Mormon families attend Sacrament meeting together, occupying entire pews with children sitting between parents. Husbands and wives conspicuously cooperate in quieting their children, and in helping them drink the water and eat the bread that constitute the Sacrament. Mature individuals are considered incomplete without a spouse and children in attendance. (The images of nuclear family togetherness stand in contrast to Tongan Wesleyan worship in which seating is segregated by sex and often by age.) Instead of listening to one individual deliver a sermon, worship consists of "talks" and "testimonies" by any one who wishes to participate. Whole families deliver "programs" with each member giving a talk related to missionary work, family cooperation, tithing, or genealogy. Children's testimonies typically consist of statements of thankfulness for living in their families, and expressions of love for their parents, siblings, and the Prophet of the Church. Mother's and Father's Days are marked by elaborate programs.[5] Mormon doctrine hammers on the theme of the home as an exclusive domain in which fathers and mothers teach their children how to be "worthy" of such blessings as stakehood, the Temple, the programs of the Church, and serving a mission. While the religious radio broadcasts in Tonga generally expound on Christian Biblical themes, the Mormons are distinctive for their messages about responsibilities of parents. When Mormons invoke the notion of *hotau ngaahi famili* ('our families'), they refer to an idealized nuclear family, and not extended kin networks that comprise most Tongan households of all religious affiliations. Even many of the most assimilated Tongan Mormon households continue to be composed of extended kin.

Mormon doctrine thus constructs a model of the family radically different from that found in the greater Tongan society. It should be noted, however, that the model is not entirely incompatible with conventional Tongan values. Mormon beliefs about men, for example, are generally compatible with Tongan constructions of gender, and kinship ideologies that designate husbands as more "chiefly" than their wives (though less "chiefly" than their older sisters; there is no representation in Mormon family model of the traditionally powerful *mehekitanga* 'paternal aunt'), and as *'ulumotu'a*, or 'heads of households' (although not leaders of extended families).[6] Many of the roles and the knowledge that the Mormon Church imparts to women are again not inconsistent with Tongan constructions of female gender. However, Mormonism explicitly precludes women from exercizing their prerogatives over their brothers and male cousins and thus obviates "chiefly" status for women. The Mormon model also ideally precludes the possibility of a woman's atttaining virtual *'ulumotu'a* status within her extended family by dint of economic and educational achievements (as men can). Mormon Tongan women are generally exhorted to focus their talents and energies within the nuclear family and learn domestic arts with this goal in mind. As we shall see below, perhaps the most radical difference between the Mormon model of gender relations and conventional Tongan ideals is in the former's virtual elimination of the *tapu* relation between brother and sister.

THE MORMON TONGAN FAMILY

Mormon doctrine projects a model of the family that is radically different from the experience of most Tongans. Much of the distinctiveness and the separation of the Mormon sub-culture in Tonga, and antagonism that the sub-culture evokes, rests directly on these key ideas about the family and salvation. So far, however, I have written primarily of ideas and ideals; a more complex picture of contextualization and subtle conflations of identity arises from an ethnographic perspective.

My data on how Tongans negotiate family identity is drawn from two communities in which I conducted fieldwork in 1982-84. The first is the pseudonymous Kolovava'u, a village in the northern island of Vava'u with the oldest continuous Mormon population in Tonga. This pluralistic setting, with its Wesleyan, Church of Tonga, and Mormon congregations, affords a glimpse of inter and intra-church cooperation and competition, and of the social boundaries of religious identity. The second setting is the highly acculturated community of Liahona, which is an enclave of 23 modern suburban homes in and around the capital of Nuku'alofa. The growth of Tonga's indigenous Mormon community and church structure has depended on a number of "strong" families to maintain its legitimacy, both in the eyes of Salt Lake City and the Tongan people. They live in the Liahona complex and sometimes return to a prosperous life in their natal villages after having attended college and worked overseas. Some of the most powerful Mormon leaders in Tonga are married to Americans they met while at Brigham Young University. The common language and code of prestige in Liahona is English. In the surrounding area are two burgeoning villages of "working class" Mormon Tongans who not possess lands on Tongatapu and who depend upon Liahona for their wages.

The degree to which Tongans reconstitute themselves as Mormons takes place along a spectrum of acculturation from isolated villages to Liahona, where the exemplary model is situated within the most successful Mormon elites. The difference between Mormons in a mixed community like Kolovava'u and an acculturated enclave like Liahona, however, is a matter of degree not kind. Mormons in both places engage in certain contexts and activities that sharply distinguish them from other Tongans; and both, in other circumstances, affirm their Tongan identity even when it conflicts with Mormon teachings.

NEGOTIATING IDENTITIES: BROTHER-SISTER RELATIONS

All Tongans place *faka'apa'apa*, or respect, of brothers for their sisters, and by extension an ideology of respect for all women, at the center of their moral system. Older sisters are considered more metaphorically *'eiki* 'chiefly' than their brothers and are subject to certain avoidance behavior. Practices that violate avoidance (*maumau e tapu*) include extended private talking, sexual joking, exposure of private parts of the body such as genitals, chest and thighs, dancing together, sitting together in a public place, and direct involvement in each other's clandestine courtships and marriages. Mixed peer groups of all ages will cease sexual joking, or any metaphorical references to courtship and sexual activity the instant an opposite sex sibling or cousin comes within earshot.

As with all non-Western Mormons, Tongan Mormons are encouraged by the Church to avoid the extremes of custom which are considered irrational and counterproductive to family solidarity and loving relations. This entails deliberately reducing the conventional distance between brothers and sisters, both inside the family and in public contexts. To do this, Tongan Mormons invent and represent Mormon-style brother-sister relations in a number of bounded, ritualized contexts, which do not necessarily extend into the areas in which baseline requirements of *tapu* are required. The fact that there *is* flexibility of the behavioral and communicative conventions surrounding the relationship also allow even the most devout Tongan Mormons to switch their frame of reference from one context to another: to observe Mormon Church standards of behavior in one, and Tongan standards of propriety in another.

One public context in which the Tongan model of sibling relations is overturned is the Mormon dance. Mormon dances are represented as clean, well lighted places for all Mormon members — and for all who conform to the dress code and standard of conduct — to enter and enjoy. They are a well-supervised setting for male and female youth to socialize with non-kinsmen — preferably returned missionaries. Like their American counterparts, the Tongan Mormon community closely regulates the behavior and life plan of adolescents. These controls and activities are lauded by other church leaders who see the ideal model of premarital chastity and the obedience and missionary zeal of Mormon youth — though not the beliefs — as a positive standard of morality.

None of the drunkenness and standing back that characterizes male behavior at other Tongan church dances occurs at the Mormon dance. The event, defined as an *'ekitiviti Siasi* 'Church activity', is carefully supervised by older married couples, and attended by Mormon leaders of various ranks. Considerable attention and expense as to appearance must be made by those who attend, including advance provisions to bring a partner. Brothers and sisters are sometimes found seated in the same general area, along with their families. One brother and sister team in Kolovava'u, both returned missionaries, were excellent ballroom dancers and would unabashedly take the floor for demonstrations. I likewise sometimes observed cousins dancing together in the early stages of the evening.

On the occasion of one such dance in Kolovava'u, I joined some members of the other two churches (Wesleyan and Church of Tonga) who often congregated outside of the modern chapel hall to socialize and comment on the activities inside. These observers considered the attention drawn to married and unmarried couples — symbolized in their physical proximity and matching "mumu-aloha" dress — to be humorous. The fact that the dances take place in the Church meeting hall was more serious — akin to polluting the sacred with the profane. Brothers actually dancing with their sisters was considered most scandalous and even animalistic. Despite the co-existence of these different church groups in Kolovava'u for 70 years, these recurring displays, continue to foster perceptions of the Mormon church as *muli* 'un-Tongan', and ties ongoing differences and boundaries in religious identity to the proper maintenance of cultural traditions.

In the wake of my first Mormon dance, (and still reeling from the public display of brother-sister contact) I questioned several Tongan sister missionaries about the *tapu* issue. Their answer confirmed my observations of brother-sister interactions in various Mormon households, that 'respectful' relations prevailed in their families in the form of physical modesty and a ban on 'swearing'. They said that it would be permissible to dance with their brothers, but only at a Mormon Church dance and not at one of the town discos which are ill-lit. The way the *kau palangi* 'Westerners' live in their families is alright for them, but not for the Tongans. These missionaries planned to teach their children to abide by the rules of 'respect'.

'FREEDOM TO CHOOSE'

While all Tongans sustain a high level of commitment to their respective churches, membership in the Mormon Church entails an even more intensive participation in a subculture which often conflicts with traditional Tongan values and representations of social institutions. In Korn's (1978) discussion of Tonga's multi-denominational society, she captured very nicely this aura of "difference" about the Mormons, but did not portray the extent to which they also shape Mormon doctrine to traditional patterns, especially at the village level. The "personal retooling" strategy which she coins as the prime motivation in converting to Mormonism is not limited to the unique opportunities for material advancement within the Mormon institutional system, but also applies to expectations and statuses that are distinctly Tongan. In other words, Mormons, like other Tongans, conflate Tongan and religious identity; they attempt to reconcile the common moral universe the two share, and the common goals to which the negotiation of religious identity through family practice is applied.

Tongan Mormons often express the license to bypass tradition in the phrase *tau'ataina ke fili* 'freedom to choose', which frequently appears in versions of Mormon scripture and Church manuals as the direct translation of "free will" (e.g., 2 Nephi2:27 in *The Book of Mormon*). The word *tau'ataina* has an equally complex meaning for Tongans as "free will" has for Europeans. It denotes freedom from accountability to rules and ranked superiors, and expresses the optative principle in Tongan social life that stands in opposition to *fuakavenga* 'obligation'. Mormon Tongans routinely invoke this idea to support certain innovations, like wearing Western clothes to church and adopting (or not adopting) a particular home economics lesson of the Relief Society. 'Freedom to choose', however, does not constitute an option in all contexts of social and economic life, particularly those situations which define a person in conventional terms as moral. Tongan Mormons must manifest proper Tongan behavior and values, both within their ward community and in relation to the wider society, if they are to maintain reputation.

One such context asserted itself in the village of Kolovava'u. A couple whom I'll call 'Isi and Sela lived with several adopted children (offspring of 'Isi's sister, a non-Mormon) in a neat wooden house with electricity and indoor plumbing, built entirely from money 'Isi earned in New Zealand where he lived with his older sister. The only other household member was 'Isi's mother. They very closely approximated nuclear family living, which Sela explained to me as living the Mormon gospel principle of self-reliance, through *tau'ataina* or freedom from oppressive obligations to other kindred: this enabled them to focus their energies on their children's 'progress' (*fakalaka*). One day they received a letter from 'Isi's older sister (also a Mormon) in New Zealand requesting that 'Isi give her his oldest daughter's unborn baby to adopt. Sela deeply resented her sister-in-law for exercising her prerogative, but she was powerless to cross either her husband or his sister. Despite the daughter's misery at parting with her baby after he was born, 'Isi made arrangements to fly him to New Zealand. Although Mormon doctrine stands in unequivocal opposition to such practices, and other Tongan Mormon villagers felt free to oppose 'Isi's capitulation to his sister, Sela explained the situation in terms of separate frames of reference for Mormon and Tongan thinking. No church in Tonga teaches disrespect and no matter what church a man belongs to, it would be 'shameful' (*fakama*) to refuse such a request. And Tongans are always Tongans, no matter what their religious beliefs.

Whatever the degree of acculturation to the Mormon model or experience overseas, Tongan Mormons in Kolovava'u, who numbered half of the village population, were arguably as equally invested in traditional modes of support and legitimation for their church as members of other denominations. When I compared a year's church-related expenses for a sampling of families from the three congregations, I discovered that the Mormons are in fact involved to an often greater extent than other Tongans in having to raise finances to put on feasts, and circulate ceremonial wealth in order to mark religious events and honor key participants. Within the Mormon Church, there are many circulating church positions which regularly receive new occupants, young missionaries who go and return from missions, chapel, and stake centers which must be dedicated, numerous conferences at the stake and ward levels throughout the year, dances, and ward socials. Tongan Mormons derive tremendous pride and moral satisfaction from being able to honor their obligations in a superior fashion, both in relation to each other, and in relation to the events staged by families of the other churches, even when it taxes the resources of the nuclear family.

All this necessitates a high degree of borrowing and resource sharing among extended kindred, activating the traditional ideologies that define those relationships. All categories of relatives borrowed from each other in Kolovava'u, though non-Mormons routinely complained that their Mormon kin rushed to borrow from them, but excluded them from the events that followed. This was a particularly serious charge because the Mormons of Kolovava'u were primarily salary earners, both inside the Church and in businesses, while the Wesleyan and Church of Tonga families had a larger proportion of farmers among them and thus a lesser cash flow. Wesleyans and Church of Tonga members claimed that they hesitated before making a request of a Mormon relative while Mormons said the opposite: their poorer relatives and neighbors were constantly borrowing from them. When the internal culture of the Mormon family did not interfere with the wider practice of resource sharing in the village, non-Mormons did not view Mormonism as constitutively foreign or unacceptable, but as a superficial badge of church affiliation that did not negate Tongan Christian morality.

It is the wealthier and more powerful Mormon Tongan elites — those who live in the Westernized enclave of Liahona — who have greater 'freedom to choose': to set examples and ground rules for interactions with extended and non-Mormon kin, and even to speak out against profligate spending on feasts. They also have greater success in substituting Mormon moral imperatives (providing for one's own children first, for example) over others (spending the children's school fees on a feast given by a sister to inaugurate a new Mormon chapel).

For these men and women, the responsibility for managing the politics of identity is weighty. By their public statements and behavior, they are expected to interpret and redefine 'the Tongan way' to resonate with Mormon ideologies in such a way that their way of life signifies a Christian ideal. Their church callings constitute a platform for them to promulgate correct living and their family lives must also conform to the model of "gospel living" in order to be considered by American Mormon leaders for higher ecclesiastical callings. In the interviews conducted by leaders to choose a Mission President, for example, several questions pertain to the activities, spirituality, and domestic skills of the wife. Both spouses have to be "good family people" and to demonstrate a commitment to "caring for their own families" in Mormon terms in order to ascend to important callings.

All of the most salient images associated with American Mormons may be observed in these people: many children, a van or microbus, Western clothing,[7] modern housing, and evidence inside their homes of considerable immersion in the activities of their church including Mormon scriptures, manuals, and journals. Husbands and wives are often seen sitting together in church and at dances, socializing in Church activities with other couples and families and entering the Temple together. Socializing as families and as married couples is particularly frequent in the mixed American-Tongan community of Liahona; in the villages, far more time is spent in sex-segregated social activities like kava-drinking for men and weaving baskets for sale to tourists and tapa-making for women. Exemplary husband and wife teams are constantly traveling to preside over the Mormon programs which appear with great frequency throughout the Tongan islands. In these Sunday night "firesides" (special programs for youth), special missionary conferences, area conferences, and ward and stake conferences, their talks often focus on the proper ways for Mormon Tongans to conduct courtship and marriage, and members are exhorted to follow the life plan that ensures celestial marriage. These spouse teams share anecdotes about their relationship, alternating joking and serious frames as American Mormons would. (In Tongan culture competitive joking between married couples signals closeness in public contexts). They urge members to adopt radical solutions to the obstacles posed to Tongan society to "celestial marriage" practices. Foremost is 'talking straight' (*lea hangatonu*) as opposed to 'lying' (*loi*) and metaphorical, indirect speech (*lea heleaki*), which are standard communicative conventions among all Tongans. Newlyweds are expected to speak in Sacrament meetings about their new commitments to each other and to the Church.

Resource sharing among extended kin must nonetheless be accomplished if Mormons are to have any credibility as Christians. The following profile of a high-ranking Mormon Tongan Church official shows how this is made possible, given his sophistication in interpreting the Tongan and Mormon cultural frameworks in terms of each other. He explained to me that his family values embrace showing "respect" and "love" for his parents, sisters, and brothers alike, even if they are not yet members of the Church. The success of his marriage with his American wife has rested on their having both agreed to compromise on the issue of providing for the economic well-being of members of his extended family (which included the immediate families of his other siblings). Such requests include contributing on occasion to education, feasts, and house-buildings of his various relatives, many of whom he personally baptized in the Church and who look to him for spiritual leadership. In order to balance the welfare of his large nuclear family with the legitimate expectations of his *kainga,* he applied the "gospel principles" of budgeting and allocating resources which he learned on his mission, as a Stake President, and as a high-ranking employee of the Church. He and his wife together set aside a portion of their household budget to lease out bush lands which he allocates to relatives to farm. He calls the collective effort produced by his *kainga* and other fellow Church members building a "testimony of love through work." He sees this as an example of a gospel principle of economic cooperation, like the communalistic United Order of the early Mormon Church. He also sees family cooperation as the "fruits of genealogy," and the products thereof as "blessings." Even though he recognizes that he is regarded as an *'ulumotu'a* 'ranked head' of his extended family, it would go against his religion to interfere in any way with the internal family decisions of his relatives. He simply sees himself as providing direction and example.

As this profile of the Church leader indicates, even the more urbanized Tongan Mormon elites are engaged in sharing with their various extended kindred, and honor the conventions of respect for ranked relations. To do otherwise would be to risk being labelled as unChristian and *ta'e 'ofa* 'without love' by fellow Mormons and Wesleyans alike. This is in keeping with Tongan thinking about the responsibilities of those with high status and wealth. It is they who are in a position to patronize, and thus to control and direct the welfare of other relatives.

CONCLUSION

The Mormon Church in Tonga pursues a policy of frequent creation of bounded events, both public and private, in which basic Tongan principles about familial relations and communicative conventions are temporarily overturned. By adopting these discourses and practices, Church leaders hope that Tongans will let go of cultural features that impede perfectibility and the attainment of celestial glory. Tongans indeed learn their Mormon identity through the accumulated experience of these bounded contexts.

By enacting Church doctrine in certain institutionalized contexts, Tongan Mormons set themselves apart as a distinct religious community within Tonga. This in turn enables them to navigate successfully through the ecclesiastical hierarchy and the Church employment system. Yet we have seen that even Mormon leaders do not necessarily extend Mormon doctrine into all frames and interactions of Tongan life. Conventional values of mutual support among extended kin continues to figure strongly in individuals' lives. Indeed, there is some indication that Mormon Tongans may at times convert Mormon activities to Tongan ends: through doing genealogy, for example, and reconstituting their known lines of descent as Mormons in Temple ritual, they also appropriate and systematize knowledge about kinship which is used toward very Tongan ends — to build alliances and cooperation among *kainga.*

Tongan members of the Mormon Church with its *mata'i muli* 'foreign face' must in fact walk a fine line between innovation and conservatism to navigate the complex social reality of the *anga fakatonga* 'Tongan way'. Tongans are able to maintain the two systems as separate frames of reference or to view one system as an ideal expression of the other. Often, what is called innovation in one context can come to be interpreted as tradition in another. Thus brothers and sisters dancing with each other at a Mormon Church function seems radically innovative given the customary *tapu* relation between siblings of the opposite sex; but to Mormons, who would never dream of allowing their children to dance in town discos, Church dances form a special way the sexes may show proper modesty and their respect towards each other.

Tongan culture continues to be selectively permeable to the adoption of Western ideas and materials, which are appropriated into a self-conscious body of tradition. There is an indigenous idea of 'progress' or 'advancement' (*fakalaka*) which in the modern sense has come to encompass the physical trappings of Western society, and the expectations and means for acquiring them. As Tongans shape their interpretation of the primary Mormon meanings into an effective representation of the Mormon family model, what emerges is convergent on processes already in motion in the political economy of modern Tonga. All Tongans are acutely aware that the emerging class structure, complicated by the traditional system of hereditary rank, has produced increasing contradictions between the importance and economic exclusivity of the Tongan *famili* in relation to extended networks of *kainga.* The Mormon "rationalization" of family practice, both in public and private contexts is a powerful means for advancement within the alternative Mormon class structure. Tongan Mormons also view their church as hastening the inevitible 'advancement' of Tonga as a whole, with themselves in the vanguard. The Tongan Mormon family thus takes on additional metaphorical dimensions in the invention and negotiation of religious identity. It is at once a symbol of a particular vehicle of salvation, of Tongan Christian identity in general, and of a new Tongan social order.

NOTES

Fieldwork in the Kingdom of Tonga was carried out from November, 1982 through August, 1984, with the support of a University of California Regents Traveling Grant and Lowie Fellowships from the Department of Anthropology, University of California Berkeley. I am extremely grateful to the Tongan Government, to many Tongans who must remain anonymous, to the Mormon leaders who were inordinately kind and helpful to me, and to Tevita Toli Hala'api'api for his insights during the preparation of this chapter. Thanks also to John Barker for helpful comments on earlier drafts.

1. Nine percent is probably a conservative figure, considering the bias inherent in the method of enumeration: although the Church appeals heavily to youthful converts, only heads of households were consulted. The LDS Statistics Office and Desert News

Almanac report a baptized population of 30,000 — nearly one-third of the entire population (Church of Jesus Christ of Latter Day Saints 1980-86). These somewhat doubtful statistics (Church records tend to retain the names of inactive members who have long since joined or returned to another church) would give Tonga the highest member-to-nonmember ratio in the world.

2. Unless otherwise indicated, historical data on the Mormon mission in Tongan was taken from the Latter Day Saints Quarterly Reports (1916-84), Nuku'alofa and Salt Lake City. See also Gordon (1988).
3. Standard works on Mormon history, theology and organizational structure include O'Dea (1957), Leone (1979) and Shipps (1985).
4. The Mormon Church in Tonga has had to adapt to a dialectic between the rhetoric of acceptance and of condemnation on the part of the King and nobility. While the King attends and becomes the focal point of all major Mormon events to which he is invited, he has also exercised his chiefly prerogative to undermine the Mormons' credibility in a number of ways. In the 1960's, he appropriated a Mormon chapel in Nuku'alofa and converted it to a restaurant. During the course of my fieldwork in 1982-84, he invited American anti-Mormon evangelists to preach and show films throughout Tonga and he also sponsored anti-Mormon gatherings of high-ranking Tongan chiefs and ministers.
5. Ironically, Tongan Wesleyans have adopted the practice of sacralizing these holidays in church from the Mormons.
6. Tongan kinship and its attendant ideologies of rank have been summarized by Kaeppler (1971).
7. Many of the woman dress in Hawaiian style, reflecting the Pan-Polynesian Mormon subculture promulgated at the Polynesian Cultural Center at Brigham Young University in Hawaii.

11

CATHOLICISM AND PULAPESE IDENTITY

Juliana Flinn

In formulating a cultural identity, people assert certain aspects of their way of life, their culture, as essential to who they are as a group. But the selection of these traits or customs — regardless of how old they may be — and their assertion as components of a group's cultural identity take place in the present (Linnekin 1983). Tradition as a key image represents a contemporary symbolic construction. People actively formulate an identity, one that relates to contemporary needs, concerns, and issues. Thus with tradition, we are likely to find both continuity and discontinuity with the past, because tradition is not simply something from the past that has persisted into the present; it is how the past is perceived, interpreted, and asserted in the present (Handler 1984; Handler and Linnekin 1984).

The concept of cultural identity and ethnic identity differ, although the two are often used in the same way, with an ethnic group treated essentially as a cultural group (Berreman 1983:289). The difference according to Berreman is a subtle one: "ethnic" has to do with how a people perceive and assert aspects of their culture whereas, "cultural" has to do with content, with what it is that a group shares. Carstens (1986:88), however, makes a different distinction. For her, both concepts deal with images. Cultural identity subsumes the entire cultural image a group has of itself, one presented both to outsiders and to each other. Ethnic identity, on the other hand, subsumes only the particular cultural traits a group selects to construct an image presented to others. These traits supposedly differentiate a group from others, so that ethnic identity emphasizes boundaries with other groups (cf. Barth 1969).

Yet these attempts to differentiate the two terms neglect the ethnocentricity of the concepts of ethnicity and ethnic identity. Linnekin and Poyer (in press), for example, maintain that ethnic identity is one type of cultural identity, one that is Western in ideology because it is based on Western notions of biology and descent. They caution against ethnocentrically applying these concepts to other formulations of identity, because other people may have other ways of organizing their beliefs about themselves and cultural others. Linnekin and Poyer describe how Pacific island notions of cultural identity are grounded in notions of the person that differ from Western ones. To Pacific islanders, a person is typically someone with a network of relations with others rather than an isolated individual. And behavior towards those others is essential to identity. In other words, cultural identity in the Pacific is based less on biology and descent than on behavior. Shared identity does not derive so much from biology as from shared food, land, companionship, and sociability. Biological connectedness may provide a model, but behavior is the determining factor. Nonetheless, much of the theory of ethnicity and ethnic identity applies to Pacific island formulations of cultural identity, particularly the notion that identities are situationally flexible and often emerge through interaction with other groups.

In formulating a cultural identity, people can creatively incorporate Christianity into the image they construct of themselves. Although Christianity is a foreign intrusion in Oceania, islanders in some ways have been able to draw meaning from Christianity to construct a positive identity, providing self-esteem in the modern context. People may even perceive Christian teachings as extolling their own traditional core values. In this way, a group both embraces the new and finds value in the old. Without having to erect a boundary between the old and the new, islanders have found ways of interpreting and embracing Christianity in ways that provide continuity with traditional values and serve their needs in the modern setting (see Gordon, Kaplan, Smith, this volume).

For the people of Truk in Micronesia, core values center on sharing, nurturing, and cooperation, particularly among kin. Goodenough (1951:31), for example, when elaborating on sibling relations, stresses the sharing of property and offering of mutual support expected of fellow lineage members. Gladwin and Sarason (1953:49) describe the ideal Trukese as someone who is "kind, generous, mild," whose personal interests are subordinated to those of the descent group. Marshall (1976, 1977, 1981) has consistently stressed a pattern of resource sharing as essential to Trukese kinship. Kin should *tong* 'love' one another, *tumwunuu, fengen* 'take care of each other', and *lilis fengen* 'cooperate' (Marshall 1976:38). In a detailed analysis of ideal character traits, Caughey (1977) points out that the islanders value both exhibiting respect and avoiding arrogant and haughty behavior, particularly toward kin. The island communities apparently vary, however, regarding attitudes towards expressing aggression and accepting assertive or competitive behavior in appropriate contexts.

Pulapese, who inhabit an atoll in the western part of Truk State, find these core values consistent with many teachings of the Catholic church. They derive meanings from Catholicism that promote notions of sharing and cooperation and reinforce ideals of matriliny. In the modern context of rapid sociocultural change, Pulapese construct an image of themselves as a people who embody these valued traits. These islanders are not simply passive victims of outside forces; they contend with them. Being among the least acculturated in Truk provides support for an identity as people who embody the highest values and standards of behavior. The islanders are proud of being Catholic and have incorporated that pride into aspects of their belief system concerning what sort of people they are and into the image they present of themselves to other islanders. Elsewhere I have described the formulation of Pulapese cultural identity (Flinn 1985a). In this paper I describe how a foreign element — Catholicism — relates to that identity, and how Pulapese use it to buttress contentions that they exhibit good, traditionally valued behavior. They also merge traits of being a good Catholic, such as taking one spouse for life, with being a good Pulapese, and thus contend they merit respect from other islanders. At the same time, Pulapese attempt to distance themselves from behavior other islanders tend to label barbaric by attributing the practices to their pre-Christian days.

THE SETTING

Pulap is one of three atolls in the Western Islands, which lie about 130 miles west of Truk Lagoon in the Federated States of Micronesia. The two inhabited islets of the atoll are Pulap and Tamatam, but Pulap is larger in both area and population. It measures 0.262 squares miles in area (Bryan 1971) and in 1980 had 432 people (United States Department of State 1980). The two other atolls in the Western Islands group are Puluwat and Pulusuk, both south of Pulap. Inter-island canoe travel remains common in the Westerns, providing opportunities for considerable inter-island interaction. Contact with other islands, however, especially Truk Lagoon, is usually by a government ship which arrives irregularly and infrequently, perhaps six times a year.

Homesites and canoe houses, many still made of thatch, line the southern, sheltered end of the islet. Each homesite is named and represents a matrilineal descent line and typically includes the women of the group, together with their husbands and children. Even though land tenure has become individualized, homesite members share use-rights and produce.

Economic activity is directed primarily toward subsistence fishing and horticulture, although islanders can earn a very modest income from selling copra and fish. Teaching at the elementary school on the island provides the only full-time employment. A number of Pulapese now live and work on Moen, however, which is the administrative and commercial center of Truk. Pulap's young people are attending secondary schools on

Moen and many are leaving to attend college in the United States. When they finish, most hope to obtain employment on Moen rather than return home, since the only opportunities on Pulap are the traditional subsistence activities.

At the present time all of Pulap is Roman Catholic. The community is part of the diocese of the Caroline and Marshall Islands. This diocese is administered by a bishop, a few Micronesian priests, several Jesuit priests (a few of whom are Micronesian), and Micronesian deacons. An American Jesuit ministers to the Western Islands. His primary residence is Puluwat, south of Pulap, but he usually manages to visit the other atolls several times a year. In his absence a Pulap deacon and Pulap catechists take charge. They hold services every morning in a church built in the central settlement area and lead the rosary every afternoon. Although only a handful may participate in these daily observances, virtually all the women and many of the men attend church on Sunday and during special services held the first Friday of each month.

Catholicism is relatively new for the Pulapese. They converted less than forty years ago through the efforts of a Mortlockese catechist who arrived on the atoll in the late 1940s. This was much later than other areas of Truk and elsewhere in Micronesia. The first attempt at conversion that Pulapese recall was made by a Protestant catechist from Truk Lagoon, who lived on the islet during the German era before World War I. Later, during the Japanese administration, a Catholic catechist from Truk is said to have stayed for about three years but was asked to leave because of carrying on affairs with island women. A similar fate met a Protestant catechist from Moen who reportedly arrived about 1940.

Oral tradition regarding conversion provides some insight into Pulapese cultural images of themselves as Catholics and as Pulapese. The notion of strength emerges quite often. Most commentary about their conversion, for example, centers on the catechist's strength of personality and of belief. And when describing the less successful earlier attempts, Pulapese comment either on the strength of indigenous beliefs or the lack of moral strength on the part of the catechist. Pulapese expected catechists to behave according to local norms and the precepts they were trying to teach. Aside from the personal persuasiveness of the Mortlockese catechists as a factor in their conversion, Pulapese probably perceived advantages to acquiescence. The catechist arrived soon after the advent of the American administration and all the evidence of *its* strength, which included defeating the Japanese and introducing some dramatically effective medical practices.

Change connected with conversion to Christianity was less thoroughgoing on Pulap than places converted earlier in Truk. Hezel (1978) has described the relatively recent move among missionaries, particularly in the Catholic Church, toward indigenization, incorporating aspects of local cultural tradition into Catholicism. Not only has this movement stressed tradition and custom, but it has contributed to a critical examination of modernization and its consequences. No longer is all that is American or Western superior to what is Micronesian. In fact, retreating from attempts to "civilize" natives, the church encourages maintenance of a strong cultural identity. Although this movement gained strength after Pulapese converted and were encouraged to abandon some of their old ways, the islanders nonetheless are reaping some of the benefits.

Missionary activity primarily affected religious practices and certain customs directly contrary to Catholic dogma, including some aspects of marriage and family life. Whereas divorce and remarriage were common in the past, they are now forbidden to couples married in the church. The Catholic church also prohibits birth control and abortion, but these bans are of little concern since Pulapese value children and large families, and they attach relatively little stigma to a woman having a child out of wedlock. The priest has tried unsuccessfully to discourage adoption, contending that mothers should not give away their children, but despite the priest's objections, the practice continues to be widespread. The priest has a certain degree of power in the area of divorce because he can refuse a second church marriage, but he has little by way of sanctions to impose in the area of adoption, which involves no church ritual.

Rituals and activities invoking ancestor spirits and other supernatural creatures were also prohibited in the early mission period. Menstrual houses, puberty rites, and magical chants disappeared. Also lost were some healing rituals and many activities associated with navigation, such as the initiation of new navigators. Traditional activities which have been retained now occur only without magical songs or chants that previously accompanied them. For example, local medicines are now administered without magical formulas. Belief in ghosts and ancestor spirits persists nonetheless, and even the educated continue to believe they can communicate with the spirits in dreams.

In their eyes, Pulapese made a distinction, with the help of missionaries, between what was "pagan" and what was "just custom." For example, Pulapese contend that the catechist went too far in encouraging them to abandon some of their ways, such as the custom of women stooping or crawling for their brothers. They felt they had to convince church authorities that the custom was one of respect and had nothing to do with paganism. Pulapese firmly believe in a difference between paganism and "our way of life." In fact, some of the older people who remember the catechist speak with pride of some "pagan" ways they chose to abandon on their own, such as magical chants from navigation. These appealed to supernatural, non-Christian, beings. Giving up the chants enabled them therefore to retain the other aspects of navigational customs.

Other parts of Truk experienced far more thoroughgoing changes in the course of their conversions than did the Pulapese. On Etal, for example, Protestant missionary emphasis on individualism contributed to a weakening of descent groups and cooperation and sharing among kin (Nason 1978). These earlier missionaries promoted Western values of social, political, and economic individualism, encouraging, for instance, individualized ownership of property rather than corporate ownership by indigenous descent groups. Before conversion, group concerns eclipsed individual interests, and cooperation and sharing were highly valued. Such behavior was particularly incumbent upon members of the same descent group but ideally extended to everyone in the community. According to Nason, ancestral spirits played a key role in maintaining the system, and clan chiefs, acting for the good of the group, mediated between members of the clan and its ancestral spirits. Missionaries undermined the priority of the group over the individual by attacking ancestral spirits and all activities and beliefs they perceived to be related to them. As a result, clan chiefs declined in importance while younger, educated people gained in status and wealth. Yet more than a mere substitution of criteria for status emerged. Whereas clan chiefs had to be concerned with the welfare of all group members, the younger men have not felt the same sort of obligation. Nason does not claim that Christianity actually caused the shift in emphasis on cooperation and sharing to individual concerns, but that it promoted the transition and provided the islanders with an ideology to explain and cope with the many changes they were experiencing.

This pattern does not appear to be inevitable, however. On the nearby islet of Kutu, considerable change occurred because of missionary influence, including the loss of ceremonies and activities connected with ancestors (Reafsnyder 1984). The Protestant missionaries attacked many traditional customs such as dancing. But cooperation, generosity, and sharing, particularly among kin remain core values for the Kutu people, and they actively discourage individualism. The people find these values consistent with Christian teachings and pride themselves on being good Christians as opposed to people of Truk Lagoon, who supposedly still retain aspects of their old religion, rituals, and beliefs. Kutu people in this regard seem to believe they have undergone more change than the people of Truk Lagoon by abandoning more behavior that is non-Christian. Thus tradition as practiced by Trukese is "evil." Traditional customs retained on Kutu, however, they construe as consistent with Christian values.

Missionary activities on Pulap have allowed for the retention of more traditional ways, and Pulapese in fact have formulated an image of themselves as the most traditional people of Truk. Change has been most dramatic for Pulap during the American administration, coming later than for Etal and Kutu. Pulapese realize that they were among the last to become Christian and that they also began attending formal schools and obtaining employment after others in Truk had successfully sought the new opportunities for wealth, power, and prestige. Thus to a certain extent, Pulapese feel disadvantaged relative to islanders already in positions of power. On the other hand, they have had an opportunity to note some adverse consequences of adopting new ways and values. For example, Pulapese perceive others in Truk as being dependent on money and thus no longer self-sufficient. And they believe that reliance on money steers people away from traditional patterns of sharing. Pulapese note that other islanders no longer have sailing canoes but purchase motorboats, which cost money, need fuel, and break down. To the Pulapese, reliance on foreign technology weakens the value of traditional skills and the prestige of those who hold specialized knowledge. Pulapese observe that young people from other islands go off to school and either do not return or return having lost respect for elders. Other islanders have come to rely increasingly on rice and other imported foods instead of the traditional foods linked by Pulapese with core values having to do with cooperation, sharing, kinship, and gender ideology. Giving up those foods implies abandoning the attached values.

Pulapese consciously attempt to retain certain customs and patterns of behavior they perceive to be traditional. These customs demonstrate in their eyes their continued commitment to core values. Through appropriate behavior, people reveal their character traits. For example, women exhibit respect by "crawling" for their brothers, and Pulapese contend that most other islanders in Truk have abandoned this behavior, and by implication the valued character trait as well. Men still make and sail their traditional canoes, a sign of self-sufficiency, skill, manliness, bravery, and strength (strength that rests with knowledge, not aggression). In asserting their cultural identity — to themselves as well as to other islanders — Pulapese deliberately practice much of this behavior in the small community they have established on Moen. For example, migrants wear lavalavas and loincloths in the village as a cultural symbol of self-sufficiency instead of reliance on money. They prepare traditional foods and distribute them to all Pulapese as evidence of their cooperation and unity and retention of kinship behavior (Flinn in press).

BEING PULAPESE AND CATHOLIC

When Pulapese discuss their cultural identity or formulate an image of what it means to be Pulapese, they stress retention of traditional patterns of behavior, especially those customs having to do with relations and behavior among kin. The individual and his or her rights have not come to overshadow the descent group or island community. Appropriate behavior toward others, particularly fellow descent group members, remains paramount. This behavior contributes to kin group solidarity and continued attention to demonstrating concern for others, especially fellow descent group members and other close kin, rather than focusing on the rights of individuals. A belief that they have retained traditional, customary behavior expected of kin is a key element of Pulapese cultural identity, and it is fundamental to their assertions of superiority over other islanders who have reputedly lost traditional ways and who supposedly exhibit less behavior indicative of *tong* 'love' and *mehonohon* 'respectfulness'.

One of the general claims Pulapese make about the sort of people they are is that they exhibit *tong*, or 'love, pity, mercy, compassion' (cf. Elbert 1972:183). Not only on Pulap, but throughout Truk, behavior exhibiting this sentiment is highly valued and held as an ideal. *Tong* is said to be strongest among matrilineal kin, who are conceptualized as a group of siblings (Flinn 1985b; Goodenough 1951:31; Marshall 1981). The expression of *tong* is linked with kinship, and demonstrating *tong* demonstrates kinship. Elsewhere I have argued that being a good 'brother' or 'sister', and in general behaving as kin ought to behave through sharing resources and showing concern, provides evidence of being a good person (Flinn 1985a). In addition to sharing of resources, Pulapese emphasize appropriate deference and respect behavior that junior siblings show senior siblings. This contributes to a reputation for being *mehonohon* 'modest, respectful', also a valued character trait throughout Truk (Caughey 1977), and again something that is exhibited through behavior toward others, especially kin.

According to conventional wisdom on the island, Catholicism has promoted such behavior and enabled Pulapese to demonstrate more easily their good qualities. Presumably they had the potential to exhibit *tong* all along, but people contend it was more fully realized and strengthened with Catholicism. For example, women speak of how they used to fight over men in their pagan days although ideally they should have been modest and respectful. Now they claim they no longer behave that way and are able to live closer to the ideal because of their new religion.

The emphasis and value placed on sharing and cooperation applies in a diffuse sense to the community as a whole. Such behavior is particularly incumbent upon kin but ideally extends to everyone on Pulap. In fact, it would be unlikely for there not to be some sort of kin tie — though distant in some cases — among all of the islanders. Although such ties are typically not activated in day-to-day activities, they emerge for feasts and other community affairs such as weekly meetings and annual elementary school graduation. Pulapese present themselves as a people who are unified, cooperating with one another, rather than divided into factions.

Being all of one faith contributes to this image for them. They assert that other islands are marked by discord and cleavages, and one type of division is one that runs along church affiliation lines. To retain their unity, Pulapese resist efforts of non-Catholic missionaries to preach on the island. One example Pulapese frequently cited concerned the visit of a Protestant mission boat from the neighboring atoll of Puluwat. Puluwat is a religiously divided community, half Protestant and half Catholic, a split Pulapese deride since it signifies lack of unity. To demonstrate that Puluwat attempts to convert them would be unwelcome, Pulapese refused to extend their customary hospitality to the visitors. A few individuals brought food to specific Puluwat relatives, but the community as a whole refused to feed them. Part of their attitude had to do with resisting Puluwatese, who, in their eyes were trying to reign over them again and impose their ways, but at the same time, Pulapese resented attempts to divide the community into two religious factions.

In the same vein, if a non-Pulap man marries a Pulap woman, and especially if he intends to settle according to the custom of uxorilocal residence, he is expected to convert to Catholicism. A man who marries off the island may or may not convert, and Pulapese understand either decision. If a man converts from Catholicism when he marries off the island, Pulapese interpret his actions not as a rejection of the truth but as a gesture of cooperation with his wife's kin and of commitment to the group and island he marries into. Again, the emphasis in their belief system and projected image of themselves is on the common interest, the community or island interest, rather than concerns of the individual. The Christian emphasis on harmony and concern for others dovetails with Pulapese concepts of cooperation and focus on descent group and community concerns. This, rather than individualism, has come to the fore.

The church building itself is a symbol of unity. The building is located together with other public buildings, including the school and the meeting house, centrally located in the settlement area on the southern end of the islet. The community views the church as public, belonging to all the people of the island, like the meeting house. In fact, Pulapese commonly hold a meeting Sundays after attending church. One of the most talked about recent events on Pulap, and the occasion of elaborate festivities, was the dedication celebration after the church was expanded and renovated.

Island feasts also demonstrate unity, and most of them in one way or another are associated with the church. Weddings, for instance, involve the entire community, and many Catholic holy days, especially Easter and Christmas, are occasions for feasts with large amounts of food and entertainment such as songs, dances, speeches, and contests. Another example is December 8, the Feast of the Immaculate Conception, when women bring cooked taro (*Colocasia esculenta*), the prestige food, as an offering to Mary, and compete to determine who has grown the largest and the best taro corms. This replaces earlier ceremonies during which people offered food to pre-Christian gods.

The work of the church associations is work Pulapese view as for the common good of the island and parallels behavior indicative of being a good relative, such as bringing food to visitors. These church organizations include a five-member Parish Council; the *Selaator*, an organization of twenty senior men; and the *Selaatora*, an organization of twenty senior women.[1] For younger people of both sexes is an organization called *Mwiiren Yasor* 'group that makes offerings'. Almost all of the forty to forty-five members are between the ages of eighteen and thirty, and they represent about three-quarters of the resident women and about sixty percent of the resident men within this age range. These young people carry out much of the physical labor involved in the upkeep and building of the church, visit and pray with the sick, and occasionally bring food to visitors on the island. *Mwiiren Yasor* raises money from the sale of pandanus mats and sennit its members make. Moreover, the members often meet together following the afternoon rosary to practice new hymns and learn Bible passages.

Pulapese assert pride in their unity, in being all of one Christian faith, and they resist attempts to convert them to another, but their resistance is based more on the potentially divisive impact of a segment of the island converting than on the rightness or wrongness of any particular denomination. Nevertheless, they do contend that being Catholic is better than being Protestant. Certain aspects of Catholicism and its ideals they assert as superior to Protestantism, and they have incorporated some elements of being a good Catholic into their notions of being a good Pulapese. In particular, they claim pride in not allowing divorce, even though it used to be common on the island, as was the case elsewhere in the area. Catholicism forbids remarriage and divorce, and once married in the church, no Pulapese has subsequently remarried unless the first spouse has died.

(They do, however, separate from a spouse they are unhappy with.) Pulapese proudly take this practice as further evidence of 'love', an aspect of their character reputedly strengthened by Catholicism.

In their eyes Catholics are more able to exhibit 'love' than other people. Some stories told on the island about Russians are revealing in this regard. Under American influence, Pulapese are extremely leery and suspicious of anyone labeled Communist and typically equate Russians with Communists (and Russia with the Soviet Union). The islanders tell a story about Russian Communists who supposedly arrived by submarine at Lamotrek, an atoll to the west in Yap State. According to the story, these Russians abused the residents, jailing some and striking others. Stories of this sort are intended to reveal the true nature of Communists and of Russians. Pulapese tell another story, however, of Russians who arrived at Pulusuk, south of Pulap in the Western Islands. These Russians behaved quite differently: like good Pulapese, they gave away goods, money, and food to the residents there. Since Russians are Communists and Communists are reputedly bad, Pulapese had difficulty understanding why the Russian visitors behaved as they did, exhibiting such uncharacteristic generosity and concern. In the end they decided that Russia must have some Catholics, and that those particular visitors must have been Catholics, because Catholics *tongey aramah* — 'love people'.

Thus Pulapese have integrated certain aspects of Catholicism with their traditional value system, claiming that Catholicism reinforces and highlights the positive aspects. In addition, however, they use Catholicism to dissociate themselves from traits which today are not highly valued patterns of behavior. In particular, displaying strength or bravery is problematic, as it borders on arrogance, disrespect, competitiveness, and aggression (cf. Caughey 1977:26; Marshall 1979:56-57). An emphasis on sharing, cooperation, and modest, unassuming behavior is widespread in Truk, and aggressive, assertive behavior is generally inhibited, although the degree to which aggressive behavior in certain contexts is tolerated or valued seems to vary. Caughey (1977) describes the value placed on *pwara* 'bravery' in certain situations on a Truk Lagoon island, carefully pointing out, however, that even on nearby islands, the relative value placed on the show of bravery differs. On one, aggressive and competitive behavior has value in certain contexts, and on another very little. Inter-district and inter-island warfare were common throughout Truk until the German administration put an end to such hostilities early in the 20th century. Aggressive behavior toward kin, particularly fellow lineage members was prohibited, and aggression expressed outside the lineage was less reprehensible but nonetheless problematic. Warfare is no longer acceptable, although bravery and signs of manliness are still valued. In Truk Lagoon, drunken comportment (Marshall 1979), competitive feasts (Gladwin and Sarason 1953:53), and baseball (Murdock 1965) apparently serve as substitutes for warfare as contexts for exhibiting bravery.

At issue is balancing the values surrounding generosity, respect, and cooperation on the one hand and bravery and strength on the other. Pulapese today contend they are kind, peaceful, respectful people, yet they want to avoid appearing weak or cowardly. In the same vein, they want to present themselves as people who are strong and brave, yet without exhibiting aggression. One way they do so is by taking pride in having been good warriors in the past, before it was outlawed. They use the fact of their conversion to Catholicism as part of their efforts to have it both ways, to be both peaceful and fierce. By highlighting their past, they point out that they are capable of successful warfare and are thus worthy of respect because of their bravery, yet converting to Catholicism means they chose no longer to do so. Thus Pulapese can divorce themselves from behavior that is interpreted today as "bad" while asserting their capacity to be brave and strong. They can claim they are people who choose to be peaceful and modest, to exhibit *tong* 'love' and they claim Catholicism has aided them in doing so.

CATHOLICISM AND CHANGE

Pulapese cultural identity and the manner in which Catholicism has been incorporated into assertion of that identity have not existed in a vacuum but in the context of American administration of Micronesia and dramatic sociocultural change. Formal education and paid employment in the port town of Moen have become increasingly available, but Pulapese have been among the last to begin seeking these options. They are among the least acculturated islands of Truk, and today they are proud of their traditionalism and assert it as a virtue. It provides, in their eyes, a model for other Trukese of appropriate behavior and customs. Nonetheless, they are increasingly interested in the resources and prestige available in today's Truk; they want access to political positions and jobs, and they want a voice in making decisions. Essential to these in their view is education, and Catholicism is associated both with the American presence and with access to the best education available in the area. Catholicism is associated with American influence in part because Pulap was converted after the U.S. took over administration of the islands following World War II and because the priest himself is an American Jesuit in a diocese run by Americans. Whatever reservations Pulapese have about changes other islanders have experienced, they nonetheless want the income, goods, jobs, and prestige available through education and employment. Being good Catholics and stressing the advantages of having converted presumably legitimate their rights to such positions.

Catholicism does provide Pulapese with access to an elite education and the prestigious positions that education makes feasible. Thus there is considerable practical advantage to emphasizing the role of Catholicism in their lives and the extent to which they are good Catholics. The private Catholic schools in Truk have a reputation for providing a superior education, and education is viewed as a key to obtaining a job, with its attendant income and prestige. Those who have been able to attend Catholic schools have indeed been among those to obtain the better jobs.

Pulapese need the support and backing of their priest, however, and in some cases from the missionary who works on Namonuito Atoll, north of Pulap. The American Jesuit who lives on Ulul in the Namonuitos plays an important role in affairs of the public secondary school on the island, a school which Pulapese students attend before continuing on to the high school on Moen. This priest is particularly concerned with the impact of the behavior of students from the more acculturated islands on Namonuito and Western Island students, whose behavior he views as more appropriately respectful, modest, and moral. His attitude reinforces Pulapese pride in their own customs. He also administers a test for admission to the Catholic high school and can make personal recommendations for the students. Pulapese thus have an incentive to be good Catholics and to stress the advantages that Catholicism has brought to them, such as enabling them to learn more consistently and effectively to exhibit 'love'.

For those who return to Pulap rather than look for jobs on Moen, a Catholic education is still an asset. They are more likely to obtain higher positions or appointments in the church organizations, positions which bring them increased prestige in the island's social life. In this way, young people can achieve positions of status which traditionally could not be acquired until one was an older adult and had accumulated knowledge and specialized skills (Flinn 1985b). New statuses, such as deacon and catechist, have been added to the social structure, along with teachers and municipal officers, and the new academic and religious knowledge is not under control of the elders, or of islanders themselves, but of outsiders. The priest may appoint people to these positions even when the islanders do not consider them to be the best suited. For the Pulapese, then, Catholicism can gain them access to outside knowledge and the opportunities and prestige it can provide.

CONCLUSION

Catholicism — introduced from the outside but embraced by the Pulapese and incorporated into their cultural identity — plays a role in allowing Pulapese to be both traditional and modern. They have a sense of continuity with their past such that they feel they are deserving of respect in the contemporary context. In fact, Pulapese contend for a position in the modern context by exhibiting what they perceive as the best of being traditional. They can be important and valued people, retaining what they believe others have lost and demonstrating behavioral traits they believe others value and esteem. These others include other Trukese, Americans, and members of the Catholic hierarchy, all of whom comprise part of the social and political environment.

Given the constraints and opportunities in the contemporary context, the people of Truk state seek an identity that is a positive one, providing them with self-esteem and the possibility of prestige among others. Christianity can be an effective resource in this process in a variety of ways. On Etal, for example, the islanders seem to have found in Christianity a way of understanding and coping with the contact situation. It at least provides an ideology to explain change. The people of Kutu found Christian values consistent with core Kutu values and present themselves to others in Truk as good Christians, in opposition to people of Truk Lagoon, who are said to practice much of their traditional ways. The people of Kutu contrast Christianity with tradition, respectfulness and generosity with arrogance and stinginess, the outer islands with Truk Lagoon.

Pulapese similarly see themselves as respectful and generous people in contrast to the people of Truk Lagoon, but they construct a different relationship between Christianity and tradition. By converting to Catholicism, Pulapese believe they became strengthened in their ability to behave according to valued patterns and to avoid ones construed in the modern context as negative. They see no dichotomy between being Pulapese and being Catholic, between being traditional and yet playing a role in the modern context, between following valued patterns of behavior and yet gaining access to modern opportunities and goods. All three groups, however, use Christianity in creative ways to understand and cope with change, and they show the range of possibilities for incorporating Christianity into the indigenous way of life, and for using identity for political and economic goals.

NOTES

The research for this paper is based on fieldwork conducted from January 1980 to March 1981 on Pulap Atoll and among Pulap migrants on Moen and in the United States. It was financed by a doctoral research grant from the National Science Foundation. A second grant from the National Science Foundation allowed further research during the summer of 1986 among Pulapese living on Moen. I wish to thank John Barker and other symposium members for their useful comments.

1. The term Selaator is derived from the Spanish *celador* 'curator' (Elbert 1972:166).

12

CHRISTIANITY AND MAORI ETHNICITY IN THE SOUTH ISLAND OF NEW ZEALAND

M. Jocelyn Armstrong

If we look back at the early definitions of ethnicity, we find the first definitions to be with reference to religion. The original "ethnics" were peoples whose religious behavior was different from the prevailing Christianity of Western Europe: the first "ethnics" were "heathens" (cf. Abramson 1980; Royce 1982). Today's anthropological definitions place common origin and background at the core of ethnicity (Cohen 1978; Keyes 1976, 1981). Ethnic identifications sort people on the basis of common descent, ancestry, birthplace, history, or other origin attribute. Beyond common origin, however, ethnicity consists of other cultural elements, the beliefs and behaviors by which people demonstrate their ethnic identities. There is no fixed set of cultural elements but, with language, religion is one of the most widely used. In addition, ethnicity consists of social factors. People use their ethnic identities to pursue social goals and interests. Most often these are political or economic in nature, but they can also be religious or have religious ingredients. In short, anthropology's definitions of ethnicity do not equate it with religion, but religion is still significantly involved.

Christianity, or another of the universalist faiths, can support an ethnic identity in a number of ways and to a varying extent. Generally, the connection occurs when variant renderings become important to the cultural content of the identity (Abramson 1980). Christian beliefs and practices are shared with other and differing groups, but over time, an ethnic group puts its own stamp of originality on the religion and this becomes accepted by members and non-members as an important aspect of the group's identity. The distinctiveness that develops may involve a significant revision of theology but relatively minor innovations such as in the setting or style of worship are also common. A similar range of variation occurs in the contribution of Christianity to a group's social goals. Accordingly, it can be argued that Christianity's reinforcement of ethnicity is stronger to the extent that a group's particular interpretation of the religion comes to define its social goals (cf. Lewin 1978; Stout 1975). However, other kinds of less direct and specific connections can be important and enduring too. This chapter examines some of the more general links between Christianity and Maori ethnicity in the South Island of New Zealand. In particular, it examines separatism and ecumenism in the organization of Christian church life as playing an important role in the shaping and pursuit of goals which are firstly Maori rather than Christian in nature, and which attach to the general goal of maintaining an identity as Maori.

CHRISTIANITY AND ETHNIC IDENTITY IN POLYNESIA

Since its introduction to the peoples of the Pacific by European missionaries in the late 18th and early 19th centuries, Christianity has been variously and firmly incorporated into the definition of social identities. In Polynesia, as elsewhere in the Pacific and throughout the world, distinctive renderings of Christianity in support of group identities have developed through the incorporation of elements of the pre-Christian indigenous religion. Specific Christian beliefs have also been interpreted in local terms and specific practices adapted to local settings. But distinctiveness is also present in the promotion of more general but important modifications or emphases, for example, in the organization of Christianity's churches and church life. This form of adaptation has some particular relevance for use of Christianity in support of ethnic forms of identity in Polynesia.

The present-day island South Pacific has been described as "the most solidly Christian part of the world," and its people as committed to giving the churches "a larger place in their life" than the people of any other region of the Christian world (Forman 1982:227). Christianity is not the only universalist faith in the Pacific but it is the oldest by far and has by far the largest number of followers. Within the indigenous segment of the population almost everyone is at least nominally Christian. This solid sharing of the one religion has certainly lent support to the recent development of inclusive ethnic identities which include both the pan-Pacific one of Pacific islander and a lower-level identity as Polynesian in contradistinction to Melanesian or Micronesian. The Pacific Conference of Churches was established by the islands' major Protestant churches in 1961, and central theological colleges to serve the entire region were opened in 1966 (for Protestants) and 1972 (for Catholics). Catholics joined the Conference of Churches in 1976. During the 1970s and 1980s, the wider identities were being advanced in the staging of conferences and arts festivals, networking, and the statements and actions of widely respected leaders, and were being increasingly appealed to for the pursuit of shared political interests (cf. Linnekin in press:33-36).

Among the major ethnic subgroups of Polynesians, Christianity has a long history as a fundamental cultural attribute of Hawaiian, Tahitian, Samoan, and Tongan as well as Maori identity. As regards general modifications or emphases, Maori Christianity diverges somewhat in bringing together separatism and ecumenism in the organization of church life in support of Maori ethnicity. Hawaiian ethnicity has drawn some support from the establishment of "Hawaiian churches," that is, churches with Hawaiian priests and, in most cases, mostly Hawaiian members. However, church life has not been formally organized along ethnic lines. Furthermore, at the group level, being Hawaiian is as much a matter of being members of the United Church of Christ in contrast to being Catholic and Filipino, for example, and being Christian in contrast to the linking of other local ethnicities, such as Japanese and Chinese, with other universalist faiths. Elsewhere in Polynesia, independent self-governing churches have emerged. Full independence was typically slow and not always smooth in coming but independence was the intention of all the Protestant missions from the start. In time, it resulted in establishment of, for example, the independent Congregational Church in Samoa, Free Wesleyan Church of Tonga, and Tahitian Protestant Church. In Samoa and Tonga, in the course of movement toward modern-day political independence and nationhood during the 1960s, prior experience with church independence provided a strong base for church involvement in nation-building, and for reference to Christian perspectives and church life in the definition and display of Samoan and Tongan as national identities (see Forman 1982:209-214). As emigrations from both places to New Zealand and the United States took on substantial proportions during the sixties and seventies, the Samoan churches set up overseas districts and the Tongan churches took up the cause of fair treatment and wages for overseas Tongans.

The emphasis on ecumenism over denominationalism in support of Maori ethnicity contrasts with the strong association of Hawaiian ethnicity with the one denomination. In the Tahitian, Samoan, and Tongan cases, Maori ecumenism contrasts with well-developed traditions of denominational independence and competition. In Tahiti, Christianity has a history of Protestant-Catholic rivalries and tensions. In Samoa and Tonga, interdenominational competition has reached the point of open conflict in the past (see e.g., Urbanowicz 1977), and in Tonga additional serious intra-denominational fracturing has occurred. In part at least the situation reflects use of denominational differences to support the maintenance and strategic management of pre-Christian identities such as those based on kinship and territory (Korn 1978; Tiffany 1978b).

In sum, within Polynesia, Maori Christianity in New Zealand appears to be somewhat distinctive not just in its emphasis on separatism and ecumenism in church life but also in its use of the two features in combination. The remainder of this chapter explores ways in which the two features, independently and as a pair, connect with the formation of Maori ethnicity in the South Island of New Zealand. The chapter combines data collected in field research on Maori ethnicity and ethnic relations in the South Island with information from historical and other secondary sources to: (1) outline the historical and contemporary setting of the interaction of Christianity and Maori identity in the South Island; (2) examine the place of separatism in organized Christianity as it relates to the definition and use of Maori identity; (3) examine the place of ecumenism and denominational cooperation in identity definition and use; and (4) consider separatism and ecumenism in Christianity as mutually-reinforcing identity supports which, as such, link significantly with endeavors by Maori as an ethnic minority to retain their identity as Maori despite substantial wide-ranging incorporation into the institutions of the Pakeha or European majority. Throughout, the chapter looks beyond the regional South Island level to events and circumstances at the national, New Zealand level for context and perspective.

THE GENERAL ENVIRONMENT OF MAORI CHRISTIANITY IN THE SOUTH ISLAND

Christianity was introduced to Maori in the South Island about the same time as to most other Pacific peoples, during the early decades of the 19th century (Pybus 1954). The new religion was widely present by the time New Zealand was annexed as a British colony in 1840, but organized European colonization provided the setting and resources for increased mission activity and church expansion, especially between the 1840s and 1860s but into the 1880s too. This chapter deals only with Maori participation in the mission churches of European origin, and essentially with the Anglican, Methodist, and Roman Catholic Churches since these have been, and remain, the strongest churches in the South Island. Maori are also involved in messianic churches established by Maori prophets for Maori people (see de Bres 1985 for a recent review). One of these, the Ratana Church (see e.g., Henderson 1972), gained a strong following in the South Island during the early years of its formation in the 1920s and, after a long dormant period, began to rebuild its activities there in the 1960s. Also present are churches of American origin, notably the Mormon Church. Beginning in the 1880s, and as part of the Church's attention to indigenous peoples throughout the Pacific, the work of the Mormon Church in New Zealand has been strongly directed at the Maori minority (see Schwimmer 1965).

The link to Maori ethnicity varies among the three groups of churches. I focus on the mission churches of European origin as the oldest group, as having over half the Maori population as professed members, and as having by far the most impact in the South Island, though their activities there have been affected by the presence of the other groups of churches, in both the past and modern times. I consider the presence of separatism and ecumenism in church life in general but some particular attention is given to how the two features are expressed in the history and contemporary character of the South Island's "Maori churches."

"Maori churches" are local churches within the major churches' fold established to serve Maori communities. Originally built in the 1860s and 1870s in most cases, the churches were located at traditional places of Maori settlement that would continue into modern times as *kainga* or 'Maori villages'. The villages are sited on "Maori land," that is, land that remained in Maori hands after European contact and continued to pass to future generations according to pre-European inheritance patterns. They are or have been the location of a *marae* (community assembly ground) with its "Maori hall," and an elementary school for village children, the "Maori school," in addition to the "Maori church." Though rural places, most of the villages are today close to or within easy driving distance of a main urban center. As a result, their churches have helped serve South Island urban Maori too. Visually, and as the language of discourse about them implies, the villages remain as pockets of Maoridom in a European-dominated environment.

Two general circumstances are important to understanding any aspect of Maori identity development in the South Island: demography and New Zealand's official policies regarding the organization of Maori-Pakeha relations (see Armstrong 1987 for a fuller account). The South Island, though larger in size than New Zealand's other main island, the North Island, is the less populous and markedly so with respect to Maori. At the 1981 census the South Island contained slightly more than one-fourth of New Zealand's total population and roughly the same proportion of the Pakeha or European population. The proportion of Maori living in the South Island has always been small. In 1981, less than 7 percent of the Maori population lived in the South Island. At close to 20,000, the South Island's Maori population was not inconsequential in numbers and, due to in-migration from the North Island, had experienced three decades of growth from only 4,000 at the census of 1951. However, while Maori made up close to 9 percent of New Zealand's total population in 1981 and 11.3

percent of the North Island's population, they represented just 2.2 percent of the South Island's total population. Maori in the South Island are very much an ethnic minority vis-à-vis the Pakeha majority in demographic terms and have been for more than a century.

As noted above, Christianity was present among Maori in the South Island prior to the onset of organized European settlement in 1840 and the consequent reduction of Maori to tiny minority status. The missionaries were committed to generally "civilize" (that is, Europeanize) as well as Christianize the Maori. They established the first European-style schools and these schools subsequently offered the first formal instruction in the English language. The missionaries also encouraged the adoption of European forms of domestic life. Europeanization proceeded rapidly among Maori in the South Island in the decades following 1840.

As early as 1850, most land in the South Island had passed from Maori to European hands. This disrupted Maori territorial associations and attachments and thereby the foundations of the pre-contact tribal system of identity and status. It also constrained the maintenance of other core elements of Maori life, in particular the *marae* and large-scale gatherings or *hui* that the *marae* accommodated. Both went into marked decline in the South Island for the next 100 years. The Maori language experienced an especially sharp decline. The pace and degree of the shift to English was such that Maori quickly came to be viewed by Maori and Pakeha alike as a "dying language" in the South Island. The rate of Maori-Pakeha intermarriage was high, sufficient to effectively remove ancestry or "blood" as a readily obvious indicator of ethnic identity for future generations of Maori in the South Island. Maori migrating from the North Island in the 1950s and 1960s found the "losses" experienced by Maori in the South Island sufficient to judge them not just "less Maori" but, in some views, "not Maori at all." On the other hand, small numbers and a century of opting for a low profile and a Europeanized style of living had helped foster comparatively "good" relations between Maori and Pakeha in the South Island. In the prevailing idiom of ethnic relations in New Zealand, "good" meant the relations were closer, more cooperative, and involved a greater measure of mutual respect.

During the 1950s the course of Maori identity development in the South Island began to change. The change traces to a complex of reasons, but two stand out. First, while the in-migrations from the North Island in no way altered the small demographic minority status of Maori in the South Island, they did contribute sufficient increases in the Maori population to make a difference. For the first time there were sizable numbers of Maori living in South Island cities. Further, since the migrants were predominantly younger adults, the in-migrations modified the typically mature character of the island's pre-1950 Maori populations. Second, a nation-wide Maori renaissance movement began to take shape. It sought a revitalization of *Maoritanga* 'Maoriness' and Maori culture. Land, language, *marae*, and *hui* were all foci of attention together with Maori forms of speechmaking, music, and other arts and crafts. The mainstream churches gave general support to the movement and church life provided settings for its work. The movement took off from a relatively low point in the South Island but, by the 1980s, the Maori presence in the South Island had reached striking new levels in activities and facilities as well as numbers. Maori ethnicity had become "more Maori" in cultural content. Use of the Maori language, for example, was newly evident as a marker of Maori identity. Identification as Maori was considered appropriate and preferred for pursuit of much wider range of interests. Maori goals concerning the nature of Maori-Pakeha relations were in the process of major revision.

Guidelines for the official management of Maori-Pakeha relations were set down in the Treaty of Waitangi signed by representatives of both groups in 1840. Maori and Pakeha were to live in unity on an equal footing and with equality of opportunity. Translation of the Treaty's goals into New Zealand's official policies for Maori-Pakeha relations has produced a sequence of four policies. The first three, which span the first 140 years of interaction, all foresaw Maori incorporation into the European-style institutions of the Pakeha. A short first stage of amalgamation (in the 1840s) was followed by a long period of assimilation (1850s-1960s). However, it is generally agreed that the two policies differed in name only, that both intended Maori assimilation. Maori were to become "absorbed" and "blended" into Pakeha society and culture with "complete loss of Maori culture" (Hunn 1961:15). A shift to a policy of integration in the 1960s was supposed to redirect relations to a more equal footing. As officially defined, integration would "combine (not fuse) the Maori and Pakeha elements to form one nation wherein Maori culture remains distinct" (Hunn 1961:15). In practice all three policies turned out to be very similar. The Treaty of Waitangi's promises of Maori-Pakeha unity and equality were sought through a Pakeha-defined uniformity. The official policies of the major churches regarding church life are in general accord; by the 1960s all the churches had established policies of "integration." The existence instead of a separate and distinctive Maori church life, its long life notwithstanding, was viewed as an interim state of affairs. Integration was encouraged but regarded as a gradual process. It should not be hurried or imposed. Additionally, it has been pointed out that the churches were not in a position to enforce nation-wide integration had they chosen to. The Protestant churches in particular but New Zealand's

Catholic Church too, lacked the tightly-knit structure and hold on their membership needed for top-level decisions to be enforced at district and local levels (Mol 1966). However, Maori use of a distinctive church life in support of Maori identity was and would continue to be significantly at issue too.

During the 1970s Maori mounted pressure for a new commitment to the Treaty of Waitangi and transition to the fourth official (government) policy of biculturalism. Under biculturalism Maori-Pakeha partnerships would prevail and New Zealand's social institutions would be reworked to accommodate equal reference to both Maori and Pakeha values and ways of doing things as well as more Maori in positions of leadership and responsibility than had previously been the case. As presented by a Maori spokesperson, a bicultural New Zealand means "one in which *taha* Maori [the Maori side] receives an equal consideration with, and equally determines the course of this country as *taha* Pakeha" (Awatere 1984:10). The experience of difference and identity development in church life provided Maori with a strong base from which to seek biculturalism in organized religion. By the late 1980s all the major churches were united in formal commitment to the new policy and prominently involved in efforts to implement it.

ETHNIC SEPARATISM IN CHURCH LIFE

The contemporary separation of Maori and Pakeha in church life in New Zealand is supported in a well-developed ethnic-based organization of the major orthodox churches. All have Maori divisions for their ministry to Maori, and Maori clergy, most of whom work in ministering to Maori. The level of activity of the churches' Maori sections has waxed and waned over time. During the period of fieldwork this chapter draws on, 1960s-1980s, it was strong and strengthening. In particular, by the 1980s, Maori leadership for Maori in the mainstream churches was undergoing significant development. The Anglican Church had had a suffragan Bishop of Aotearoa[1] to serve Maori throughout New Zealand since 1928, but the position was given full episcopal status in 1978 and, in 1981, the bishop was elected by the Maori people. Also during the 1980s, two Maori ministers served one-year terms as President of the Methodist Church in New Zealand. In 1986, a delegation of Maori Catholics traveled to the Vatican to request representation on New Zealand's conference of Catholic bishops. The existing conference of Pakeha bishops lent strong support and the first Maori Catholic bishop was appointed in 1987. It is expected that this new national-level Maori leadership will, among other things, further work by Maori clergy to develop a Maori theology involving the synthesis of Christian and traditional Maori religious beliefs and practices for today's Maori Christians.[2]

It was as missions to Maori that the major churches began their work in the South Island. As colonization increased the European population to majority proportions, the missions were continued as separate sections for ministry to the Maori minority and paved the way for development and maintenance of a separate Maori church life. As noted, most of the South Island's Maori churches were built in this period (1860s and 1870s). From the churches' standpoint, the practical obstacles to maintaining separate ministries for the South Island's small Maori population have, in the years since, often loomed large. From time to time, the practice has come under attack at national church conferences as "unchristian" and "racist" and as such something the churches should not condone much less support. The situation came under particular scrutiny with the introduction of integration as the official government policy concerning Maori-Pakeha relations in the 1960s. A study commissioned by the National Council of Churches in New Zealand to review the churches' positions regarding integration (Mol 1966), found the Anglican, Methodist, and Catholic Churches all firmly committed to integration as their "ultimate" goal but all pursuing an "interim" policy of Maori-Pakeha separation. Both the Anglican and Methodist Churches reported pressures from segments of their Pakeha clergy and membership to dissolve the Maori sections. However, as New Zealand interpreted integration in the 1960s, Pakeha receptivity to Maori ambitions and inclinations should prevail. It was largely in response to Maori preference and pressure that the separate church sections remained, became stronger rather than weaker, and grew beyond the organization of worship to include a variety of separate social services and social and recreational activities.

Maori independence within the main orthodox Christian churches in the South Island is presently administered by an Anglican Maori Mission, a Roman Catholic Maori Mission, and the Maori Division of the Methodist Church. The last comprises a single parish, the Otautahi-Te Waipounamu (Christchurch-South Island) Parish. All three bodies have their headquarters in Christchurch, the South Island's main city. They have essentially similar policies regarding the churchly side of their work: for districts with a significant Maori population, there is a commitment to use of Maori places of worship, Maori clergy, and the Maori language. All three resources have been in short supply and been supplemented by the use of Maori halls and *whare hui*, 'meeting houses' as well as churches as places of worship, Maori-speaking Pakeha as clergy, and use of the Maori language according to competencies of clergy and congregations. By the late 1980s, however, there were signs of renewal. Development of *marae* throughout the South Island and the establishment of urban churches for Maori had added new places of worship. The Anglican Maori Mission was staffed by a team of Maori ministers rather than by the missioner alone as previously, and the minister for the Methodist Maori parish was a Maori rather than a Pakeha as in the past. In both churches, the use of lay readers, which had thrived in the early days of mission work in the South Island, was under renewal. The Maori language renaissance was aiding a return to more use of Maori as the language of worship.

All three churches are also actively involved in the administration and support of separate social services and in the organization of separate church-affiliated social and recreational activities. In Christchurch, for example, the Anglican Church operates Te Wai Pounamu Maori Girls' College, one of a small number of residential secondary schools for Maori in New Zealand and the only one in the South island. All three churches have been involved in the establishment and management of places of accommodation for working Maori youth in Christchurch. The Methodist Church had a pioneer role in the development of urban *marae* in Christchurch, sponsoring establishment of Te Whatu Manawa Maoritanga o Rehua, or "Rehua *marae*," in 1960. Its meeting house was the first traditional-style one to be built in the South Island in more than 100 years. For more than a decade, Rehua was the only *marae* in a main city in the South Island. By the 1980s it was the busiest *marae* in the South Island, the setting for local, regional, and national *hui* hosted by all kinds of groups. The Catholic Church has responded to the need for urban facilities with the building and operation of the first Maori community center in Christchurch, Te Rangimarie opened in 1969. In the same year, the Anglican Maori Mission moved to a new location in the city which it has since been developing as Te Rau Oriwa Marae and Community Centre.

Some of the city's more active Maori clubs and culture groups, whose aims include education in Maori arts and crafts, language, music, and other behaviors considered important to public display of a Maori identity, are church-affiliated. Concert parties such as those organized by the Catholic Academy of Maori Culture (Te Whetu Ariki o Kahukura) and the Anglican-affiliated Te Wai Pounamu Maori Girls' College have made a major contribution to the revitalization of *haka* 'posture dances and chants' and *waiata* 'songs' in the South Island, hence of *marae* protocol as well as Maori input to the public ceremonial of the community at large. These and other concert parties have also given new life to Maori entertainment in the South Island and their standards of performance have gained national recognition.

This concentration of separate church-related facilities, organizations, and activities in the South Island's main city can satisfy Maori at large that Maori independence in organized religion is being upheld, and it constitutes a significant communication of the circumstance to Pakeha observers. Nearby rural-living Maori have ready access to the city's activities and many are regular participants. Maori throughout the island travel to Maori gatherings or *hui* staged under church auspices or at church facilities in Christchurch.

Urban Maori also travel to participate in the religious life of rural places. Within easy driving distance of Christchurch in particular are four *kainga* 'villages' that Maori living in the city frequently visit. Some have kinsmen or workmates in the *kainga* but a known connection is not a standard motivation, nor is it grounds for welcome. Here Maori churches are the main setting for the practice and public display of separatism in organized religious life. As noted earlier, a church as such is not necessary for the conducting of separate services, but where there is a church, the building itself is an important concrete sign of a continuing separate church life. To the Maori concerned, the church is a valued venue for worship not only in the company of other Maori but in a Maori setting and one enhanced by extension beyond the church to the surrounding Maori village and its other elements of Maori identity, including all-important links with ancestors and the land. In a very deep sense, Maori are "at home" worshipping in Maori churches.

In the 1980s, Maori church development in Christchurch was looking ahead to comparable venues for urban worshipers. As noted, the Anglican Maori Mission's church complex was being developed as Te Rau Oriwa *Marae.* The church in particular was undergoing major remodeling of its interior to accommodate a variety of Maori events in addition to church services. The original sanctuary was being rebuilt as a chapel and the body of the church to serve as a *whare hui* 'meeting house.' The Methodist Otautahi (Christchurch) Maori Parish had recently acquired its first separate church complex — parsonage and hall as well as church — and was beginning a similar project. The buildings had become available as a result of consolidation of the city's Pakeha parishes. The Maori parish leadership had passed up earlier opportunities to take over redundant Pakeha facilities because they offered a church only. It had waited until facilities that could accommodate Maori meetings as well as church services became available. But the acquired church was considered "all very Pakeha" and in need of remodeling to turn it into "a Maori place" which could be variously used "during the week as well as on Sundays." In short, with urban Maori Anglicans, parish members were seeking a place that would provide some of the feelings and serve some of the functions of a *marae.*

For their churches in particular, both projects — Anglican and Methodist — also shared the goal of a church design suited to "a Maori service." That is, to the informal, loosely-structured and family-centered style of service preferred by most Maori. The original churches were both older buildings and designed for the typically more structured and person-centered Pakeha-style of worship. With their adjacent halls and ground, both churches could also accommodate the after-service fellowship that most Maori associate with church-going and count as an important distinguishing feature of a Maori service. At one Anglican Maori service I attended in 1987 where the congregation included a number of visitors from outside the parish, Pakeha as well as Maori, the officiating minister closed with a reminder of how to behave: "Don't just get up and go but stay, talk to each other. Start with the traditional Maori greeting: Where do you come from? and go from there. The chances are you'll find a bond."

All in all, Maori churches, rural and urban, old and new, afford Maori valued freedoms of expression in religion. Not surprising, one of the most valued is, and has been, freedom as to language of expression.

The Maori language has already been presented as coming close to "dying" in the South Island. The first European missionaries had learned Maori out of necessity. They continued to work in it even as Maori knowledge of English was spreading and encouraged their Maori teaching and preaching assistants to use Maori though most had competence in English (cf. Pybus 1954). Partly as a result, use of Maori remained stronger for longer in church life than in most other public domains and it never completely disappeared. However, against the general decline of the language and, later, with the dearth of Maori or Maori-speaking clergy, the early level of church use could not be sustained. The general decline began sharply with the onset of large-scale European colonization, 1840s-1860s, and continued for the next 100 years. Then, with the help of the growing numbers of Maori-speaking in-migrants from the North Island and as part of the wider Maori renaissance of the 1960s, a campaign to rescue the language took shape. Maori is still very much a minority language in the South island but by the 1980s it was newly evident and important as a marker of Maori identity there.

Having Maori as the language of present-day Maori church services is thus partly important toward the communication of Maori difference to non-Maori. Services at which only the hymn singing will be in Maori, a not uncommon format, are regularly announced or talked about as being "in Maori." But the Maori language is also a valued component of the services in Maori churches because it "helps us to feel Maori" and "reminds us that we still are Maori." All Maori in the South Island speak English and few use Maori as their home language but, irrespective of personal competencies, most people will agree that Maori is "in place" at any service in a Maori church, that it sounds "right." One Anglican Maori missioner who limited his use of Maori on grounds that his congregations would not understand it was considered "too Pakeha" in his position on Maori language use in Maori churches. A Methodist Maori minister was more receptive to his parishioners' preference for services that were at least partly in Maori but he, too, viewed the mix of competencies in any South Island congregation as grounds for concern. The printing of service booklets in both Maori and English has aided participation but does not guarantee comprehension. Among lay persons, however, the prevailing position is that it is not necessary to understand what is being said in order to enjoy listening to it, nor, for that matter, to get something out of it. On the contrary, a sermon in Maori has "more meaning" because its language is "in your blood." To some people, use of the Maori language, even limited use, is the crucial feature of independence in Maori Christian worship: "If we don't have this we may as well go along to the Pakeha church."

ECUMENISM

Like separatism, ecumenism has been a feature of Maori Christianity in the South Island for most of the religion's history there. It contrasts with a strong tradition of denominationalism in Pakeha Christianity. The divisions among the major orthodox churches imported by the European colonists in the 1840s-1860s have been preserved. At times, intra-denominational fracturing has obtained. At the time of importation, the main divisions were reinforced by a regional organization of settlement which, for example, established Presbyterian dominance in one part of the South Island and Anglican dominance in another. In modern times, Protestant interaction and joint endeavors at the national level have occurred under the National Council of Churches in New Zealand formed in 1941. During the 1960s and 1970s, several of the Protestant churches formulated plans for union but the attempts at implementation were localized and often short-lived and the plans eventually collapsed. The 1980s produced initiatives for a new national body that would bring more churches, including the Catholic Church, together and led to formation of the Conference of Churches in Aotearoa-New Zealand in 1987. A new and separate Maori Council of Churches, Te Runanga Whakawhanaunga i Nga Hahi o Aotearoa, had been constituted by the Maori sections of the major churches five years earlier, in 1982.[3] The move was a significant assertion of Maori identity and independence in contemporary New Zealand church life. However, it was equally a reflection of the relative strength and historical depth of Maori ecumenism at local and regional levels.

According to their self reports, clergy working at the local level of the Maori sections of the major churches, whether Maori or Pakeha in their own ethnic origins, expect to become involved with a denominationally diverse community of Maori, and see themselves as different in this respect from the clergy of general or Pakeha parishes whose work is typically first and foremost specific to their own denominations. As exemplified among Anglican clergy, the Anglican vicar in the Church's Maori section expects not just to minister to those in his community who call themselves Anglican, but instead to be "a kind of Chaplain to the community" as a whole. He or she expects to be "part of the life of that place, of the life of the *Maori* people" (New Zealand Anglican Board of Missions 1982). Clergy who do not achieve this level of involvement are less successful in the eyes of their Church and subject to Maori disapproval. A Maori Anglican missioner working in the South Island during one of my fieldwork periods was liked as a person and respected as a hard worker but criticized in private as "too Anglican" in his attitudes and activities.

In another area of ecumenical thinking and behavior of long standing, Maori can regularly accommodate the specialists and rituals of several denominations under one religious roof, at a single church service, or in the religious segment of a public ceremony. In Christchurch, when weekly services were held at the Methodist-affiliated Rehua meeting house in the 1960s and 1970s, the conducting of the services rotated among several clergy of diverse denominations. Rehua also provided Maori at large with the city's only traditional-style setting for a *tangihanga* 'funeral.' As other churches have developed additional Maori places of worship in Christchurch, there has been less need for a sharing of the Rehua facilities. However, they remain generally available and are used by various churches both independently and jointly for a variety of purposes other than Sunday services. In 1987, they were in use for Ratana as well as Methodist services. At Rehua, as at other *marae,* interdenominational services are normal procedure at planned *hui,* including those for which one or another particular church is organizer or sponsor.

Policies of open recruitment to the major churches' separate social services for Maori in the South Island also reflect the de-emphasizing of denominational allegiances and, furthermore, stimulate the behavior. The Anglican-affiliated Te Wai Pounamu Maori Girls' College in Christchurch has always been open to and attended by students of all denominations. Methodist connections have not been a requirement for residence at Rehua Maori Hostel, the Methodist-founded accommodation for working

Maori youth in the city. A group does not need to be Catholic or have a Catholic spokesperson to use Te Rangimarie, the Maori community center established by the Catholic Maori Mission in Christchurch. On the contrary, initial fund raising for the center, as for the meeting house established by the Methodist Church, drew contributions from Maori at large and from the North Island as well as all parts of the South Island, and it was always understood that the facilities would be utilized accordingly, that is, by people who identify as Maori rather than by sub-groups of Maori Catholics or Maori Methodists. The church-sponsored Maori clubs and culture groups have memberships that are diverse as to denomination and use names that clearly identify the group as Maori but do not specify the home church. In their cultural pursuits, their goal is to bring Maori — and, further, interested Pakeha — together for the learning, promotion, and enjoyment of Maori expressive culture. The clubs often recruit on the basis of age and sex but not denomination.

Limited concern with denominational attachments is also evident at the individual and family levels. Metge (1976) has noted that, while few Maori declare themselves to have "no religion" on census forms, substantially higher proportions of Maori than Pakeha "object to state" or fail to specify religious affiliation. The explanations may include objection to the census as an invasion of privacy and/or a Pakeha imposition, or adherence to beliefs and groups not officially recognized, but I suggest that we are also seeing another expression of ecumenical inclinations.

Even among regular church-goers, a professed denominational affiliation is not necessarily considered binding or confining. Husbands and wives with differing Christian backgrounds do not feel pressed to resolve the difference, and the examples include professed Catholics and Mormons for whom greater church pressure for family conformity can be assumed. Nor are children necessarily guided into the church of their parents. Infrequency of contact with the personnel or services of the parents' church or churches is sometimes at issue, but it is also widely held that "they're all the same after all" and that "one minister can't bless you any better than the next one." In similar vein, in one South Island Maori family that I knew well, both parents and children were in the habit of attending "the lot" which, at the time, meant Anglican, Catholic, Baptist, and Salvation Army services and, speaking on behalf of their children, the parents said: "They agree with them all and believe in them all and that's all right with us." The father of another family presented his own and his family's position as: "We're Anglicans and Methodists by confirmation, but we go to them all — Methodist, Presbyterian, Anglican, even the Roman Catholics." And, shifting to comment on Maori divergence from the Pakeha model: "They've been trying to tell us for a hundred years that one God is better than the other, but they haven't managed to convince us yet." In the words of one of the South Island's Maori clergy: "I'm Anglican, but don't hold that against me because the God I believe in is bigger than that. If He's not, I'm not interested in Him."

The Maori churches in *kainga* 'villages' in the South Island are, in most cases, explicitly interdenominational or non-denominational, or, if administratively linked to a particular denomination, they are made available to and are used by others. A long history of Methodist association, for example, obtains in the case of Rapaki, one of the four *kainga* in the vicinity of Christchurch, but the church has been regularly used for both Anglican and Methodist services and, in modern times, Baptist and Ratana services as well. At the *kainga* of Taumutu, also in the Christchurch vicinity, the name of the church, Hone Wetere (John Wesley) Church records its Methodist beginnings in the 1860s but through the years it has been used by most denominations and has been regarded by the district's Pakeha as well as Maori residents as the community church. Such arrangements could well be explained as commonsense economy on the part of the participating churches in the past or since, especially given the limited resources for a separate Maori church life in the South Island which were discussed earlier and the typically small size of local congregations. But such an explanation would be secondary at best. Rather, the churches were built on land next to or near the local *marae* and with labor, lumber, and money from the local Maori population at large. They were thus long ago established as a kind of extension of the *marae* and, as such, properly vested in and available to the community as a whole. Action to the contrary had been vigorously contested in the *kainga* of Arowhenua. An original church built in the 1860s and designated as non-denominational had been subsequently incorporated into the local Anglican parish and when a new church was built in 1931 it was dedicated as Holy Trinity (Anglican) Church. Local non-Anglicans, mostly Ratana and Catholic at the time, voiced strong opposition. They were not successful in contesting a court decision to vest part of the original church site, a Maori land reserve, in the Anglican Church Property Trustees. However, their opposition did incite a formal Anglican statement confirming the new church's availability for non-Anglican services (cf. Taylor 1950). In fact, it has seen less shared use than most of the South Island's *kainga* churches but, in 1987, clergy of several local parishes had a multi-denominational schedule of services arranged.

Services at each of the *kainga* churches near Christchurch are normally conducted by ministers based in the city. The visiting minister is likely to bring a carload of Christchurch Maori with him. Both they and the local members of the congregation will more than likely be diverse as to denomination. After the service, the visitors must be suitably hosted which usually entails an invitation to stay and eat together. Further, since the services at most of the South Island's Maori churches are typically infrequent, they are often the occasion of a memorial service or other special event for which attendant social activities are again appropriate. In short, the services tend to take on the character of a traditional Maori gathering to which the community at large is attracted and at which, by tradition, everyone is welcome. The church services become integral parts of occasions when participants are much more concerned about presentation of themselves as Maori than as members of this versus that Christian denomination.

SEPARATISM, ECUMENISM, AND MAORI IDENTITY

Separatism and ecumenism in church life occur as distinctive features of Maori Christianity throughout New Zealand. Other writers speaking from research or mission work among Maori in the North Island have offered a variety of comment on the meaning of the two features.

In one view of separatism, it is a reaction to the focus on church-going and church-based worship in Pakeha-style organized religion; in maintaining their own sections of the major churches, Maori have sought "something more conformable" to the Maori pattern of a more personal and pervasive relationship between people and their religious leaders (Ngata and Sutherland, 1940:366-373). Another recurring view stresses the general conditions and style of most mainstream Pakeha Christian worship, especially the level of structure and formality, as a deterrent to Maori participation and, hence, a cause of pressure for maintenance of separate services. In the view of a long-term Supervisor of the Methodist Maori Mission, his own and the other major mission churches had continued to contain just too much that was "foreign to the Maori spirit" (Laurenson 1964:45). A separate church life has also been discussed as nurtured by Maori as a refuge in the face of increasing involvement in the Pakeha way of life in most other public domains (Mol 1965).

Intra-Maori ecumenism has also received a variety of explanation, though mostly in terms of denominational "looseness" or "casualness." In 1940, Ngata and Sutherland (1940) reported on the practice in the North Island as a relatively new but pronounced form of "tolerance between Maori members of different churches." Ethnographic research led the Beagleholes to the conclusion that most Maori were using church membership for "reasons other than that of satisfying spiritual needs" such as social or economic advantage (Beaglehole and Beaglehole

1946:208-210). Ritchie has since suggested that the evidence of limited denominational loyalty implied Maori belief in a "sort of generalized Christianity" on the one hand and the assumption that "religious beliefs are not strongly held" on the other (Ritchie 1963:124). Another interpretation by Schwimmer (1968:52-53) refers to the preservation of pre-contact practices. Religious life was the communal concern of Maori *hapu*, localized sections of tribes, and the same function continues in local modern-day Maori populations diversity as to tribal, or church, affiliation notwithstanding. Metge (1976) has pointed to the general guidelines for efforts at ecumenism as available in two core Maori ways. The first, *aroha* 'love,' incorporates helping and caring for other Maori as virtues, and an openness in group recruitment as an expected expression. The other, *kotahitanga* 'unity,' embodies explicit recognition of differences as preliminary to their resolution. It is therefore not surprising that Maori pride themselves on overlooking the denominational differences of organized Christianity in the cause of community and Maori welfare.

Some of these interpretations would seem to have more merit than others. Some are supported in this chapter's South Island case material, others are not. However, relative merit or evidence in support aside, all of them can lend weight to a viewing of separatism and ecumenism in organized Christianity as linked to larger issues of Maori identity management. Separatism allows Maori participants in Catholic church life, for example, to identify themselves as groups of Maori Catholics in contradistinction to Pakeha Catholics rather than following the Church's Pakeha-defined ideal and joining forces with them as ethnically mixed groups of Catholics. Ecumenism brings Maori Catholics together with Maori Anglicans and Maori Methodists for identification as Maori Christian, in opposition again to the Pakeha model of consolidation as Catholic or other, or, when broader levels of cooperation are appropriate, as ethnically mixed groups of Christians. Separatism and ecumenism both put being Maori in contrast to Pakeha first; they put an ethnic form of identification ahead of a non-ethnic (religious) one. Both state a preference for performance according to Maori standards and communicate the expectation that the interpretation of Maori behavior by others will be according to the standards that apply to the ethnic identity first and the religious ones second. And the two features allow use of Maori interaction in organized Christianity for pursuit not only of religious interests but also interests that are primarily or essentially ethnic in nature.

The South Island situation also indicates that efforts to remain Maori over time are increasingly at issue; or, more precisely perhaps, the situation brings the process into sharper focus. A separate Maori-style church life has both required and encouraged the preservation of Maori behaviors — notably language, *marae*, and *hui* — which are important among the cultural elements of Maori ethnicity and, therefore, important resources for identification as Maori in other spheres of life too. As mentioned, with colonization, the small Maori population of the South Island experienced relatively rapid, general Europeanization and massive losses in most areas of Maori culture. Remaining separate in religious life offered opportunities first for stemming the losses and then for repairing some of them. The Maori response has been to safeguard those opportunities and, toward a new general assertion of Maori difference and independence in modern times, to exploit them.

Ecumenism has had at least three long-term implications for Maori efforts to retain an identity as Maori. First, it has facilitated the pooling of limited, sometimes diminishing, cultural and social resources for remaining Maori in religious life. Second, this experience has supported a return to stronger self-identifications as Maori for a wide variety of purposes in other, non-religious domains. Third, ecumenism has served the maintenance and, in modern times, wider use of Maori identity through the strength in numbers it allows. Again, though a factor of potential advantage to Maori throughout New Zealand, special meaning for the small Maori minority in the South Island draws attention to it. Additionally, ecumenism has perhaps come to aid Maori identity-building efforts in a fourth, rather different way. As pioneers of ecumenism in New Zealand, Maori have provided leadership and example in an endeavor that Pakeha Christians have long claimed to support but have been slow to reach agreement and take action on. As negotiations for a new general ecumenical council for New Zealand's churches proceeded during the 1980s the example set by formation of the Maori council in 1982 received repeated public acknowledgment (see e.g., Steering Committee of the New Ecumenical Body 1986). In private discussions, Pakeha church leaders would often recognize the precedence of the Maori council by referring to it as "the ecumenical council." Positive outcomes for Maori identity maintenance through a new source of self- and other-esteem are suggested.

Following from the above, it becomes important to see separatism and ecumenism in Christianity as related, mutually-reinforcing supports of Maori identity with, over time, growing implications for its management not only in religion but in other major spheres of life too. As such, they have been shaped by and also helped shape official (government) policy regarding Maori-Pakeha relations. As noted, guidelines for the policy are contained in the 1840 Treaty of Waitangi under which Maori and Pakeha agreed to a future of unity and quality. Maori distinctiveness in organized religion developed under a policy of assimilation and was upheld under conditions of growing Maori despair with the policy's outcomes. Under assimilation, Maori were to lose their culture, adopt Pakeha culture and become absorbed and blended into Pakeha society. Despite the policy's long life, 1850s-1950s, assimilation did not occur. Maori experienced substantial cultural loss but rather than being assimilated into Pakeha life, they became socially adrift and culturally deprived. Remaining distinctive in religious life subsequently provided a base for resistance to the policy of integration introduced in the 1960s. Integration was supposed to return Maori-Pakeha relations to a more equitable state by combining rather than blending the Maori and Pakeha elements of society. It acknowledged Maori concerns about the revitalization of Maori culture in its provision for Maori culture to remain distinct. To many Maori, however, integration in practice turned out to be assimilation by another name; it, too, sought Maori-Pakeha unity through a Pakeha-defined uniformity. Separatism and ecumenism in religion first gave Maori some control over the extent and manner of integration and then provided resources for its displacement. In facilitating and otherwise supporting the revitalization of Maori culture and in affirming a continuing Maori interest in ethnic-based social interaction, religious separatism and ecumenism helped prepare both Maori and Pakeha for formulation of a new and different and policy of biculturalism.

Biculturalism requires equal reference to both Maori and Pakeha beliefs and values in the shaping of New Zealand's social institutions. The policy rests on a reading of the Treaty of Waitangi as recognizing the status of Maori as *tangata whenua* 'people of the land' in New Zealand and promising Maori-Pakeha unity through partnership. Biculturalism became the Maori agenda during the 1970s. To some Pakeha observers, it had been a Maori "aspiration" for several decades (see Schwimmer 1968). Looking beyond New Zealand, it has been nurtured by the marked growth in ethnic revivals worldwide and has drawn support from specific connections and exchanges with the identity redefinition efforts of Aborigines in Australia, Hawaiians in Hawaii, and American Indians in Canada and the United States. Within international Christianity, biculturalism finds echoes in the growing openness to indigenization, and in the modern missionary approach to local cultures which typically replaces the opposition of the past with interest and a desire to promote preservation and development (Forman 1978; cf. Flinn chapter 11; Smith chapter 8).

By the mid 1980s, adjustments towards bicultural institutions were being made in law, education, social welfare, health, tourism, and radio and television as well as the major churches. The changes would not have been possible without Pakeha receptivity and support but they had been set in motion largely as a result of Maori pressure and effort. An illustration from organized Christianity has already been mentioned in reference to developments in the ecumenical movement. The formation of Te Rununga Whakawhanaunga i Nga Hahi, the Maori Council of Churches, in 1982, not only put Maori ahead in reform at the national level. It was also taken as a challenge by the planners of the new general ecumenical body that their proposals were not bicultural, that they continued the monocultural and Pakeha-dominated character of the inter-church organizations of the past (see Steering Committee of the New Ecumenical Body 1986). In response, in 1983, the negotiating churches decided to shelve a constitution for the new body that had been several years in the making and entered into three more years of discussions. When the new body was established in 1987 it was named Conference of Churches in Aotearoa-New Zealand as an expression of its commitment to biculturalism, and its goals gave prominence to seeking "bicultural partnerships" at all levels of operation. At the national level, the Conference would seek, partnership with Te Rununga Whakawhanaunga i Nga Hahi. It was anticipated that both bodies would belong to international organizations and that each would be free to send representatives to international meetings.

The connections between separatism and ecumenism in organized Christianity and Maori identity development examined in this chapter are only a part of the total linkage between Christianity and Maori ethnicity. However, they are sufficient to show the complexity of such linkages and some of the implications for additional research of the Maori and other cases. We should expect Christianity to connect in a variety of ways with both the cultural and social dimensions of ethnicity. We should look for interaction and an exchange of influence between the two general strands of the link. We should look for the past in the present but also for rearrangements and new outcomes over time.

NOTES

This chapter draws on field research in the South Island which began in the late 1960s and has continued into the 1980s. The initial period of research, 1967-68, resulted in the author's Ph.D. dissertation and was supported by a Woodrow Wilson Foundation Fellowship. Nine shorter periods have been completed since — one in 1969, four during the 1970s, and four during the 1980s, the latest in June-July 1987. The research has been on Maori ethnicity and ethnic relations in general. It has been conducted island-wide but, as the case material presented in this chapter will show, most in-depth work has been done in the main city of Christchurch and a selection of the island's "Maori villages," the name used for traditional places of Maori settlement in rural locations. Research concerning the role of Christianity in Maori identity has included: inquiry into religious attitudes and behaviors in a sample survey of Maori households in the South Island; participation in the church life of all denominations, including those not featured in this chapter and covering the churches' secular as well as religious activities; numerous informal conversations; and informal interviews with a large pool of key informants such as church leaders, the officers and staff of church-related secular activities, members of ethnic, and national ecumenical bodies. All the many persons who have supported and contributed to this work are most gratefully and warmly acknowledged. In addition, I thank John Barker and Charles Forman for many helpful comments on earlier drafts of this chapter and Marcia Siders and Joyce Wolverton at the University of Illinois for careful preparation of the manuscript.

1. 'Aotearoa' is the Maori name for New Zealand. According to tradition it was originally given to the North Island by the Maori explorer Kupe. At least until the time of European colonization, the South Island was designated separately as 'Te Waipounamu.' Te Waipounamu has continued as a regional name but Aotearoa came to be used for the country as a whole and adopted as the Maori name for New Zealand by Pakeha. Present-day usage of Aotearoa in the naming of positions, organizations, etc., serves two purposes. It can specify an organization, for example, as Maori or, in the case of a bi-ethnic or multi-ethnic organization it can recognize Maori indigenousness.
2. For a major contribution see Marsden (1977), and for a summary of work as of the 1980s by a Pakeha researcher of Maori religion, de Bres (1985).
3. The history and modern foci of the general ecumenical movement in New Zealand are reviewed in detail in Brown (1985). For a full account with comment of the building of the new Conference of Churches in Aotearoa-New Zealand, see Steering Committee of the New Ecumenical Body (1986).

13

AFTERWORD

John Barker

The purpose of the seminars of which this book is the product was to explore Oceanic Christianity ethnographically through detailed studies of local communities. This book, therefore, cannot be said to represent Oceanic Christianity as a whole or even to provide an overview. It is a set of case studies, weighted towards Melanesia. Each study describes unique historical and cultural situations; and each study reflects the personal experiences, discussions, and insights of individual ethnographers and Oceanic people. Given the immense differences between the case studies and the communities they describe — between Tongan Mormons and Maisin Anglicans, for example, or between the Kove and Maori experience of religious pluralism — that common themes stubbornly emerge is all the more impressive.

In each of the studies we find Christian forms and ideas at the nexus of local communities and the outside world. The ethnographies make it clear that Christianity does not simply represent the outside to Pacific peoples, as it did during the early missionary period. In each case, Christianity has become an integral part of people's sense of their cultural and historical selves, as a part of who they authentically are. Pulapese, Kragur villagers, and Maisin have no difficulty identifying aspects of Christian teaching with traditional values and behaviors and proclaiming themselves exemplary Christians on that basis. Indeed, some New Britain peoples and western Fijians go much further and claim Christianity as their original religion — once lost to the Europeans but now reclaimed. While outsiders might focus on the recent advent of Christianity in the Pacific, then, these studies indicate that for at least some Pacific peoples — and we suspect most — many aspects of Christianity have been appropriated into daily life to the extent that Christianity, along with received customs and traditions, forms a fundamental part of people's cultural identity.

This is what I have called the internal face of Oceanic Christianity. But Christianity, of course, extends well beyond local communities, linking them through historical, organizational, and ideological bonds into regional and international networks. Each case study explores to some degree how Pacific peoples grapple with Christian organizations and ideas as they experience, explore, and attempt to shape their relations with encompassing levels of society. Thus Kragur and Maisin villagers have gradually internalized Western notions of time and discipline over years of attending church services and mission schools; thus Misiman islanders have explored the convergences between imported Christian teachings, received notions of spirituality, and the persistant aspirations of cargoism; thus Maori leaders on the South Island of New Zealand have found in the churches a means to preserve and promote their language, customs, and sense of self in the face of a long history of assimilation. Different as these experiences are, they are all facets of the external face of Christianity in Oceanic communities. Christian elements permeate the discourse between people in local communities and those outside. Sometime the language of this discourse becomes blunt — as in the overt Americanization of Tongan Mormons. But the studies in this book explore more subtle and multi-leveled discourses: the varied cultural identities of Pulapese and their neighbors that are at once Christian and unique to their islands or the attempts of Lobodan villagers to translate patriarchal sermons and prayers into their own egalitarian and matrilineal cultural experience. In all these studies we find Pacific peoples struggling to define themselves in relation to the outside world through the medium of Christian institutions and ideas.

Macintyre observes that students of indigenous Christianity "have stressed the ways in which converts subsume elements of the new cosmology into familiar or traditional frames or reference... Equally, there is a tendency to convert known categories so that they accommodate innovations" (page 86). This two way process suggests two frameworks for comparing local versions of Christianity: indigenous religious assumptions and the cosmological framework of the incoming Christian sect. The case studies in this book, reflecting the anthropological orientation of most of the authors, concentrate on the first process. A number of comparisons seem suggestive. The Kove and Mengen situations in New Britain, for example, are very similar, reflecting common cultures, colonial histories, and indigenous responses. There are clear similarities as well between the coastal Melanesian societies studied in this book — notably the recurrent attempts to situate Christianity in their own past and within their sense of traditional values. At the moment, however, it is hard to go much further than these generalizations. As these case studies make clear, there are simply too many factors that go into the emerging religions of the Pacific to facilitate easy comparison. The situation is complicated not only by the syncretic process alluded to by Macintyre but by the reality of religious pluralism. Most Oceanic peoples have been exposed to a variety of local and regional religious influences. And they continue to encounter (along with the rest of the world) new religious messages and ideologies broadcast by ever more penetrating radio and television signals as well as old fashioned missionary efforts. The few easy generalizations of the past — notably between the "hierarchical" Polynesian churches and the "egalitarian" congregations of Melanesia — are turning out to have been too simple and too reliant upon other increasingly questionable assumptions about culture regions (cf. Thomas 1989). Possibly the most important generalization that emerges out of a comparison of the studies is the degree of diversity in the ways Oceanic peoples understand and practice Christianity. Clearly conversion to Christianity has not, as some early critics feared, led to cultural homogeneity across the region.

The book as a whole, then, provides important generalizations and contributes to regional comparisons, while exploring the nuances of popular religion among Oceanic Christians in a variety of locations. The authors provide another important contribution by expanding the range of ethnographic analysis in Oceanic communities. The effects of the recent critiques of conventional ethnographic research and writing are apparent in these studies. Although the authors describe distinct peoples, they situate them within history and in terms of their connections with encompassing social systems. Most importantly, they view Pacific islanders as active knowledgeable people who play an important role in shaping their societies.

Still, most of the chapters concentrate on a conventional anthropological concern — what Geertz (1983) calls "local knowledge." The authors present local knowledge as the practical religion of villagers and congregations: their understandings, often tacit, of Christian teachings, received customs and knowledge, and their own place within the encompassing society. All of this is important; yet Christianity has also introduced a new social organization of knowledge into communities: official knowledge that is neither entirely local or entirely external. Dealing with Christianity ethnographically challenges us to include in our analyses organizations, ideas, and forms that are more than local: the church personnel, the sermons, the liturgies, and the church government. I make an effort in this direction in my discussion of the station in Maisin society. But Thune addresses this challenge the most seriously by considering and interpreting some of the most authoritative forms of Christian knowledge, which include prayers, Biblical passages, sermons, and testimonials of conversion.[1] In the future, ethnographers of Pacific Christianity will need to expand the scope of ethnographic inquiry much further than we have, so that it includes phenomena like church services, church organization, self-help groups, women's organizations, youth movements, and Oceanic theologies.[2] In addition, ethnographers may also consider new venues for ethnographic research into Christianity. The urban churches, for example, are enormously important in integrating rural peoples into the towns, yet remain largely unstudied.

Anthropologists have long dominated the study of many parts of Oceania, notably the Melanesian countries. Yet as anthropologists become more interested in macro-developments like colonialism and conversion to Christianity they need to rely more on the research of colleagues in different disciplines. The ethnographic study of Christianity has gained enormously from recent historical and ethnohistorical research into the missionary period. But we also need more studies of Christianity from sociological and political perspectives. Although the churches now coordinate much of their work through regional and international organizations, and although many have created powerful media and commercial organizations, there are presently no good studies of the regional impact of church organizations. Sociological surveys of the relation between religious affiliation and class status are also long overdue. As Forman points out in chapter two, we still know little of the extent or significance of Christian rhetoric in nation-building. The ethnographic approach to Christianity is valuable, but it is not privileged and should not become a sub-discipline. We can only benefit by sharing information between studies on Christianity in anthropology, sociology, history, politics, theology, and missiology.

I suggested earlier that this book reflects a wider shift in anthropology away from intensive studies of exotic cultures — seen as out of time and place — towards more historically situated accounts. This trend will doubtless continue as a new generation of anthropologists, from Oceania as well as industrialized countries, turns its attention to the situation of Oceanic peoples.

A class I teach uses Eric Wolf's monumental *Europe and the People without History* (1982). Rather than deal with the book as a whole through lectures and discussions, I divide the students into four regional groups. Each group puts together a class presentation on Asia, Latin America, North America (excluding Mexico), or Africa. They are encouraged not simply to summarize material from the text, but to expand upon some of the examples of the impact of the world system and, most importantly, to explore how each of these regions is reflected in the cultural mosiac of Vancouver. The presentations have been very successful. The students use slides, music, food, and drama to draw their audiences into an experience of the parts of the world they are discussing. By exploring these histories and cultures in Vancouver itself, they bring home to the class the fact that ethnography is not limited to exotic "others." The world has become too small a place for that.

The most affecting presentation I have seen dealt with North America.

The students arranged the audience along three walls of the classroom. As the students described and ilustrated massacres, epidemics, land grabs, and assimilationist policies of church and state towards Native Americans, a solitary figure wearing an eerie white mask slowly strode along the perimeter of the room, placing cards on most members of the audience — "dead," "sick," "shoot," and "dying." During this time, the main narrator standing at the front of the room, a British Columbian Native woman, gradually removed parts of the traditional costume she was wearing to signify the loss of indigenous culture. She ended the presentation with a moving talk of her own experience. Now middle aged, she was taken from her reservation at an early age first to attend residential schools and then to be put in foster homes. Only recently had she returned to her home and was now, with great effort, learning the language of her people. She told us of her political involvement with international organizations of aboriginal peoples and of her people's Catholicism. She expressed the hope that the presentation showed us something of what Native Peoples had suffered and lost. Still, she confessed a worry that we might get the wrong idea — that, as many observers predicted in the early twentieth century, the loss of population and customs meant the loss of a distinct people. Much had changed, yet Indian people struggled on in the present world. "I'm still here," she said.

Oceanic peoples are still here too, despite many years of economic, political, and religious domination by outsiders. They have shown a remarkable ability to absorb and adapt the institutions and ideas that have resulted from Western colonization and its aftermath. They are more than ever linked into economic, political, and ideological networks that now embrace the world. They are vulnerable, like all of earth's people, to the depredations of military competition, resource depletion, and pollution. For all these changes and for all of the increasing participation in the world system, Oceanic peoples continue to draw from the unique heritage of their place, as do all peoples who maintain a sense of their own histories. Ironically, ethnographers are only beginning to catch up with the transformations in the societies they study. Our task now, as reflected in this and other recent volumes in Pacific ethnography, is to seek Oceanic peoples where they actually are rather than where we imagine they were before or where they should be.

NOTES

1. Geoffrey M. White (1987), for example, presented at the ASAO Monterey session in 1987 a fascinating study of conversion narratives from Santa Isabel in the Solomon Islands.
2. Two papers presented at the ASAO meetings but not included in this collection deal directly with church organizations. Elizabeth Roach (1987b) has studied women's church groups in Samoa, looking at their important moral and economic roles in villages and the country as a whole. Mac and Leslie Marshall (1986) discussed the enormous influence of women's temperance groups in Truk. (see Marshall and Marshall 1990).

REFERENCES

Abramson, Harold J.

1980 Religion. *In* Harvard Encyclopedia of American Ethnic Groups. Cambridge, MA: Harvard University Press.

Ahrens, Theodor, and Walter Hollenweger

1977 Volkschristentum und Volksreligion im Pazifik. Frankfurt: Verlag Otto Lembeck.

Anderson, Benedict

1983 Imagined Communities: Reflections on the Origin and Spread of Nationalism. London: Verso.

Anonymous

1968 Buk Bilong Beten end Sing-Sing Bilong Ol Katolik (Prayer Book and Hymnal for Catholic Natives of New Guinea). Westmead: Westmead Printing.

Arbuckle, Gerald A.

1978 The Impact of Vatican II on the Marists in Oceania. *In* Mission, Church and Sect in Oceania. James A. Boutilier, Daniel T. Hughes, and Sharon W. Tiffany, eds. pp. 275-299. ASAO Monograph No. 6. Lanham, MD: University Press of America.

Armstrong, M. Jocelyn

1987 Maori Identity in the South Island of New Zealand: Ethnic Identity Development in a Migration Context. Oceania 47:195-216.

Awatere, Donna

1984 Maori Sovereignty. Auckland: Broadsheet.

Babadzan, Alain

1982 Naissance d'une Tradition: Changement Culturel et Syncretisme Religieux aux Iles Australes (Polynésie Français). Paris: Travaux et Documents d'Office de la Recherche

Scientifique et Technique d'Outre-Mer.

Bailoenakia, P., and F. Koimanrea
1983 The Pomio Kivung Movement. *In* Religious Movements in Melanesia Today 1, W. Flannery, ed. pp. 171-189. Point Series, Vol. 2. Goroka: Melanesian Institute.

Baptismal Register
Ms. Baptismal Register, C[atholic] M[ission] Malmal. Malmal.

Barker, John
1979 Papuans and Protestants. A Sociological Study of the London Missionary Society, Methodist and Anglican Missions in Papua, 1870 to 1930. M.A. thesis. Anthropology and Maori Studies Department. Victoria University of Wellington.
1985*a* Maisin Christianity: An Ethnography of the Contemporary Religion of a Seaboard Melanesian People. Ph.D. dissertation. Department of Anthropology and Sociology. University of British Columbia.
1985*b* Missionaries and Mourning: Continuity and Change in the Death Ceremonies of a Melanesian People. *In* Anthropologists, Missionaries, and Cultural Change, Darrel L. Whiteman, ed. pp. 263-94. Williamsburg: Studies in Third World Societies, No. 25.
1986 From Boy's House to Youth Club: A Case Study of the Youth Movement in Uiaku and Ganjiga Villages, Oro Province. *In* Youth and Society: Perspectives from Papua New Guinea, Maev O'Collins, ed. pp. 81-107. Political and Social Change Monograph 5. Canberra: Department of Political and Social Change, Research School of Pacific Studies, Australian National University.
1987 Optimistic Pragmatists: Anglican Missionaries among the Maisin of Collingwood Bay, Northeastern Papua, 1898-1920. Journal of Pacific History 22:66-81.
1989 Western Medicine and the Continuity of Belief: The Maisin of Collingwood Bay, Oro Province. *In* A Continuing Trial of Treatment: Medical Pluralism in Papua New Guinea, Stephen Frankel and Gilbert Lewis, eds. pp. 69-94. Dordrecht: Kluwer.
Ms. Christianity in Melanesian Ethnography. *In* Tradition, History and Articulation in Melanesian Anthropology, James G. Carrier, ed.

Barnett, Homer G.
1942 Applied Anthropology in 1860. Applied Anthropology 1: 19-32.

Barr, J.
1983 A Survey of Ecstatic Phenomena and 'Holy Spirit Movements' in Melanesia. Oceania 54:109-132.

Barr, John, and Garry Trompf
1983 Independent Churches and Recent Ecstatic Phenomena in Melanesia: A Survey of Materials. Oceania 54:48-72, 109-32.

Barrett, D.B.
1968 Schism and Renewal in Africa. Nairobi: Oxford University Press.

Barth, Frederik
1969 Introduction. *In* Ethnic Groups and Boundaries. Frederik Barth, ed. pp. 9-38. Boston: Little, Brown and Company.

Beaglehole, Ernest
1957 Social Change in the South Pacific: Rarotonga and Aitutaki. London: Allen and Unwin.

Beaglehole, Ernest, and Pearl Beaglehole
1946 Some Modern Maoris. Wellington: New Zealand Council for Educational Research.

Beckett, Jeremy
1978 Mission, Church, and Sect: Three Types of Religious Commitment in the Torres Strait Islands. *In* Mission, Church, and Sect in Oceania. ASAO Monograph No. 6. James A. Boutilier, Daniel T. Hughes, and Sharon W. Tiffany, eds. pp. 209-229. Lanham, MD: University Press of America.

Beidelman, T.O.
1982 Colonial Evangelism: A Socio-Historical Study of an East African Mission at the Grassroots. Bloomington: Indiana University Press.

Belshaw, C.S.
1957 The Great Village; the Economic and Social Welfare of

Hanuabada, an Urban Community in Papua. London: Routledge and Kegan Paul.

Berde, S.
1974 Melanesians as Methodists: Economy and Marriage on a Papua New Guinea Island. Ph.D. dissertation. Department of Anthropology. University of Pennsylvania.

Berreman, Gerald D.
1983 Identity Definition, Assertion and Politicization in the Central Himalayas. *In* Identity: Personal and Socio-Cultural, A Symposium. Anita Jacobson-Widding, ed. pp. 289-319. Uppsala, Sweden: Almquist and Wiksell.

Biddlecomb, Cynthia
1982 Pacific Tourism. Suva: Pacific Conference of Churches.

Black, Robert H.
1963 Christianity as a Cross-cultural Bond in the British Solomon Islands Protectorate as Seen in the Russell Islands. Oceania 33:171-181.

Bodrogi, T.
1951 Colonization and Religious Movements in Melanesia. Acta Ethnographica 2:259-292.

Böhm, Karl
1983 The Life of Some Island People of New Guinea. A Missionary Observation of the Volcan Islands. Berlin: Reimer.

Boseto, Leslie
1983 I Have a Strong Belief. Rabaul: Unichurch Books.

Bott, E.
1981 Power and rank in the Kingdom of Tonga. Journal of the Polynesian Society 90: 7-81.

Boutilier, J.A., D.T. Hughes, and S.W. Tiffany, eds.
1978 Mission, Church, and Sect in Oceania. ASAO Monograph No. 6. Lanham, MD: University Press of America.

Brady, Ivan
1975 Christians, Pagans, and Government Men: Culture Change in the Ellice Islands. *In* A Reader in Culture Change, I. Brady and Barry Isaac, eds., vol. II pp. 111-145. Cambridge, Mass.: Schenkman Publishing Co.

de Bres, Pieter H.
1985 Maori Religious Movements in Aoteroa. *In* Religion in New Zealand Society, 2nd ed., Brian Colless and Peter Donovan, eds. pp. 30-55. Palmerston North: Dunsmore Press.

Brewster, A.B.
1922 The Hill Tribes of Fiji. Philadelphia: J.B. Lippincott Company.

Brigg, S., and L. Brigg
1967 The 36th Australian Infantry Battalion. Sydney: 36th Australian Infantry Batallion (St. George's English Rifle) Regiment.

Britsch, R.L.
1986 Unto the Islands of the Sea: A History of the Latter-Day Saints in the Pacific. Salt Lake City: Deseret Books.

Bromilow, William E.
1929 Twenty Years Among the Primitive Papuans. London: The Epworth Press.

Brown, Colin
1985 Ecumenism in New Zealand: Success or failure? *In* Religion in New Zealand Society, 2nd ed., Brian Colless and Peter Donovan, eds. pp. 81-98. Palmerston North: Dunsmore Press

Brunton, Ron
1980 Misconstrued Order in Melanesian Religion. Man 15:112-28.

Bryan, Edwin H., Jr.
1971 Guide to Place Names in the Trust Territory of the Pacific Islands. Honolulu, Hawaii: Pacific Scientific Information Center, Bernice P. Bishop Museum.

Bürkle, Horst, ed.
1978 Theologische Beiträge aus Papua Neuguinea. Erlangen: Verlag der Evangelishe-Lutheranische Mission.

Burridge, K.O.L.
1960 Mambu: A Melanesian Millennium. London: Methuen.
1965 Tangu, Northern Madang District. *In* Gods, Ghosts and Men in Melanesia, Peter Lawrence and M.J. Meggitt, eds. pp. 224-49. Melbourne: Oxford University Press.
1969 New Heaven, New Earth: A Study of Millenarian Movements. Oxford: Basil Blackwell.
1973 Encountering Aborigines: Anthropology and the Australian Aboriginal. New York: Pergamon Press.
1978 Introduction: Missionary Occasions. *In* Mission, Church, and Sect in Oceania. James A. Boutilier, Daniel T. Hughes, and Sharon W. Tiffany, eds. pp. 1-30. ASAO Monograph No. 6. Lanham, MD: University Press of America.

Calvert, James
1983 [1858] Mission History. Fiji and the Fijians, Vol. II: Suva: Fiji Museum.

Capell, A.
1970 A New Fijian Dictionary. Suva: Government Printer.

Carrier, James G.
1980 Knowledge and Its Use: Constraints upon the Application of New Knowledge in Ponam Society. Papua New Guinea Journal of Education 16:102-26.

Carrier, James G., and Achsah H. Carrier
1987 Brigadoon, or; Musical Comedy and the Persistence of Tradition in Melanesian Ethnography. Oceania 57:271-293.

Carrithers, M., S. Collins, and S. Lukes, eds.
1985 The Category of the Person: Anthropology, Philosophy, History. Cambridge: Cambridge University Press.

Carstens, Sharon
1986 Public and Private Definitions of Cultural Identity in a Chinese Malaysian Settlement. *In* Cultural Identity in Northern Peninsular Malaysia. Sharon A. Carstens, ed. pp.

75-91. Monographs in International Studies, Southeast Asia Series, Number 63. Athens, Ohio: Ohio University Center for International Studies, Center for Southeast Asian Studies.

Catholic Directory

1982 Catholic Directory, Papua New Guinea and Solomon Islands: Pipel Bilong God. Port Moresby: Catholic Apostolic Nunciate of Papua New Guinea and the Solomon Islands.

Caughey, John L.

1977 Faanakar: Cultural Values in Micronesian Society. University of Pennsylvania Publications in Anthropology, No. 2. Philadelphia: Department of Anthropology, University of Pennsylvania.

Chowning, A.

1969 Inter-tribal Acculturation in Papua New Guinea. Journal of Pacific History 4:27-40.

1972 Ceremonies, Shell Money, and Culture Change among the Kove. Expedition 15(1):2-8.

1974 Disputing in Two West New Britain Societies. *In* Contention and Dispute, A.L. Epstein, ed. pp. 152-197. Canberra: Australian National University Press.

1977 History of Research in Austronesian Languages: New Britain. *In* New Guinea Area Languages and Language Study, S. Wurm, ed. pp. 179-195. Canberra: Australian National University Press.

Chowning, A., and J.C. Goodale

1965 The Passismanua Census Division, West New Britain Open Electorate. *In* the Papua-New Guinea Elections 1964, D.G. Bettison, C.A. Hughes, and P.W. van der Veur, eds. pp. 264-279. Canberra: Australian National University Press.

Chowning, A., A.L. Epstein, T. S. Epstein, J.C. Goodale, and I. Grosart

1971 Under the Volcano. *In* The Politics of Dependence: Papua New Guinea 1968, A.L. Epstein, R.S. Parker, and M.Reay, eds. pp. 48-90. Canberra: Australian National University Press.

Christiansen, P.

1969 The Melanesian Cargo Cult: Millenarianism as a Factor in Cultural Change. Copenhagen: Akademisk Forlag.

Church of Jesus Christ of Latter-Day Saints
1978 The Book of Mormon. Salt Lake City: Utah
1980-86 Deseret News Church Almanac. Provo: Deseret.

Clammer, John
1975 The Perception of Tradition in Fiji. *In* Anthropology and the Colonial Encounter, Talal Asad, ed. New York: Ithaca Press.

Clifford, James
1980 The Translation of Cultures: Maurice Leenhardt's Evangelism, New Caledonia 1902-1926. Journal of Pacific History 15:2-20.
1982 Person and Myth: Maurice Leenhardt in the Melanesian World. Berkeley: University of California Press.

Cohen, Ronald
1978 Ethnicity: Problem and Focus in Anthropology. Annual Review of Anthropology 7:379-403.

Cohn, Bernard
1981 Anthropology and History in the 1980s. Journal of Interdisciplinary History 12:2.

Comaroff, Jean
1985 Body of Power, Spirit of Resistance: The Culture and History of a South African People. Chicago: University of Chicago Press.

Comaroff, Jean, and John Comaroff
1986 Christianity and Colonialism in South Africa. American Ethnologist 13:1-22.

Corbin, H.
1964 Histoire de la Philosophie Islamique. Paris: Gallimard.

Counts, Dorothy A.
1978 Christianity in Kaliai: Response to Missionization in Northwest New Britain. *In* Mission, Church, and Sect in Oceania, J.A. Boutilier, D.T. Hughes, and S.W. Tiffany, eds., pp. 355-394. ASAO Monograph 6. Lanham, MD: University Press of America.

Crocombe, Ron, ed.
1983 Religious Cooperation in the Pacific Islands. Suva: Institute of Pacific Studies.

Crocombe, Ron, and Marjorie Crocombe, eds.
1968 The Works of Ta'unga. Records of a Polynesian Traveler in the South Seas, 1835-1896. Canberra: Australian National University.

Culhane, P.H.
1939 Bibel Katolik as Sina. Vunapope: Sacré Coeur.
1954 Katekismo e Katolik ora ra Maege Me. T. O'Neill, rev. Vunapope: Sacré Coeur.

Cummings, David W.
1961 Mighty Missionary of the Pacific: The Building Program of the Church of Jesus Christ of Latter-Day Saints, Its History, Scope, and Significance. Salt Lake City: Bookcraft.

Daniélou, J.
1964 The Theology of Jewish Christianity. J.A. Baker, trans. *In* The Development of Doctrine before the Council of Nicea, vol. 1, J. Daniélou, ed. London: Darton, Longman and Todd.

Davenport, W., and G. Coker
1967 The Moro Movement of Guadalcanal, British Solomon Islands Protectorate. Journal of the Polynesian Society 76:123-175.

De'Ath, Colin
1981 Christians in the Trans-Gogol and the Madang Province. Bikmaus 2:66-88.

Dening, Greg
1980 Islands and Beaches: Discourses on a Silent Land: Marquesas 1774-1880. Honolulu: University Press of Hawaii.

Desroche, H.
1979 The Sociology of Hope. London: Hudd.

Derrick, R.A.
1950 A History of Fiji. Suva: Government Press.

Deverell, Gweneth and Bruce Deverell, eds.
1986 Pacific Rituals, Living or Dying? Suva: Institute of Pacific Studies.

Donner, William
1985 Sikaiana Social Organization. Ph.D. dissertation. University of Pennsylvania.

Douglas, Norman
1974 Latter-Day Saints Missions and Missionaries in Polynesia, 1844-1960. Ph.D. dissertation. Australian National University.

Elbert, Samuel H.
1972 Puluwat Dictionary. Pacific Linguistics, Series C, No. 24. Canberra: Linguistic Circle of Canberra.

Epstein, A.L.
1969 Matupit: Land, Politics and Change among the Tolai of New Britain. Canberra: Australian National University Press.

Epstein, T.S.
1968 Capitalism, Primitive and Modern: Aspects of Tolai Economic Growth. Canberra: Australian National University Press.

Etherington, Norman
1976 Mission Station Melting Pots as a Factor in the Rise of South African Black Nationalism. The International Journal of African Historical Studies 9: 592-605.
1983 Missionaries and the Intellectual History of Africa: A Historical Survey. Intinario 2:27-45.

Fabian, Johannes
1981 Six Theses Regarding the Anthropology of African Religious Movements. Religion 11:109-26.

Fergie, D.
1981 Prophecy and Leadership: Philo and the Inawai'a Movement. *In* Prophets of Melanesia, G. W. Trompf, ed. pp. 89-104. Port Moresby: Institute of Papua New Guinea Studies.

Fernandez, James W.
1978 African Religious Movements. Annual Review of

Anthropology 7:195-234.

Firth, Raymond
1970 Rank and Religion in Tikopia. London: George Allen and Unwin.

Flannery, W., ed.
1983-84 Religious Movements in Melanesia Today, 2-3. Point Series, vols. 3-4. Goroka: Melanesian Institute.

Flinn, Juliana
1985*a* We Still Have Our Customs: Being Pulapese in Truk. Paper presented at the annual meeting of the Association for Social Anthropology in Oceania, Salem, Massachusetts.
1985*b* Kinship, Aging, and Dying on Pulap, Caroline Islands. *In* Aging and Its Transformations: Moving Towards Death in Pacific Societies, Dorothy Ayers Counts and David R. Counts, eds. pp. 65-82. ASAO Monograph No. 10. Lanham, MD: University Press of America.
In press Tradition in the Face of Change: Food Choices Among Pulapese in Truk State. Food and Foodways. Forthcoming.

Fore, G.
1981 Koriam and the Little Book. Ms., typescript, inserted in the Pomio sub-district files.

Forman, Charles W.
1978 Foreign Missionaries in the Pacific Islands During the Twentieth Century. *In* Mission, Church, and Sect in Oceania. James A. Boutilier, Daniel T. Hughes, and Sharon W. Tiffany, eds. pp. 35-63. ASAO Monograph No. 6. Lanham, MD: University Press of America.
1982 The Island Churches of the South Pacific: Emergence in the Twentieth Century. Maryknoll, N.Y.: Orbis Books.
1984 'Sing to the Lord a New Song': Women in the Churches of Oceania. *In* Rethinking Women's Roles: Perspectives from the Pacific, Denise O'Brien and Sharon W. Tiffany, eds. pp. 153-72. Berkeley: University of California Press.
1985 Playing Catch-up Ball: The History of Financial Dependence in Pacific Island Churches. *In* Missions and Missionaries in the Pacific, Char Miller, ed. pp. 91-118. New York and Toronto: Edwin Mellen Press.

1986 The Voice of Many Waters. The Story of the Life and Ministry of the Pacific Conference of Churches in the Last 25 Years. Suva: Lotu Pasifika Productions.

1987 Christianity in the Pacific Islands. *In* Encyclopedia of Religion. New York: Macmillan.

Fortune, Reo

1963 Sorcerers of Dobu. New York: E. P. Dutton and Company.

Fountain, O.C.

1971 Some Roles of Mission Stations. Practical Anthropology 18:198-207.

1966 Religion and Economy in Mission Station - Village Relationships. Practical Anthropology 13: 49-58.

France, Peter

1969 The Charter of the Land: Custom and Colonization in Fiji. Melbourne: Oxford University Press.

Fugmann, Gernot, ed.

1986 The Birth of an Indigenous Church: Documents of Lutheran Christians of Papua New Guinea. Goroka: Melanesian Institute.

Fugmann, Wilhelm

1985 Bischof Zurewec Zurenuo; Ein "Untergebener" der Neuendettelsauer Mission? Zeitschrift für Mission 1:42-46.

Fullerton, Leslie Douglas

1969 From Christendom to Pluralism in the South Seas: Church-State Relations in the Twentieth Century. Ph.D. dissertation. Drew University.

Garrett, John

1982 To Live Among the Stars: Christian Origins in Oceania. Geneva and Suva: World Council of Churches and the University of the South Pacific.

Garrett, John, and John Mavor

1975 Worship the Pacific Way. Suva: Lotu Pasifika Productions.

Geertz, Clifford
1983 Local Knowledge. New York: Basic Books.

Gerritson, R., and M. Macintyre
1985 Social Impact Study of the Misima Gold Mine. An IASER Report. (Two volumes).

Gerritson, R., R.J. May, and M.A.H.B. Walter
1981 Cargo Cults, Community Groups and Self-Help Movements in Papua New Guinea. Department of Political and Social Change, Working Paper 3. Canberra: Research School of Pacific Studies, Australian National University.

Gesch, Patrick
1985 Initiative and Initiation: A Cargo Cult-Type Movement in the Sepik Against its Background in Traditional Village Religion. St. Augustin, West Germany: Anthropos-Institut.

Gill, S.R.M.
1929 Committee Appointed to Enquire into the Interrelationship between Native Ideas and Christianity. Anglican Archives, University of Papua New Guinea, Box 25.

Gilson, Richard
1980 The Cook Islands: 1820-1950. Wellington: Victoria University.

Gladwin, Thomas, and Seymour B. Sarason
1953 Truk: Man in Paradise. Viking Fund Publications in Anthropology, No. 20. New York: Wenner-Gren Foundation for Anthropological Research.

Goodenough, Ward H.
1951 Property, Kin, and Community on Truk. Yale University Publications in Anthropology, No. 46. New Haven: Yale University Press.

Gordon, Tamar
1988 Inventing Mormon Identity in Tonga. Ph.D. dissertation. Department of Anthropology. University of California, Berkeley.

Government of Tonga
1982 Census. Nuku'alofa: Government Printing Office

Gregory, C.A.
1980 Gifts to Men and Gifts to God: Gift Exchange and Capital Accumulation in Contemporary Papua. Man 15:626-52.

Guenther, Mathias Georg
1977 The Mission Station as 'Sample Community': A Contemporary Case from Botswana. Missiology 5: 457-65.

Guiart, Jean
1956 Un Siècle et Demi de Contacts Culturells à Tanna, Nouvelles-Hebrides. Paris: Musée d 'Homme.
1959 Destin d'une Église et d'un Peuple. Nouvelle-Calédonie 1900-1959. Étude Monographique d'une Oeuvre Missionarie Protestante. Paris: Mouvement du Christianisme Social.

Gunson, Niel
1965 Missionary Interest in British Expansion in the South Pacific in the Nineteenth Century. Journal of Religious History 3:296-313.
1969 The Theology of Imperialism and the Missionary History of the Pacific. Journal of Pacific History 5: 255-65.
1978 Messengers of Grace, Evangelical Missionaries in the South Seas, 1797-1860. Melbourne: Oxford University Press.

Gutman, Herbert G.
1973 Work, Culture, and Society in Industrializing America, 1815-1919. American Historical Review 78:531-588.

Hall, Clarence
1980 Miracle on the Sepik. Costa Mesa, Cal.: Gift Publications.

Hall, Edward T.
1983 The Dance of Life: The Other Dimension of Time. New York: Anchor Press/Doubleday.

Handler, Richard
1984 On Sociocultural Discontinuity: Nationalism and Cultural Objectification in Quebec. Current Anthropology 25:55-71.

Handler, Richard, and Jocelyn Linnekin
1984 Tradition, Genuine or Spurious. Journal of American Folklore 97:273-290.

Hannett, L.
1970 Church and Nationalism. *In* The Politics of Melanesia, Marion W. Ward, ed. pp. 654-65. Port Moresby and Canberra: University of Papua New Guinea and Australian National University.

Hefner, Robert W.
1987 The Political Economy of Islamic Conversion in Modern East Java. *In* Islam and the Political Economy of Meaning, William R. Roff, ed. pp. 53-78. London: Croom Helm.

Heise, David R.
1967 Prefactory Findings in the Sociology of Missions. Journal for the Scientific Study of Religion 6: 39-58.

Henderson, J. McLeod
1972 Ratana: The Man, the Church, and the Political Movement. 2nd ed. Wellington: Reed.

Hess, M.
1982 Misima — 1942, An Anti-colonial Religious Movement. Bikmaus 3:48-54.

Hesse, K., and T. Aerts
1982 Baining Life and Lore. Port Moresby: Institute of Papua New Guinea Studies.

Hezel, Francis X.
1978 Indigenization as a Missionary Goal in the Caroline and Marshall Islands. *In* Mission, Church, and Sect in Oceania. James A. Boutilier, Daniel T. Hughes, and Sharon W. Tiffany, eds. pp. 251-273. ASAO Monograph No. 6. Lanham, MD: University Press of America.
1983 The First Taint of Civilization. A History of the Caroline and Marshall Islands in Pre-Colonial Days, 1521-1885. Honolulu: University of Hawaii Press.

Hilliard, David L.
1974 Colonialism and Christianity: The Melanesian Mission in the Solomon Islands. Journal of Pacific History 9:93-116.
God's Gentlemen: A History of the Melanesian Mission, 1849-1942. St. Lucia: University of Queensland Press.

Hobsbawm, Eric, and Terence Ranger, eds.
1983 The Invention of Tradition. Cambridge: Cambridge University Press.

Hocart, A.M.
1929 The Lau Islands. Honolulu: Bishop Museum Bulletin no. 62.
1950 Caste. New York: Russell and Russell.
1969 [1927] Kingship. Oxford: Oxford University Press.
1970 [1936] Kings and Councillors. Chicago: University of Chicago Press.

Hogbin, H. Ian
1939 Experiments in Civilization: The Effects of European Culture on a Native Community of the Solomon Islands. London: Routledge and Kegan Paul.
1951 Transformation Scene: The Changing Culture of a New Guinea Village. London: Routledge and Kegan Paul.
1958 Social Change. London: C.A. Watts.

Hooper, Anthony, and Judith Huntsman, eds.
1986 Transformations of Polynesian Culture. Auckland: Polynesian Society, Memoir no. 45.

Horton, Robin
1971 African Conversion. Africa 41:85-108.
1975 On the Rationality of Conversion. Africa 41:85-108.

Horton, R., and J.D.Y. Peel
1976 Conversion and Confusion: A Rejoinder on Christianity in Eastern Nigeria. Canadian Journal of African Studies 10:481-98.

Howard, Michael C.
1983 Vanuatu: The Myth of Melanesian Socialism. Labour, Capital, and Society 16:176-203.

Huber, Mary Taylor

1987 Constituting the Church: Catholic Missionaries on the Sepik Frontier. American Ethnologist 14:107-125.

1988 The Bishops' Progress: A Historical Ethnography of Catholic Missionary Experience on the Sepik Frontier. Blue Ridge Summit, Pennsylvania: Smithsonian Institution Press.

Hughes, Daniel T.

1985 The Effects of Missionization on Cultural Identity in Two Societies. *In* No. 26. Anthropologists and Missionaries: Part 2, Frank A. Salamone, ed. pp. 167-182. Studies in Third World Societies. Williamsburg: College of William and Mary, Department of Anthropology.

Hunn, J. K.

1961 Report on Department of Maori Affairs with Statistical Supplement (24 August 1960). Wellington: Government Printer.

Inglis, John

1890 Bible Illustrations from the New Hebrides; With Notices of the Progress of the Mission. London: Thomas Nelson and Sons.

Jaspers, R.

1981 An Historical Investigation into the Foundation of the Catholic Church in Papua New Guinea and the Solomon Islands. Ms., mimeograph. Port Moresby: Holy Spirit Seminary, Bomana.

Jorgensen, Dan

1981*a* Life on the Fringe: History and Society in Telefolmin. The Plight of Peripheral People in Papua New Guinea. Volume 1: The Inland Situation, pp. 59-79. Occasional Paper 7. Cambridge, Mass.: Cultural Survival.

1981*b* Taro and Arrows: Order and Entropy in Telefol Religion. Ph.D. dissertation. Department of Anthropology and Sociology. University of British Columbia.

Kaeppler, A.

1971 Rank in Tonga. Ethnology 10:174-93.

Kahn, Miriam
1983 Sunday Christians, Monday Sorcerers: Selective Adaptation to Missionization in Wamira. Journal of Pacific History 18:96-112.
1986 Always Hungry, Never Greedy: Food and the Expression of Gender in a Melanesian Society. Cambridge: Cambridge University Press.

Kale, J.
1985 The Religious Movement among the Kyaka Enga. *In* New Religious Movements in Melanesia, C.E. Loeliger and G.W. Trompf, eds. pp. 45-74. Suva and Port Moresby: Institute of Pacific Studies and University of Papua New Guinea Press.

Kaltefleiter, Werner
1984 Südsee Christen in einer jungen Kirche. Pattlach: Aschaffenburg.

Kamma, F.C.
1972 Koreri: Messianic Movements in the Biak-Numfor Culture Area. The Hague: Nijhoff.

Kaplan, Martha
1988*a* Land and Sea and the New White Men: A Reconsideration of the Fijian 'Tuka' Movement. Ph.D. thesis. Anthropology Department. University of Chicago.
1988*b* The Coups in Fiji: Colonial Contradictions and the Post-Colonial Crisis. Critique of Anthropology 8:93-116.

Keesing, Felix M.
1942 The South Seas in the Modern World. London: George Allen & Unwin.

Keesing, Roger M.
1987 Anthropology as Interpretive Quest. Current Anthropology 28: 161-176.

Keesing, R., and R. Tonkinson eds.
1982 Reinventing Traditional Culture: The Politics of Kastom in Island Melanesia. Mankind, special issue, 13(4).

Keyes, Charles F.
1976 Toward a New Formulation of Ethnic Group. Ethnicity

3:202-213.

1981 The Dialectics of Ethnic Change. *In* Ethnic Change, Charles F. Keyes, ed. pp. 4-30. Seattle: University of Washington Press.

Keysser, Christian

1950 Eine Papuagemeinde. 2nd ed. revised and enlarged. Neuendettelsau: Freimund Verlag.

Korn, Shulamit R. Decktor

1978 After the Missionaries Came: Denominational Diversity in the Tonga Islands. *In* Mission, Church, and Sect in Oceania, J. Boutilier, D. Hughes, and S. Tiffany, eds. pp. 395-422. ASAO Monograph No. 6. Lanham, MD: University of America Press.

Laitin, David D.

1986 Hegemony and Culture: Politics and Religious Change Among the Yoruba. Chicago: University of Chicago Press.

Lal, Brij

1988 Power and Prejudice: The Making of the Fiji Crisis. Wellington: New Zealand Institute of International Affairs.

Langmore, Diane

1982 A Neglected Force: White Women Missionaries in Papua 1874-1914. Journal of Pacific History 17:138-57.

Lanternari, V.

1962 Messianism: Its Historical Origin and Morphology. History of Religions 2:52-72.

1963 The Religions of the Oppressed: A Study of Modern Messianic Cults. L. Sergio, trans. New York: New American Library.

Laracy, Hugh M.

1976 Marists and Melanesians: A History of Catholic Missions in the Solomon Islands. Canberra: Australian National University Press.

Latter Day Saints Mission Quarterly Reports

1916-84 Nuku'alofa and Salt Lake City.

Latukefu, S.
1974 Church and State in Tonga. Canberra: Australian National University Press.
1978 The Impact of South Seas Islands Missionaries on Melanesia. *In* Mission, Church, and Sect in Oceania. J. Boutilier, D. Hughes, and S. Tiffany, eds. pp. 91-108. ASAO Monograph No. 6. Lanham, MD: University Press of America.
1988 Noble Traditions and Christian Principles as National Ideology in Papua New Guinea: Do Their Philosophies Complement or Contradict Each Other? Pacific Studies 11:83-96.

Laufer, C.
1955 Aus Geschichte und Religion der Sulka. Anthropos 50:32-64.

Laurenson, George I.
1964 The Maori and Religion. *In* Maori and Pakeha: Studies in Christian Responsibility, pp. 41-45. Christchurch: Women's Committee of the National Council of Churches in New Zealand.

Lawrence, Peter
1964 Road Belong Cargo: A Study of the Cargo Movement in the southern Madang District New Guinea. Manchester: Manchester University Press.
1987 Cargo Cults. *In* The Encyclopedia of Religion, Vol. 3, pp. 74-81. New York: Macmillan.

Lawrence, Peter, and M. Meggitt, eds.
1965 Gods, Ghosts and Men in Melanesia: Some Religions of Australian New Guinea and the New Hebrides. Melbourne: Oxford University Press.

Leach, J., and E.R. Leach, eds.
1983 The Kula: New Perspectives on Massim Exchange. Cambridge: Cambridge University Press.

Leenhardt, Maurice
1979 Do Kamo. New York: Antheneum.

Leone, Mark P.
1979 Roots of Modern Mormonism. Cambridge, MA: Harvard

University Press.

Levy, Robert I.
1969 Personal Forms and Meanings in Tahitian Protestantism. Journal de la Société des Océanistes 25:125-136.
1973 Tahitians. Mind and Experience in the Society Islands. Chicago: University of Chicago Press.

Lewin, Frank W.
1978 Religion and Ethnic Identity. *In* Identity and Religion: International, Cross-Cultural Approaches. Hans Mol, ed. pp. 20-38. London: Sage Publications.

Leymang, Gerard
1969 Message Chrétien et Mentalité Néo-hébridaise Journal de la Société des Océanistes 25:239-255.

Lieber, Michael D., ed.
1977 Exiles and Migrants in Oceania. ASAO Monograph No. 5. Honolulu: University Press of Hawaii.

Linge, Hosea
1978 An Offering Fit for a King. The Life and Work of the Rev. Hosea Linge, Told by Himself. Translated by N. Threlfall. Rabaul: United Church of Papua New Guinea and the Solomon Islands.

Lini, Walter
1980 Beyond Pandemonium: from the New Hebrides to Vanuatu. Wellington: Asia Pacific Books.

Linnekin, Jocelyn S.
1983 Defining Tradition: Variations on the Hawaiian Identity. American Ethnologist 10:241-252.
In press The Politics of Culture in Oceania. *In* Cultural Identity and Ethnicity in the Pacific, Jocelyn Linnekin and Lin Poyer, eds. Honolulu: University of Hawaii Press.

Linnekin, Jocelyn, and Linette Poyer, eds.
In press Cultural Identity and Ethnicity in the Pacific. Honolulu: University of Hawaii Press.

Linton, R.
1943 Nativistic Movements. American Anthropologist 45:230-240.

Loeliger, Carl
1974 The Church and National Life in Papua New Guinea. Lutheran World 21: 211-217.

Loeliger, Carl, and Garry Trompf, eds.
1985 New Religious Movements in Melanesia. Suva and Port Moresby: Institute of Pacific Studies and the University of Papua New Guinea Press.

Longgar, W.
1975 The Johnson Cult of New Hanover. *In* New Religious Movements in Melanesia, C.E. Loeliger and G.W. Trompf, eds. pp. 25-35. Suva and Port Moresby: Institute of Pacific Studies and University of Papua New Guinea Press.

Lundsgaarde, Henry P.
1966 Cultural Adaptation in the Southern Gilberts. Eugene, Oregon: Department of Anthropology, University of Oregon.

Lutkehaus, Nancy
1983 Introduction. *In* The Life of Some Island People of New Guinea, by Böhm, Karl. Berlin: Reimer.

Maburau, A.
1985 Irakau of Manam. *In* New Religious Movements in Melanesia, C.E. Loeliger and G.W. Trompf, eds. pp. 2-17. Suva and Port Moresby: Institute of Pacific Studies and University of Papua New Guinea Press.

Macintyre, M.
1983 Changing Paths: An Historical Ethnography of the Traders of Tubetube. Ph.D. Thesis. The Australian National University.

Macnaught, Timothy
1971 The Subjugation of the Hill Tribes of Fiji. M.A. thesis. Australian National University.
1982 The Fijian Colonial Experience: A Study of the Neotraditional Order Under British Colonial Rule Prior to World War II. Pacific Research Monograph 7. Canberra: Australian

National University.

Maden, P.
1977 A Myth from the Mengan Area and the Cargo Cult in the Pomio Sub-province. Ms., handwritten. Goroka: Goroka Teachers College.

Mair, L.P.
1958 Independent Religious Movements in Three Continents. Comparative Studies in Society and History 1:113-136.

Malinowski, Bronislaw
1961 [1922] Argonauts of the Western Pacific. New York: E.P. Dutton.

Marcus, G.E.
1980 The Nobility and the Chiefly Tradition in the Modern Kingdom of Tonga. Wellington: Polynesian Society Memoir No. 42.
1981 Power on the Extreme Periphery: The Perspective of Tongan Elites in the Modern World System. Pacific Viewpoint 22:48-64.

Marsden, Maori
1977 God, Man and Universe: A Maori View. *In* Te Ao Hurihuri. The World Moves On., Michael King, ed. pp. 143-163. Wellington: Hicks Smith/Methuen.

Marsella, A.J., G. Devos, and L.K. Hsu, eds.
1985 Culture and Self. Asian and Western Perspectives. New York: Tavistock.

Marshall, Mac
1976 Solidarity or Sterility? Adoption and Fosterage on Namoluk Atoll. *In* Transactions in Kinship: Adoption and Fosterage in Oceania. Ivan Brady, ed. pp. 28-50. ASAO Monograph No. 4. Honolulu: University Press of Hawaii.
1977 The Nature of Nurture. American Ethnologist 4:643-662.
1979 Weekend Warriors: Alcohol in a Micronesian Culture. Palo Alto, California: Mayfield Publishing Company.
1981 Sibling Sets as Building Blocks in Greater Trukese Society. *In* Siblingship in Oceania. Mac Marshall, ed. pp. 201-224. ASAO

Monograph No. 8. Ann Arbor: University of Michigan Press.

Marshall, Mac, and Lesile B. Marshall
1986 Temperance in Truk: The Involvement of Church Women's Groups. Paper presented at the Annual Meeting of the Association for Social Anthropology in Oceania, New Harmony, Indiana.
1990 Silent Voices Speak: Women and Prohibition in Truk. Belmont, California: Wadsworth.

Marx, Gary T.
1967 Protest and Prejudice: A Study of Belief in the Black Community. New York: Harper and Row.

Maude, A.
1973 Land Shortage and Population Pressure in Tonga. *In* The Pacific in Transition: Geographical Perspectives on Adaptation and Change, edited by H. Brookfield. New York: St. Martin's Press.

May, John D'Arcy, ed.
1985 Living Theology in Melanesia: A Reader. Goroka: Melanesian Institute.

May, R.J., ed.
1982 Micronationalist Movements in Papua New Guinea. Political and Social Change Monographs, Vol. 1. Canberra: Australian National University Press.

McConkie, Bruce R.
1979 Mormon Doctrine. Salt Lake City: Bookcraft.

McSwain, Romola
1977 The Past and Future People: Tradition and Change on a New Guinea Island. Melbourne: Oxford University Press.

Mead, Margaret
1956 New Lives for Old: Cultural Transformation, Manus 1928-1953. New York: New American Library.
1964 Continuities in Cultural Evolution. New Haven and London: Yale University Press.

Metge, Joan
1976 The Maoris of New Zealand. London: Routledge and Kegan Paul.

Miller, Elmer S.
1970 The Christian missionary, agent of secularization. Anthropological Quarterly 43:14-22.

Misa
Ms. [Untitled manuscript]. N.p.

Mol, J. J. [Hans]
1965 Integration versus segregation in the New Zealand churches. British Journal of Sociology 16:140-149.
1966 Religion and Race in New Zealand. Christchurch: National Council of Churches.

Monberg, T.
1962 Crisis and Mass Conversion on Rennell Island in 1938. Journal of the Polynesian Society 71:145-150.
1967 An Island Changes its Religion: Some Social Implications of the Conversion to Christianity on Bellona Island. *In* Polynesian Culture History: Essays in Honor of Kenneth P. Emory, G.A. Highland *et al.*, eds. pp. 565-590. Honolulu: Bishop Museum Press.

Monckton, C. A. W.
1922 Taming New Guinea. New York: Dodd Mead and Company.

Moritzen, Niels-Peter
1974 Tok Bilip Bilong Yumi, Eine Darlegung des Glubens in Neuguinea. Evangelische Missions-zeitschrift 31:80-92.

Murdock, George P.
1965 Culture and Society. Pittsburgh: University of Pittsburgh Press.

Mumford, Lewis
1963 [1934] Technics and Civilization. New York: Harcourt, Brace and World.

Naingis, M.
1977 Cargo Cult: The Koriam Cult Movement. Ms., handwritten. Goroka: Goroka Teachers College.

Namunu, S.
1983 Ancestors and the Holy Spirit. B.D. Thesis. Rarango Theological College, Papua New Guinea.

Narokobi, Bernard
1977 What is Religious Experience for a Melanesian? *In* Christ in Melanesia, pp. 7-12. Goroka: Melanesian Institute.

Nason, James D.
1978 Civilizing the Heathen: Missionaries and Social Change in the Mortlock Islands. *In* Mission, Church, and Sect in Oceania James A. Boutilier, Daniel T. Hughes, and Sharon W. Tiffany, eds. pp. 109-137. ASAO Monograph No. 6. Lanham, MD: University Press of America.

National Census
1981 1980 National Census; East New Britain Provincial Counts. Mimeograph. Port Moresby.

Nelson, H.
1969 European Attitudes in Papua, 1906-1914. *In* The History of Melanesia, K.S. Inglis, ed. pp. 593-624. Port Moresby and Canberra: University of Papua New Guinea and the Australian National University.
1976 Black, White and Gold: Goldmining in Papua New Guinea, 1878-1930. Canberra: Australian National University Press.

Nerhon, Acoma
1969 Histoire de Ma Vie. La Monde non-Chrétien 89:38-78.

New Zealand Anglican Board of Missions
1982 Aotearoa. Te Pihopatanga o Aotearoa. The Church and the Bishopric. Wellington. New Zealand Anglican Board of Missions.

Newton, Henry.
1914 In Far New Guinea. London: Seeley Service.

Ngata, Apirana T., and Sutherland, I. L. G.
1940 Religious influences. *In* The Maori People Today. I. L. G. Sutherland, ed. pp. 336-373. Christchurch: Whitcombe & Tombs.

O'Dea, Thomas F.
1957 The Mormons. Chicago: University of Chicago Press.

Oliver, Douglas
1981 Two Tahitian Villages: A Study in Comparisons. Laie, Hawaii: Institute for Polynesian Studies.

Oram, N.D.
1971 The London Missionary Society Pastorate: The Emergence of an Educated Elite in Papua. Journal of Pacific History 6:115-37.

Orr, J. Edwin
1976 Evangelical Awakenings in the South Seas. Minneapolis: Bethany Fellowship, Inc.

Panoff, F.
1969 Some Facets of Maenge Horticulture. Oceania 40:20-31.
1970*a* Maenge Remedies and Conception of Disease. Ethnology 9:68-84.
1970*b* Food and Faeces: A Melanesian Rite. Man 5:237-252.

Panoff, M.
1968 The Notion of the Double-Self among the Maenge. Journal of the Polynesian Society 77:275-295.
1969*a* Inter-Tribal Relations of the Maenge People of New Britain. New Guinea Research Bulletin vol. 30. Port Moresby: Australian National University.
1969*b* The Notion of Time among the Maenge People of New Britain. Ethnology 8:153-66.
1969*c* Les Caves du Vatican; Aspect d'un Cargo Culte Melanésien. Les Temps Modernes 25:2222-2244.
1969*d* An Experiment in Inter-Tribal Contacts: The Maenge Labourers on European Plantations, 1915-42. Journal of Pacific History 4:111-125.

Papua New Guinea National Gazette
1981 Papua New Guinea National Gazette. No. G69, 10 Sept., 1981.

Waigani.

Patre, C.
1977 Religion in Melanesia — the Mengan Culture Area. Ms., handwritten, Holy Spirit Seminary.

Pihofr, Georg
1961-63 Die Geschichte der Neuendettelsauer Mission in New Guinea. 3 vols. Neuendettelsau, Bavaria: Freimund Verlag.

Piven, Frances Fox, and Richard A. Cloward
1982 The New Class War: Reagan's Attack on the Welfare State and Its Consequences. New York: Pantheon Books.

Point
1975 Urbanization in Papua New Guinea. Point, no. 1. Goroka: Melanesian Institute.
1977 Christ in Melanesia. Point, no. 1. Goroka: The Melanesian Institute.
1980 Christian Worship in Melanesia. Point, no. 1. Goroka: Melanesian Institute.

PF (Pomio Sub-District Files)
1959*a* File 51-1-2, C. Fleay/H. West
1959*b* 51-1-2, F. Reitano
1959c 51-1-2, C. Fleay/G.O. Oakes
1965 51-1-2, anon. marked 'Cargo Cults — W. Mengan'
1966 51-1-10, J.K. McCarthy
1967*a* 51-1-12, A. Bottrill
1967*b* 51-1-10, Hoskins sub-district Report
1967c 51-1-10, H. Dickinson/H.West
1968 51-1-2, M. Davis
1979 7-1-1, A. Bos

Puloka, T.T.
1979 Toward Contextualization: An Attempt at Contextualizing Theology for the Tongan church. D. Min. dissertation. School of Theology. Claremont

Pybus, T. A.
1954 Maori and Missionary: Early Christian Missions in the South Island of New Zealand. Wellington: A. H. and A. W. Reed.

Quain, Buell
1948 Fijian Village. Chicago: University of Chicago Press.

Rambo, Lewis R.
1982 Current Research on Religious Conversion. Religious Studies Review 8:146-159.

Ranger, Terence O.
1978 The Churches, the Nationalist State and African Religion. *In* Christianity in Independent Africa, Edward Fashole-Luke, Richard Gray, Adrian Hastings, and Godwin Tasie, eds. pp. 478-502. London: Rex Collings.

Rath, D.
1980*a* The Languages and Communities of the Mengan Region. *In* Language, Communication and Development in New Britain, R.L. Johnston, ed. pp. 197-214. Ukarumpa: Summer Institute of Linguistics.
In press The Melanesian Big Man in the Mengan Society; Comparisons and Contrasts. Dallas Anthropology Museum Monograph Series.

Read, K.E.
1952 Missionary Activities and Change in the Central Highlands of Papua and New Guinea. South Pacific 6:229-238.

Reafsynder, Charles B.
1984 Emergent Ethnic Identity in an Urban Migrant Community in Truk State, Federated States of Micronesia. Ph.D. Dissertation. Department of Anthropology. University of Indiana.

Rimoldi, D.M.
1971 The Hahalis Welfare Society of Buka. Ph.D. dissertation. Research School of Pacific Studies. Australian National University.

Risenfeld, A.
1950 The Megalithic Culture of Melanesia. Leiden: E.J. Brill.

Ritchie, James E.
1963 The Making of a Maori. Wellington: A. H. & A. W. Reed.

Roach, Elizabeth

1987*a* From English Mission to Samoan Congregation. Ph.D. dissertation. Anthropology Department. Columbia University.

1987*b* Women's Roles in the Samoan Congregational Church. Paper presented at the annual meetings of the Association for Social Anthropology in Oceania, Monterey, California.

Robin, Robert W.

1982 Revival movements in the Southern Highlands Province of Papua New Guinea. Oceania 52:320-43.

Rodgers, Daniel T.

1978 The Work Ethic in Industrial America: 1850-1920. Chicago: University of Chicago Press.

Rodman, Margaret, and Matthew Cooper, eds.

1983 The Pacification of Melanesia. ASAO Monograph No. 7. Lanham, MD: University Press of America.

Rodman, William L., and Dorothy Ayers Counts, eds.

1983 Middlemen and Brokers in Oceania. ASAO Monograph No. 9. Lanham, MD: University Press of America.

Roheim, Geza

1950 Psychoanalysis and Anthropology. New York: International Universities Press.

Rokowaqa, Epeli

1935 Ai Tukutuku Kei Viti. Ms., National Archives, Suva, Fiji.

Rosentiel, Annette

1953 The Motu of Papua New Guinea: A Study of Successful Acculturation. Ph.D. dissertation. Anthropology Department, Columbia University.

Ross, Harold M.

1978 Competition for Baegu Souls: Mission Rivalry on Malaita, Solomon Islands. *In* Mission, Church, and Sect in Oceania, J.A. Boutilier, D.T. Hughes, and S.W. Tiffany, eds. pp. 163-200. ASAO Monograph 6. Lanham, MD: University Press of America.

Routledge, David
1985 Matanitu: The Struggle for Power in Early Fiji. Suva: University of the South Pacific.

Rowley, C. D.
1965 The New Guinea Villager: A Retrospect from 1964. Sydney: F. W. Cheshire.

Royce, Anya Peterson
1982 Ethnic Identity: Strategies of Diversity. Bloomington: Indiana University Press.

Rutherford, N.
1971 Shirley Baker and the King of Tonga. Melbourne: Oxford University Press.

Rutherford, N., ed.
1977 The Friendly Islands: A History of Tonga. Melbourne: Oxford University Press.

Sahlins, Marshall
1972 Stone Age Economics. Chicago: Aldine-Atherton.
1981 Historical Metaphors and Mythical Realities: Structure in the Early History of the Sandwich Islands Kingdom. ASAO Special Publication, No. 1. Ann Arbor: University of Michigan Press.
1985 Islands of History. Chicago: University of Chicago Press.

Scarr, Deryck
1984 A Short History of Fiji. Sydney: George Allen and Unwin.

Schieffelin, Edward L.
1981*a* Evangelical Rhetoric and the Transformation of Traditional Culture in Papua New Guinea. Comparative Studies in Society and History 23:150-56.
1981*b* The End of Traditional Music, Dance, and Body Decoration in Bosavi, Papua New Guinea. *In* The Plight of Peripheral People in Papua New Guinea, Robert Gordon, ed. pp. 1-22. Cultural Survival, Occasional Paper No. 7.

Schoeffel, Penelope
1977 The Origins and Development of Women's Associations in

Western Samoa 1830-1977. Journal of Pacific Studies 2:1-21.

Schoorl, J.W.
1978 Salvation Movements among the Muyu of Irian Jaya. Irian 7:3-35.

Schwartz, Theodore
1968*a* The Paliau Movement in the Admiralty Islands, 1946-54. New York: Anthropology Papers of the American Museum of Natural History, vol. 49, No. 2.
1968*b* Cargo Cult: A Melanesian Type-Response to Culture Contact. Paper presented at De Vos Conference on Psychological Adjustment and Adaptation to Culture Change, Hakone, Japan, 1968 and the 8th International Congress of Anthropological and Ethnological Sciences, Toyko.
1976 Cultural Totemism: Ethnic Identity Primitive and Modern. *In* Ethnic Identity: Cultural Continuities and Change, George De Vos, ed. pp. 106-131. Palo Alto, California: Mayfield.

Schwimmer, Eric
1965 The Cognitive Aspect of Culture Change. Journal of the Polynesian Society 74:149-181.
1968 The Aspirations of the Contemporary Maori. *In* The Maori People in the Nineteen-sixties. A Symposium. Eric Schwimmer, ed. pp. 9-64. Auckland: Blackwood & Janet Paul.
1973 Exchange in the Social Structure of the Orokaiva: Traditional and Emergent Ideologies in the Northern District of Papua. New York: St. Martin's Press.
1979 The Self and the Product: Concepts of Work in Comparative Perspective. *In* Social Anthropology of Work, Sandra Wallman, ed. pp. 287-315. New York: Academic Press.

Sennett, Richard, and Jonathan Cobb
1972 The Hidden Injuries of Class: New York: Vintage Books.

Sharp, N.
1976 Millenarian Movements: Their Meaning in Melanesia. Melbourne: LeTrobe Sociology Papers, Vol. 25.

Shipps, Jan
1985 Mormonism: The Story of a New Religious Tradition. Urbana: University of Illinois Press.

Siikala, Jukka

1982 Culture and Conflict in Tropical Polynesia: A Study of Traditional Religion, Christianity and Nativistic Movements. Helsinki: Academia Scientiarum Fennica.

Siwatibau, Suliana and David Williams

1982 A Call to a New Exodus. An Anti-Nuclear Primer for Pacific People. Suva: Lotu Pasifika Productions.

Smith, Jean

1974 Tapa Removal in Maori Religion. Journal of the Polynesian Society 83:1-43; 84:44-96.

Smith, Michael French

1978 Good Men Face Hard Times in Kragur: Ideology and Social Change in a New Guinea Village. Ann Arbor: University Microfilms.

1980 From Heathen to Atheist: Changing Views of Catholicism in a Papua & New Guinea Village. Oceania 51:40-52.

1982*a* Bloody Time and Bloody Scarcity: Capitalism, Authority, and the Transformation of Temporal Experience in a Papua New Guinea Village. American Ethnologist 9:503-18.

1982*b* The Catholic Ethic and the Spirit of Alcohol Use in an East Sepik Province Village. *In* Through a Glass Darkly: Beer and Modernization in Papua New Guinea, Mac Marshall, ed. pp. 271-288. Institute of Applied Social and Economic Research Monograph 18. Boroko: Papua New Guinea Institute of Applied Social and Economic Research.

1984 'Wild' Villagers and Capitalist Virtues: Perceptions of Western Work Habits in a Preindustrial Community. Anthropological Quarterly 57:125-138.

1985 White Man, Rich Man, Bureaucrat, Priest: Hierarchy, Inequality and Legitimacy in a Changing Papua New Guinea Village. South Pacific Forum 2:1-24.

1988 From Heathen to Atheist on Kairiru Island. *In* Culture and Christianity: The Dialectics of Transformation, George Saunders, ed. Westport, Conn.: Greenwood Press.

1989 Business and the Romance of Community Cooperation on Kairiru Island. *In* Sepik Heritage: Tradition and Change in Papua New Guinea. Durham, N.C.: Carolina Academic Press.

Snowden, C.
1982 A History of the Cooperative Movement in Papua New Guinea. Masters dissertation. History Department. University of Papua New Guinea.

Steering Committee of the New Ecumenical Body
1986 Ecumovement: Towards a New Ecumenical Body in Aotearoa. Christchurch: National Council of Churches in New Zealand.

Steinbauer, Friedrich
1979 Melanesian Cargo Cults: New Salvation Movements. St. Lucia: University of Queensland Press.

Stokes, Randall G.
1975 Afrikaner Calvinism and Economic Action: The Weberian Thesis in South Africa. American Journal of Sociology 81: 62-81.

Stout, Harry S.
1975 Ethnicity: The Vital Center of Religion in America. Ethnicity 2:204-224.

Strathern, A.J.
1984 A Line of Power. London: Tavistock.

Strayer, Robert W.
1976 Mission History in Africa: New Perspectives on an Encounter. African Studies Review 19:1-15.
1978 The Making of Mission Communities in East Africa: Anglicans and Africans in Colonial Kenya, 1875-1935. London: Heinemann, and Albany: State University of New York Press.

Strelan, John
1978 Search for Salvation. Adelaide: Lutheran Publishing House.

Struggling for Lutheran Identity
1983 (Report of a Conference of African and Papua New Guinea Theologians). Neuendettelsau, West Germany: Evangelical Lutheran Church of Bavaria.

Sundkler, B.G.M.

1961 [1948] Bantu Prophets in South Africa. London: Oxford University Press.

Talmon, Y.

1966 Millenarian Movements. Archives Européennes de Sociologie 7:159-200.

Taylor, W. A.

1950 Lore and History of the South Island Maori. Christchurch: Bascands.

Theissen, G.

1978 Sociology of Early Palestinian Christianity. Philadelphia: Fortress Press.

Thomas, Nicholas

1989 The Force of Ethnology: Origins and Significance of the Melanesia/Polynesia Division. Current Anthropology 30:27-41.

Thompson, E.P.

1967 Time, Work-Discipline and Industrial Capitalism. Past and Present 38: 56-97.

Thornley, A.W.

1979 Fijian Methodism, 1874-1945. The Emergence of a National Church. Ph.D. dissertation. Australian National University.

Thune, Carl

1980 The Rhetoric of Remembrance: Collective Life and Personal Representations in Loboda Village. Ph.D. dissertation. Princeton University.

1981 Normanby Island Historiography. Bikmaus II:3-9.

1987 Aliens, Brothers, Fathers, and Sons: Insiders and Outsiders in Loboda Village 'Contact' Literature. Paper presented at the annual meetings of the Association for Social Anthropology in Oceania. Monterey, CA.

Ms.a. Equalitarian Historiography: The Representation of the Past on Normanby Island, Papua New Guinea, manuscript.

In press The Making of History: The Representation of World War II on Normanby Island, Papua New Guinea. *In* The Pacific

Theater: Island Representations of World War II, Geoff White and Monty Lindstrom, eds. Honolulu: University of Hawaii Press.

Ms.b. From Blood to Landscape: Death and Matrilineal Reincorporation on Normanby Island. *In* Death and Life in the Societies of the Kula Ring, Fred Damon and Roy Wagner, eds.

Tiffany, Sharon W.

1978*a* Introduction: Indigenous Reaction. *In* Mission, Church, and Sect in Oceania, J. Boutilier, D. Hughes, and S. Tiffany, eds. pp. 301-305. Lanham, MD: University Press of America.

1978*b* The Politics of Denominational Organization in Samoa. *In* Mission, Church and Sect in Oceania, J. Boutilier, D. Hughes, and S. Tiffany, eds. pp. 423-456. Lanham, MD: University Press of America.

Tippett, Alan R.

1954 The Christian (Fiji 1835-1867). Auckland: The Institute Printing and Publishing Society.

1967 Solomon Islands Christianity: A Study in Growth and Obstruction. London: Lutterworth Press.

1971 People Movements in Southern Polynesia. Studies in the Dynamics of Church-planting and Growth in Tahiti, New Zealand, Tonga, and Samoa. Chicago: Moody Press.

1977 The Deep Sea Canoe: The Story of Third World Missionaries in the South Pacific. South Pasadena: William Carey Library.

1980 Oral Tradition and Ethnohistory: the Transmission of Information and Social Values in Early Christian Fiji 1835-1905. Canberra: St. Marks Library.

Tirpaia, C.

1975 The Kivung Lavurua Movement among Sections of the Tolai Community of East New Britain Province. Ms., handwritten. Port Moresby: University of Papua New Guinea.

Tomasetti, Friedegard

1976 Traditionen und Christentum in Chimbu-Gebiet Neuguineas: Beobacktungen in der Lutherischen Gemeinde Pare. Wiesbaden: Steiner.

Tovalele, P.

1977 Pomio Cargo Cult — East New Britain. *In* Socio-Economic Change — Papua New Guinea, R. Adams, ed. pp. 123-139. Lae: University of Technology Press.

Trompf, G.W.

1977 Secularisation for Melanesia? *In* Christ in Melanesia, pp. 208-25. Goroka: The Melanesian Institute.

1980 Religion and Money: Some Aspects. The Young Australian Scholar Lecture Series, Vol. 1. Adelaide: Charles Strong Trust.

1981 Melanesian 'Cargo Cults' Today. Current Affairs Bulletin 58(1):19-22.

1983 Independent Churches in Melanesia. Oceania 54:51-72, 122-132.

1984*a* What has Happened to Melanesian Cargo Cults? *In* Religious Movements in Melanesia Today 3, W. Flannery, ed. pp. 29-51. Point Series, Vol. 4. Goroka: Melanesian Institute.

1984*b* Missiology and Anthropology: A Viable Relationship? Oceania 55:148-53.

1986 Competing Value Orientations in Papua New Guinea. *In* Ethics and Development in Papua New Guinea, G. Fugmann, ed. pp. 17-34. Point Series, Vol. 9. Goroka: Melanesian Institute.

1989*a* Introduction. *In* The Cargo and the Millennium: Trans-Oceanic Comparisons and Connections in the Study of New Religious Movements, G.W. Trompf, ed. pp. 15-16. Religion and Society, J. Waadenburg, gen. ed. Berlin: de Gruyter.

1989*b* Doesn't Colonialism Make You Mad? *In* Papua New Guinea: A Century of Colonial Impact, 1884-1984, S. Latukefu, ed. Port Moresby: University of Papua New Guinea Press.

In press Payback: The Logic of Retribution in Melanesian Religions.

Trompf, G.W., ed.

1987 The Gospel is not Western. Black Theologies from the Southwest Pacific. Maryknoll, N.Y.: Orbis Books.

Trompf, G. W., and A. Kasaminie

1981 The Druze and the Quaker: The Social Implications of Mysticism. Prudentia (Supp. Vol. The Via Negativa):187-205.

Trompf, G. W., and L. Longi
1981 Fieldnotes. Unpublished manuscript.

Tuaivi, Maretu
1983 Cannibals and Converts: Revolutionary Change in the Cook Islands. Marjorie Crocombe, ed. Suva: Institute of Pacific Studies.

Turner, H.W.
1967 A Typology of African Religious Movements. Journal of Religion in Africa 1:1-34.
1983 New Religious Movements in Primal Societies. *In* Religious Movements in Melanesia Today, vol. 1, W. Flannery, ed. Point Series 2. Goroka: Melanesian Institute.

Tuza, E.
1975 The Emergence of the Christian Fellowship Church. M.A. dissertation. History Department. University of Papua New Guinea.
1977 Cultural Suppression? Not Quite. Catalyst 7:106-126.
1981 Silas Eto of New Georgia. *In* Prophets of Melanesia, G.W. Trompf, ed. pp. 65-88. Port Moresby: Institute of Papua New Guinea Studies.

United States Department of State
1980 Annual Report to the United Nations on the Administration of the Trust Territory of the Pacific Islands.

Urbanowicz, Charles F.
1977 Motives and methods: Missionaries in Tonga in the early 19th century. Journal of the Polynesian Society 86:245-263.

Valentine, C.A.
1958 An Introduction to the History of Changing Ways of Life on the Island of New Britain. Ph.D. dissertation. University of Pennsylvania.
1963 Social Status, Political Power, and Native Responses to European Influence in Oceania. Anthropological Forum 1:3-55.

Valeri, Valerio
1985 Kinship and Sacrifice: Ritual and Sacrifice in Ancient Hawaii.

Chicago: University of Chicago Press.

van Baal, J.
1979 The Role of Truth and Meaning in Changing Religious Systems. *In* Official and Popular Religion, H. Vrijhof and J. Waardenburg, eds. Religion and Society, J. Waardenburg, gen. ed. The Hague: Mouton.

Vicedom, Georg
1961 Church and People in New Guinea. London: Lutterworth.

Vogel, H.
1911 Ein Forshungsreise im Bismark-Archipel. Hamburg: Hamburgische Wissenschaftliche Stiftung.

Walsh, A.C.
1972 Nuku'alofa: A Study of Urban Life in the Pacific Islands. Wellington: Reed Education.

Walter, M.A.H.B.
1983 Cargo Cults: Forerunners of Press. *In* Religious Movements in Melanesia Today 1, W. Flannery, ed.pp. 190-204. Point Series, Vol. 2. Goroka: Melanesian Institute.

Webb, Malcolm C.
1986 Why Our Civilization Can Never Be "Moral:" The Cultural Ecology of Christian Origins. *In* the Burden of Being Civilized: An Anthropological Perspective on the Discontents of Civilization, Malcolm C. Webb and Miles Richardson, eds. pp. 101-119. Southern Anthropological Society Proceedings, No. 18. Athens: University of Georgia Press.

Weber, Max
1958 [1920] The Protestant Ethic and the Spirit of Capitalism. Talcott Parsons, transl. New York: Charles Scribner's Sons.

Weiner, Annette B.
1976 Women of Value, Men of Renown. New Perspectives on Trobriand Exchange. Austin: University of Texas Press.

Westermark, George
1987 Church Law, Court Law: Competing Forums in a Highlands

Village. *In* Anthropology in the High Valleys, L.L. Langness and Terence E. Hays, eds., pp. 109-135. Novato, CA: Chandler and Sharp.

Wetherell, David
1973 Monument to a Missionary: C. W. Abel and the Keveri of Papua. Journal of Pacific History 8:30-48.
1977 Reluctant Mission: The Anglican Church in Papua New Guinea, 1891-1942. St. Lucia: University of Queensland Press.
1978 From Fiji to Papua: The Work of the Vakavuvali. in: Journal of the Polynesian Society. 8:153-72.

White, Geoffrey M.
1978 Big Men and Church Men: Social Images in Santa Isabel, Solomon Islands. Ph.D. dissertation. Anthropology Department. University of California at San Diego.
1987 "Histories of Contact, Narratives of Self: Missionary Encounters in Santa Isabel." Paper presented at the annual meetings of the Association for Social Anthropology in Oceania, Monterey, California.

Whiteman, Darrell L.
1983 Melanesians and Missionaries: An Ethnohistorical Study of Social and Religious Change in the Southwest Pacific. Pasadena, Ca.: William Carey Library.
1985 The Use of Missionary Documents in Ethnohistorical Research. *In* Anthropologists, Missionaries, and Cultural Change, Darrel L. Whiteman, ed. pp. 295-322. Williamsburg: Studies in Third World Societies, No. 25.

Whiting, S.
1975 Death and Leadership on Misima. An Anthropological History of a Massim Village. M.A. Thesis. Monash University.

Williams, F.E.
1930 Orokaiva Society. London: Oxford University Press.
1944 Mission Influence Among the Keveri of South-east Papua. Oceania 15:89-141.
1976 'The Vailala Madness' and Other Essays. Erik Schwimmer, ed. St. Lucia: University of Queensland Press.

Williams, R.G.
1972 The United Church in Papua New Guinea and the Solomon Islands. Rabaul: Trinity Press.

Wiltgen, Ralph M.
1969 Catholic Mission Plantations in Mainland New Guinea: Their Origin and Purpose. *In* The History of Melanesia, K.S. Inglis, ed. pp. 329-362. Canberra and Port Moresby: Australian National University, and University of Papua New Guinea.

Winkler, James
1982 Losing Control. Towards an Understanding of Trans-National Corporations in the Pacific Context. Suva: Pacific Conference of Churches.

Wolf, Eric
1982 Europe and the People Without History. Berkeley: University of California Press.

Wood-Ellem, E.
1983 Salote of Tonga and the problem of national unity. Journal of Pacific History. 18:163-192

Worsley, Peter
1968 The Trumpet Shall Sound: A Study of "Cargo Cults" in Melanesia. New York: Schocken Books.

Wright, Malcolm
1966 The Gentle Savage. Melbourne: Lansdowne Press.

Yagas, A.
1985 The Begesin Rebellion and the Kein Independence Movement: Preliminary Analyses. *In* New Religious Movements in Melanesia, C.E. Loeliger and G.W. Trompf, eds. pp. 18-25. Suva and Port Moresby: Institute of Pacific Studies and University of Papua New Guinea.

Young, Michael W.
1977 Doctor Bromilow and the Bwaidoka Wars. Journal of Pacific History 12:130-53.
1980 A Tropology of the Dobu Mission. Canberra Anthropology 3:86-104.

1983 Magicians of Manumanua. Berkeley: University of California Press.

CONTRIBUTORS

M. JOCELYN ARMSTRONG (Ph.D., Anthropology, University of Illinois at Urbana-Champaign, 1971) is currently Assistant Professor in the Institute for Research on Human Development at the University of Illinois. Between 1974 and 1985 she taught anthropology at the University of Hawaii at Manoa. She has conducted field research and published articles on aspects of ethnic identity and ethnic change in Malaysia and Hawaii as well as New Zealand.

JOHN BARKER is Assistant Professor in the Department of Anthropology and Sociology at the University of British Columbia. He received his M.A. (1979) from Victoria University of Wellington and Ph.D. (1985) from the University of British Columbia. He has conducted research in Papua New Guinea and in British Columbia on religious innovation, art, and the history of ethnographic research. His most recent publication is "Western Medicine and the Continuity of Belief: the Maisin of Collingwood Bay, Oro Province," in *A Continuing Trial of Treatment: Medical Pluralism in Papua New Guinea,* edited by Stephen Frankel and Gilbert Lewis (1989).

ANN CHOWNING is Professor of Anthropology at Victoria University of Wellington in New Zealand. A graduate of Bryn Mawr College, she took her M.A. and Ph.D. at the University of Pennsylvania. She held a Senior Research Fellowship at The Australian National University, and has taught at Bryn Mawr College, Barnard College (Columbia University), and the University of Papua New Guinea. Ann Chowning has been carrying out long-term research in Papua New Guinea since 1954, working in four different societies on New Britain and Fergusson Island. Among her numerous publications is *An Introduction to the Peoples and Cultures of Melanesia* (1973, 1977).

CHARLES W. FORMAN is Professor Emeritus of Missions at Yale University Divinity School. He received his Ph.D. at the University of Wisconsin in 1941 and M.Div., S.T.M. at Union Theological Seminary in 1944. The author of many books and articles on churches in Oceania, his most recent publications include *The Island Churches of the South Pacific: Emergence in the Twentieth Century* (1982) and *The Voice of Many Waters: The Story of the Life and Ministry of the Pacific Conference of Churches in the Last Twenty-five Years* (1986).

JULIANA FLINN is Associate Professor of anthropology at the University of Arkansas at Little Rock. She attended Bernard College (A.B. 1972), Stanford University (Ph.D. 1982), and Columbia University (M.P.H. 1984). In 1980-81, she conducted field research on Pulap Atoll and among Pulap migrants living elsewhere in Micronesia and the United States. She returned to Micronesia in 1986 for further research in the Pulap migrant community on Moen.

TAMAR GORDON is Assistant Professor at Bard College. She attended Yale University (B.A. 1977) and the University of California at Berkeley (Ph.D. 1988). She conducted field research in Tonga in 1982-84 and has worked with Tongans in the United States.

MARTHA KAPLAN received her Ph.D. in anthropology from the University of Chicago in 1988 following fieldwork and archival research in Fiji in 1982, 1984-85, and 1986. She has taught anthropology at the College at the University of Chicago and at New York University. In addition to her continuing interest in Fiji, she is pursuing research on 19th century British colonialism in India. Her most recent publication is "Luve ni Wai as the British Saw It: Constructions of Custom and Disorder in Colonial Fiji," in *Ethnohistory* (1989).

MARTHA MACINTYRE is Lecturer in Social Anthropology at La Trobe University, Bundoora, Victoria, Australia. A teacher and a historian before she turned to anthropology, she was educated at the Universities of Melbourne and Cambridge, and received her Ph.D. from the Australian National University. Compiling *The Kula: A Bibliography* (1983) inducted her into the Massim area of Papua New Guinea and she has since carried out research on Tubetube and Misima islands. Her most recent publication is a collection of essays, jointly edited with M. Jolly, *Family and Gender in the Pacific: Domestic Contradictions and the Colonial Impact* (1988).

MICHAEL FRENCH SMITH is Director of Research for Public Sector Consultants, Inc. in Lansing, Michigan. He received his Ph.D. in anthropology from the University of California, San Diego (UCSD) in 1978. He has conducted field research in East Sepik and Manus Provinces in Papua New Guinea and in southwest Virginia. His most recent publication is "From Heathen to Atheist on Kairiru Island," in *Culture and Christianity: The Dialectics of Transformation*, edited by George Saunders (1988).

CARL E. THUNE received his Ph.D. from Princeton University in 1980, based on research in Loboda village, Milne Bay Province, Papua New

Guinea conducted between 1975 and 1977. He has published articles dealing with Loboda village oral literature, traditional economic systems, and ideology. He currently works for Prudential Insurance where he researches and supports advanced computer system analysis and implementation methodologies.

GARRY W. TROMPF is Associate Professor and Head, Department of Religious Studies at the University of Sydney. He was educated at the Universities of Melbourne, Monash, and Oxford, and took his doctorate from the Australian National University. His main research fields include the history of Western historiography, the sociology of millenarism, and the history of Melanesian religion. His major publications include *Friedrich Max Müller The Idea of Historical Recurrence on Western Thought* and *In Search of Origins* and he has edited *Prophets of Melanesia The Gospel is not Western*; and *New Religious Movements in Melanesia.* His latest book, *Melanesian Religion,* will appear in 1990.

INDEX

abortion, 225
acculturation, 18, 174, 175, 197, 205, 242, 255
Adam and Eve, 6, 45, 136, 167, 207
adoption, 214, 225
affinal relations, 56, 97, 98, 119, 121, 123, 125
aggression, 222, 227, 231
alcohol, 5, 21, 212, 264
ancestors, 45, 47, 70, 72, 90, 134, 139, 146, 157, 190, 208, 247
ancestral spirits, see also "death," "spirits," 11, 33, 50, 48-53, 88, 91-93,93 97-98, 181
  and Christianity, 97, 119, 225, 226
  in cargo cults, 44, 63, 64, 67, 69, 71, 73, 75, 85, 87, 94-95, 166-167
  punishment by, 98, 160, 171
  relations with humans, 72, 98-99
  seances with, 48, 49-50, 51, 93, 94, 95, 96
Anglican missions and churches, 3, 4, 18, 28, 175-178, 195, 199, 240, 244, 245-246, 247-248, 250, 251, 252
anthropology,
  research on Pacific Christianity, 1, 7-10, 22-23, 25, 26-27
Australian aborigines, 175, 206
authority, see also "hierarchy," "inequality," 177, 182, 187-188, 206
Baha'i missions, 36, 40, 57
baptism, 11, 37, 41, 133, 155, 177, 204, 206, 207, 208, 216
Baptist missions and churches, 204
Bible, 6, 14, 53, 105, 114-115, 118, 142, 190, 205, 230
  translation of, 124, 202
biculturalism, see also "religious pluralism," 21, 173, 182-183, 192-194, 244, 256-257
big men, 106-107, 108, 114, 153
Brisbane flood, 74
Bromilow, W.E., 103, 108, 115, 124
cargo cults, see also "indigenous perceptions," "Kove," "Kivung," "Kragur," "Losevasevan," "Mengen," "millenarianism," "new religious movements," 8, 23-24, 27, 59, 78, 79, 81, 83
Catholic missions, see "Roman Catholic missions"
chiefs, 128-129, 131-132, 134-135, 140-144, 199, 200, 201, 205, 226
children, 36, 37-38, 50, 90, 104, 119-120, 181, 205, 209, 251
Christianity, see also "Adam and Eve," "ancestral spirits," "Bible," "confession," "conversion," "cultural identity," "death," "devil," "ecumenism," "ethnic identity," "God," "hell," "hymns," "indigenous clergy," "inequality," "Jesus Christ,"

"local churches," "Mary," "missionaries," "missions," "missionization," "paganism," "prayer," "religious pluralism," "sectarianism," "secularization," "sermons," "services," "sickness," "sin," "sorcery," "Sunday," "Ten Commandments," "theology," "translation," and listings under individual denominations,
and arts, 28, 174, 246, 255
and colonial incorporation, see also "colonial systems," 7, 15, 16-17, 18, 96, 149-152, 156, 158-162, 168-171, 173, 174, 176, 177, 183, 192-194, 232-233, 260
and indigenous values, 14, 20-21, 27, 83, 137-140, 158, 162-164, 172, 188, 205-206, 207, 222, 227, 228-232, 233, 234
and nationalism, 7, 30, 127, 140-145, 239
as a Pacific religion, i, 1-2, 21, 22-23, 27, 29, 30-31, 76-77, 81, 88, 238-239, 259-260
cultural adaptation of, 5, 8-9, 10, 13-15, 27-28, 79, 97, 99, 151, 181, 200-201, 209-210, 213-218, 226, 244-245, 254, 259-260, 261
global face of, 2, 15-21, 31, 191, 259-260
indigenous perceptions of, 9, 14, 34, 49, 54, 61, 77, 86, 105-121, 115, 118, 123, 128-129, 134, 157-158, 160, 163-164, 168, 189-192, 198
in urban areas, 5, 30, 241, 242, 246-247, 261-262
local face of, 2, 10-15, 259
prohibitions of, 35-36, 40-41, 57, 96, 112-114
research, 1-2, 10, 22-23, 25-32, 257-258, 262
Christmas, 83, 138-139, 230
churches, see "local churches"
Church Missionary Society, 3
Church of Tonga, see "Methodist missions"
clergy, see "indigenous clergy," "missionaries," "missions, teacher-evangelists"
colonial systems, see also "Christianity, and colonial incorporation," 20, 81, 101, 130-131, 144-145, 177, 178, 193, 232, 263
resistance to, 12, 23-24, 34, 41-42, 61, 62-63, 67, 69, 75, 76, 77-78, 87, 130-131, 152, 162, 165-167, 169-171, 232
community solidarity, 159, 187-188, 229-230, 254
conception and birth, 89, 90, 108-109, 117, 125
confession, 72, 158
conversion 3, 5-6, 35-36, 129-130, 133-134, 145, 177, 189-190, 196, 200, 201, 202, 204, 224-227, 229, 230, 232, 234, 261, 264
motives for, 156-157, 173, 197, 213, 224, 229, 232-233, 253-254
research, 8, 10-11, 15, 22, 24, 26
Cook Islands, 28
cooperative associations, 21, 23-24, 64, 66, 73, 178, 191
cosmology, 16, 19-20, 24, 81, 96, 150, 158
cultural identity 170, 172, 173, 211,

215, 221-222, 222-223, 224, 227, 228, 234
Christian influences on, 17, 20, 143, 162-164, 169, 222, 225, 234, 238-240, 244, 247-248, 259-260
curing, 18, 51, 52, 171, 181, 225
dance, 206, 211-212, 215, 218, 226
death, see also "ancestral spirits," "funerals," "spirits," 48-49, 54-55, 120, 166, 203, 207-208
Christian influences, 49, 52-53, 119-120
on Misima, 13, 86, 88, 92-93, 96, 97-98
devil, 49, 50, 53, 97
divorce, 57, 177, 225, 230-231
Dobu, 91, 103, 107, 108, 110, 111, 115, 124
Drauniivi village, see also "Fiji," "Navosavakadua," 14, 17, 127-128, 129, 130, 132-140, 144, 146
dreams, 48, 49, 51, 84, 93, 98, 225
economic advancement, 160-162, 198, 253-254
economic development, 21, 61, 73-75, 82, 85, 94, 96, 178, 185, 218, 223, 232-233
ecumenism, see also "Maori, separation," 53, 238, 239-240, 241, 249-257, 258
education, 5, 18, 29, 178, 183, 186, 195, 199, 216, 223-224, 232-233
egalitarianism, 8, 14, 101, 103, 122, 123, 125, 187, 188, 260, 261
elders, 113, 118-119, 182, 187, 189, 191, 193, 227, 233
emotions, 91-92
Etal island, 226-227, 234
ethnic identity, 221, 237, 241-243, 244
Christian influences, 21, 237-240, 253-257
ethnohistory, 1, 9, 128
Evangelical missions and churches, 1, 5, 29, 199
exchange, see also "feasts," "reciprocity," "sharing," 56, 83, 93, 97-98, 103, 107-110, 155, 164, 168, 176, 179, 184-185, 191, 194, 214-215
gifts, 72, 97-98, 103, 107-108, 110, 137, 164, 182
family, 19, 198, 203, 206, 207-210, 218
feasts, 93, 98, 121, 185, 188, 189, 191, 199, 201, 205, 214, 215, 216, 230, 247
Fiji, see also "Drauniivi village," "Navosavakadua," 3, 4, 14, 24, 84, 147
cultural logic of, 14, 127-128, 134, 136-137, 139-140, 140-145, 146
Methodists in, 129-130, 132-133, 143, 145, 146, 147
military coup in, 14, 128, 140-141, 143, 145
Free Wesleyan Church, see "Tonga, Methodists"
funerals, 48, 50, 53, 57, 81, 90, 92, 93, 96-97, 99, 100, 120, 250
gender, 133, 208-210, 227
God, see also "Lord's Prayer," 116-118, 251-252
as father, 110-111, 114, 119, 123
as leader, 85, 106-107, 108
autochthonous origin of, 11, 14, 33, 39, 42-47, 54, 55-56, 58, 84-85, 132, 134-137, 139, 144, 146, 156-157, 162-163, 172
belief in, 39, 54, 82, 83

indigenous perception of, 16, 19-20, 33-34, 42, 44, 54, 63, 65, 82, 106-111, 129, 140-141, 190
power of, 106, 108-109, 111-114, 123, 133
punishment by, 27, 33, 39-40, 49, 57, 72, 112, 207
relations with indigenous deities, 65, 86, 135-137, 142
relations with humans, 70, 105-111, 115, 121, 123, 164, 205, 207
Hawaii, 201, 203, 204, 219, 239
heaven, 48, 54, 56, 92, 111, 135, 157
hell, 57, 157
hierarchy, see also "inequality," "rank,"8, 101, 122-123, 133, 142, 144, 261, 187, 161, 162
husband and wife, 208-210, 215-216
hymns, 1, 28, 83, 105, 133, 230, 248
indigenous clergy, see also "missions, teacher-evangelists," 82, 93, 104-105, 133, 149, 156, 178, 179, 180, 200, 206, 224, 244-245, 245-246, 250
attitudes towards local cultures, 99, 184-185, 189-190, 205, 249
work of, 118, 124, 181-183, 186, 202-203, 252-253
indigenous elites, 7, 150, 161-162, 165, 166-167, 211, 215-217
indigenous perceptions, see also "Christianity," "God," "Jesus Christ," "money,"
of Americans, 34, 38-39, 43-44, 46-47, 56, 62-63, 212-213, 232
of Europeans, 16-17, 46-47, 54, 83, 84-86, 137-138, 157-158, 159-162, 164, 166-167
of space, 174, 180, 192
of time, 135, 150, 152, 158, 159-161, 168, 171-172, 174, 177, 180-181, 192
of work, 16-17, 55-56, 159-161, 169-170, 171-172, 174, 175, 178, 181, 187-188
indirect rule, 178
individualism, 14, 20, 89, 101, 134, 188, 226, 229
inequality, see also "hierarchy," "rank," 5, 15, 125, 152, 159
Christian expressions of, 14, 106-111, 114, 122-123
creation of, 141-143, 149-150, 158, 187
justification of, 85, 142-144, 161-162, 168, 170
Jehovah's Witnesses, 36
Jesus Christ, see also "Kivung, messiahism in," 1, 12, 111, 115-118, 186
indigenous perceptions of, 44, 51, 55, 57, 119-121, 132, 137-138, 143, 146, 2 202, 205
relations with humans, 105-106, 115, 121-122
relations with local deities, 63, 64, 70, 79, 132
relation to leaders, 65, 76-77, 79-80, 138, 205
Kairiru island, 152-153
Kaliai, New Britain, 36, 42-43, 46
kastom, see "tradition"
kin groups, 102-103, 107, 109, 112-114, 119, 121-122, 134-136, 146, 153, 178, 180, 187, 189, 191, 196, 206, 223, 226, 228
kinship, 16, 58, 89, 98, 109, 119-122, 125, 133, 178, 179, 201, 208, 209, 214, 216, 219, 222, 227, 228-229, 231

Kivung, see also "cargo cults," "Mengen," 12, 20, 60-80
Christian influences, 75-78
laws and punishments of, 67, 69-70, 75-76
messiahism in, 76-77, 79-80
organization of, 64-65, 67, 73-74
origins of, 60-61, 64-69, 77, 78
politics of, 61, 68, 70, 74-75
teachings and rituals of, 66, 67-68, 70, 72-73, 79-80
Thursday in, 63, 64, 67, 68, 70, 72
knowledge, 119, 146, 153, 189, 233
Kove, 11, 33-58
cargo cult in, 11, 33, 34, 38-39, 41-47, 48, 52, 54, 55-56, 57, 58
religious affiliations of, 40-41
Roman Catholic mission in, 11, 33, 35, 36-38, 49, 56
Seventh Day Adventist mission in, 11, 33, 35-36, 36-38, 40-41, 49
Kragur village, 16-17, 55, 149-172
cargoism in, 17, 166-167, 169-170
Catholicism in, 16-17, 149, 155-156, 157, 158-159, 160, 165-166, 169-170, 171
kula system, 24, 110
Kutu island, 226-227, 234
land, 97, 128-129, 131-132, 140-144, 190-192, 222, 241, 242, 243
language, 21, 97, 181, 182, 196, 242, 243, 245-246, 248-249, 255
church languages, 124, 195, 196
leadership, see also "big men," "chiefs," "elders," 28-29, 85, 106-107, 178, 182, 185, 186-188, 209-210, 216-217, 244, 255
Leenhardt, Maurice, 6
life, 90-91
literacy, 82, 177
Loboda village, 13-14, 101-125
Methodist church in, 103-105, 124
local church, 37, 61, 82, 83, 180, 202-204, 204, 205-206, 231-233
and community solidarity, 187-188, 229-230, 247-248
associations and councils, 178, 186, 230, 230
buildings and resources, 133, 229-230, 245-246
community support of, 83, 104-105, 139, 178-179, 183, 184, 205
festivals, see also "feasts," 139, 185, 187-188, 230
local government councils, 42, 56, 79, 153-154, 185, 187
London Missionary Society, 3, 4
Lord's Prayer, 111-114, 123
Losevasevan, 13, 81, 82, 93-96, 99-100
Christian influences, 88-89
origins and growth, 83-87
love, 106, 107-108, 137-138, 141, 205, 209, 216-217, 222, 228, 231, 254
Lutheran missions and churches, 4
Magic, 28, 95, 99, 106, 154, 157-158, 176, 225
Maisin, 18, 173-196
Malaita, 39, 55
Manam island, 39
Maori, see also "ecumenism," "New Zealand," 3, 10, 21, 237-258
assimilation of, 243, 255-256
ethnic separation of, 238, 240, 241, 244-249, 253-256
Maori churches, 241
Maori Council of Churches,

249-250, 255, 257
marriage, 36, 48, 79, 121, 136, 177, 216, 223, 229, 230
Mary, 1, 115-118, 119-120, 121, 123, 149, 157, 167, 230
Melanesia, 3-4, 8
Melanesian Institute for Pastoral and Socio-Economic Service, 26
men, 28, 41, 58, 89, 208-210, 227
Mengen, see also "Kivung," 12, 60-79
cargo cults in, 61-64
Roman Catholic mission in, 62, 65, 67-68, 78
Messianic churches, 240
Methodist missions and churches, see also "Fiji," "Misima," 3, 4, 14, 24, 56, 103-105, 124, 240, 244, 245-246, 246, 247-248, 250, 250
migration, see also "wage labor," 154-155, 178, 199-200, 204, 239, 242-243, 248
millenarianism, see also "cargo cults," 4, 8, 157-158, 165-166
Misima, see also "Losevasevan," 12-13, 81-100
Methodists on, 13, 81, 82, 89, 93, 95, 96-97, 99, 100, 101,
missionaries, 23, 149-150, 166-167
effects of, 93, 158-159, 225, 226
perceptions of indigenous peoples, 5-6, 47, 49, 56, 130, 157, 206-207
missions, see also "Christianity," "conversion," "missionaries," "missionization," and entries under individual denominations, 2-5
catechists, see "mission, teacher-evangelists"
localization of, 104, 178-179, 197-198, 203, 224-225, 239, 256
medical services, 7, 35, 104, 124, 174, 224
plantations, 156, 158, 160, 171, 174, 202
research, 5, 23, 26, 262
resistance to, 34, 39, 47, 77-78, 150, 225, 229
rivalry, see "sectarianism"
schools, 7, 35, 36, 37, 38, 56, 82, 104, 124, 152, 155-156, 158, 160, 174, 177-178, 179, 201, 202, 203, 233, 242, 246
stations, 18, 35-36, 173-176, 179-183, 183-194, 192
teacher-evangelists, 35, 37, 38, 56, 103, 129-130, 155, 176-177, 180, 181-183 , 195, 224, 225, 233
missionization, 1, 5-10, 17, 22, 81, 150-152, 174, 194
modernity, 180, 183
Moen, 223-224, 232, 233
money, 41, 66, 74, 84, 94, 95, 137, 138, 141, 149, 154-155, 161, 164, 164-165, 166-167, 172, 182, 191, 206, 227
Moro movement, 26, 76
morality, 14, 160-161, 172, 205, 206, 211, 212, 213, 215
Mormon missions and churches, 3, 6, 19, 197-220, 240-241, 251, 252
mortuary rituals, see "funerals"
names, 36, 56
Navosavakadua, see also "Drauniivi," 127, 130-132, 144-145, 147
and Christianity, 133-134, 138-139

New Britain, 4
New Caledonia, 6
new religious movements, see also "cargo cults," 24, 59-60, 70
New Tribes Mission, 36, 52
New Zealand, 3, 4, 21, 203, 214, 237-258
oratory, 28, 205
Pacific Council of Churches, 21, 238
paganism, 5, 16, 93, 96, 130, 133, 139, 177, 180, 190, 225-226, 228, 237,
Paliau movement, 65, 69, 76, 79, 83
Papua New Guinea, 3-4, 17, 18-19, 20, 23, 26, 30, 60, 65, 69, 74, 81, 94, 149, 162, 173, 192, 194,
Peli movement, 76, 166
Pentecostal missions and churches, 5, 29, 199
personhood, 13, 33, 50, 81, 88-92, 89, 98-99, 100, 103, 112, 125, 221-222, 228, 231-232
politics, 21, 61, 78, 87, 94, 95-96, 147, 168-170, 193
polygamy, 39, 57, 177
Polynesia, 3, 6, 8, 19, 238-240
Pomio sub-province, East New Britain, see "Mengen"
popular religion, 10, 12, 13, 15, 22-23
power, 65, 108-110, 114, 138, 198
practical religion, 173
prayers, 14, 83, 103, 122, 124, 133, 139, 160, 166, 173, 205, 230
  texts and exegesis, 105-111, 111-114
Presbyterian missions and churches, 3, 28, 249, 251, 252
Protestants, see also individual denominations, 3, 224, 229, 230, 238, 243, 249
Pulap, 17, 20-21, 221-235
  Catholicism in, 222-223, 224, 228-232, 232-233, 234
rank, 180, 189, 196, 199
Ratana church, 240, 250, 252
reciprocity, see also "exchange," "sharing," 61, 63, 66, 72, 73-75, 77, 78, 109-110, 137, 199, 205
religious innovation, 11, 12, 17-18, 19-20, 22
religious pluralism, 53-54, 76, 82-83, 87-89, 93, 95-96, 99-100, 143-144, 197, 210, 215, 250
  in oceania, 11, 13, 18-20, 30, 260-261
respect, 205, 213, 216, 228
ritual, 13-14, 56, 131-132, 133, 134, 138-139, 146, 147, 203, 205, 208, 225
Roman Catholic missions and churches, see also "Kove," "Kragur Village," "Mengen," "Pulap," 2-3, 4, 28-29, 79, 82, 130, 195, 199, 200, 204, 206, 238, 240, 244, 245, 246, 249, 251, 252
sacrifice, 134-135, 146, 191
Salvation Army, 251, 252
Samoa, 3, 19, 30, 84, 201, 239
sectarianism, 4, 11, 19, 34, 35-38, 53-54, 55, 197-198, 201-202, 204-206, 206-207, 210, 212, 219, 229, 239, 249
secularization, 4, 7, 12, 162, 194
sermons, 1, 29, 54, 102, 105, 114-115, 118-119, 122, 123, 196, 205, 209
  text and exegesis, 115-121
services, 14, 18, 37, 38, 67, 82, 101, 102, 104-105, 122, 124,

132-133, 139, 149, 150, 158, 160, 181, 196, 209, 215, 216, 224, 237, 245-246, 247-249, 252-253, 261
Seventh Day Adventist missions and churches, see also "Kove," 3, 4, 56, 58, 130, 199, 206
  prohibitions of, 35-36, 37, 40-41
sharing, see also "reciprocity," 14, 214-215, 216, 222, 226, 227, 228
siblings, 125, 205, 210, 211-213, 218, 227, 228
sickness, 11, 48, 50, 51-52, 88, 89-90, 92, 93, 96, 99, 146, 160, 171, 181
  Christian influences, 40, 184, 186, 207, 230
sin, 70, 72, 85, 108, 111-112, 113-114, 134, 135, 143, 146, 157, 160, 164
Solomon Islands, 2, 26-27
Somare, Michael, 167
sorcery, see also "witchcraft," 49, 52, 82, 90, 91, 92, 96, 98, 99, 103-104, 108, 112, 114, 160, 166, 181, 182, 188
  Christian influences on, 39, 66, 97, 100, 104, 108, 176
soul, 33, 49, 51, 92, 97, 206
South Sea Evangelical Church, 3
spirits, see also "ancestral spirits" 13, 92, 93, 157, 226
Sunday, 11, 36, 37, 40, 41, 57, 66, 68, 70, 81, 82, 83, 104, 186, 206, 224, 230
syncretism, 11, 81
Tahiti, 3, 19, 28, 201, 239
taxes, 41, 95, 153-154, 179
Ten Commandments, 11, 12, 40, 44, 53-54, 66, 67, 68, 69-70, 70-71, 75, 76, 205
theology, 6, 23, 105, 207, 237, 245, 261
  Pacific, 6, 23, 89, 244-245, 261-262
Thursday cult, see also "Kivung," 63-64
time, see "indigenous perceptions, time"
Tolai, 60, 61, 68, 69, 78, 79
Tonga, 3, 11, 19, 24, 84, 197-219, 239
  Methodists in, 197, 199, 200, 201-202, 205-206, 210, 212, 215
  religious identity in, 198, 201, 212, 213, 217, 218
tradition, 20, 27-28, 70, 76, 101-102, 163-164, 179-180, 189, 191-192, 195, 198, 211, 214-217, 221-222, 226, 228, 234
  invention of and neo-tradition, 7, 15, 17, 19, 20-21, 70, 75, 142-143, 145, 179, 191, 195, 197-198, 211, 218, 221
translation, 6, 65, 91, 97, 105, 108, 115, 124, 125, 196
Trobriand Islands, 124-125
Tuka movement, see "Navosavakadua"
United Church of Papua New Guinea, see "Loboda village," "Misima"
Vanuatu, 3, 5-6, 20, 26, 28, 30
Vatican II, 4, 20, 156
wage labor, see also "migration," 101, 122, 149, 156, 161, 169, 211
warfare, 47, 93, 129, 132, 142, 146, 160, 177, 189, 191, 200, 231-232
witchcraft, see also "sorcery," 84,

92, 93
women, 28, 38, 39, 58, 82, 82, 89, 96, 104, 132-133, 178, 191, 203, 208-210, 219, 225, 227, 228, 230, 261, 264
work, see "indigenous perceptions, work"
World Council of Churches, 4
World War II, 38, 47, 62, 78, 86, 103, 122, 224, 232
Yali movement, 76, 84, 166
youth, 21, 56, 82, 82, 178, 186, 187, 202, 212, 227, 230, 261